Two Churches

ENGLAND AND ITALY
IN THE THIRTEENTH CENTURY

Two Churches

ENGLAND AND ITALY

IN THE THIRTEENTH CENTURY

Robert Brentano

WITH AN ADDITIONAL ESSAY

BY THE AUTHOR

UNIVERSITY OF CALIFORNIA PRESS

BERKELEY, LOS ANGELES, LONDON

University of California Press
Berkeley and Los Angeles, California

University of California Press, Ltd.
London, England

© 1968 by Princeton University Press
Paperback edition © 1988 by
The Regents of the University of California

Printed in the United States of America
1 2 3 4 5 6 7 8 9

Library of Congress Cataloging-in-Publication Data
Brentano, Robert, 1926–
    Two churches : England and Italy in the thirteenth century /
Robert Brentano, with an additional essay by the author.
        p.   cm.
    Includes bibliographical references and index.
    ISBN 0–520–06098–9 (pbk. : alk. paper)
    1. England—Church history—Medieval period, 1066–1485.
2. Italy—Church history—476–1400.   I. Title.
BR750.B755 1988   87–12530
274.2'05—dc 19

CONTENTS

PREFACE TO NEW EDITION

$\mathcal{I}$ should like to thank the University of California Press, and particularly its director, Mr. James Clark, for reprinting this twenty-year-old book and also to thank two especially encouraging colleagues in the department of history at California, Randolph Starn and Irwin Scheiner. It was Scheiner's idea to append the essay "Bishops and Saints," which I had written for Perry Curtis's collection *The Historian's Workshop* to explain the composition of *Two Churches* as exactly and openly as I could when that composition was still fresh in my mind. Although the essay is rather heavily and uninhibitedly personal, and so perhaps annoying, I hope that its explanation of process will prove interesting to some readers of the book. For her help in and responsibility for the original publication of the book by Princeton University Press, I should like again to thank Miss Miriam Brokaw.

I should also like to thank recent colleagues at Emory and Smith for having stimulated me to think again even about this part, and particularly to thank Jean Wilson at Smith, who lured me into history in the first place, and George Cuttino at Emory, who first taught me to read documents.

The present edition is a reprinting. I have not tried to rewrite the book or to incorporate within it research that has been done in recent years or even to make it reflect changes in my own attitudes. The basic contrast within the book was meant, as I wrote in its conclusion, to provoke closer observation of the thirteenth-century church; its parts were not meant to be "fixed and permanent structures." If I were now beginning to write the Italian half of my contrast, I would write and shape it somewhat differently. I have spent the years since the 1960s studying Italy and its church in areas—most intensely a band of territory stretching from Rome through Rieti to Sulmona and L'Aquila—which I did not then know very well. In my study I have been aided by the work and often the presence of effective Italian historians; and in this period the study of local Italian ecclesiastical history has been revolutionized. I have tried to describe the revolution and to suggest some part of my debt to its participants in a recent review essay, "Italian Ecclesiastical History: The Sambin Revolution."[1] Subjects which my book touches, moreover, like the pieve and the will-testament, have exploded into general visibility and interest.[2]

More specifically, I made a Rieti notary die too early, and I failed to take a crusading cardinal away from Citeaux.[3] Perhaps I made too sharp a break in provision at 1265 and used the word *bull* too casually. Certainly I read too trustingly the description of the condition of the Rieti chapter in a papal mandate. This list could continue. One correction I really do want to make. It concerns a man who was bishop of Rieti from 1278 to 1286. In *Two Churches* he was called, as he has been conventionally called, Pietro Gerra; but the careful research of Norbert Kamp makes it seem wise to discard the "surname" Gerra and to call Pietro, who was successively bishop of Sora and Rieti and then archbishop of Monreale and Capua and finally patriarch of Aquileia, Pietro da Ferentino or Pietro Romano or "Egiptius." When I wrote *Two Churches*, Pietro seemed to me simply a political bishop, and I thought there was nothing to indicate that he was "troubled by the thought of

---

[1] *Medievalia et Humanistica*, NS, 14 (1986), 189-197.

[2] *Pievi e Parrocchie in Italia nel basso Medioevo (sec. XIII-XV)*. Italia Sacra, Studi e documenti di storia ecclesiastica, 35-36 (Rome, 1984); for wills, see most recently: *Nolens intestatus decedere. Il testamento come fonte della storia religiosa e sociale* (Settore Bibliotheche e Archivi della Giunta Regionale dell'Umbria, 1985); but also the pivotal work of Agostino Paravicini Bagliani, *I testamenti dei cardinali del Duecento* (Rome, 1980).

[3] For the notary, see my "Localism and Longevity: The Example of the Chapter of Rieti in the Thirteenth and Fourteenth Centuries," in *Law, Church, and Society: Essays in Honor of Stephan Kuttner*, ed. Kenneth Pennington and Robert Somerville (Philadelphia, 1977), 293-310, 300; for the cardinal, Agostino Paravicini Bagliani has forced us to recognize that Eudes de Châteauroux was not a Cistercian (*Cardinali di Curia e "familiae" cardinalizie dal 1227 al 1254*, Italia Sacra, 18-19 [Padua, 1972], I, 200-201).

pastoral care." This now seems to me a partial and superficial view of him. Evidence from Rieti, Ferentino, and Udine has changed my mind. Pietro now seems to me potently to exemplify my old statement: "Any single Italian bishop could, perhaps, if there were sufficient evidence, be moved in our perception, and his character completely changed."[4]

After *Two Churches* had been published, two kind and eminent scholars, Richard Hunt and Daniel Waley, sent me particularly helpful suggestions and ideas. Anyone interested in Celestine V should now turn to the work of Peter Herde. Finally, a book which deals with Italian dioceses should not now be published without specific reference to the work of the historian who has in recent years done more, I think, than any other to expose the structure and texture of a single Italian diocese, Antonio Rigon of Padua.[5]

[4] Norbert Kamp, *Kirche und Monarchie im Staufischen Königreich Sizilien.* I. *Prosopographische Grundlegung: Bistümer und Bischöfe des Königsreichs 1194-1266* (Munich, 1972-1975), I, 105; see below pp. 183, 221.

[5] Peter Herde, *Cölestin V (1294), (Peter vom Morrone), Der Engelpapst* (Stuttgart, 1981), and "Celestino V, papa," in *Dizionario biografico degli Italiani,* XXIII. Rigon's work is discussed in "Italian Ecclesiastical History: The Sambin Revolution," cited in note 1 above.

PREFACE
AND ACKNOWLEDGMENTS

N 1952 I finished a dissertation about ecclesiastical institutions in the north of England at the end of the thirteenth century. I had tried to see the connections between English institutions and both the Roman curia and the
common law of the church; but as I had written I had become
increasingly dissatisfied with a sort of flatness in my English
definition. Definition seemed to me to require comparison.
Comparison of York with Canterbury and Rouen, which I
had tried, seemed insufficient. Canterbury and Rouen were
too close. I decided that a comparison with the south of Italy,
a place directly across the enclosure of the Roman church, at
its other side but clearly within its doctrinal and legal boundaries, would be ideal for giving depth and dimension to a description of English ecclesiastical institutions. The two places
seemed, on the surface, very far apart to me: one still encrusted
with the riches of Greece, the other (north of York) barely
having been touched by the warmth of Rome.

At first I had intended to compare only the two institutions
that I knew best, metropolitan archbishops and papal judges
delegate, in the two areas. Research changed my mind. I
found that I could not properly explain archbishops and
judges if they were disentangled from the surrounding church.
The differences between types of archdeacons, between
bishops, between all sorts of different but surprisingly related
institutions and ideas seemed pressingly pertinent. Their related consideration seemed unavoidable, and also attractive.
The difference, always particularly apparent to the archival
historian, between the kinds of records that had been written
and that survived, in the two countries, seemed clearly connected with a general difference between the ways in which
the two churches had thought about themselves.

At the same time I was more and more convinced that the
two churches had, in general, thought of themselves as units.
In spite of the fact that the English church was composed of

two quite independent provinces and that the Italian church was scattered through a very various collection of political states, each seemed as real as, for example, Bede's "English nation." The inhabitants of each assumed, I feel sure, that they lived within a national, that is an Italian or English, church (as the Camaldolese did when they counted out the cardinals by nation). The assumption was matched and formed by, and formed, local institutions. Assumptions and institutions ran together.

My belief in these "national" units and my interest in comparing them has encouraged me to talk less of regional differences than might be expected from a casual appraisal of the two areas. There is certainly plenty of difference within the Italian church. One can feel it, even now, too easily. In Umbria, in high romantic mood, one walks with the saints on the palm of God's hand: Benedict, Francis, Gregory's stories inhabit the green and pious-seeming valleys. In Campagna, above the sea, the god is Aphrodite and the dialogues are Norman Douglas's. Umbria and Northumbria can be made to seem more like each other than either is like Campagna, Calabria, or Milan. I think, however, that too much that is facile has been said already about regional, particularly Italian regional, differences. The most familiar cliché, the difference between north and south, has, I think, saved many observers from the pain of careful observation and analysis. It is a very simple machine. I have talked of this difference only when I thought it really pertinent. I have tried not to make the Italian-English difference an equally simple machine.

This book is not meant to be a definitive exploration of the whole of the two churches in any case. The attempt would be absurd. But the book is not meant, either, to be an intense exploration of "certain aspects" of the two churches. It is meant rather to be an extended essay about the connected differences between the two churches, to use "aspects" as touchstones for comparison. It is meant to be a comparison of two total styles. These are not architectural styles, although there is a marked and significant difference between English and Italian ecclesiastical architecture in the thirteenth century. The nonarchitectural style of the thirteenth-century Italian church might in fact be called sustained Romanesque, or perhaps sustained Burgundian.

Comparing England (or Britain) with Italy in order to expose more fully one or both is not a new idea. Historians, like Tacitus and Collingwood, have made the comparison, and so have poets, like Browning and, with superb intellectuality, Clough. This is, at least locally, where angels feared to tread. The famous Venetian Anonymous wrote from the other side in his *Relation* (of about 1500), and condensed for us his comparison in the observation that unlike the Italians the English felt no real love, only lust. The spring bough and the melon-flower, Collingwood's city and field—the long continuity of the difference is startlingly apparent. Explaining the continuity (and perhaps there is no more difficult sort of historical explanation—its difficulty is painful to the mind) is not the job that this book sets itself. But it would be dull and dishonest to ignore the fact that the continuity exists. All that this book has to say may be no more than that the thirteenth-century Italian church was in fact, as Browning warned, a melon-flower. The book may be only a gloss on *amore*. The symbol is more inclusive, more evocative, less guilty of excluding the essential but undefined, than detailed description can be. Melon-flower and *amore*, however, fortunately for the purpose of this book, say very little about the intricate, connected detail of administrative history. Collingwood's (after Tacitus's) city against field presses less deeply but says more. The general difference between the styles of the English and Italian churches has a great deal to do, and very directly, with the fact that the inhabitants of Italy were continually city-dwellers and the inhabitants of Britain were essentially not.

Although this book is about both England and Italy, it approaches them differently. The thirteenth-century Italian church is, particularly in English and French, practically unknown. Before it can be explained or analyzed, it must be recreated, formed again in detail. The job is in part really archaeological. The outline of past existence must be uncovered. This is not at all true of the thirteenth-century English church. It has been well explored. This disparity in past observation forces my book to talk much more of Italy than of England;

but, if it is a book about one church rather than the other, it is a book about England. England is meant to be seen, for a change, against what it was not. In this sort of profile it has a different look. England may no longer seem a country in the frozen North, incapable, in the distance, of responding fully to Lateran enthusiasm. Its full response to ecclesiastical government may seem clearly connected with its, of course relatively, full response to secular government.

Italy and England were not in every way opposites within the universal church. In some ways they were more alike than the French and German territories that separated them were like either. A case in point is the general absence from both England and Italy of those highly aristocratic ecclesiastical corporations, willing to receive only members of the greatest families of their realms, which have sometimes been considered characteristic of the medieval church. Neither of the very different societies of Italy and England was an ideal setting for this sort of convent or chapter. Both Italy and England were in their different directions rather apart from the main patterns of continental feudalism. They were connected with each other through the wool trade. In fact a number of English churches, particularly northern ones, were more involved with active northern Italian mercantile towns than were many churches in Italy.

In various ways, however, the churches placed between England and Italy were like one or the other of the two. Northern and western French churches had archdeacons and archdeaconries like those of England; they were similarly divided into provinces, and they had similar vicars general and officials. Vacancy administration in France seems to have been similar to that in Italy; and, as in Italy, almost no French bishops in the thirteenth century kept episcopal registers. In general the characteristics of the French church seem to shade into those of the English and Italian churches. That shading is not considered here. Here only the two poles are considered, for the better definition, it is hoped, of each and of the total church of which both formed a part—for the sharper delineation of two disparate styles.

It will be clear that this book is not, as its title might imply, a study of the connection between the Italian and English churches. Still, a study of differences seems to demand an initial consideration of what sorts of connections there were. The book's first chapter is thus a study of that about which the book is not—but also an indication of what sort of place or thing the center of the official thirteenth-century church was. In this chapter I have wanted the reader not just to know but also to feel the lack of connection, the dizzying repulsion, between the two churches. I have pushed rather hard to get a sense of this repulsion into the prose.

For a pretended essay on two styles of ecclesiastical behavior, this book may seem incredibly long and detailed (and the detail may not carry its intended color to the reader for whom the names of Italian towns do not hold visual memories—sunlight on the archives' walls; the priest's housekeeper pouring wine). The detail has several explanations. The Italian church has to be established, recreated, as I have said (and I have tried to do this particularly in Chapters II and IV). The details are meant to be a series of connected empirical syllogisms. I myself, like Lucien Leuwen's father, or perhaps Ranke, find no truth or conviction without detail. I am also much attracted to a sort of pebbled surface which, although it is always difficult, when it works, gives a helpful dimension to historical writing, breaks the flat surface. The technique seems to me to have succeeded really in only two books that I have read, Tawney's *Business and Politics* and Powicke's *Thirteenth Century*; but it also seems to me that these are the two "great" books of history that I have read from the last generation, and that they perfect an historical style worth even the failing effort.

Although this work may seem very unlike any work of Powicke's, it is meant to be of, or from, his tradition, and so of course the tradition of Maitland. It is meant to be a study of "those hidden processes of mind and matter which lie beneath the structure of government." It was written, in its beginning, for Powicke to read, and it is dedicated to his memory.

A book like this carries such a weight of indebtedness to various archivists and historians in several countries that a mere list of their names would make the length of a long chapter. I must therefore name only a few of them. The work carries the imprint, unmistakable, I should think, however distorted, of two of my teachers, Dr. W. A. Pantin and Miss Kathleen Major. Professor Gene Brucker has been helpful to me in very many ways, among them introducing me to things Italian and trying to save me from at least some errors in dealing with them. Professor Sheldon Rothblatt repeatedly helped me get parts of the manuscript back and forth from Italy to the United States, and encouraged me, particularly when, during a mail strike, the manuscript was temporarily lost. My wife, Carroll Winslow Brentano, has helped me continuously through the ten years in which this book was being put together, and she has shared with me the mixed pleasures of the archive trail. Professor Stephan Kuttner encouraged me through rather difficult periods during the writing of this book; Professor George Guttridge read parts of the manuscript, and his reaction helped me in shaping the rest of it. Mr. Peter Herde has lent me two of his manuscripts and advised me very helpfully about processes at the curia; my use of his written work is readily apparent in my notes. Miss Barbara Harvey, Professor Anne Pippin Burnett, and Mr. W. Urry have sent me photographs, photostats, and microfilms; and Mr. Urry searched in the Canterbury archives for documents that would help me. The late Professor Walther Holtzmann, the late Professor Leopoldo Cassese, Professor Gerard Caspary, and Dom Angelo Mifsud of Cava all helped me with their advice. I have profited from conversations about southern Italy with Mr. Paul Mosher and from listening to Mrs. Susan Millinger Smith on saints' lives. Don Emidio de Sanctis has generously granted me repeated access to the capitular archives at Rieti. Dom Giovanni Mongelli graciously helped me in procuring an illustration which he had also used in his edition of Montevergine documents; the Biblioteca Medicea Laurenziana permitted me to use their manuscript of Federigo Visconti's sermons and sent me a microfilm of it. Some of the material in Chapter V, below, appeared earlier in an article, "Sealed Docu-

ments of the Mediaeval Archbishops at Amalfi," first published
in *Mediaeval Studies*, xxiii (1961), 21-46; and I should like to
thank the editor of *Mediaeval Studies* for permitting me to use
it again here. I should similarly like to thank the editors of
Traditio and the Fordham University Press for permission
to use again, also in Chapter V, material from an article, "The
Bishops' Books of Città di Castello," first published in *Traditio*, xvi (1960), 241-254. I should like to thank the editors of
the *Monumenta Iuris Canonici,* Series C: Subsidia, vol. 1:
*Proceedings of the Second International Congress of Medieval
Canon Law* (Vatican City, 1965) and His Excellency the
Secretary of the S. Congregation of Seminaries and Universities for permitting me to use in Chapter II, below, material
that first appeared in an essay, "Three Thirteenth-Century
Italian Cases in Ecclesiastical Courts," in the *Proceedings*, 311-
319. I should like to acknowledge the permission of: the Art
Reference Bureau, for Alinari and Anderson, for permission
to publish Figs. 1, 5, 6, 8, and 19; the Art Reference Bureau,
for Bildarchiv Foto Marburg, for permission to publish Fig. 2;
the Gabinetto Fotografico Nazionale, Rome, for permission
to publish Figs. 3, 4, 7, 9, 10, 11, 12, 14, 15, and 18; the Gabinetto Microfotografico of Montevergine for Fig. 16; Editions
Arthaud for permission to use Fig. 13. I should like to thank
Mrs. Adrienne Morgan, who drew the maps, and Georg
Westermann Verlag and the Biblioteca Apostolica Vaticana
for permission to use the maps upon which they were, in part,
based. Map 1 is based in part upon "Die Kirche im Spät-
mittelalter" from *Westermanns Atlas zur Welt Geschichte*,
II: *Mittelalter* (Braunschweig, 1956), 88-89; Map 2 is based
upon maps from Studi e Testi, *Rationes decimarum Italiae
nei secoli XIII e XIV*: Campania, Umbria.

Although I am unable to thank by name all those courteous
archivists in Bari, Città di Castello, Venice, Bologna, Verona,
all over Italy, who helped me, I should like specifically to
thank two of them for whom I shall always have the greatest
admiration and affection. Among all those provincial ecclesiastical archivists whom I met, some of them sometimes over-
worked, a few tired or distracted or involved in nonecclesiastical work to the point of churlishness, most much more

pleasant than one could expect, these two stood out. Don
Mariano Dionigi at the Duomo in Assisi and my dear friend
Don Gabriele Vissicchio at the Duomo in Amalfi (with his
kind assistant Don Riccardo Arpino), dividing their time between their orphanages, their chanceries, and their music,
proved to me that sanctity and utility are still, or now, alive
in the provincial Italian church.

ILLUSTRATIONS

MAPS

Two Churches

ENGLAND AND ITALY
IN THE THIRTEENTH CENTURY

I · THE CONNECTION

N November 1237, as heavy winds blew and black tower-like clouds formed and the planets were said to be gathering together under the sign of Capricorn, the cardinal legate Otto sat on a high seat raised in the west end of Saint Paul's in London and presided over a council of the church in England. The prelates of England, tired and peeved by the winter roads and the legate's insistence, gathered together around and beneath the cardinal's throne.[1] It was, in the long run of the century, a remarkably, a surprisingly, successful council. The legate preached from the text "And in the midst of the throne, and round about the throne, were four beasts, full of eyes before and behind."[2] And to this text succeeding English prelates were as a sea of glass. The English bishops of the later thirteenth century were—as close as their political humanity could come to it—the ideally vigilant bishops of the reformed Roman church of Innocent III's Lateran Council of 1215, reasserted and made pointedly local by Otto's London council with its flaming text.

Otto was one of a series of thirteenth-century Roman legates who, in their persons, brought the elevating connection of Rome to England.[3] Otto's most distinguished successor, Otto-

[1] Matthew Paris, *Chronica Majora*, ed. H. R. Luard, Rolls Series (London, 1872-1883), III, 414-420.

[2] *Ibid.*, 419; Revelations 4:6; the canons (glossed) of Otto's council may be found in *Constitutiones Legatinae . . . D. Othonis et D. Othoboni Cardinalium . . .* (Oxford, 1679), 3-73, printed with William Lyndwood's *Provinciale*; they are also printed in David Wilkins, *Concilia Magnae Britanniae et Hiberniae* (London, 1737), I, 649-656. (Also see F. M. Powicke and C. R. Cheney, *Councils and Synods with Other Documents Relating to the English Church*, II. i [Oxford, 1964], 237-259.)

[3] For legates to England through Guala (1216-1218) see Helene Tillmann, *Die päpstlichen Legaten in England bis zur Beendigung der Legation Gualas (1218)* (Bonn, 1926); it is hoped that this book will do something toward substantiating the extravagant claim for the English bishops; I think that my estimate's being higher than, say, that of Miss Gibbs' and Miss Lang's book is due to my looking at English bishops in comparison with the bishops of another church:

buono Fieschi, later briefly Pope Hadrian V, scion of a brilliant but morally rather ambiguous Genoese-papal family, caught the wracked England of the 1260's and helped to raise it toward the ideal of the Christian feudal kingdom.[4] Otto's predecessor, Nicholas, cardinal bishop of Tusculum, had, in 1213, with an Italian Cistercian abbot in his train, descended upon the abbey of Evesham and rid it of Roger Norreys, its disgustingly immoral abbot, who had been plundering it and deforming it for years.[5] These men cut through petty local boundaries and fought to make the universal church work. They were, at their best, great men of high purpose, and their most serious work knew no nationality.

In the spring of 1238 the legate Otto came to Oxford and stayed in the abbey at Osney. His presence and that of his Italian, trans-Alpine, Roman household excited the clerks of Oxford to nationalist riot. The riot started, according to Matthew Paris, with the raised Roman voice of an Italian porter.[6] The riot of Oxford and the council of London, it must with difficulty be remembered, circled around the same man. The international church of the thirteenth century was also for the most part an Italian church; and the presence of the international church's representatives in England meant the presence of Italian clerks who had been brought up in its ways and taught to think in its terms—although it is possible that some

---

cf. Marion Gibbs and Jane Lang, *Bishops and Reform, 1215-1272* (Oxford, 1934), 174-179.

[4] For Ottobuono see particularly F. M. Powicke, *King Henry III and the Lord Edward* (Oxford, 1947), I, 246 n. 1; II, 557-558, 562-563; for Ottobuono's unpopularity because of his connection with the tenth of 1266, *ibid.*, II, 559-561.

[5] *Chronicon Abbatiae de Evesham*, ed. W. D. Macray, Rolls Series (London, 1863), 230-256, particularly 250; for the legate Giovanni of Ferentino's activities, C. R. Cheney, "The Papal Legate and English Monasteries in 1206," *English Historical Review*, XLVI (1931), 443-452; and "Cardinal John of Ferentino, Papal Legate in England in 1206," *English Historical Review*, LXXVI (1961), 654-660.

[6] Matthew Paris, *Chronica Majora*, III, 482; and see Powicke, *Henry III*, I, 353, and Dorothy M. Williamson, "Some Aspects of the Legation of Cardinal Otto in England, 1233-41," *English Historical Review*, LXIV (1949), 145-173, particularly 171-173.

of them, perhaps Guala or Ottobuono, prepared no doubt by the pervasive thought of Paris, may have come to prefer the ways of the English church.

Just before the beginning of the century a sharp-eyed, sharp-tongued monk and proctor from Christ Church, John Bremble, wrote back to Canterbury to tell the monks at home what the curia, in which they had become involved, was like. "This I'll tell you," he wrote, "at Rome I have found all Romans, and the pope [Clement III, Paolino Scolare] is a Roman, both by birth and by type."[7]

John Bremble meant that the pope was greedy. Greed is the quality that Matthew Paris most constantly connected with Italians. Matthew created, in his *Chronica Majora*, an intensely and critically observed England-centered world for the years from 1235 to 1259, and in it he watched Otto at last set sail from Dover leaving a kingdom desolated by him as a vineyard might have been by a wild boar. Matthew's Otto had, with quadruple greed, extorted English money and dispersed English livings for himself and for the pope.[8] Greed and nationalism are both major themes in Matthew's work; and Matthew is particularly interesting on the international church as an Italian church because it upset him in both guises. He was made intensely uncomfortable by any sort of central reform that threatened or might seem to threaten the heavy properties of the rich houses of the old religious orders, and he was a xenophobe. Directly and in quotation Matthew's sulphurous billows of disturbed image find bellow-mouths and sponge-bellies at Rome and Italian spies poking into and discovering the secret treasury of England.

Matthew was, however, not more concerned than Robert Grosseteste. Grosseteste, from 1235 to 1253 the scholar bishop of Lincoln, of all bishops most thoughtfully aware of the pastoral function and like Stephen Langton the mirror of thirteenth-century episcopal excellence, found the provided Italian

[7] *Epistolae Cantuarienses* (vol. II of *Chronicles and Memorials of the Reign of Richard I*), ed. William Stubbs, Rolls Series (London, 1865), 194.

[8] Matthew Paris, *Chronica Majora*, IV, 84-85; for a considerably fuller discussion of Matthew Paris as historian see Chapter V, below.

and the Italian legate a threat to the cure of souls and to the integrity of ecclesiastical administration.[9] The careful, painful letters with which Grosseteste tried, in obedience, to resist Otto's provisions have none of Matthew's facility and bombast.[10] They preserve a quite different tone of opposition, and record its awful necessity in the mind of this spiritually sensitive administrator.

The problem of the Roman church was a serious one. Rome needed to support its necessary servants. Its sources of current income were insufficient and insufficiently elastic.[11] But rich livings, deposited by the past and not all of much contemporary value in service to the ecclesiastical community, lay scattered about the provincial church. Some of these, collected through shrewdly elaborated reversions, the papacy could, with a good deal of haggling, parcel out to the various governments that supported clerks, and particularly to royal governments and its own. In a century when the papacy was Italian this process produced anti-Italian feelings of at least two sorts. Those who haggled with the papacy for incomes for their clerks (or for their brothers) while admitting the system, hated Italian successes; and their attitude was connected with that of those who hated concentrations of property, at least of other people's property, and not less when the concentration was in Italian hands.[12] There were also those, like

[9] See particularly D. A. Callus, ed., *Robert Grosseteste* (Oxford, 1955) and within that collection particularly the essay by W. A. Pantin, "Grosseteste's Relations with the Papacy and the Crown," 178-215; see also: Powicke, *Henry III*, I, 78, 356; Brian Tierney, "Grosseteste and the Theory of Papal Sovereignty," *Journal of Ecclesiastical History*, VI (1955), 1-17; Robert Grosseteste, *Epistolae*, ed. H. R. Luard, Rolls Series (London, 1861). For a fuller discussion of Grosseteste see Chapter III, below.

[10] Robert Grosseteste, *Epistolae*, 144-145, 151-154.

[11] The whole business of provisions is sharply examined in Geoffrey Barraclough, *Papal Provisions* (Oxford, 1935); Ann Deeley, "Papal Provision and Royal Rights of Patronage in the Early Fourteenth Century," *English Historical Review*, XLIII (1928), 497-527, remains an extremely helpful essay.

[12] See Hugh MacKenzie, "The Anti-Foreign Movement in England, 1231-1232," *Anniversary Essays in Mediaeval History by Students of Charles Homer Haskins*, ed. C. H. Taylor (Boston, 1929), 183-203;

Grosseteste—or at least there was Grosseteste himself—who hated the potential abuses connected with the system of provisions. Grosseteste might have, must have, fully sympathized with the fiscal problems of the international church, but to him they were of a different and lesser order from the necessity of having a responsible pastor in every parish. And it was perfectly clear by the later years of Grosseteste's career that provisions, and most noticeably the provisions of foreigners who would be absent, or if present locally inept, were a threat not only to superfluous canonries but also to livings with the cure of souls. Thus the representative of the Italian church in England, no matter how innocent of personal vice, was to this perceptive bishop the agent of evil; and, in Matthew Paris's distortion, Grosseteste hated provided Italians as he hated the poison of snakes.[13]

Of Italians in England, although there are varieties of expression, money is always—almost always—the theme. The merchants collecting their wool shade into the bankers making their loans. In complement to the Italian holders of livings scattered through the English countryside, there was, from 1229 to the close of the thirteenth century, the central office of the papal collectors, with its staff of from four to seven men, its Italian notary, and its household, in the New Temple in London.[14] In the early century the collectors general were

see also *Registrum Roberti Winchelsey, 1294-1313*, ed. Rose Graham, Canterbury and York Society (London, 1917-1953) [hereafter *Winchelsey*], 792 (1304) for Italian clerks in Somercote jail. The attitude toward property is nicely suggested, in connection with Robert Tweng's rising in 1231-1232, in the annals of Dunstable, *Annales Monastici*, ed. H. R. Luard, Rolls Series (London, 1864-1869), iii, 129.

[13] Matthew Paris, *Chronica Majora*, v, 257; see too Pantin, "Grosseteste's Relations," in Callus, 194, 195, using Eccleston to show Grosseteste's wanting his men to be good and present, but not necessarily speaking English, because example speaks. (Thomas Eccleston, *De adventu fratrum minorum in Angliam*, ed. A. G. Little [Manchester, 1951], 92; the nephews of cardinals are bad not because they speak no English but because they are interested only in temporalities.)

[14] W. E. Lunt, *Financial Relations of the Papacy with England to 1327* (Cambridge, Mass., 1939), 581; see also Emilio Re, "La Compagnia dei Riccardi in Inghilterra," *Archivio storico italiano*, LXXII

sometimes the legates, but this practice ended with Otto's departure in 1241. The collectors were almost always Italian, and they seem, reasonably enough, to have been generally unpopular. For almost the whole last quarter of the century the office was held by Goffredo of Vezzano, who was sufficiently effective to provoke the English clergy to a joint complaint about his methods to Nicholas III.[15] Goffredo was succeeded, as the century turned, by Bartolomeo of Ferentino, an Italian providee who had been variously employed around England so long that he had the "interests of an English prelate."[16] As early as 1246 the collector had been Berardo of Ninfa near Rome, a papal chaplain and scribe, the rector of Langley in the diocese of Lincoln, who died, in England, in 1258. Through Berardo's agency, in connection with Richard of Cornwall's diversion of the crusading money collected in 1249, according to Matthew Paris, scandal arose and devotion cooled.[17]

Bartolomeo of Ferentino's activities within the church and realm of England were not solely fiscal. Italian names, like his and Giovanni of Lucca's or the Italian notary Ildebrandino Bonadoce's, occur variously in English ecclesiastical activities.[18] Archbishop Pecham of Canterbury was served by the

---

(1914), 87-138, for the instruments of Peter of Valle Cimaria, Camerino diocese, at the New Temple, 126-129; and see W. E. Rhodes, "The Italian Bankers in England," *Historical Essays*, ed. T. F. Tout and James Tait (Manchester, 1907), 137-168.

[15] Lunt, 585.

[16] Lunt, 588.

[17] Lunt, 613; Matthew Paris, *Chronica Majora*, v, 74 (and 707); Peter Herde, *Beiträge zum päpstlichen Kanzlei- und Urkundenwesen im 13. Jahrhundert*, Münchener Historische Studien (Kallmünz, 1961), 27-28; and, as Herde suggests, index listings under "Berardus de Nimpha" in *Les Registres d'Innocent IV*, ed. Elie Berger, Bibliothèque des écoles françaises d'Athènes et de Rome (Paris, 1884-1911) [hereafter *Innocent IV*]. It is interesting to note in a forgery scandal, with which Berard had to deal, the involvement of Walter Scammell and Gilbert of Saint Leofard early in their careers (*Innocent IV*, III, 458).

[18] See, for example, C. M. Fraser, *A History of Antony Bek* (Oxford, 1957), 36, 38; Decima L. Douie, *Archbishop Pecham* (Oxford, 1952), 109; Robert Brentano, *York Metropolitan Jurisdiction and Papal Judges Delegate (1279-1296)* (Berkeley and Los Angeles, 1959), 126, 128, 130, 132, 138, 140, 161, 184, 186, 188-194, 197, 247.

Florentine clerks and brothers Vicio.[19] A more famous man, Enrico of Susa, who was to become the great canonist bishop of Ostia, was a special adviser to Henry III. Hostiensis may seem little more Italian than Boniface of Savoy; but Accursius, who advised Edward I, recalls quite clearly the Italian connection that meant for England borrowed legal learning as well as legalistic shrewdness.[20] Bologna was in Italy, and its alumni and its thought connected the two churches, as they did the whole of western Christendom.

On 10 September 1224 nine followers of Francis of Assisi landed at Dover. Of these, three were English and five Italians.[21] It is possible that through the thirteenth century, in which the Franciscans meant so much to England, an occasional Englishman consciously thought that Francis was Italian and a product of the Italian church. It is possible that someone reading Aquinas thought of the country around Salerno, that Englishmen occasionally remembered Norcia or Gregory's house on the Coelian. Quite certainly Englishmen dreamed of pilgrimages, and went on them, to sacred and Italian Rome. The Romans Oderico and Pietro worked with marked Italian effect, echoing in very alien distance Cosmatesque Rome, within French Westminster on Edward the Confessor's shrine and Henry III's own tomb.[22] And the saints upon whose dismembered bodies the great churches of Italy were built were not forgotten in London and York. But these beauties are distractions.

The Italian church was present in England and visible

[19] Douie, *Archbishop Pecham*, 61.

[20] See Powicke: *Henry III*, I, 272-273; II, 695, 777; *The Thirteenth Century* (Oxford, 1953), 135-136, 285-286, 469-470, 626.

[21] D. Knowles, *The Religious Orders in England*, I (Cambridge, 1956), 130-131; T. Eccleston, *De adventu fratrum minorum in Angliam*, 3-6.

[22] For Pietro and Oderico (Pietro's father?), see Peter Brieger, *English Art, 1216-1307*, Oxford History of English Art (Oxford, 1957), 120; Edward Hutton, *The Cosmati, The Roman Marble Workers of the XIIth and XIIIth Centuries* (London, 1950), 23-27, frontispiece, pls. 63 and 64; Powicke, *Henry III*, II, 589 n. 1; and, particularly, Royal Commission on Historical Monuments (England), *An Inventory of the Historical Monuments in London*, I: *Westminster Abbey* (London, 1924), 25, 26, 28, 29, pls. 38, 39, 44-49, 185, and frontispiece. Cf. J. White, *Art and Architecture in Italy, 1250-1400* (Baltimore, 1966), 57.

within the church of England. Innocent IV in 1253 in an effort to make its presence more palatable offered to limit papal provisions of Italians to English livings to an annual total value of 8,000 marks.[23] In the short run, in terms of the Italian church that was actually felt, known, and recognized as Italian by thirteenth-century Englishmen, the five friars at Dover could not compete with the busy office in the New Temple. Even the wretched bishop of Cervia, driven from his split, salt-rich see on the Adriatic, looked, of necessity, a financial obligation to Grosseteste in Lincoln.[24]

The English church was dappled with scattered members of the Italian church, leech-spotted with them; together they formed the tentacles of the fiscal offices of the church of Rome. They also formed the whips with which the church of England was sometimes flicked to reformation and enthusiasm. The image of the English clerics in Italy is quite different from, almost the reverse of, that of their Italian counterparts in England. In Italy the English rolled together with the members of other provincial churches in the tangled briar patch, the sticky tar pit, that surrounded the holy purpose of the Roman curia as it moved to Rieti, Perugia, Viterbo, and Orvieto, to summers at Tivoli, or political summers at Lyons. English clerics at Viterbo or Rieti, there to seek a privilege, a judgment, or a stay of judgment from a papal office, found themselves living, by chance, in an Italian cathedral city at the heart of an Italian diocese. A good many thirteenth-century Englishmen thus, in a way, got to know the Italian church rather well.

In the late 1270's and the 1280's a monk from Christ Church Canterbury, Robert of Selsey, was following the curia as proctor both for his house and for Archbishop Pecham. By 1280 Robert as proctor for Christ Church had borrowed 250 marks from merchants of Pistoia and left his bond with an interested papal official.[25] On 12 August 1280, Robert, at Viterbo, bor-

---

[23] Powicke, *Henry III*, 278-281.

[24] Grosseteste, *Epistolae*, 337.

[25] Historical Manuscripts Commission, *Report on Historical Manuscripts*, v (London, 1876) [hereafter Hist. MSS Comm.], *Fifth Report*, 451 (Doc. Ch. Ant. P 56); for Selsey, see also Douie, *Pecham*, 182.

rowed fifty marks (at the twice-quoted equivalence of thirteen shillings, four pence sterling to the mark) with letters of credit from the convent, from curial Florentine merchant-bankers, the Abbati (the family of St. Albert of Messina), who seem to have catered to English Benedictines, the money to be returned on the following Feast of Saints Philip and James (1 May) at Saint Omer or Paris or the curia.[26] In 1283 Robert was being sent to Matteo Orsini, cardinal deacon of Santa Maria in Porticu, by Pecham in the difficult attempt to make the house of Christ Church a mirror of virtue for the church of England, worthy of the martyr Thomas's honor.[27] On 23 December 1286, Robert was paying debts at the curia, as John de Capella, the Englishman, witnessed, and the notary Giovanni Amati de Guarcino redacted and notarized the creditors' receipts. Vanni di Nicola di Bruno of Viterbo, a butcher who followed the curia, got, in the house in which he was staying at Rome, the fifteen shillings nine pence Tournois gross and the twenty florins that Robert owed him for the meat he had bought from him.[28] In the house in which he was staying, Fico of Perugia, a poulterer who followed the curia, got the seventeen shillings and four pence Tournois gross that Robert owed him for chickens and capons and game and meat.[29] Both Fico and Vanni, suppliers from curial towns who followed the higher prices and expanded markets that the

[26] Canterbury Cathedral Chapter Archives, Ch. Ant. C 1286, to which one of the witnesses is Benedict or Benet of Southwell ("de Suellis"), a clerk of Archbishop Wickwane's of York who was active for Wickwane at Southwell in October 1281 and at Northampton in December 1282 (Brentano, *York Metropolitan Jurisdiction*, 206, 130); for the Abbati, whose involvement in English affairs does seem to occur more frequently than chance survival would dictate (e.g. Brentano, *York Metropolitan Jurisdiction*, 224-225), see G. A. Brucker, "An Unpublished Source on the Avignonese Papacy: the Letters of Francesco Bruni," *Traditio*, XIX (1963), 356-357 n. 24; and Edouard Jordan, *De mercatoribus camerae apostolicae saeculo XIII* (Rennes, 1909), 85, 96, 97.

[27] *Registrum Epistolarum Fratris Johannis Peckham, Archiepiscopi Cantuariensis*, ed. Charles Trice Martin, Rolls Series (London, 1882-1885) [hereafter *Peckham*], II, 545-546.

[28] Canterbury Cathedral Chapter Archives, Ch. Ant. P 58.

[29] Canterbury Cathedral Chapter Archives, Ch. Ant. P 59.

curia brought to the town in which it at the moment stood, promised not to harass Robert of Selsey any more.

The year before, on 13 July 1285, in the great church at Tivoli, Robert of Selsey had made protest before another redacting notary, Benesalute of Cermignano in the diocese of Penne, and before witnesses including another Christ Church proctor, Robert of Elham, and Master Riccardo de Spina, and Master Reginald of Saint Alban's, a professional English proctor at the curia.[30] Robert of Selsey proclaimed that if he had the money to pay the debts that he had contracted at the curia in negotiating the affairs of the church of Canterbury and to pay for the trip back to Canterbury he would go home without any further delay, but he did not have the money, so he could not leave. Selsey had to forego the pleasures of Canterbury for those of Tivoli, to stay at the curia with his expenses swelling. He was like a heavily and increasingly interested debt for his convent.

Robert of Selsey was one of a number of contemporary or approximately contemporary Canterbury proctors who moved back and forth to the curia. Anselm of Eastry, who was active at the same time as Selsey and through the nineties, had, like Selsey, been present in Pecham's chamber at Lambeth on 7 February 1282, with William de la Corner and Gilbert of Saint Leofard, important clerks in both English provinces and future bishops, and Selvagio of Florence, who called himself the chaplain of Matteo Orsini, when Robert Lacy, acting under Pecham's special mandate, had sent letters to the suffragans of Canterbury to excommunicate Thomas Canti-

[30] Canterbury Cathedral Chapter Archives, Ch. Ant. P 57; Ricardo de Spina is elsewhere (Ch. Ant. C 1286) described as a clerk of the diocese of Bath, and although I think he was a Spina, he could have been a Thorn (he was a rough contemporary of Nicholas de Spina, Abbot of Saint Augustine's, Canterbury)—a constant sort of difficulty when the church is using its international language; for the curia's causing prices to rise, see Daniel Waley, *The Papal State in the Thirteenth Century* (London, 1961) 80-81, and his information from Cesare Pinzi, *Storia della Città di Viterbo* (Viterbo, 1887-1913), II, 59n. For Selsey see, too, Jane Sayers, "Canterbury Proctors at the Court of the *audientia contradictarum litterarum*," *Traditio*, XXII (1966), 311-345, 323, 320.

lupe, the rebellious bishop of Hereford and future saint, and had given the letter to Thomas himself.[31] Anselm was at the curia by October 1282 trying to recover property that had been held by Robert Kilwardby, who had died there shortly after having been translated from the see of Canterbury to the cardinal bishopric of Porto.[32] In 1277 Robert Poucyn, the then new proctor for Christ Church, was going about Viterbo with a notary and witnesses paying off the debts of his predecessor, John of Battle: to Chiara, the poor widow of Giacomo, twenty shillings for wine; to Salimbene di Rainerio two marks, ten shillings for poultry and candles; to Angelo di Girardo one mark, four shillings, four pence for fodder and wine; to Biagio di Girardo money for hay and wine; to Pelegrino the blacksmith money for shoeing horses; to Giacomo of Viterbo money for grain; to Robert Nicola of Orvieto, tavern-keeper, money for wine; to Robert the Englishman for unspecified services, twenty-one shillings.[33] At the end of the century Canterbury proctors at the curia were searching for strayed property and were enmeshed in debts, and one at least said, before a notary, that he was greatly grieved that he could not go home.

Almost one hundred years before Robert of Selsey's proclamation in Tivoli the then monks of Christ Church Canterbury had received a depressing letter from Innocent III. "Because, in fact," he, or one of his chancery clerks, wrote, "it has pleased God to exact from your two monks at the Holy See their debt to nature, we advise you now to send to our presence other prudent and discreet men who know how to, and are able to, defend your rights."[34] Death at the curia, or on the road to or

---

[31] *Peckham*, I, 299-300; for Anselm, see *Winchelsey*, 528, 538, index, and also *Register of Bishop Godfrey Giffard*, ed. J. W. Willis Bund, Worcestershire Historical Society (Oxford, 1902) [hereafter *G. Giffard*], II, 490.

[32] *Peckham*, III, 1058.

[33] Hist. MSS Comm., *Fifth Report*, 451; I have not actually seen this Canterbury Chapter document, identified in the report as S.B. c.9 1277, and unfortunately I do not think there was time in the commission's preparation of the report for it to achieve the fullness and exactness which would permit its readers to have complete trust in it.

[34] Stubbs, *Epistolae Cantuarienses*, 443, 445.

from it, further darkened a case that seemed terrible enough without it for the monks of Christ Church, "co-athletes with St. Thomas," fighting to prevent the archbishops Baldwin and Hubert Walter from establishing a secular college at Canterbury. The new deaths reminded them of older deaths, of the predecessors of proctors' predecessors. In the early phases of the case John Bremble had written back telling his co-athletes what people said of the curia. He quoted Horace on the leech, and he said that certainly for Rome true and sound advice was found in the passage from Matthew, "And if any man will sue thee at the law and take away thy coat, let him have thy cloak also."[35] Better, it was said, to fall among thieves than to be taken in the snares of the Roman curia. Intricately woven delays would never let a case end or let loose the litigants until all their financial resources were clearly exhausted. Even then the Romans had ways of getting money from the moneyless. There was some hope when Clement III became pope at the end of 1187 that the sun of justice had risen and that all had been made new.[36] But by March of 1188, when the Canterbury messenger ("our boy, R.") had returned home, lamentations were again in order. Benedict Humphrey wrote back to Canterbury that the music was stilled, "our dance is turned into mourning."[37] Clement III was by then showing himself a Roman of Rome.

In the century between John Bremble and Robert of Selsey generation after generation of Canterbury monks, entrammeled in the curia's snares, could have repeated the reflections of a Canterbury proctor in 1188 on the disillusionment that a fresh proctor felt as he learned after his arrival at Rome the hard lessons that experience of the curia taught: "How sweetly innocent are the days of youth, the child playing at his games, unaware of future care; how delicious, how blessed they seem from the hard age of man."[38] In the longer span of time from John of Salisbury to the author of the *Life of Edward II*

[35] *Ibid.*, 214, reference to Matt. 5:40.
[36] Stubbs, *Epistolae Cantuarienses*, 190, references to Ps. 9:4 and 2 Cor. 5:17.
[37] Stubbs, *Epistolae Cantuarienses*, 191-192, reference to Lam. 5:15.
[38] Stubbs, *Epistolae Cantuarienses*, 191-192.

few Englishmen who knew the curia doubted that Lady Money ruled there, and by tyrannical and exacting whim.[39] A dominant, pervasive, penetrating cliché, in its bloated form, shaped history through men's minds—a sense of present greed that cloaked a misunderstanding of the demands of a necessarily growing bureaucracy, probably;[40] but the cliché was given its detail by the actual, constant, petty greed of the grasping followers of the curia. An image was formed in which shell and kernel had the same texture: "e dopo il pasto ha più fame che pria."

Christ Church Canterbury had more to spend and more to lose than the majority of English religious corporations. It must have been more involved with the Roman curia than was the dead average of English houses. But all that seems really unusual about Christ Church is that it was so exquisitely and sadly vocal, that it was blessed with proctors who could mingle quotations from Horace and the Scriptures so pointedly, and that its bills survive in poulterer and butcher detail.

In contrast, however, with the monks of Canterbury, led generation after generation like grumbling lambs to their Roman slaughter, Thomas of Marlborough, monk of Evesham, relished his Roman experiences. In his account, westcountry garrulous perhaps, of his trials at Rome, horns no longer hang mute on walls, and the cynical foreknowledge of expensive defeat is replaced by delight in learning the ropes—

[39] John of Salisbury, *Historia Pontificalis*, ed. Marjorie Chibnall, Nelson's Medieval Texts (Edinburgh and London, 1956), 49, 80 (and see 76 for swarms of German appellants, like disturbed bees); *Vita Edwardi Secundi*, ed. N. Denholm-Young, Nelson's Medieval Texts (Edinburgh and London, 1957), 45-48, particularly 46, a strong statement about curial venality that compares unfavorably the contemporary greed of Clement V with that of preceding Italian popes, and so turns the cliché. See too George B. Parks, *The English Traveller to Italy*, I (Palo Alto, 1954), 117-136, for a nice collection of loud lament and discussion of travelers', including proctors', experiences.

[40] For a recent discussion, see John A. Yunck, "Economic Conservatism, Papal Finance and the Medieval Satires on Rome," *Mediaeval Studies*, XXIII (1961), 334-351. The material appears again in Yunck's book, *The Lineage of Lady Meed* (Notre Dame, 1963), in which see p. 86 n. 3.

and how to hang the bishop of Worcester in them.[41] Marlborough, who later became prior and then abbot of his house, and who enriched it with his history, with buildings and glass, a library and advice, was a learned and capable man.[42] He had been taught by Stephen Langton. He was considered an expert in the law by the monks of his house.

It was because of Marlborough's learning, and his rousing and acute marshaling of the opposition, when Bishop Mauger of Worcester, informed of his duty, attempted to visit the house, that Marlborough was made the convent's proctor and sent off to Rome in 1204.[43] His difficulties were formidable; one can imagine them in Bremble's mouth. The worst difficulty was his wretchedly immoral and peculiarly erratic, but tenacious, abbot, Roger Norreys, who went by a separate route to Rome. Marlborough and Norreys were old enemies. At Rome, although Norreys refused to speak, they lived together until Marlborough was warned that Norreys might kill him. But in spite of his abbot, who besides being a personal annoyance was a grave danger to the abbey's immunity, Marlborough persevered, and with zest. When Innocent III and Cardinal Ugolino suggested that it would be wise for Marlborough to prepare himself for waging his case by spending six months in the schools of Bologna, he went—from April to October 1205.[44] Whether or not he learned much law in the schools, he came back with a list in his mind of the graded reputations of Italian legists from Azo down. He was able to get his party the best advocates in Rome, and he had learned a lot about how to handle Innocent III's crustiness. This the chief of the bishop of Worcester's proctors had not learned, evidently, for he bored the pope to rebuke with a lengthy proemium and again irritated him by saying, "Holy Father, we have learned in the schools, and this is the opinion of the

[41] Macray, *Chronicon Abbatiae de Evesham*, 109-170; David Knowles, *The Monastic Order in England* (Cambridge, 1940), 331-345 ("The Case of Evesham").

[42] Macray, *Chronicon Abbatiae de Evesham*, 264-278.

[43] *Ibid.*, 109, 141.

[44] *Ibid.*, 147-150.

masters, that prescription does not hold against episcopal right." To which Innocent replied, characteristically, "Then you and your masters had been drinking too much of your English beer when you were learning." And according to Marlborough, Clipston, the Worcester proctor, perhaps not believing that he had heard correctly, repeated his statement and Innocent his reply.[45]

Marlborough, himself, in spite of his initial gifts had not been spared Innocent's temper, but on the whole Innocent's potent governing personality—strangely like King John's—stimulated him. Innocent and Marlborough looked at each other, as Jocelin of Brakelond's Henry II and Samson had, with pleased approval.[46] In the end, with an important decision for his house, Marlborough, lacking money for the proper presents, sneaked out of Rome, splendidly undefeated. He returned home to write his advice to future monks who would have to fight again in a curia that could not restrain itself from ambiguous decisions:

> I tell you this because the behavior of the court of Rome is like that of a devoted mother who consoles in her embraces her children whom their father has just whipped. Thus cases in the court, like ours, are often divided so that each side may bear the sentence, and neither go away sad. . . . I have written this for you so that when the time comes you will act like men and remember because I have told you, and pray for me.[47]

Again, against the poignant Canterbury lamentation from the end of the twelfth century, can be read the harsh fury of Prior Richard Claxton of Durham, another cathedral monastery, from the late thirteenth century. Claxton, in hot rhetoric, tried to direct from Durham the activities of three Durham

[45] *Ibid.*, 152, 189; Helene Tillmann used the Marlborough incidents in her work on Innocent: Helene Tillmann, *Papst Innocenz III* (Bonn, 1954), 50, 238.
[46] *Ibid.*, 142, 143.
[47] *Ibid.*, 229.

proctors at the curia: two local men, Henry of Teesdale, a monk, and Thomas of Normanton, a clerk; and a professional English proctor, Adam of Fileby.[48] Claxton was anxious not to be the innocent northern dupe of southern sophistication, but rather to be devious among the devious.

Robert Grosseteste, early in his episcopate, sent his proctor (S. of Arden) to the curia under the protection of a curious collection of letters. In one of these, to a papal notary (whom he did not know, he said, but knew of, through Giovanni of Ferentino, papal chaplain and subdeacon and archdeacon [Italian] of Norwich), Grosseteste coyly, or at least fussily, apologized should he have distorted or truncated his correspondent's title.[49]

Grosseteste's early uncertainty of tone seems a small concession to the threatening curia's wiles when it is compared with the indecision of Thomas Cantilupe, bishop of Hereford from 1275 to 1282, because Cantilupe's indecision was literally a matter of pounds and pence and how to spend them. In the maneuverings of these two men one can compare the maneuverings of the saintly with the maneuverings of the "saint." Cantilupe wrote in confusion, in 1281, to John of Bitterley and William Brun, his proctors in the curia. He had just one hundred pounds (a conventional sum) to send to the curia, and he wanted it divided in the most expeditious way, and so as not, if possible, to include a direct bribe to the pope. Thirty marks were to be given to the English cardinal, but the other lesser gifts should be adjusted profitably.[50] Cantilupe also involved himself curiously with his proctors. He, for example, once wrote a queer, apologetic, ambivalent letter to his proctor, the Italian professional Bardo of Poggibonsi. Cantilupe explained that John of Bitterley was coming to join Bardo, in no way to replace him or to make him less Canti-

---

[48] Brentano, *York Metropolitan Jurisdiction*, 208-217 (Durham Dean and Chapter Archives, M.C. 5820, "8 Instruments," 1, 3, 4, 5, 6).

[49] Grosseteste, *Epistolae*, 130-131.

[50] *Registrum Thome de Cantilupo, Episcopi Herefordensis*, ed. R. G. Griffiths and W. W. Capes, Canterbury and York Society (London, 1907) [hereafter *Cantilupo*], 274-275; Brentano, *York Metropolitan Jurisdiction*, 125.

lupe's proctor. Cantilupe hoped, rather, that John would be able to stimulate Bardo and Cantilupe's other curial friends to prosecute Cantilupe's various affairs more vigorously.[51] Although Cantilupe's register includes a great deal that it might have seemed discreet not to copy, it also includes a notation of secret instructions to Brun and Bitterley, too secret to copy even in this candid register.[52]

The nervous insecurity with which the early Grosseteste and Cantilupe and practically all visible thirteenth-century English prelates viewed the curia was bred partly of inexperience, but it was not bred of the lack of at least some personal knowledge. These prelates came back to England not only from making appeals and petitions, but sometimes from expensive and confusing confirmations of their elections. They may occasionally have been inspired to great governance at the curia, as it has been suggested that Pecham was by Nicholas III, or as Langton may in a way have been by Innocent III.[53] But they also came back with that common, frightening, thirteenth-century disillusionment, the loss of innocence upon having seen the curia: "Vidi, vidi caput mundi."[54]

The insecurity took its most violent symbolic form in the belief that poison was rampant in the curia. People whose deaths would seem to have helped no one were constantly thought in danger. Archbishop Wickwane of York, in 1281, warned Hugh of Evesham, the then new English cardinal (whose poisoning might, in fact, have come to seem a boon), to keep dangerous concoctions away from his house.[55] And when Evesham died in 1287 the Worcester chronicler wrote that he had been poisoned. (It was also suggested, Evesham so provoked to symmetry, that he, the famous physician who

[51] *Cantilupo*, 276.

[52] *Ibid.*, 273.

[53] See David Knowles, "Some Aspects of the Career of Archbishop Pecham, II" *English Historical Review*, LVII (1942), 178-201, 180.

[54] *Latin Poems Commonly Attributed to Walter Mapes*, ed. Thomas Wright, Camden Society (London, 1841), 217 (line 13).

[55] *The Register of William Wickwane, Lord Archbishop of York*, ed. William Brown, Surtees Society 114 (Durham, 1907) [hereafter *Wickwane*], 195.

had come to cure the malarial fevers of Rome, another symbol of its hot, deadly horror, had died of them.)[56]

Wickwane, whose great enemy was Claxton, kept active a
little company of proctors at the curia. At one point, after two
years of office, he quashed all his early proctorial appointments
and started a fresh collection. Wickwane's tone wavers, in letters to different correspondents, between worry about the
quicksands of Roman subtlety and hope that somehow the
proper negotiation, the properly solicitous letter, properly delivered, may turn the subtlety to his advantage or at least turn
it from harming his church. The registers of English prelates
and the documents of English religious houses record in painful repetition the same sentiments and images, as the guardian
of the church's state at home guides and coaxes those athletes
sent on the actual six weeks' journey (over Alpine passes high
as heaven but cold as hell) into the flaying legalistic vortex.[57]

The flask of poison, the mysterious curial swamps, were generally to be found beyond the Alps in Italy. But although the
English traveled farther and higher to parcel out their money,
their trip seems otherwise similar enough to the trip of local
Italian proctors. In the 1230's Nicola di Manuele, canon and
proctor of Saint Nicholas in Bari, and Biandemiro, the same
convent's prior, were forced to involve their house with greedy
and litigious Roman merchants.[58]

In the same decade, Grifo, the prior and proctor of the con-

---

[56] A. B. Emden, *Biographical Register of the University of Oxford*
(Oxford, 1957-1959), I, 656; Luard, *Annales Monastici*, IV, 494, and
see below, note 155.

[57] For Wickwane, *Wickwane*, 203-204, 206-208, for Alpine passes
see Bremble in Stubbs, *Epistolae Cantuarienses*, 181. See Stubbs,
Epistolae Cantuarienses, lxiii, for the time the trip took, e.g. January
9-February 27.

[58] *Codice diplomatico barese*, ed. Commissione provinciale di arche-
ologia e storia patria [hereafter *C.d.b.*], VI: "Le Pergamene di S. Nicola
Bari (1195-1266)," ed. Francesco Nitti di Vito (Bari, 1906), 87-88 no.
56, 91-94 nos. 58-59, 101 no. 65, 107-108 no. 71 (proctor of San Nicola
kept by imperial edict within the Regno); see too Giovanni Mongelli,
"Le Abbadesse Mitrate di S. Benedetto di Conversano," *Archivi*, 2nd
ser., XXVI (1959), 342-401, 379, for the appointment of Conversano's
proctor, Manetto de Horatiis, in 1272. I am indebted to Mr. Paul
Mosher for this reference.

vent of Ognissanti in Cuti, a suburb of Bari, testified before a
Roman cardinal to the heavy expenses his house had incurred
in sending proctors to Rome; and Grifo's abbot could use as,
one must assume, a plausible excuse for not sending original
documents to Rome, the dangers of the long winter road.[59]
Tomasuccio, the monk proctor of the Cistercian house of
Fiastra in the March of Ancona, for whose expenses in the
curia it was necessary to alienate a tenement for three generations, had creditors' receipts (including that of Galgano,
presumably the familiar papal scribe) scribbled on one of the
instruments he carried about.[60] The monk Matteo of Agri-
gento was sent off by his house, Monreale, to beg a confirmation of privileges from the discouraging, delegating complexi-
ties of Nicholas III's court.[61] In September 1263 Altegrado
Angeli of Loreto, proctor of the house of San Giuliano over
Spoleto, a convent swaying between the Benedictine and Cistercian orders, found it necessary to return to Spoleto to consult his employers. He appointed a subproctor to carry on
his work at the curia in Orvieto, a man called Lanzelotto of
Loreto (a name that sounds like a romantic pastiche but that
assures a geographical if not familial connection between the
members of this little proctorial company).[62]

In 1299, on Friday, July 31, the proctor of a litigious house
of Dominican nuns, Sant'Agnese in Bologna, stood before the
papal palace in Anagni and asked to go in.[63] The proctor,
Tiberto di Giacomo, a *conversus* of the house and not the
order's proctor, whom the nuns used for some routine im-

[59] *C.d.b.*, I: "Le Pergamene del Duomo di Bari (952-1264)," ed.
G. B. Nitto De Rossi and Francesco Nitti di Vito (Bari, 1897), 179;
C.d.b., VI: "Le Pergamene di S. Nicola Bari (1195-1266)," ed. Fran-
cesco Nitti di Vito, 97-98; see also below, Chapter II.

[60] Rome, Archivio di stato, Pergamene di Fiastra, no. 1351; for
Fiastra's involvements see below, Chapter IV.

[61] G. L. Lello, *Descrizione del Real Tempio e Monasterio di Santa
Maria Nuova di Morreale, vite de' suoi arcivescovi, abbati, e signori,
col sommario de i privilegi della detta Santa Chiesa* (Palermo, 1702),
14-15.

[62] Rome, Archivio di stato, Pergamene di Fiastra, no. 1275, and see
also no. 1291.

[63] Bologna, Archivio di stato, 7/5597, F 392.

petrations, discussed entering the palace with the gate-keeper Rodolfo before the gate through which those who could went to the room in which Boniface VIII held public consistories.[64] Tiberto had the discussion notarized, and the professional proctor Pietro of Treviso acted as a witness, so that it could be officially proved that an essential, initially futile attempt had been made. Archbishops and bishops, Benedictines, Cistercians, Dominican nuns, and Camaldolese monks from Italian dioceses and religious houses created proctor after proctor and sent them off to the curia, proctors empowered to borrow money and to defend their houses and their churches as best they could.

A group of Camaldolese documents from the late 1250's and from the diocese of Arezzo is a fair sample of the urgent repetitiveness of proctorial arrangements, of the insistent, felt, necessity for adequate local representation at the curia (and adequate meant, particularly, with properly formulated instruments of appointment). These documents were produced in connection with a series of interrelated disputes between Guglielmino degli Ubertini, bishop of Arezzo, on one side, and Camaldoli and its Aretine daughter houses, on the other. The dispute stretched from 1258, when Alexander IV granted the Camaldolese a general exemption, their use of which Bishop Guglielmino felt violated his episcopal rights and made impossible the performance of his duties, to 1268, when the contesting parties made formal a compromise that was in fact a victory for the Camaldolese.[65]

On 12 February 1258 in the cloister of San Michele in Arezzo the imperial notary Paolo Gambiera notarized the in-

[64] For an example of the use of the order's proctor see Bologna, Archivio di stato, bolle, busta 1, no. 11 (Urban IV, Viterbo, 13 September 1261).

[65] *Annales Camaldulenses*, ed. J. B. Mittarelli and Anselmo Costodoni, v (Venice, 1760), 33-34, 135-142, 201; *Documenti per la storia della città di Arezzo*, ed. Ubaldo Pasqui (Florence, 1899—), ii, 164-165, 350, 407-413; for an introduction to Camaldoli in its later medieval form see P. J. Jones, "A Tuscan Monastic Lordship in the Later Middle Ages: Camaldoli," *Journal of Ecclesiastical History*, v (1954), 168-183; for a discussion of Guglielmino as bishop see below, Chapter III.

strument through which Martino, prior of Camaldoli, acting
for his house and the whole order, recorded his making Giovanni, prior of San Bartolomeo of Anghiari (who was present), and Guglielmo, claustral prior of Sant'Apollinare in
Classe in the diocese of Ravenna (who was not present), proctors for the order at the papal curia for the order's dispute with
the bishop of Arezzo.[66] (In November 1257 Alexander IV
had confirmed to the prior the order's privilege of constituting
a proctor general for the order at the curia.)[67] On 16 February,
in the cloister of San Salvatore at Selvamonda, Guido, abbot
of that monastery, made the same two priors, neither of whom
was present, the proctors of his specific monastery in the dispute with the bishop in the curia; and the imperial notary,
Paolo Gambiera, who had notarized Martino's instrument,
notarized Guido's.[68] On 28 March, in the cloister of San Bartolomeo in Anghiari, the prior, Giovanni, himself the order's
proctor in the previous month, named Guglielmo of Sant'-
Apollinare, Master Compagno of Volterra, Monaco, a clerk
of Pisa, and Pelle, a *conversus* of Anghiari, proctors of his
monastery in disputes with the bishop of Arezzo, his vicar,
and the bishop elect of Volterra, in or out of the curia, before
any auditor, but particularly before Pietro Capocci, cardinal
deacon of San Giorgio in Velabro (the auditor designate for
the dispute).[69] On the following day Ventura, abbot of
Tuoma, in the cloister of his monastery, made Guglielmo,
Giovanni, Compagno, and Monaco his monastery's proctors;
and on 31 March, Mauro, abbot of San Salvatore, Berar-
denga, at his monastery, made the same men its proctors.[70]
Similar actions were taken on 1 April in Pozzo at the house

[66] Florence, Archivio di stato, Conventi soppressi, Camaldoli, 12
Febb. 1258; I am grateful to Mr. P. J. Jones for his having written
to me of the richness of this fond.
[67] Florence, Archivio di stato, conventi soppressi, Camaldoli, 8 Nov.
1257.
[68] Florence, Archivio di stato, conventi soppressi, Camaldoli, 16
Febb. 1258.
[69] Florence, Archivio di stato, conventi soppressi, Camaldoli, 28
Marz. 1258.
[70] Florence, Archivio di stato, conventi soppressi, Camaldoli, 29 Marz.
1258; 31 Marz. 1258.

of a Ventura di Mabilia by Benedetto, prior of San Quirico delle Rose, for his house, and on 2 April at Pieve di Chio (before the rectors of Petreto and San Martino) by Deodato, prior of San Savino Val di Chio, and on the same day by the gate of Castiglion Aretino by Simone, prior of the nearby house of Pozzo.[71] On 3 April, Radulfo, prior of Fieri sopra Cortona, in his cloister, acted similarly.[72] On 4 April, Martino, prior of Camaldoli, again in the cloisters of San Michele in the city of Arezzo, but acting with a notary different from the one he had used in February, made Guglielmo, Giovanni, Compagno, who were absent, and the *conversus* Pelle, his house's and order's proctors, particularly in the case with the bishop of Arezzo, his vicar, and the elect of Volterra, and especially before the cardinal deacon of San Giorgio as auditor; by this time Martino also found it wise to include a clause empowering the proctors to receive absolution for members of the order from sentences of excommunication pronounced by the bishop of Arezzo.[73] In two months ten notaries had collected from this circle of Aretine Camaldolese houses increasingly elaborate statements making a slightly varying group of men proctors to act for them in the Roman curia, and, in the later instruments, particularly before a specific auditor.

A quarter of a century later, on 3 September 1281, in his chapter house, Paolo, abbot of the Camaldolese monastery of San Silvestro of Monte Subasio in the area of Spello (that narrow strip of the diocese of Spoleto which stretched between the dioceses of Assisi and Foligno and touched the diocese of Nocera Umbra), made proctors for his house. An imperial notary from Spello, Pietro di Filippo, notarized the abbot's two quite separate instruments. In one the abbot made Dom Francesco Rustichelle and Petrillo Andree of Assisi proctors in actions before Orlando, bishop of Spoleto, vicar

[71] Florence, Archivio di stato, conventi soppressi, Camaldoli, 1 Apr. 1258; 2 Apr. 1258.

[72] Florence, Archivio di stato, conventi soppressi, Camaldoli, 3 Apr. 1258.

[73] Florence, Archivio di stato, conventi soppressi, Camaldoli, 4 Apr. 1258.

in spiritualities within the duchy of Spoleto, or before Andrea
or Giacomo, his vicars, or before Biagio, canon of San Lorenzo, Spello, or Ranaldo, canon of Santa Maria, Spello, the
bishop's officials or *custodes*. In the other instrument Abbot
Paolo made the Camaldolese monk Giacomo Visconti "sin-
dicum, procuratorem, actorem, et nuncium specialem" of the
convent in the Roman curia with the variety of powers necessary for a proctor who participated in cases.[74]

On 7 September 1244 the nuns of the convent of Cosma e
Damiano in Mica Aurea (San Cosimato) in Trastevere within
the city of Rome, who were of the order of Claresses, made
Girardo Odonis their proctor in their disputes with a miscellany of heirs in a full but undifferentiated instrument.[75] Up
and down the peninsula and in the islands, at Vercelli,
Bologna, Siena, Fiastra, Cava, Avellino, Bari, Monreale,
everywhere, religious corporations gathered at the sound of
their bell, or at the accustomed hour, in chapter houses and
cloisters and parlors and abbots' chambers to make men they
knew or trusted, or were advised to trust, their proctors to
represent them, to be themselves, legally, so that they might in
corporate person act in various courts including the highest
ones, those of the Roman curia. And in this activity monasteries and houses of friars were not different from secular
chapters of priests and clerks.

Nothing seems more central to the thirteenth century and
to the connections and contingencies of its units than its assumed necessity for representation by proctors. A difficult level
of sophistication demanded that the absent be parties to important and potentially expensive actions and that they act as
if they were present and capable individuals. Thus the absent
and the corporate and the inept created proctors for themselves
through elaborate and formally exact actions, recorded in
sealed or notarized documents. A flaw in one of these instruments could postpone or invalidate an action, and it was important that this should not accidentally occur. Formularies

---

[74] Florence, Archivio di stato, conventi soppressi, Camaldoli, 3 Sett.
1281 (both); see Waley, *Papal State*, 320.

[75] Rome, Archivio di stato, Pergamene di Santi Cosma e Damiano,
252.

guided local writers; and scribes and notaries quickly gained practice in the form.

The thirteenth century, again, constantly acted through proctors.[76] Proctors received grants of land and loans; they

[76] This constant action through proctors is obviously very closely connected with extremely important contemporary institutional developments in various directions, with the various faces of the ideas of representation and corporation, see, e.g.: Gaines Post, "Plena Potestas and Consent in Medieval Assemblies: A Study in Romano-Canonical Procedure and the Rise of Representation, 1150-1325," *Traditio*, I (1943), 355-408; Martin Weinbaum, *The Incorporation of Boroughs* (Manchester, 1937), 1-27, and G. H. Martin, "The English Borough in the Thirteenth Century," *Transactions of the Royal Historical Society*, 5th ser., XIII (1963), 123-144; John T. Noonan, *The Scholastic Analysis of Usury* (Cambridge, Mass., 1957), 133-153; Brian Tierney, *Foundations of the Conciliar Theory* (Cambridge, 1955); and, too, Hastings Rashdall, *The Universities of Europe in the Middle Ages*, ed. F. M. Powicke and A. B. Emden (Oxford, 1936) (and see note 177 below), and Powicke, *Henry III*. For a recent, thorough, and sophisticated exploration of the theoretical, legal problems of corporation (and of related problems) in thirteenth-century canonical writings, see an unpublished Harvard Ph.D. thesis: Gerard E. Caspary, "The King and the Two Laws: A Study of the Influence of Roman and Canon Law on the Development of Ideas on Kingship in Fourteenth-Century England," 190-270. The formularies that discuss the making of proctors survive too numerously and too familiarly to require a list of examples, but a nice example of an unfamiliar formulary that includes letters for making proctors and that is unpretentiously filed among the other surviving documents of a Benedictine convent is Durham Dean and Chapter Archives, Locellus XX. 24; for the importance attached to the form of the instrument see *Die Summa Aurea des Willelmus de Drokeda*, ed. Ludwig Wahrmund, Quellen z. Geschichte des römisch kanonischen Processes im Mittelalter, vol. II, pt. 2 (Innsbruck, 1914), 94-171; Brentano, *York Metropolitan Jurisdiction*, 220-225; for various terms used and legal definitions from Ulpian through Hostiensis, see Donald E. Queller, "Thirteenth-Century Diplomatic Envoys: *Nuncii* and *Procuratores*," *Speculum*, xxv (1960)—the mid-thirteenth-century documents that I have used often, as Queller suggests, equate syndic, proctor, actor, and yconomus; see, too, William Diekamp, "Zum päpstlichen Urkundenwesen des XI, XII, und der ersten Hälfte des XIII Jahrhunderts," *Mitteilungen des Instituts für österreichische Geschichtsforschung*, III (1882), 565-626, 603-604; see for comparison: G. *Giffard*, 258, 275; *Cantilupo*, 106-107; *Registrum Ricardi de Swinfield, Episcopi Herefordensis*, ed. William W. Capes, Canterbury and York Society (London, 1909) [hereafter *Swinfield*],

appeared for the parties in law suits, and sought privileges from governments. They negotiated treaties; and, at Rome, they selected judges delegate. In a nice example of the reverse of the sort of proctor-making most frequently to be found, Gentile de Fighino, a notary working at the Roman curia, acting within the parish of San Salvatore in Campo "Sancti Francisci" in Rome in March 1289, made three Servites, Lothoringo the prior general, whoever should be prior of the house in Florence, and Sostegno of Florence, his proctors and special nuncios particularly for collecting rents and debts.[77]

Lists of proctors' names, their towns and countries, their commissions, their employers, their bankers, may well seem long and tedious. But this tedious intricacy is of the utmost importance. This dry machine is the heart of the administrative church. The connections between employer and proctor and banker and papal official are that heart's vital tissues. Because thirteenth-century proctors have lost their biographies and retained only their names and places and bits of their business, because they are so cell-like or corpuscular, they look dull at first sight; but, to modify the image, their valences connect the ecclesiastical world.

Through this system of proctors the world's person was formally present at the curia. Saint Cuthbert of Durham and Saint Nicholas of Bari could stand side by side on the streets of Tivoli. Their corporate persons were represented almost as personally as were the archbishop of York, the archbishop of Bari, or the king of England, and in much the same way.

Although local proctors were constantly being sent to the curia, and although they were undoubtedly the most trust-

---

67; *Registrum Johannis de Pontissara, Episcopi Wyntoniensis*, ed. Cecil Deedes, Canterbury and York Society (London, 1913-1924) [hereafter *Pontissara*], 271-272; and see *Winchelsey*, 544-545. I was unable to read Miss Sayers's article on Canterbury proctors (see above, note 30) before writing this section. I have made references to some of the more obvious connections, but the entire article is pertinent to this discussion.

[77] Florence, Archivio di stato, conventi soppressi, Santissima Annunziata, 31 Marz. 1289; for Evesham's making a proctor in England, *G. Giffard*, II, 266. Curial persons had to be present at home, too.

worthy kind of proctors, they were not the only or the most expert proctors to be found in the curia. The curia had collected around it, by the second half of the thirteenth century, a large community of resident or intermittently resident professional proctors specifically expert in the vagaries of its offices and personalities.[78] Their names appear in the little nests of curial figures, like papal scribes, in witness lists, particularly witnessing recorded actions before officers like cardinal auditors or the *auditor contradictarum litterarum.*[79] There is occasional reference to the place where a proctor lived, like the house in Perugia where, in 1265, Waldinus, the proctor at the Roman curia, and his companions (?associates, perhaps even partners, *socii*) stayed.[80]

Henry the Poet, in his versified contemporary satire on the curia, had his parting sophisticate answer the questioning, foolish German, coming to Rome, who had asked if he might not find some proctor in the city who could help him. One would be more likely, said the sophisticate (parodying, in passing, Cassiodorus), to find an infant child deserted by its mother, grazing grasses by their herds, green waters by their fish, a pond by its croaking frogs, a bride by her young husband, a mother's breast by her suckling babe, than find the Sacred City deserted by its proctors.[81] Henry the Poet "might

[78] See: Rudolf von Heckel, "Das Aufkommen der ständigen Prokuratoren an der päpstlichen Kurie im 13. Jahrhundert," *Miscellanea Francesco Ehrle,* II, Studi e Testi, 38 (Vatican City, 1924), 290-321; Herde, *Beiträge,* particularly 80-100; Robert Fawtier, in *Les Registres de Boniface VIII,* ed. Georges Digard, Maurice Faucon, Antoine Thomas, and Robert Fawtier, Bibliothèque des écoles françaises d'Athènes et de Rome (Paris, 1907-1939) [hereafter *Boniface VIII*], IV, xxxiii-xxxviii; Robert Brentano, "Peter of Assisi as Witness," *Quellen und Forschungen aus italienischen Archiven und Bibliotheken,* XLI (1961), 323-325.

[79] E.g. Rome, Archivio di stato, Pergamene di Fiastra, 1476; Florence, Archivio di stato, conventi soppressi, Cestello, 23 Sett. 1295.

[80] Heckel, "Das Aufkommen," 84; Herde, *Beiträge,* 85 and n. 26; *Les Registres de Clément IV,* ed. Édouard Jordan, Bibliothèque des écoles françaises d'Athènes et de Rome (Paris, 1893-1945) [hereafter *Clément IV*], 84.

[81] Hermann von Grauert, *Magister Heinrich der Poet in Würzburg und die römische Kurie,* Abhandlungen der königlich bayerischen

weep like Xerxes:—so many serried rows sit perched there like winged creatures, alighted out of heaven," or laugh like Innocent III understanding Robert Clipston to have said that the supply of advocates in the curia had been exhausted.[82]

It was the custom of the English involved with the curia to combine the services of these wily but uncommitted professionals with those of the proctors whom they had sent from home. In September 1282 Anselm of Eastry, acting as proctor at the curia for Archbishop Pecham of Canterbury, was empowered not only to contract a loan but also to appoint a curial proctor; and in the same month the archbishop appointed as curial proctors the important resident professional Filippo of Pomonte along with Giacomo of Trevi.[83] One of the problems of Richard Claxton, prior of Durham, in dealing with his curial proctors in the years 1284 and 1285 had to do with which letters of instructions should be read only by his local proctors. One letter was to be read only by the Durham monk Henry of Teesdale, very specifically by no other person. Another letter Adam of Fileby, the professional proctor, must show to Henry. A third was directed to either Henry or Adam, and a fourth to either Henry or Thomas of Normanton, the Durham clerk proctor.[84]

The names of the curial proctors who were responsible for the impetration of bulls, for actually procuring them, were often, in the later thirteenth century, written on the tops of the bulls' dorses. These dorses seem inarticulate pieces of evidence; but in combination numbers of bulls can build a picture, always fragmentary of course, of the pattern of proctors' business operations.

Filippo da Pomonte (Philippus, Phylyppus de Pomonte), sometimes alone, sometimes with Nicola da San Vittore (N de Sancto Victore), was active for three great Franciscan

Akademie der Wissenschaften, philosophisch-philologische und historische Klasse, xxvii (1912), vv. 127-133.

[82] Macray, *Chronicon Abbatiae de Evesham*, 189.

[83] *Peckham*, iii, 1058.

[84] Brentano, *York Metropolitan Jurisdiction*, 214-217, 208-213 (Durham Dean and Chapter Archives, M.C. 5820, "8 Instruments," 5, 6, 1, 3).

communities, San Francesco in Assisi, Santa Croce in Florence, and the Frari in Venice.[85] Nicola appears alone acting for Santa Croce and San Francesco.[86] Filippo was appointed a proctor by the Franciscan Pecham, and he had represented Canterbury's Benedictine chapter, Christ Church, in 1277, before Pecham's nomination.[87] Both Nicola and Filippo appear on a 1289 Canterbury receipt.[88] Nicola was also active for Bavarian Minorites in the 1280's and for the chapter of Paris in 1294.[89] In the late 1270's and 1280's Filippo and Nicola would seem to have formed a partnership, perhaps not constant, employed, but not exclusively, by Franciscan congrega-

[85] Assisi, Archivio communale, San Francesco, no. 213 (1, 2)—with Nicola; Florence, Archivio di stato, conventi soppressi, Santa Croce, 18 Genn. 1286—with Nicola; Venice, Archivio di stato, Frari di Venezia, II, 43, 44—alone. For Filippo see Sayers, "Canterbury Proctors," 318–320, 327–328; for Nicola, 328—for Nicola as a "literate" witness see Rome, Archivio di stato, San Cosimato, 259.

[86] Assisi, Archivio communale, San Francesco, nos. 212 (1, 2), 215; Florence, Archivio di stato, conventi soppressi, Santa Croce, 18 Genn. 1286—identified by the same archival reference as the jointly proctored, similarly dated, Honorius IV bull in the note above, but with a different scribe—"O. Laud" instead of the jointly proctored bull's "F.R." (For F.R. see Fawtier, Boniface VIII, xxi; Florence, Archivio di stato, conventi soppressi, San Francesco di Pistoia, 18 Genn. 1283—a Franciscan proctorial privilege; Robert Brentano, "'Consolatio defuncte caritatis': a Celestine V letter at Cava," English Historical Review, LXXVI [1961], 298-303, 300 nn. 1, 3—there is possibly a suggestion, no more, that F.R. may have been a scribe in some way favored by Franciscans. For O. Laud see e.g. Bologna, Archivio di stato, bolle, busta 1, no. 7—Nicholas III bull, 1279.)

[87] Pecham, see above, note 83; Christ Church, Canterbury Cathedral Archives, Ch. Ant. C 285. I am very grateful to Mr. Hugh Lawrence for having told me of this Canterbury document and for then describing it to me in detail. It is a littera (or littere) conveniencie issued from Viterbo by Gerard of Parma, auditor contradictarum litterarum on 22 April 1277. In it Filippo the convent chapter's proctor has chosen as his judge in a dispute the Benedictine prior of Rochester; his opponent has chosen for a disputant, who was a rector, the archdeacon of Rochester; while the auditor granted as the common third judge the bishop of Rochester: an important representative of regular interests, of secular interests, and a third man who must in theory represent the total interest of his flock—a very patterned selection.

[88] Hist. MSS Comm., Fifth Report, 451 (C 224).

[89] Herde, Beiträge, 95; Fawtier, Boniface VIII, IV, xxxvi.

tions. Nicola and Filippo were not, even for these congregations, the only specifically named proctors—that is, proctors
not designated in the bull as being simply for the Minorites.[90]
A proctor named Bonaspes of Assisi, who may have been
Nicola and Filippo's predecessor, was called proctor of the
nuns of Assisi in 1277.[91] He had acted for the nuns, Franciscan Claresses, of Santi Cosma e Damiano (San Cosimato) in
Trastevere in 1272, and in 1274 for the Frari, but in 1276 for
the Cluniacs.[92]

Archbishop John Romeyn of York used a proctor named
Guido of Novara, pretty obviously Italian; one of Romeyn's
contemporaries at Canterbury, Archbishop Robert Winchelsey, used a proctor who appears as "W de Donnebroke," as
obviously insular.[93] The imposing proctor "N de Vico"
(?Nicola Novelli de Vico) was active for England and Italy
as he was for France, for great figures like the King of England and the commune of Bologna.[94]

[90] For "Minor'," see Venice, Archivio di stato, Frari di Venezia, ii,
17, 18, 19, 21, 22, 28, 30, 32, 33, 34, 37, 39 (Minorum), 40, 41—but
these are all from the 1240's, 1250's, and 1260's, before Filippo and
Nicola's Franciscan work, as is Herde's example from Saint Agnes,
Würzburg (Beiträge, 100, cf. 95). The "Minor'" bulls from the Frari
are interrupted by one procured in 1260 by the proctor Fr. R. who,
like Nicola da San Vittore, appears on Saint Agnes, Würzburg bulls
(Herde, Beiträge, 100: Fr. R. in 1257 [3] and 1258 [1]; Nicolà in
1284 [1]). Michael Petri is another proctor, from the 1280's, preserved at Santa Croce: Florence, Archivio di stato, conventi soppressi,
Santa Croce, 18 Genn. 1282 (1, 2).
[91] Todi, Archivio communale, iv, ii, 39.
[92] Rome, Archivio di stato, Pergamene di Santi Cosma e Damiano,
no. 292 ("Bonaspes pro Roma"); Venice, Archivio di stato, Frari, ii,
42; London, British Museum, Additional Charter 1547 (John XXI for
Cluniacs); also, see Herde, Beiträge, 89, 98: for the college of Altötting
in 1267, and for the Benedictines of Seeon, twice in the same year.
[93] London, Public Record Office, S.C. 7, 51(3), Honorius IV to
King Edward for John (for Guido, see also Herde, Beiträge, 99);
London, Public Record Office, S.C. 7, 9(7), Celestine V to King Edward
for Winchelsey (scribe: O. Laud)—see "Dunbridge" in Winchelsey,
564-565, 568-569, 578, 639, 658, 670, 680, 1052-1054, 1060-1061.
[94] London, Public Record Office, S.C. 7:6(1), 6(12); Bologna,
Archivio di stato, bolle, busta 1, no. 16; see Fawtier, Boniface VIII,
xxxvi, and also xi.

There were at least three Poggibonsi proctors active at the curia in the late thirteenth century: "Francus," "Jacobus," and "Bardus." Giacomo was active for the Servites of Florence in 1291, for the Spedale of Siena in 1281, and for the Benedictine house of San Salvatore, Castiglione in 1288.[95] Bardo was employed by Bishop Thomas Cantilupe of Hereford in 1275 and at least through 1279.[96] Franco had a more apparently varied career, but one that suggests a connection, perhaps of blood, perhaps of partnership, with Giacomo. Franco like Giacomo worked for the Spedale of Siena; one Spedale dorse, from 1281, corrects his name to Giacomo's.[97] But Franco was also active for the Benedictine prior and convent of Durham, and for the Minoresses of the English house of Waterbeach, in 1302 and 1295.[98] The fragments of people that these men must remain contrast with the at least larger fragment of Pietro of Assisi.

A man named Pietro of Assisi (perhaps a succession of men acting under the same name) was a prominent curial proctor throughout the second half of the thirteenth century.[99] Toward the end of the century his name is frequently coupled with that of Filippo (generally "Phy" and not infrequently following the Assisi abbreviation). Again as in the case of Pomonte and San Vittore and of the Poggibonsi proctors, there is every suggestion of a partnership or an agency (after all, proctors could look at contemporary bankers). The suggestion is strengthened by the later existence of Angelo of Assisi

[95] Florence, Archivio di stato, conventi soppressi, Santissima Annunziata, 28 Agosto 1291 (1, 2, 3), 23 Luglio 1291; Siena, Archivio di stato, Spedale, 28 Agosto 1281; Naples, Archivio di stato, Archivio Caracciolo di Santo Bono, Castiglione, Abbazia di San Salvatore, no. 3.

[96] *Cantilupo*, 12-13, 15, 18, 19, 213-214, 250 (Bardo was dead before 15 August 1280); cf. *Peckham*, III, 1003, payment of a pension to Bardo.

[97] Siena, Archivio di stato, Spedale: 31 Agosto 1281; 31 Ottobre 1285 (1, 2, 3, 4); 25 Agosto 1281.

[98] Durham Dean and Chapter Archives, 3, 2, Pap. 4, 5, 6: to abbot of Whitby, for prior and convent of Durham; London, British Museum, Cart. Cott., xi, 19—cf. Fawtier, *Boniface VIII*, xxxiv.

[99] Heckel, "Das Aufkommen," 319-320; Herde, *Beiträge*, 85-86; Brentano, "Peter of Assisi."

and I of Assisi, and the earlier existence of Bonaspes.[100] At the
very least Assisi was peculiarly productive of proctors in the
thirteenth century, as it was of saints, and it is not unlikely that
the proctors were helped to prominence by the growing order
at home—that is, that the saints and the proctors were connected. (The places from which proctors took their names
suggest general patterns of advancement, although not very
rigid ones: Orvieto, Aquila, Montepulciano, Assisi, Pontecorvo, Pisa—curial places, places connected with great prelates
and orders, reminiscent of those baronial, episcopal and
prebendal manors and towns, from Ninfa to Nassington, from
which administrative clerks were advanced to importance in
the thirteenth century.)[101] It seems possible, too, that even the
single names on the bulls' dorses sometimes refer to an office
or agency rather than to a simple person (but admittedly when
these generally rather shadowy figures do appear in any substance, it is, except for Waldinus in his house in Perugia, the
substance of an individual man).

[100] For Angelo and I, see Herde, *Beiträge*, 92, 95. For a discussion
of the table of organization of medieval merchant companies, see
Armando Sapori, "Il Personale delle Compagnie mercantili del
medioevo," *Studi di storia economica medievale* (Florence, 1940),
435-503.

[101] E.g.: P. de Orvieto (Durham Dean and Chapter Archives, 4, 1,
Pap. 2, 28); B. de Pontecorvo (Cava, Badia, Arc. Nuov., o.1, 2, and
Brentano, "*Consolatio defuncte caritatis*," 299); P. de Montepulciano
(Florence, Archivio di stato, Montepulciano, 7 Luglio 1280); Helyas
de Spoleto (Palermo, Archivio di stato, Tabulario del Monastero di
Santa Maria Maddalena di Valle Giosafat, Pergamena no. 153);
Angelus Josaphat (Palermo, Archivio di stato, Santa Maria Maddalena,
127); Michael de Aquila (Palermo, Archivio di stato, 121); Johannes
Pisanus (Florence, Archivio di stato, conventi soppressi: Badia, 28
Mag. 1281 and 17 Giug. 1281; Camaldoli, 25 Febb. 1286; and see
Heckel, "Das Aufkommen," 320 n.1, Fawtier, *Boniface VIII*, iv, xxv,
and Herde, *Beiträge*, 95, 98); P. (?Pandulfo) da Milano (de Mediolan')
reminds the reader of the various patrons available for the initial
promotion of clerks in some areas (Palermo, Archivio di stato, Cefalù,
Mensa vescovile, no. 73, where, as the dorse states, P. acts for the
bishop of Cefalù, in 1306), as also does V. (?) da Orvieto, acting for
the bishop and in favor of the chapter of Orvieto (Orvieto, Archivio
capitolare, bolle, 5 Nov. 1297 [1, 2]); Angelo of Giosafat, and B. (Benedetto) of Pontecorvo, also point up the difficulty of telling a local
from a curial proctor; see further below.

Man, men, or agency, Pietro of Assisi was employed by religious corporations in at least Germany, France, England, and Italy.[102] He was perhaps particularly adept at the difficult negotiations involved in disputes and the selection of judges before the *auditor contradictarum litterarum*.[103] He was certainly for a time the proctor general of the Cistercians.[104] He was connected with Cistercian houses in France and Germany (Foigny, Ebrach, Langheim, Waldsassen).[105] In his work for the German daughters and granddaughters of Morimond he was in 1289 and 1291 associated with Filippo; and once, in 1290, for Ebrach, a house with particularly frequent, preserved, connections with Assisi proctors, he was replaced by Filippo.[106] Pietro worked in 1281 and 1282, again with Filippo, for the Cistercian monastery of San Salvatore Settimo, near Florence.[107] But Pietro was not monopolized by the Cistercians. He worked for the bishop and chapter of Bamberg.[108] He worked for the two great English Benedictine convents of Westminster and Durham.[109] More significantly perhaps he worked for the Franciscans of Assisi; he in fact got them their copy of *Clericis laicos*.[110] In 1254 a Pietro of Assisi had been provided to a canonry of the cathedral church of San Rufino

[102] And in areas it is even less easy to fit into simple national categories: for his work for Magdenau, see Anton Largiadèr, "Die Papsturkunden des Zisterzienserinnenklosters Magdenau," *Mitteilungen des Instituts für österreichische Geschichtsforschung*, LXVIII (1960), 140-155, 142 and n. 9, 152-153 (1251).

[103] See Brentano, *York Metropolitan Jurisdiction*, 218-219 (Durham Dean and Chapter Archives, Loc. XIV.4.j; Westminster Abbey Muniments, 32644—seal strip).

[104] Brentano, "Peter of Assisi," 324, 325.

[105] Fawtier, *Boniface VIII*, IV, xxxvii; Herde, *Beiträge*, 91-92, 93-94, 99, and particularly 86.

[106] Herde, *Beiträge*, 91-92.

[107] Florence, Archivio di stato, conventi soppressi, Cestello, 15 Ott. 1281, and 18 Genn. 1282; for San Salvatore Settimo, see P. J. Jones, "Le Finanze della badia Cistercense di Settimo nel XIV secolo," *Rivista di storia della chiesa in Italia*, X (1956), 90-122.

[108] Herde, *Beiträge*, 90.

[109] See above, note 103, and Durham Dean and Chapter Archives: 2, 2, Pap. 1; 4, 1, Pap. 1 and 13; 4, 2, Pap. 8.

[110] Assisi, Archivio communale, San Francesco, nos. 239, 240, 242 (*clericis laicos*).

in Assisi; and in 1263 a Pietro, canon of the cathedral of church of San Rufino in Assisi and notary, was active as the proctor for San Rufino before a canon of Todi acting as papal executor.[111] In 1260, Filippo, clerk and proctor of the chapter, acted for the church before cardinal auditors in a case between the chapter and an archpriest pretending to a canonry.[112] These could, little more can be said, be the right canon Pietro and Filippo.[113] Pietro was active for a very long time, and it is this length that argues his divisibility most strongly. He worked for the Cistercian house of Hardehausen in 1241, for Langheim in 1297.[114]

What, beyond his endurance and activity, and in spite of the doubt about his number, makes Pietro a more imposing fragment than most of his fellows is that he breaks silence, and silence is broken about him. He is not completely caught in the repeated mime of the bull's dorse or the seal strip of the auditor's letter, or even in contract or receipt. In the sickening congestion of Henry the Poet's proctors crowding around the papal curia, "Petrus ab Assisio" is given a specific if difficult and unattractive form. He exists, although not in an abundance of descriptive detail, in the passing attack of the poem. Henry mocks him, the "Cistercian abbot."[115]

[111] *Innocent IV*, III, 386 no. 7368; Assisi, Archivio capitolare di San Rufino (within the Duomo), fasc. 3, no. 114. (It would, of course, be a serious error to assume cordial relations between San Francesco and San Rufino.)

[112] Assisi, Archivio capitolare di San Rufino, fasc. 3, no. 101.

[113] The Pietro of Durham Dean and Chapter Archives, Loc. XIV.4.j, is called canon of Assisi.

[114] Heckel, "Das Aufkommen," 319-320; Herde, *Beiträge*, 94. Herde (86 and n. 37) discusses this length. It is remarkable, but not impossible, that a proctor should be so long active. (Napoleone Orsini was a cardinal from 1288 to 1342.) I do not believe, as some historians who have involved themselves with this problem have, that proctors necessarily wrote their own names on the dorses of bulls (see Brentano, "*Consolatio defuncte caritatis*"); if they did, there were certainly several Pietros. If they did not, there still may have been, as I think, several clerks working under his name.

[115] Grauert, *Magister Heinrich*, vv. 171-178; Herde (*Beiträge*, 86) is persuaded by this and the evidence from a 1259 Alexander IV bull ("P de Ass Cister abbas") that one Pietro was in fact a Cistercian

Pietro is also preserved, of course in fragment, through an odd and fortunate survival, but an undated one, in the act of talking about his office on the witness stand.[116] On 30 August in about the year 1265, presumably in the court of a cardinal auditor, in a dispute between the Cistercian house of Chiaravalle di Fiastra in the March of Ancona and the semi-filiated house of San Giuliano over Spoleto, Pietro was asked what he knew of letters impetrated the last Easter by the proctor of San Giuliano, and what of the selection of judges delegate by the proctors of both sides. He said San Giuliano's proctor had come and appealed; he knew because he had seen the letter and held it in his hands and because he had met with the San Giuliano proctor for selecting judges. Asked who the judges were, Pietro could not remember, except that he thought that the third judge, the supposedly impartial member of the bench, who was given by the auditor and who was often the center of much intrigue, had in this case been the prior of San Venanzio (who was in fact a papal scribe financially connected with Fiastra).[117] Peter could not remember

abbot. I find it unlikely. I think that on the tongue of the satirist the constant Cistercian proctor was a mock abbot; and I think that it is possible to explain the dorse notation by the fact that patrons are sometimes recorded there. But it would be foolish to dismiss any Herde judgment lightly. His work is based not only upon his own industrious and perceptive searching, but also on information and suggestions from Heckel's notes, presumably from Prof. Acht of Munich, and from the "Schedario Baumgarten," Baumgarten's records of the notations on papal bulls, which are preserved within the Vatican archives, and which are just now in process of publication: *Schedario Baumgarten, Descrizione diplomatica di Bolle e Brevi originali da Innocenzo III a Pio IX*, ed. Giulio Battelli, i-ii: *Innocenzo III-Innocenzo IV, 1198-1254; Alessandro IV-Benedetto XI, 1254-1304* (Città del Vaticano, 1965-1966). Herde's is an epoch-making book for the study of the chancery; still on this point I think he has weighed his pieces of specific evidence incorrectly, and too heavily against the general evidence existing about Pietro; see my review of his book in *Speculum*, xxxix (1964), 153-155.

[116] Brentano, "Peter of Assisi" (Rome, Archivio di stato, Pergamene di Fiastra, no. 2225); see a full discussion of this case in Chapter IV, below.

[117] Rome, Archivio di stato, Pergamene di Fiastra, no. 1388, and Brentano, "Peter of Assisi," 323 n. 1; for the process of selecting

if he had seen the letter bulled. He did not know if it had been bulled or if, in connection with it, the parties had been cited; but he did know that the letter of confirmation sought by Fiastra had touched upon the same business. He protested finally that his "convencionem judicum" should not be prejudicial to the house of Fiastra because he was not the special proctor of that house but rather the proctor for the whole Cistercian order. The testimony is difficult because it assumes too much knowledge in its reader, but it throws a silhouette of a proctor's memory and of his job. And the fullness of his job seems to have crushed Pietro's memory, if he was being at all candid—but of course candor is not a quality to be expected on a witness stand, nor, as Henry the Poet heavily pointed out, was it to be expected among curial proctors.

Pietro of Assisi was the Cistercian proctor general. The Camaldolese under Alexander IV found it worth the expense to have their privilege of maintaining a proctor general in the curia confirmed. In 1259 the Templars maintained Fra Lamberto as their proctor in the Roman curia.[118] The corporate representation of both Franciscans and Dominicans in the middle and later thirteenth century is clear from the "Minor" and "Predicatorum" of many of their documents.[119] The Franciscans retain talk of their proctor general and the Dominicans lists of theirs from 1256.[120] In 1278 Rainaldo of Aquila was proctor general for the Hospitallers.[121] A sensible

judges see Brentano, *York Metropolitan Jurisdiction*, 153-158, and also see Geoffrey Barraclough, "Audientia litterarum contradictarum," in *Dictionnaire de droit canonique*, ed. R. Naz, 1 (Paris, 1935), 1387-1399.

[118] Florence, Archivio di stato, conventi soppressi, Camaldoli, 8 Nov. 1257; Gelasio Caetani, *Regesta Chartarum* (Caetani), 1 (Perugia, 1925), 36.

[119] "Predicatorum"—e.g. Florence, Archivio di stato, conventi soppressi, Sant'Agnese Montepulciano, 13 Febb. 1296; see G. R. Galbraith, *The Constitution of the Dominican Order* (Manchester, 1925), 136.

[120] See J. J. Berthier, *Le Couvent de Sainte Sabine à Rome* (Rome, 1912), 290-291; the Assisi *Bullarium*, for first year of Martin IV: the *Bullarium* was published by Francesco Pennacchi in the *Archivum Franciscanum Historicum*, vols. VIII, X, XI, XII—for this reference see vol. X (1917), pp. 191-192.

[121] Westminster Abbey Muniments, 9181.

desire for security suggested to later thirteenth-century regulars that they use at the curia a professional proctor connected somewhat permanently with their orders, which were, with or without a permanent connection, less frail than individual houses.

Something of a related desire for security coupled with the hope that one might thus deal with a man not too strange, unpredictable, and invulnerable probably led both English and Italians to their noticeable practice of choosing relatively local men among professional proctors. It is sometimes difficult to be certain, because of this practice, whether the proctor named on a bull's dorse is a local *ad hoc* proctor (these seem still sometimes to have impetrated) or a professional from the neighborhood. Thus Benedetto of Pontecorvo, who acted for the Benedictines of Santissima Trinità at Cava between Naples and Salerno, seems in fact to have been a local Cava proctor.[122] Giovanni Pisano might seem almost equally local if only his work for the quasi-Camaldolese Benedictines of San Savino in the diocese of Pisa and the Augustinian hermits of Sant' Anna in Prato had survived.[123] But he also worked for the Hermits of Paris and for the south German houses of Schönthal and Niederviehbach; and for both the Hermits and Schönthal, in 1299 and 1300, he worked with the same "partner," Bianco da Forno.[124] The problem—local or professional —is pushed similarly toward the same resolution in the cases of Giacomo of Naples who worked for Cava (and who might possibly be the same as the "Neapolis" used by San Nicolà at Bari) and of Giacomo of Reggio who worked for the Hermits of Sant'Agostino in Naples.[125] Giacomo of Naples also worked for the hospital in Eichstätt; Giacomo of Reggio worked with Giovanni Pisano for Niederviehbach.[126]

[122] This is argued in Brentano, "*Consolatio defuncte caritatis,*" 299, from Cava, Archivio di Badia, bolle o.1 and o.2, and arca LVIII, no. 6.

[123] Florence, Archivio di stato, conventi soppressi: Camaldoli, 25 Febb. 1286; Badia, 28 Magg., 17 Giug. 1281. For Sant'Anna, see "De conventu Pratensi S. Annae," *Analecta Augustiniana,* XIX (1943), 20-60.

[124] Fawtier, *Boniface VIII,* IV, xxxv; Herde, *Beiträge,* 98, 95.

[125] Cava, Badia, Arca Nuova N. 43; Bari, San Nicola, 8/20, 9; Naples, Archivio di stato, Sant'Agostino Napoli, no. 5 (catalogued no. 9).

[126] Herde, *Beiträge,* 92, 95.

When proctors for English houses have names like Leonardo of Venafro or Bartolomeo of Bologna for the prior and convent of Durham, they were presumably professionals.[127] But when English proctors have names like the Cistercian Ruffard's Thomas of Brampton or Bishop Ralph Irton of Carlisle's Nicholas of Hexham their status is less certain, although their nationality seems secure.[128] The Durham proctor Peter of Saint Andrew's would seem safely British if he had not also worked for Fürstenfeld, Medlingen, Steingaden, and the Katharinenspital in Regensburg.[129] It is not possible to be sure into which language "Sancto Andrea" should be translated. The uncertainty about the status of proctors is due in part to the fact that Englishmen liked to use English professional proctors and that continentals, and particularly Italians, seem sensibly enough almost never to have used them.[130]

"J de Burton" and Reginald of Saint Alban's are clear examples of the English professional proctor. The Augustinian canons of Holy Trinity Aldgate, London, employed Burton repeatedly; and at least once he procured a bull for the prior and convent of Durham.[131] Reginald, acting for William Wickwane, archbishop of York, matched wits in the selection of judges with Pietro of Assisi, acting for the prior and con-

[127] Leonardo: Durham Dean and Chapter Archives 4, 2, Pap. 7 (Leonardo seems to have been linked particularly with Adam of Fileby as proctor in the affair of Fileby and the executors of Bishop Robert of Holy Island in 1284—Durham Dean and Chapter Archives, 4, 2, Pap. 4, and as witness to Adam's borrowing forty marks sterling from the Abbati in a notary's house in Orvieto in 1283—Durham Dean and Chapter Archives M.C. 7028); Bartolomeo: Durham Dean and Chapter Archives, 3, 2, Pap. 9.

[128] Thomas: London, British Museum, Cart. Harl, III A. 26; Nicholas: London, Public Record Office, S.C. 7, 29 (10).

[129] Durham Dean and Chapter Archives; 1, 2, Pap. 1, 5, 6, 7, 8, 9, 10; 4, 1, Pap. 12, 19 (from 1257 to 1262); Herde, *Beiträge*, 93, 94, 97, 99 (from 1259 to 1261).

[130] Although it would seem unlikely that Italians ever used non-Italian proctors, it would be foolish to be too positive about it; see, for example, the proctor, J. de Hyrberia, who probably worked for the Augustinian Hermits in several parts of Europe: Siena, Archivio di stato, Sant'Agostino, 7 Lugl. 1288, confirming privileges of Augustinians against the pretensions of the Bishop of Paris.

[131] London, Public Record Office, S.C. 7:19(8), 28(20), 29(1); Durham Dean and Chapter Archives, 4, 1, Pap. 29.

vent of Durham—and did a good job of it.[132] Reginald, nine
years later in 1290, again before the *auditor contradictarum
litterarum*, acted for the abbot and convent of Westminster
against the abbot and convent of Pershore.[133] Reginald had
been present in 1285 in Tivoli at Robert of Selsey's declaration about wanting to go home to Canterbury, as had Riccardo
de Spina, exactly two months before he, Riccardo, made formal
his settlement with Westminster over his disputed back salary
as their ex-proctor and over the letters he had got for them but
not given to them.[134] Reginald may possibly have had an extended relationship with Westminster, but he was certainly
capable of changing his professional allegiance from York to
Durham, for whose bishop he eventually worked. One must
presume that Reginald was purely professional in the sense
that he furthered the interests of his employer of the moment.
He was like some contemporary sailing Italian merchant who
could "receive a dozen or several dozen commissions" for the
same trip at the same time.[135]

Flocks of English proctors swarm in the peculiarly articulate
registers of the west country bishops Thomas Cantilupe
(1275-1282) and Richard Swinfield (1283-1317) of Hereford
and Geoffrey Giffard (1268-1301) of Worcester. Letters of
encouragement, reproof, account, detailed instruction, and
fairly detailed description went back and forth from the curial
towns of central Italy to the episcopal manors in the marches.
Proctors change shape. Edmund Warefeld, a Westminster

---

[132] Durham Dean and Chapter Archives, Loc. xiv.4.j; Brentano,
York Metropolitan Jurisdiction, 218-219, and 158-159 for the eventual
results of the selection.

[133] Westminster Abbey Muniments, 22498. For Reginald see, too,
Barbara F. Harvey, ed., *Documents Illustrating the Rule of Walter de
Wenlok, Abbot of Westminster, 1283-1307*, Camden Society (London,
1965), 246.

[134] Canterbury Cathedral Chapter Archives, Ch. Ant. P 57; Westminster Abbey Muniments, 22942.

[135] *Registrum Palatinum Dunelmense*, ed. Thomas Duffus Hardy,
Rolls Series (London, 1873-1878), i, 28-31, for merchants and the
quoted phrase: Gino Luzzatto, *An Economic History of Italy*, tr.
Philip Jones (London, 1961) [hereafter Luzzatto-Jones], 119.

proctor, emerges in Giffard's register as a proctor of Worcester, Westminster's enemy, as well as of Hereford.[136] Evidently
he was a generally employed English proctor. The economic
rise of a more local proctor, Robert Wych, is apparent at
Worcester.

John of Bitterley, a proctor for both Worcester and Hereford, sent to Bishop Giffard from Rome a letter that reached
Worcester on 30 November 1286.[137] Bitterley had arrived
after the feast of the Nativity of the Virgin (8 September) and
had taken the bishop's letters to the English cardinal and to
Berard of Naples in Tivoli, where Honorius IV's court then
was. Bitterley had in October received the bishop's further letters, a letter on merchants for 105 pounds, and questions
about expenses. By January he was able to compose a letter
in which he managed to suggest something of imminent but
precarious general success. He had been trying to enrich the
Worcester *mensa* with the living of Bishop's Cleeve (Clyve).
He had managed to get himself an audience with the pope
and to tell him about the death of Worcester flocks, the steril-
ity of Worcester fields, the rebuilding of Worcester manors,
and the destructiveness of armies. Finally Bitterley had succeeded in getting the pope to say that he would think about
Worcester's difficult economic situation and about the living
of Cleeve.

After the audience Bitterley had talked to Berard of Naples,
and the two of them had decided that the pope's thought
needed a monetary stimulant. Berard and Bitterley then went
to the other Berard, the pope's secretary, an always necessary
agent for anything difficult, according to Bitterley. They

[136] *G. Giffard*, II, 275; Westminster Abbey Muniments, 9181; *Cantilupo*, 12-15, 18, 210, 243, 248-250, 273-283. In an important dispute
with the chapter of Canterbury, a group of bishops from the province
of Canterbury, in 1271, named as one of their proctors at the curia,
Alan Creppyng, a doctor of civil law (*G. Giffard*, I, 146; for Creppyng,
the civil law, and Creppyng's books, see Brentano, *York Metropolitan
Jurisdiction*, 131, 151, and n. 16).

[137] Worcester, Archives within Saint Helen's (Branch of the Worcestershire Record Office), Register of Bishop Giffard, fo. 263, calendared
in *G. Giffard*, 301-302.

promised Berard the secretary 200 pounds for the papal camera before the decision about Cleeve should be made, and they promised forty marks for Berard himself.

Bitterley continued his letter to Giffard by listing exactly what he was managing to get for Worcester and by praising Berard of Naples. He admitted that he had done nothing about a petition against nonresidents that Giffard had sent him, but promised to present it at an opportune time. Then he got down to specific required sums. He insisted that he must pay lesser curial officials at least 160 pounds, that he needed 200 pounds by letters on Italian merchants quickly, that everyone at the curia believed he had the money already, that if they knew it were not true Giffard's affairs and Bitterley's person would be in danger, that if the whole deal did not work out Bitterley would return everything he had not spent for gifts and precious stones.

By all this Giffard was not taken in. With a calm shrewdness seldom evident in English episcopal letters to Rome, he explained precisely the ways in which Bitterley had proved unsuccessful, and he stated clearly his intention not to forward 200 pounds.[138] It was a bad year for Bitterley. Although Cantilupe seems to have supported him with relative confidence in the past, Swinfield was writing to demand an account of his Hereford expenses.[139] The Hereford account reveals that Bitterley had an annual expense-salary of ten marks from Hereford (part of which was brought him by the prior of Holy Trinity Aldgate); he was in 1286 receiving a pension of forty shillings from Worcester.[140]

---

[138] Worcester, Saint Helen's, Register of Bishop Giffard, fo. 263v; *G. Giffard*, 302-303; but Giffard wrote that he had gotten Bitterley the promised living at Badminton.

[139] *Swinfield*, 246-247; or see *A Roll of the Household Expenses of Richard de Swinfield*, ed. John Webb, Camden Society (London, 1854), 202-209.

[140] *G. Giffard*, II, 286; it is constantly interesting to note the moving back and forth from England to the curia of assistants, clerks, "boys": Bitterley's cited letter to Giffard (Worcester, Saint Helen's, Register of Bishop Giffard, fo. 263) concludes with the statement that after the letter had been written (*post confectionem presencium*), Giffard's boy John of Gledesey had come to Bitterley, and that Bitterley was

"Ista credo posse expedire si pecunia non defuerit in hac parte," John of Bitterley wrote to Bishop Giffard.[141] And his words are a text upon which all thirteenth-century curial proctors preached to their patrons. With money everything was possible, without it nothing. Money for Selsey to pay the vintner and the poulterer, money for Marlborough to buy Innocent III's silver cup, money for Fileby to give the English cardinal, money spent and money needed, fill the letters and accounts that the proctors sent back home, money that really must arrive a few weeks after Christmas, money lacking that endangered life and prospects.

Letters begging and excusing, and sometimes expanding into accounts of money spent, are still capable of provoking the suspicion that provincial patrons must have felt, that, for example, Bishop Swinfield must have felt when he read the account of Richard Puddleston, a particularly untrustworthy proctor. (Puddleston had procured a Hereford benefice for himself in Rome, but, back in England in 1291, he was allowed to resign it; and before returning to Rome, in the Kensington house of the abbot of Abingdon, he swore a special oath of loyalty to the bishop.)[142] Puddleston blamed losses on the mistaken actions of his Italian colleague Cursio of San Gemignano.

Swinfield may have doubted Puddleston's account; Giffard reacted sharply to a proposed account of Bitterley. An occasional expense was questioned, but the principle was unquestioned. To placate the curia it was of course necessary, it was assumed, to act as, for example, Prior Ringmere of Canterbury acted in 1275, to send off Romeward one's money and an ornament of gold.[143] The greedy supplicant assumed that the vice that often drove him to Rome must exist in peculiar purity there, and the curia was in fact greedy, "a cliché com-

---

keeping John with him until he should see how things turned out. See, too, P. M. Baumgarten, *Aus Kanzlei und Kammer. Erörterung zur kurialen Hof und Verwaltungsgeschichte im XIII., XIV. und XV. Jahrhundert* (Freiburg im Breisgau, 1907).

[141] Worcester, Saint Helen's, Register of Bishop Giffard, fo. 263.
[142] *Swinfield*, 256, 278-279.
[143] Hist. MSS Comm., *Fifth Report*, 451 (B.205.1275).

ing true." But there was something else, and it was, perhaps, less rational—the distrust that societies, with, in contrast, quite different economic and social ways of life, sometimes feel for each other. Through the very special lens of the curia, the agricultural, rustic provincial (or so he could there think himself), deprived of the diversifying qualifications of actual existence at home or in the Italian countryside, faced with fearful fascination the urban, mercantile Italian. In the distorting curial medium the difference between them looked clear and national, to the non-Italian; and he responded to it with the sort of hysterical language that men, thinking of themselves as of the country, frequently use of the city. Act conformed with speech: money, the banker-merchant's grain, was the rustic's only protection against the urban evil eye.

Since this sort of sentiment prevailed, a great many distantly provincial litigants and petitioners were anxious to get money to the curia, and, of course, a great many proctors and prelates in the curia were anxious to have it come. The trip from most of the English sources of this money to most of the curial towns toward which it moved took six arduous, even dangerous, weeks. This would seem to have posed a very serious problem in the transport of silver. But so many types of avarice were not to be frustrated by lack of a system; another form of avarice responded to their need. Englishmen who sent proctors to the curia sent them with letters through which they could negotiate loans in curial towns from associates of Italian merchant bankers in northern Europe or England.[144] Thus

[144] For an example of a slashed bond for a debt of 40 marks borrowed by Adam of Fileby for the prior and convent of Durham from Florentine curial merchants, the Abbati, in Orvieto, 15 July 1283, see Durham Dean and Chapter Archives, M.C. 7028, edited Brentano, *York Metropolitan Jurisdiction*, 224-225; see *Wickwane*, 203-207 (payments); *Winchelsey*, 538 (Florentine merchants); *G. Giffard*, I, 48 (letters for proctors to any merchant), 303 (fo. 263v), 273 (bond to Luccan merchants in London for payment of John Lacy and William de la Corner at the Roman curia); *Swinfield*, 98-99; *Cantilupo*, 276 (for the—for these purposes—important Spina of Pistoia). For the suggestive connection of an Italian notary, Ildebrandino Bonadoce, with English ecclesiastical affairs, and the Florentine wool trade: Durham Dean and Chapter Archives, Loc. XIV.4.1 and Loc. VII.74; *G. Giffard*, I, 148-149; Florence, Archivio di stato, conventi soppressi,

proctors were spared the necessity of carrying the bulk of their silver and thus of being robbed before they reached the curia. This relief meant, of course, that more money needed to be provided.

In 1286 Adam of Fileby wrote Giffard of Worcester an account of his curial expenses—an account which, like Tomasuccio of Fiastra's receipts, included a payment to Galgano, here identified as the papal scribe.[145] Fileby's account specified a fee of fifteen marks to his merchant, probably Bentino de Ananzato of Florence, for actually negotiating the loan of 100 pounds (that is, a fee of 10 percent), and well over another mark for the instrument that recorded it, a sum that is more realizably sizable when it is compared with the twelve marks that bought the black palfrey which Adam gave Berard the pope's secretary, or even with the greater sum of thirty marks for the English cardinal, who here as elsewhere was placated with the plurality of an English account's marks.

Letters to merchants were the necessary beginnings of hard debts of the sort that Thomas of Marlborough exalted in paying off and that distorted with their heaviness the accounts of Robert of Holy Island, bishop of Durham.[146] The borrowing

---

Badia, 4 Magg. 1284; Brentano, *York Metropolitan Jurisdiction*, 192-193. For an introduction to letters of credit and methods of payment in the later Middle Ages, see Robert Lopez and Irving W. Raymond, *Medieval Trade in the Mediterranean World* (New York, 1958).

[145] G. *Giffard*, II, 292 (Register, fo. 256v), and 258 (letter, 100 pounds), 292 (letter from Bentino).

[146] Thomas: Macray, *Chronicon Abbatiae de Evesham*, 256 (and see 225 for the business of Roman creditors' securities confiscated by John during the interdict and thus of Evesham instruments moving into the royal treasury); Robert of Holy Island: *Historiae Dunelmensis Scriptores Tres*, ed. James Raine, Surtees Society (London, 1839), app., lxxxix-xc, in which the expenses are divided between the prior and the bishop—there is a group of heavy debts in the form of letters obligatory then remaining in the hands of Adam of Fileby. Fileby's expensive connection with Robert of Holy Island is commemorated in a Durham letter of justice still bearing its leaden seal, in which letter Martin IV's chancery responded, from Orvieto on 8 January 1284, to Adam's appeal by ordering the subprior of Durham to investigate Adam's claims against Robert's executors, Durham Dean and Chapter Archives, 4, 2, Pap. 4 (*Durham Seals* no. 3680a).

thus respectably, and expensively, begun could then be encouraged into habit by the obvious availability of the money-lenders and the felt need of the borrowers. The clerks and monks of Bari fell as helplessly as the monks of Canterbury into the hands of curial merchant bankers. The increased borrowing, however, seems to have been accompanied by a sensation of nervous agitation on both sides. The lender was anxious to lend as much, but only as much, as could be, with its natural growth, recovered. The borrower was anxious to survive, but not to make future survival impossible. Bitterley felt that he must pretend to have more money than he had, and Bremble less—or so they pretended. The documents of Bobo di Giovanni di Bobo, a Roman merchant involved with San Nicola Bari, show a curious vacillation dictated, no doubt, by his difficulty in deciding whether to satisfy the desire for recovery or the desire for further profitable delay.[147] Bobo's difficulty was in defining his palate, unless, of course, his vacillation was meant to frighten San Nicola to higher pledges.

The involvement of Bitterley with the great curial figure Berard of Naples and a disingenuous tone in Bitterley's letters to his employers provoke the suspicion that his demands for money for curial figures may not have been completely disinterested; but there is nothing to hint that Berard was not the dominant figure in the intrigue with Bitterley, if there was intrigue. This is not true of the most notorious of late thirteenth-century English curial proctors, Adam of Fileby.

A considerable amount of information about Adam's negotiations survives from various English sees, Durham, Worcester, and Hereford. Fileby was deeply involved in Cantilupe's affairs and he knew Cantilupe's vocabulary. (It is unfortunate that his opinions about Cantilupe's sanctity are irrecoverable; they might prove hagiographically scintillating.)[148] There is nothing to suggest that Fileby himself was

[147] *C.d.b.*, VI: "Le Pergamene di S. Nicola Bari (1195-1266)," ed. Francesco Nitti di Vito, 87-108, nos. 56-71; for Bobo, see Jordan, *De mercatoribus*, 9-10 (Bobo is Jordan's first—1232—papal banker).

[148] *Cantilupo*, 244: one would know a great deal if one could be at all sure what Fileby thought as he wrote this letter, what frame of mind it reflected, what tone it was meant to strike. For a murder-

anything but a tough, wary, and very sophisticated professional, a really Italianate, or curialized, Englishman, more at
home in the Roman stew than in his English archdeaconries.
He seems completely to have outgrown the disadvantages of
his rustic birth (although through Cantilupe's narrowly aristocratic eyes Adam may always have been seen as somehow
still a local and simple clerk engaged with his brother in taking western business to the curia).[149]

A letter to Fileby, oddly preserved in Giffard's register, is
worth constant reconsideration. It was written by Adam's
clerk, John of Postwick (Postwick was a Fileby living), probably in 1286. It suggests Fileby's position in the curia in an
unusually pictorial way.[150] Postwick had met Berard of
Naples as Berard came from papal audience. Berard had succeeded in gaining Honorius IV's favor for some of Fileby's
Worcester business but not for some of his Ely business.
Berard was pleased with himself. He insisted, immediately,
right at the papal palace, that Postwick rush off to Fileby's
house and tell him the good news, because, of course, he
thought Fileby was still at the curia. This happened on Friday. Postwick was forced to tell Berard that on Monday evening Fileby's messenger had arrived from England with let-

---

ous attack by Fileby's servants, in Essex in 1285 and, in general for
Fileby, see Emden, *Biographical Register of the University of Oxford*,
II, 683-684; see also, for example: *Cantilupo*, lxix, 13-14, 112-113, 136-
138, 140, 168, 187, 209-210, 234-235, 253-254, 273-276; *G. Giffard*, II,
258, 274, 275, 292; *Swinfield*, 99, 113-115, 152-153; *The Registers of
Walter Bronescombe and Peter Quivil*, ed. F. C. Hingeston-Randolph
(London, 1889), 366; Harvey, ed., *Documents*, 9n., 50. For the continuing problem of Fileby's will see: Douie, *Pecham*, 223; *Winchelsey*,
1148-1153 (a perplexity of disputed property, composed, in fact, of
debt and credit as well as current holdings).

[149] Durham Dean and Chapter Archives, Loc. xiv.4.b, dorse of document, from 1282: "Magistro Ade de Fyluby per fratrem suum, R. de
eadem" (see Brentano, *York Metropolitan Jurisdiction*, 239-248); for
Robert of Fileby: *Swinfield*, 263-266; *Rotuli Ricardi Gravesend, diocesis
Lincolniensis*, ed. F. N. Davis, C. W. Foster, and A. Hamilton Thompson, Canterbury and York Society and Lincoln Record Society (Oxford, 1925) [hereafter *Gravesend*], 120.

[150] Worcester, Saint Helen's, Register of Bishop Giffard, fo. 256;
G. Giffard, II, 291-292.

ters and with things to say, and that Fileby, having heard the state of his affairs in England, left Rome for England at dawn on Tuesday. When he heard this Berard was very sad. He told Postwick to find out what he could about the church of Cleeve. Postwick asked and found out from Master R. de Langeford that Cleeve looked for collation to the bishop of Worcester, was vacant through Walter Scammel's elevation to the see of Salisbury, and had cure of souls. But Berard would not admit Postwick to his presence to hear the things he had found out, nor would he receive them in writing. Postwick asked a Florentine merchant at the curia, and one much involved with English affairs, if Adam had ever said anything to him about this business, and the merchant replied not a word and that he did not want to have anything to do with Berard about it.

Berard, Adam, Postwick, Langeford, the Florentine are a little tangle of people playing a curial game too hidden and too intricate to disentangle. One can only guess at their specific relations with each other. But for once Berard does not seem the most sophisticated and sought-after figure in the late thirteenth-century church, not clearly so at any rate. And at least one Englishman, Fileby, does not in this and other letters seem in a position to have seen himself in the characteristic pose that the English relished, as if at the curia they were visiting angels without a Lot to protect them.

Pietro of Assisi, as the Cistercian proctor at Rome, found his complement in the Cistercian cardinal, John of Toledo. John of Toledo was also the "English cardinal," the successor of Stephen Langton, Robert Curzon, and Robert Somercote, the predecessor of Hugh of Evesham and Robert Kilwardby.[151] Although John was more apparently Cistercian

[151] Langton, cardinal priest of San Crisogono (1206-1207) (see below, Chapter III); Curzon, cardinal priest of Santo Stefano in Monte Celio (1216-1219); Somercote, cardinal deacon of Sant'Eustachio (1239-1241) see also Sayers, "Canterbury Proctors," 324-326; Toledo, cardinal priest of San Lorenzo in Lucina (1244-1262) and cardinal bishop of Porto (1262-1275); Kilwardby, cardinal bishop of Porto (April 1278-September 1279); for a convenient guide to the cardinalate see Conrad Eubel, *Hierarchia catholica medii aevi*, I (Münster, 1913), 3-13. Gregorovius, particularly on the basis of a letter in Rymer, emphasizes John of Toledo's expensive part in getting Richard of Cornwall elected

than English, he seems at least occasionally to have taken a specific interest in English affairs, as he did in the canonization of Edmund of Canterbury.[152] In the later thirteenth century cardinals continued to represent interests other than national ones and particularly to represent the interests of religious orders; but they were thought of, both in England and Italy, as being national and representatives of national interests.[153]

Roman senator and in forming the English connection with the Roman Guelfs: Ferdinand Gregorovius, *History of the City of Rome in the Middle Ages*, tr. Annie Hamilton, v.ii (London, 1906), 344, 346 n. 2; see too Friedrich Bock, "Le Trattative per la senatoria di Roma e Carlo d'Angiò," *Archivio della società romana di storia patria*, LXXVIII (1955), 69-105, 78, for the Anglophile party.

[152] Matthew Paris, *Chronica Majora*: IV, 354, 578-579; V, 306. C. H. Lawrence, *St. Edmund of Abingdon* (Oxford, 1960), 15, 17-18, 46, 322, 324; Hermann von Grauert, "Meister Johann von Toled," *Sitzungsberichte der philosophisch-philologischen und der historischen Klasse der k. b. Akademie der Wissenschaften zu München* (1901) I, 111-325, 116 (length of time at curia), 117 and n. 1 (Cistercian activities); and see below, Chapter IV.

[153] A clear example of this occurs in a Camaldoli register now in Florence (Florence, Archivio di stato, conventi soppressi, Camaldoli, Regist. general., vol. 20 for 1283 to 1288, fo. 21v). In part of the register written, as he says (fo. 28), by the monk Alberto Vangaio as scriptor for the prior Gerardo, there is a list of the cardinals then, 1285, existing in the Roman church. The list, in which later deaths were noted into 1287, is divided into the three ranks of cardinal bishops, priests, and deacons, with occasional notes like "nunc legatus in Lombardia" and "nunc legatus in Apulia" for the cardinal bishops of Porto and Sabina. The nationality of each cardinal is noted. Eleven are called Italian; four, French; one, Provençal; one, Spanish; and one, Hugh, English. Awareness of nationality was probably sharpened by change in the nation that held the college majority (as well as the sort of nation it was) after the move to Avignon, when, for extreme example, Philip VI found sixteen out of nineteen an insufficient number of French cardinals (Norman P. Zacour, *Talleyrand: The Cardinal of Perigord (1301-1364)*, Transactions of the American Philosophical Society, 50:7 [Philadelphia, 1960], 10); and see above, note 39, for the *Vita Edwardi Secundi*'s comparison of Italian with non-Italian. The approaching Hundred Years' War found papacy and college in the hands of a partisan nation organized to use its patronage to national advantage; but in the later thirteenth century, the nationality of cardinals was already clearly noticeable and it was considered poten-

Hugh of Evesham, cardinal priest of San Lorenzo in Lucina from 1281 to 1287, is the one thirteenth-century English cardinal for whom this national connection is overwhelmingly apparent. This is true perhaps because of the length of his cardinalate (as opposed to Kilwardby's), perhaps because of the survival of a number of contemporary English episcopal registers, perhaps partly because people thought increasingly in national terms (and because in Hugh attention is not distracted by flamboyant intellectual or spiritual qualities). As John of Toledo complemented Peter of Assisi for the Cistercians, Hugh complemented Adam of Fileby and his colleagues in the representation of England at Rome. In doing so he was not, as John had been and Robert Kilwardby was to be, bishop of an Italian diocese, but he was prelate of an Italian place officially connected not only with the central government of the universal church but also with its most distinguished see.

Just before his elevation, Hugh himself, had, with the clerk Stephen of Patrington, been a proctor at the curia for Archbishop Wickwane of York. Wickwane sent Hugh to Rome accompanied by a shower of letters, asking for him the protection of cardinals and calling him "our canon of York" and "precordialem et predilectum clericum nostrum."[154] Wickwane's description, in isolation, is misleading. Hugh had been a king's clerk in 1272, and in 1275 he had been noted as long in the service of the king and his mother.[155]

Hugh's household, once he had become cardinal, was a center of political activity. His position seems sometimes almost an excuse for the existence of an office through which the king of England could hold diplomatic commerce with Medi-

---

tially valuable to the cardinals' co-nationals, a point that is made abundantly clear in the repeated references to Hugh, "the English cardinal," in English episcopal records (for particular examples see *Cantilupo*, 273-275; *G. Giffard*, ii, 292—Register of Giffard, fo. 256v).

[154] *Wickwane*, 183-184.

[155] There are helpful short biographies of Hugh: Josiah Cox Russell, *Dictionary of Writers of Thirteenth-century England* (being Special Supplement no. 3 of the *Bulletin of the Institute of Historical Research*) (London, 1936), 49-51; Emden, *Biographical Register of the University of Oxford*, i, 656; there is also a biography by Charles Trice Martin in the *Dictionary of National Biography*.

terranean kings without inventing an anachronistic diplomatic service, an office in which a man like Stefano da San Giorgio could work without provoking to tiring new definition the contemporary bureaucratic mind.[156] Certainly Hugh's circle was one of those places in which at least two of those distinct but interwoven webs that joined the western world met in a single node—the chivalric-establishment web of Edward I's and Charles of Salerno's world, the clerical web of Durham and Bari.

Hugh of Evesham, although variously competent and variously employed, was famous for his skill as a physician. Hugh's name has been particularly connected with cures of the fever, and it has been believed that he was brought to, or kept in, Rome to rid it of malaria. It is likely that he was made cardinal so that Martin IV might keep him close to the curia to attend his health.[157] Hugh was not the only thirteenth-century cleric to rise to high ecclesiastical office because of his medical skill.[158] It seems now a peculiar approach to the sacred college, but it was at least innocuous, and not all approaches to the college need be innocuous:

> Tales regunt Petri navem
> Tales habent Petri clavem.[159]

Robert Grosseteste had, as he dies in Matthew Paris, called to his deathbed the Dominican physician John of Saint Giles,

[156] See Ernst H. Kantorowicz, "The Prologue to *Fleta* and the School of Petrus de Vinea," *Speculum*, XXXII (1957), 231-249, particularly 237-239 and notes, and see also Paris, Bibliothèque Nationale, cod. lat. 8567, with which Professor Kantorowicz has worked intricately and of which he had promised a partial edition; see particularly Kantorowicz's n. 25 on p. 238, where earlier descriptions of the MS are cited.

[157] Russell (*Dictionary*, 49) lists the known, or reputed, titles of Hugh's medical works.

[158] Nicholas Farnham, bishop of Durham, for example. For a recent and more general view of Farnham's attainments, see J. R. L. Highfield, *The Early Rolls of Merton College Oxford*, Oxford Historical Society (Oxford, 1964), 15-18, and Matthew Paris, *Chronica Majora*, IV, 86.

[159] Wright, *Latin Poems*, "The Ruins of Rome," 217-222, 220, v̇v. 103-104; *Moralisch-Satirische Gedichte Walters von Chatillon*, ed. Karl Strecker (Heidelberg, 1929), 26: poem 2, lines 109-110.

who was also a learned theologian and a preacher he much admired, that he might be consoled by him at once both in body and mind.[160] But no evidence appears that Englishmen applied this happy cliché to Hugh of Evesham's ministrations. Hugh, as cardinal, occasionally sent back to English prelates advice which might suggest that he thought himself qualified to cool the fevers of the spirit. He suggested that Archbishop Pecham treat with the party of Canterbury monks opposed to his support of Prior Ringmere.[161] But the effect of the persuasions of this—one really must admit in the end—surprisingly chosen cardinal, plucked from a church that had a good many more obviously, ecclesiastically, endowed candidates, can hardly have been cooling.

In fact Hugh seems to have maintained his office of connecting the English church with the church of Rome in remarkable inertia. He was, however, taken very seriously by English prelates and their Roman proctors. This is clearly shown by the letters written to him from England and by the money given to him in Rome.[162] He was occasionally active, as in his speaking to the pope in favor of the affairs of the bishop of Worcester. But as one watches Hugh he seems an immobile idol—the wax figure of Herodian's Septimius, the funeral effigy of a late medieval king—sitting in his palazzo and receiving his thirty-mark gifts, given out of an almost superstitious fear in the givers that if gifts were withheld actions would fail.

From this ecclesiastical stillness there comes a surprising movement. Among the material that survives from Hugh's college of chaplains, in a manuscript which includes in a little collection of identified aphorisms Ecclesiastes's "There is nothing new under the sun," Stefano da San Giorgio, Hugh's chamberlain, preaches a sermon on Christ's nativity to his co-chaplains.[163] Stefano preached the mystery of the incarnation

[160] Matthew Paris, *Chronica Majora*, v, 400; for John, see William A. Hinnebusch, *The Early English Friar Preachers*, Istituto Storico Domenicano (Rome, 1951), 358-360, 263, 317.

[161] Douie, *Pecham*, 182.

[162] *Wickwane*, 199-203.

[163] Paris, Bibl. Nat., cod. lat., fos. 17v-18v (for Ecclesiastes, fo. 32v); and see above, note 156.

as a mystery of love. He evoked the living Christ, the loving virgin mother, and made the cluster of clerks by the Via Lata see the choir of angels over Bethlehem. It is hard to think of Hugh's clerks concerning themselves with the nativity except as a convenience in dating. Their sitting, in natural positions, listening to its wonder, unsettles a fixed vision of the Palazzo Fiano. Hugh of Evesham's own insecure corpus includes a sermon;[164] and one feels that in his century, in the evidence or in fact, any figure or office may turn completely—it is after all the century of Francis of Assisi, the century in which Celestine V was carted into the papacy like a Merovingian king blessing.

Hugh of Evesham is last seen preparing for the unloosening of the frail bonds of his mortal complexity, planning the dispersal of the accumulations of his lifetime in the provisions of his will.[165] Money is to go back to those English places from which it has been drained. The pastor who did not feed sheep spiritually plans to send them bread. Hugh, the medical doctor, is an ironically physical fisher of fish. He is also a man who in the shadow autobiography of his bequests points, in a medium shaped by convention, to the places and things to which he was attached, by love or guilt or memory, through accident of life, the taste of his times, or his hope of heaven.

Hugh left money for his sister Muriel and for his nephew Henry, money for the fabric of Saint Peter's York and Saint Peter's Rome and for Saint John Lateran, for ornaments for his titular church, San Lorenzo in Lucina, where he was in fact to be buried, and quite a lot of money (twenty pounds sterling) for buying a cope to be worn in the choir of Saint Peter's York. He left money for the fabric of eight bridges, particularly in the York and Worcester-Evesham areas, in a century when death by accidental drowning filled English

---

[164] Russell, *Dictionary*, 49: Oxford, Bodl. Lib., MS Bodl. 50, fo. 299v: "Sic currite ut comprehendates [sic]"; it is identified in the manuscript as "per magistrum Hugonem de Evesham."

[165] Worcester, Saint Helen's, Register of Bishop Giffard, fos. 345v-347. Hugh's relations with the legatees are not always clearly expressed in the will. John de Ullinton to whom he left twenty marks is elsewhere identified as a kinsman: *G. Giffard*, II, 406. For an interesting comparison, see Merton's will in Highfield, 31, 49-50.

court rolls. He left money to servants including whatever boy should be serving him when he died, money and the marriage of the young heir to the lady of the manor of Clopton, money to the recluses of Rome, the anchoress of Preston in Amounderness, and, half as much, to an anchoress in the parish of Howden, money to every house of lepers in Yorkshire, money for masses and funeral celebrations and the distribution of bread and future obits for himself at Saint Peter's York.[166] He left money for a passage to the Holy Land for the soul of Simon of Evesham, once archdeacon of Richmond and before that precentor of York and then archdeacon of the East Riding (and a debt to Simon's executor further points up Hugh's closeness to him).[167] Hugh provided dowers for poor girls in his English parishes of Hemingbrough, Goxhill, Spofforth, and Bugthorpe, and money for the parish paupers, and money for distributions to the poor of Hemingbrough (a parish that had paid Hugh particularly well and that in each case got more than the other parishes),[168] Goxhill, Benefield, Welton, Claverdon, and Acton.

A group of Hugh's bequests centered around the two universities of Oxford and Paris: money (forty pounds sterling) for poor scholars in arts and theology at Oxford; money for Franciscans and Dominicans at Oxford, less (ten marks as opposed to ten pounds) for the Franciscans against whom he had sided in their 1269 poverty debate with the Oxford Dominicans;[169] considerably less (forty shillings each) for the

[166] Choir cope: *ad emendum capam chori*—so just possibly fabric repair in choir; recluses: *reclusis*—but in context I do not think that this means Claresses.

[167] For Simon, see *York Minster Fasti*, ed. Charles Travis Clay, Yorkshire Archaeological Society Record Series, cxxiii, cxxiv (1958, 1959): i, 14, 42, 48; ii, 82.

[168] For Hemingbrough, see Record Commission, *Taxatio ecclesiastica auctoritate P. Nicholai IV c. 1291* (London, 1802), 302, 336; for Bugthorpe, *York Minster Fasti*, ii, 15.

[169] A. G. Little, *The Grey Friars in Oxford*, Oxford Historical Society (Oxford, 1892), 331, 333-334; the problems of the Franciscans and their money in the later thirteenth century always seem both tragic and ironic, and there is certainly something ironic in Hugh's leaving less money to the other side in the poverty dispute. For a lucid and complete account of the problems of Franciscan poverty in the thir-

Oxford Augustinian friars, the Carmelites, and the Hospital of Saint John by the Pettypont (Magdalen Bridge);[170] the same amount (forty shillings) for the nuns of Godstow, their pittances, and the nuns of Littlemore, and six marks for the nuns of Studley; more (100 shillings) for the Augustinian canons of Saint Frideswide;[171] money (forty marks to be divided evenly) for the Franciscans and Dominicans studying at Paris, and (forty pounds) for English students at Paris in arts, philosophy, and theology. Hugh made a number of other bequests to various congregations of friars: to the Franciscans, Dominicans, and Augustinians of Rome; to the Franciscans, Dominicans, and Carmelites of York; the Franciscans and Dominicans of Beverley; the Franciscans of Grimsby and Worcester (a particularly heavy gift); and to the Franciscans, Dominicans, and Augustinians of the place in which he should die. The Franciscan and Dominican bequests are always larger than the others, except in the case of Rome where the Augustinian friars were left the largest bequest to an order, but one not so large as that to Hugh's own church, San Lorenzo.

Hugh mentioned four of his books in this will: his postills over the whole Bible to go to the scholars of Oxford;[172] his great Bible to the prior and convent of Durham; his "pentalogue" in two volumes to the prior and convent of Bridlington; and his little, use of Beverley, missal to the nuns of Nunburnholme, along with their twenty shillings. Hugh also left ten marks for carrying the books to London. Hugh named

teenth century, see M. D. Lambert, *Franciscan Poverty* (London, 1961).

[170] See H. E. Salter, *Medieval Oxford*, Oxford Historical Society (Oxford, 1936), 29, and for places connected with other bequests, *passim*.

[171] The will gives a nice sense of the contrast between the newer, freer orders of men and the old, relatively enclosed houses.

[172] For postills see Beryl Smalley, *The Study of the Bible in the Middle Ages* (Oxford, 1952), 270-271; see Richard Mather, "The Codicil of Cardinal Comes of Casate and the Libraries of Thirteenth-century Cardinals," *Traditio*, xx (1964), 319-350; in general, see Michael M. Sheehan, *The Will in Medieval England*, Pontifical Institute of Mediaeval Studies, Studies and Texts, 6 (Toronto, 1963), particularly 258-265.

three sets of executors: York dignitaries for the archbishopric; west country clerics for the diocese of Worcester; cardinals and Stefano da San Giorgio for the curia and Italy.

On 15 November 1286 Hugh's will was witnessed and sealed by several members of the British, or insular, colony in Rome: Richard (Corre), bishop of Lismore in the province of Cashel; Ralph, archdeacon of Wiltshire; Ralph de Bosco, papal chaplain and canon of Dunkeld; William Brun, earlier a proctor at Rome and here described as Hugh's chaplain. On 18 August 1287, after Hugh's death, and during a papal vacancy, his will was proved in Rome by four of his cardinal colleagues.[173] The will stretches between the two churches, of Italy and of England, dividing its commonplaces and enthusiasms as well as its money between them. It plots the dissolution of a lifetime's accumulation of wealth, and particularly wealth from livings, churches, successfully sought. It plans the return to earth of a man and scholar who had realized very high ambitions but also surely (a man with the map of Oxford in his mind) spiritual disappointment. The will divides the achieved ambition, into body and soul, and into money, bread, and books, for Rome, York, Worcester and the vale of Evesham, for Oxford and Paris, for the places of Hugh's life and livings, for bridges and lepers, and brides' dowers, for anchoresses and nunneries and very noticeably for friars, for great churches, for prayers.

The official English church in Italy was that of Hugh of Evesham, Adam of Fileby, John of Bitterley, and their colleagues. But there were of course other clerics there. Prelates went to their confirmations and to get their palliums; they came to Rome for Innocent III's great council at the Lateran.[174] Pilgrims still sought the holy places. William of Derby, a monk of Saint Mary's York, who had been to southern Europe before, to Lyons in 1274, who had been prior of Saint Bee's and his own house (not because of his goodness

[173] Worcester, Saint Helen's, Register of Bishop Giffard, fos. 345v and 347.

[174] For this council, which is extremely important to the whole matter of this book, see C. J. Hefele and H. Leclercq, *Histoire des conciles* (Paris, 1907-1921) [hereafter Hefele-Leclercq], v:2, 1316-1398.

but because of his 100 marks), and who, though he had been a builder, had been recently deposed, came to Rome with great numbers of pious tourists in 1300.[175] He traveled in a little company of important Benedictine pilgrims, a brother of his own house and two other priors. William of Derby went to see the Veronica.[176] He pressed forward in a great crowd of people to see the relic. His leg was crushed. He died and was buried at the curia.

Students came to Italy too. Bologna and Padua were equipped to receive foreigners. Bologna's law was the law of the church. By 1265 "England" was one of the fourteen Ultramontane nations.[177] John of Pontoise, of the English nation, and at law a successful Bolognese, was asked by Modena to come and teach law there.[178] A thirteenth-century Durham formulary includes among its types a letter from a student at Bologna to the prior of Durham asking the prior to take care of the student's proctor and goods for the three years of the student's absence, that he might study in greater tranquility at the schools of Bologna.[179] Ambitious young lawyers from the provinces went, if they could, to Bologna. The legal commonplace with its ancient Italic background attracted and moved out into the whole church, much as did the Gothic pattern of commonplace and learned belief, that informed all the provincial patterns, from Paris and the lesser theological schools. Bologna was probably less potent than Paris, but its pattern was not, on the whole, less international. Although the law it taught came particularly from Italian sources, it was not taught in terms of peculiarly Italian church and society.

[175] *The Chronicle of St. Mary's Abbey, York*, ed. H.H.E. Craster and M. E. Thornton, Surtees Society (Durham, 1934), 31, 132, 24 (Saint Bee's), 28-29 (buying and building), 30 (deposition).

[176] *Ibid.*, 31; and for the Veronica, see Brieger, *English Art, 1216-1307*, 137 n. 1.

[177] Rashdall, *The Universities*, ed. Powicke and Emden, I, 182 and n. 4 (and in general, for Bologna, I, 87-268, for Padua, II, 9-21).

[178] *The Register of Walter Giffard, Lord Archbishop of York*, ed. William Brown, Surtees Society (Durham, 1904) [hereafter *W. Giffard*], 246.

[179] *Durham Annals and Documents of the Thirteenth Century*, ed. Frank Barlow, Surtees Society (Durham, 1945), 150.

English relics, the church's vitals, rested in Italy. At the splendid consecration of Santa Maria del Fiume at Ceccano in 1196, among the relics planted in the new church were, with a stone of Saint Stephen's stoning, part of the clothing of Thomas Becket; by 1197 in Bari a church beyond the walls by the spring well had been dedicated to Thomas of Canterbury.[180] Thomas was a saint to dedicate to in Italy. His cult was prominent in and near Anagni (see Fig. 3 in illustration section). The bishop of Catania, in 1179, gave permission for a mosque to be made into a church and dedicated to him. Thomas was put into mosaic in Monreale. His feast was (and is) painted into the calendar on the wall of the oratory of San Silvestro at the Quattro Coronati in Rome, and it was added to the ancient calendar of Città di Castello.[181] Among various connections, that between Santo Spirito in Sassia and England was still pressed.[182] Henry III and the legate Guala enriched Sant'Andrea in Vercelli with English money and perhaps English ideas and an English dedication.[183] In Vercelli Roger Norreys,

[180] "Annales Ceccanenses," ed. G. H. Pertz, *Monumenta Germaniae Historica, Scriptores* [hereafter *M.G.H., SS.*] xix (Hanover, 1866), 275-302, 292-294 (293); *C.d.b.*, vi, 14-15 no. 6.

[181] R. Ambrosi de Magistris, *Storia di Anagni* (Anagni, 1889), ii, Bk. iii, 144-147, and docs. nos. 91-92 (146-148); Lynn T. White, *Latin Monasticism in Norman Sicily* (Cambridge, Mass., 1938), 115; Evelyn Jamison, "Alliance of England and Sicily in the Second Half of the Twelfth Century," *Journal of the Warburg and Courtauld Institutes*, vi (1943), 20-32; Giovanni Muzi, *Memorie ecclesiastiche e civili di Città di Castello* (Città di Castello, 1842-1844), iii, 179. See R. Davidsohn, *Storia di Firenze*, i (Florence, 1956), 1055-1056, by 1188 an altar in San Donato outside the city and perhaps even earlier at Santa Reparata; and see too W. and E. Paatz, *Die Kirchen von Florenz* (Frankfurt am Main, 1941-1955), v, 241, and the church dedicated to Saint Thomas at Porto San Giorgio, which Professor Jean Wilson pointed out to me.

[182] See *W. Giffard*, 151-152; for Santo Spirito see Ottorino Montenovesi, "L'Archiospedale di S. Spirito in Roma," *Archivio della società romana di storia patria*, ns v (1939), 177-229.

[183] Vittorio Mandelli, *Il Comune di Vercelli nel medio evo* (Vercelli, 1857-1861), iii, 127-130; Guido Marangoni, "Il Sant'Andrea di Vercelli, intorno alle asserite sue origini Inglesi," *Rassegna d'Arte*, ix (1909), 122-126.

going home further to ravish Evesham, found the literate, teaching Evesham monk, Adam Sortes.[184]

Italy was a path to the crusade as well as the curia. Great Englishmen clerical and lay paraded through the peninsula. Richard of Cornwall watched Frederick II's eastern dancers and, in Cremona, an elephant. Richard's son Henry stopped for his death in a church in Viterbo. The Lord Edward, on his way home Edward I, passed in and out of Trapani.[185] The splendid cope of English work (recently bandited and returned) that Nicholas IV gave to Ascoli Piceno physically recalls the manifold Anglo-Italian connection of the thirteenth century—the crusade, the wool trade, the cousinage of kings. But for the official church the important connection was the curia, where, in Priscian's pattern, the ablative ruled over the dative.[186]

When in Matthew Paris, William, cardinal bishop of Sabina, in 1251 dreamed his death dream, he dreamed that he went into a terribly crowded place, like a general council, and there was no place for him to sit, until his recently dead friend, the Cardinal Otto, came and led him to a seat that he had saved for him.[187] The world of thirteenth-century prelates and proctors was, like William's dream and Henry's poem, a small, crowded place in which everyone was jostled and looked for his seat, rather than, or at least as well as, empty green fields over which tinkling church bells called to each other. And, although there was constant fear in England that the Italians were marauding the green fields, it was in the

[184] Macray, *Chronicon Abbatiae de Evesham,* 147.

[185] Matthew Paris, *Chronica Majora,* iv, 147, 164; Powicke, *Henry III,* ii, 609-610, 599-600; Ernst H. Kantorowicz, *Frederick the Second* (London, 1931), 323; M. Setton, R. L. Wolff, H. W. Hazard, *History of the Crusades,* ii (Philadelphia, 1962), 517.

[186] A joke English proctors repeated to decorate a discussion of greed points up the obliquity of the Italo-English connection: Stubbs, *Epistolae Cantuarienses,* 230. See too Walter of Chatillon, Strecker, 111: poem 10, stanza 4.

[187] Matthew Paris, *Chronica Majora,* v, 230. For the crushing crowd of an actual Council see Stephan Kuttner and Antonio García y García, "A New Eyewitness Account of the Fourth Lateran Council," *Traditio,* xx (1964), 115-178, 130-131.

crowded little place, the stage of the curia, that, essentially, the two churches met.

It was a stage in which, by the second half of the century, proctor actors sat with exchangeable masks marked "Durham," "Westminster," "Fiastra," "King of England," ready to meet other actors labeled "York," "Worcester," or "Spoleto," or merely to beg a privilege. (And the actors were tied to directing provincials by those traveling, letter-bearing boys, nuncios, brothers.) At the center of the stage sat the pope, brilliantly unmasked and personal like Innocent III facing Marlborough, early in the century, or screened and hidden by cardinals and officials like the two Berards, as, in the late century, Honorius IV was from Adam of Fileby's clerk. And the change from Innocent to Honorius was not just accidental or personal; the swelling bureaucracy of the thirteenth century muffled the pope's will and person.

The sense of this scene's stage is best recaptured in the piazza of duomo and palazzo of one of the smaller curial towns, like Orvieto. If one can imagine away the pretty elegance of the duomo's façade and imagine back the almost interminable building process, it is possible to see there the physically displaced bishop, the agitated merchants swooning with profit and fatigue, the crowded, cosmopolitan, courtier-making court, its swarming followers thronging like the peripheral moth-figures in a Guardi audience.

The combined existence of this stage-court and of the outstretched tentacles of Rome meant that the English church and the Italian church, in connection with the curia, could not be, and cannot be, considered two untouching things lying disparate and unconnected on their distant shores. They were intricately involved with each other and aware of each other. But their involvement, so unrelentingly monetary and dominated by cliché, did not generally suggest the almost unconscious exchange and interpenetration of institutions that it might have, had their tithe-fields marched, had they met in some border Savoy. Only occasionally can specifically English and Italian ecclesiastical institutions have met at all seriously even in a thirteenth-century mind—perhaps when Hostiensis glossed the problem of whether or not the archdeacon had a *territorium*,[188] or when Hadrian V looked ahead to what he thought would be the problems of his papacy.

[188] Henricus de Segusio, *Commentaria* (Venice, 1581), e.g. vol. 1, fo. 126v (to c. 7, X,i,23, a.v. *terminari*). Perhaps I underestimate the awareness in readers of the "national" origins of foreign writers; cf. the list (485-489) in Auguste Pelzer, "Prosper de Reggio Emilia des Ermites de Saint-Augustin" (468-507), in his *Études d'histoire littéraire sur la scolastique médiévale*, Philosophes Médiévaux, VIII (Louvain, Paris, 1964).

II · PROVINCES, DIOCESES, AND PATHS OF APPEAL

*T*HE distance between, the separation of, the thirteenth-century Italian and English churches is quickly and graphically exposed in the difference between the shapes and patterns of their dioceses and provinces. The principles of cohesion in the province of Canterbury and the province of Benevento, or of Amalfi, were quite clearly different. The northern church was defined, territorial, administrative, composed of contiguous, variously colored areas on a map. The southern church was distracted, unformed, a church of cult centers and extended cities, a map of dots and rayed lines, of indeterminate and unimportant borders, a pointillist affair of shrines and colleges and monasteries. Even geographically, in the simplest and most numerical sense, the churches of Stephen Langton and Saint Francis, of Grosseteste and Benizi, of Winchelsey and Celestine V expressed their characteristic antitheses. This said, it is immediately clear that in each church there were strong elements of what, in opposing them, one would call characteristic of the other—of the church of Pecham in that of Ottone Visconti or of Federigo Visconti, of the church of Cava or Montecassino in Durham or Saint Albans. These elements of similarity are obvious in the structure of the two churches, but so obvious, so easily assumed, that they may escape notice. The two churches were divided into dioceses similar enough in purpose and government so that their differences can seem significant.

The secular province of Calabria, the toe of the Italian peninsula, is one-tenth the size of England and Wales. In the thirteenth century Calabria was divided into twenty-two dioceses, England and Wales into only twenty-one. One can walk in a straight line for fifty-eight kilometers without leaving the diocese of Rochester, the least long in England and Wales.[1]

[1] Ecclesiastical maps of much of late thirteenth- and early fourteenth-century Italy are to be found inserted in the *Rationes decimarum Italiae nei secoli XIII e XIV* volumes of Studi e Testi (vols. 58, 60, 69, 84, 96,

One cannot walk two kilometers in any direction without leaving the diocese of Ravello, nor three without leaving those of Scala or Minori, nor five that of Bitetto. It is hard to walk at all and stay within their thirteenth-century borders. It is true that the diocese of Ely narrows at its middle to a width of less than fifteen kilometers; the diocese of Tertiveri narrows to less than two and one-half kilometers at its waist. Quite a long list could be compiled of really very small Italian dioceses—with an area of less than one hundred square kilometers—for the most part in the south. There were also many Italian dioceses that would not have looked peculiarly small in England or France. But, although there was even more variety in the size of Italian dioceses than in that of English and Welsh dioceses, the most startling apparent difference between the mapped organization of the two churches is the great number and small size of the Italian dioceses. The sizes and shapes of Italian dioceses had essentially been determined by the conditions of the early Italian church, but the making of small dioceses, even unpressed by population, was not finished by the end of the thirteenth century.[2] In 1320 Macerata was formed.[3]

Small dioceses were often poor dioceses, too poor perhaps to finance grandiose episcopal efforts at reform or to attract to themselves bishops with any grandiose ideas at all. In 1310 the total annual income of the bishop, chapter, and clergy of Tertiveri was valued at four *once*. But, again, there was much variation. Bitonto and Bitetto may sound the same to uninter-

---

97, 98, 112, 113, 128, 148); there is an excellent medieval map of Britain, in two sheets, north and south, *Map of Monastic Britain*, published by the Ordnance Survey. It is hoped that both sets of maps will be used by anyone who reads this chapter. In using the Italian maps it is necessary to remember that diocesan borders fluctuated and to note the actual date for which the map is illustrative; it is also important to remember that an assessment map of this sort omits a large number of important ecclesiastical corporations.

[2] The origins of Italian dioceses are discussed in Francesco Lanzoni, *Le diocesi d'Italia dalle origini al principio del secolo VII*, Studi e Testi, vol. 53 (Faenza, 1927), particularly pp. 1059-1092, and also in Giuseppe Forchielli, *La pieve rurale*, Biblioteca della Rivista di storia del diritto italiano, no. 17 (Bologna, 1938), 38-43.

[3] Otello Gentili, *Macerata Sacra* (Recanati, 1947), 8-10.

ested ears, but in the tenth assessment of 1310 the *mensa* of the bishop of Bitonto was valued at 150 *once* and Bitetto at forty *once*.[4] They cannot have seemed the same to episcopal candidates.

A related peculiarity of some Italian dioceses is their shape, which on a purely political map appears incomprehensible. The Emilian dioceses of Faenza, Forlì, and Forlimpópoli are queer, parallel strips on the map. The strip of Forlì, about seven to ten kilometers broad and almost sixty kilometers long, stretched northeastward toward the Adriatic, from the diocese of Fiesole to the diocese of Ravenna. It and its adjacent dioceses were shaped by riverbeds (or by political divisions shaped by riverbeds). Their simplicity in being dominated by a single geographical factor, in being such simple neighborhoods, again distinguishes them from British dioceses (even from those that had grown up in areas as simple as the old kingdom of Kent). In, at their extremes, very different terrains—the sweet, lush, intertwined fields of the valley of the Thames, or the allotments of Kent, against Alvaro's villages like butterflies swarming on their harsh hills (thought back 600 years)—dioceses had taken different shapes. Italian dioceses had formed and maintained themselves in islands, in circles around isolated hill towns, along the paths of rivers, within ancient Roman boundaries; and the conventional, to northern Europe, shape and size of (incidentally very populous) dioceses like Florence and Arezzo do not destroy the apparent and important distinction, or restrict the distinctly Italian diocese to the south. The different shapes were, moreover, differently decorated. Of the twenty-one dioceses of England and Wales in the thirteenth century two had archbishops; of the twenty-two of Calabria four had archbishops [Map 1].

Beyond physical shape and topographical organization there are immediately apparent differences between the substance of Italian and of English dioceses. They were hard and soft in different places; they had different areas of sharp reality and of lifeless vagueness. They expressed their structural differences in a number of ways: in the kinds of subordinates, like

[4] Domenico Vendola, *Rationes decimarum . . . Apulia-Lucania-Calabria*, Studi e Testi, vol. 84 (Vatican City, 1939), 74-75.

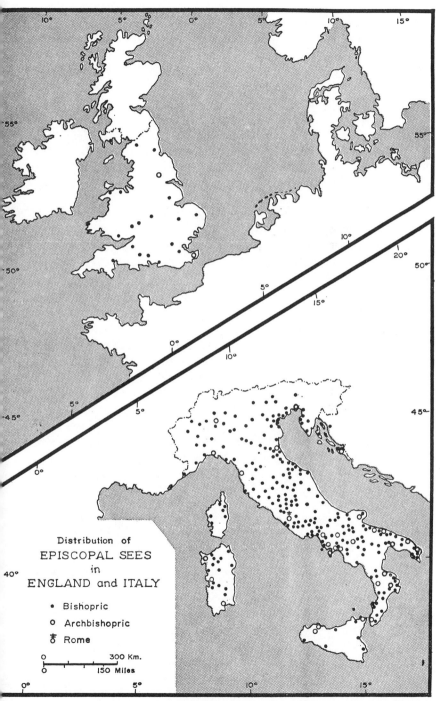

Distribution of
EPISCOPAL SEES
in
ENGLAND and ITALY

- Bishopric
○ Archbishopric
♰ Rome

0   300 Km.
0   150 Miles

Map I

vicars, that their bishops had; in what happened to them during episcopal vacancies; in the way they combined themselves
into provinces; in the positions of their cathedral chapters.
Most quickly apparent is the difference between their
archdeacons.

English dioceses, like many of their French neighbors, were
divided into geographical archdeaconries.[5] In exceptional dioceses, all quite small, the archdeaconry was coterminous with
the diocese. Although this fact almost inevitably had an effect
upon the relations between the two jurisdictions, the bishop's
and the archdeacon's, these unique archdeacons seem to have
been seen by contemporary English prelates almost as ordinary
archdeacons within the English pattern.[6] Italy of course had
archdeacons—and not just the flock of Italian clerks provided
to the archdeaconries of northern European dioceses. There
was an archdeacon among the dignitaries of most Italian
cathedral chapters. A late thirteenth-century archdeacon, Giovanni de Capite at Monreale (interesting because Monreale
had the only Italian Benedictine cathedral chapter and so a
not quite normal archidiaconal stall), died leaving a sister,
Matilda, and her daughter; they remained, these archidiaconal
relicts, entangled with the archdeacon's church through their
life interests in a vineyard which Matilda granted to Monreale.[7] "The Archdeacon" was an Italian and archdeacon of
Bologna. But the archdeacons of Italy did not have archdeaconries. The northern European process, through which
the cathedral dignitary, multiplied or divided, moved out and
connected his portion of the dissected diocese with the central see, did not occur.[8]

[5] On European archdeaconries see Alexander Hamilton Thompson,
"Diocesan Organization in the Middle Ages: Archdeacons and Rural
Deans" (Raleigh Lecture on History), *Proceedings of the British
Academy*, XXIX (1943), 153-194.

[6] Irene Churchill, *Canterbury Administration* (London, 1933), I,
43-53; Brentano, *York Metropolitan Jurisdiction*, 84-85, nn. 5 and 6,
and references therein.

[7] Carlo Alberto Garufi, *Catalogo illustrato del tabulario di Santa
Maria Nuova in Monreale, Documenti per servire alla storia di Sicilia*,
1st ser., XIX (Palermo, 1902), 63 no. 136.

[8] For the development of the connection between the rule of the
archdeaconries and the person of the archdeacon within the cathedral

Stillborn, ungrowing, the Italian office of archdeacon in the thirteenth century remained that of a cathedral dignitary. Often, in perhaps half of the dioceses of Italy, the archdeacon was the chief cathedral dignitary.[9] In this position the archdeacon, heir to the bishop's rivals, might be very active as personal representative of the bishop, as the "bishop's eye"; but in a diocese in which the difficulty of the archdeacon's position has been particularly noted, in Orvieto, the dignity of the office within the cathedral declined so sharply and fell so in the shadow of the office of the cathedral archpriest that the fifteenth-century chapter found it necessary to reinstitute the office and to restrict by legislation the future aggressiveness of the archpriest's office.[10]

The archdeacon, as he is understood in western European literature, both academic and popular, did not really exist in thirteenth-century Italy. Norman Italian dioceses were often too small to encourage the sort of division that occurred in northern Norman areas. Even the large dioceses of Italy seem not to have suggested archdiaconal subdivision to Italian prelates. The jurisdictional holdings of a large monastery under heavy northern influence, like Cassino, may have suggested something of the sort, but in the clearest case, that of Cassino's archdeacon of San Germano, the archdeacon was second dignitary to an archpriest in a collegiate *pieve* to whose total parochial area his jurisdiction was limited.[11] In some little part, the archdeacon's lacking an archdeaconry is explained by

---

chapter in the sample case of York, see: Charles Travis Clay, "Notes on the Early Archdeacons in the Church of York," *The Yorkshire Archaeological Journal* xxxvi (1944-1947), 269-287, 409-434, and *Early Yorkshire Charters,* iv, Yorkshire Archaeological Society, Record Series, extra ser. 1 (Wakefield, 1935), xxii-xxvi; Alexander Hamilton Thompson, *The English Clergy and Their Organization in the Later Middle Ages* (Oxford, 1947), 58-60.

[9] Thompson, "Diocesan Organization," 158 (counting, from Ughelli, at least 141 of 285).

[10] Vincenzo Natalini, "Il Capitolo del duomo di Orvieto ed i suoi statuti inediti," *Rivista di storia della chiesa in Italia,* ix (1955), 177-232, 225-227 no. 6, and 205-206.

[11] A. M. Caplet, *Regesti Bernardi I Abbatis Casinensis Fragmenta* (Rome, 1890), 193-197 nos. 442-445.

(or explains) the unusual importance of another local dignitary's office. But this is clearly not a case of the northern subdividing process having occurred with another name. The Italian diocese was not divided into geographical administrative units because it was not in that sense a geographical or an administered thing.

The office that forces itself into obvious view in the rural archdeacon's absence is that of the rural archpriest. The archpriest's office in thirteenth-century Italy resembled that of the rural dean in England and France north of the Loire, but it was tied to the Italian, cult-celebrating, sacrament-dispensing, tithe-gathering past. As in the case of archdeacon and dean, there is constant danger, for the historian, of confusion between the rural archpriest and the archpriest who was a cathedral dignitary.[12] In northern and central Italy the rural archpriest was often (or had been) the principal cleric in a collegiate church, called the *pieve*, which was located in an important village, which collected the area's tithes (or part of them), baptized its infants, buried its dead, and which dominated a surrounding cluster of chapels (and which recalls the old English minster). The *pieve*'s archpriest was regularly called *plebanus* or *pievano*. In parts of the north, like Genoa and Verona, the system of *plebanus*-archpriest, *pieve*, and surrounding chapels seems to have produced a curious clotted structure in the church. In the thirteenth-century diocese of Verona there seem to have been fifty-five rural *pievi*, and five more collegiate churches within the city, around which the religious or at least clerical life of the diocese was theoretically focused.[13] But, by the thirteenth century at least, the significance of the *plebanus*'s office seems to have been uncertain and

[12] Capitular archpriests were sometimes and in some places, as in thirteenth-century Orvieto, very important. In 1284 the archpriest of Orvieto intended to be off to acquire the "scientie margaritas" in the schools; his very real importance is suggested by the chapter's action in making for themselves a full proctor and vicar in his absence: Natalini, 215; and, see again Natalini, 205-206, for the archpriest's position.

[13] Forchielli, *passim* and more specifically 2-5, 6-9; see, too, Catherine E. Boyd, *A Cistercian Nunnery in Mediaeval Italy: The Story of Rifreddo in Saluzzo, 1220-1300* (Cambridge, Mass., 1943), 54-55.

to have varied from place to place even in the areas of its prominence.

In the unusually visible diocese of Lucca, in 1260, there were fifty-nine rural *pievi*. It seems clear that by then the Lucchese *pievi* had lost something of their ancient hegemony. They had to some extent been successfully challenged by the rival and insubordinate pretensions of independent parishes. They had also, and presumably unself-consciously, adapted themselves to a new world by increasingly assuming the appearance of ordinary collegiate churches. Lucchese *pievi* and *pievani* still seem generally, however, to have maintained certain important, if diminished, rights: the control of the baptismal fonts themselves; the right of the *pievani* to install dependent rectors; rights for the *pievani* of precedence and hospitality at the dependent churches; the right to demand that the inferior clergy assist at *pievi* functions; a part, one fourth normally, of the parochial tithe; rights in burial, if no longer the right always actually to bury the body of the dead parishioner. A series of twelfth- and thirteenth-century disputes reveals the Lucchese *pieve* and subaltern parish adjusting to their new relations with each other—in, for example, rights of sepulture between 1127 and 1223. In a dispute of the latter year it was declared that the parish clergy involved in the case had the customary right to bless the first fire in a new house within the parish (and the house is a unit of great importance in this relationship). These defining disputes seem to have been sharper in urban areas with their tangles of close houses and difficult borders than in rustic areas with relatively easy and empty boundaries.

At the same time that the Lucchese *pievi*'s old hegemony was thus weakening, some of them were finding for themselves a new and peculiar sort of reality. Lucchese *pievi*—of course not all, but many—were, in the twelfth and thirteenth centuries, becoming elective *pievi* with as their collective electing patrons the laity of their communities (or a significant *"universitas"* portion of them). Some Lucchese communities evidently felt that the churches built and maintained largely by themselves were their own; they were willing and able to compete with private patrons, clergy, and bishop for their

churches' patronage. One can see electing laity active in Fibbialla, Ciciana, Picciorano, and many other places. Their nom-
inees had of course to be approved, instituted, and installed by
ecclesiastical authority; the giving of the symbolic books, keys,
biretta, bell-ropes, and altar cloths remained clerical. But even
in some *pievi* which remained officially in the hands of another patron, the lay electorate seems to have had a direct
voice in the selection of the *pievano*: in 1228 the clerks, *consoli,*
and men of Padule, together with the local noble Orlandino
Ingherammi de Capannole presented to the bishop as their
nominee for *pievano* of the vacant *pieve*, Ugo, chaplain of
(significantly no doubt) Capannole; the bishop quashed their
illegal election; but he himself chose the same Ugo as *pievano*;
for this his hands were kissed by the clergy, and the laity cried
out, "Deo gratias, domine, multos annos!"[14]

Occasionally thirteenth-century Italian archpriests tried or
were forced to define aspects of themselves—to say who and
what they were. In 1240 Giacomo archpriest of Nervi on the
Ligurian coast southeast of Genoa publicly stated to Giovanni
archbishop of Genoa that his *pieve* had been established and
built in the patrimony of the archbishopric. The archpriest
said that the rights of patron and founder pertained to the
archbishop, that the right of electing and confirming an archpriest to the *pieve* belonged to the archbishop and no other,

[14] All of the information about Lucchese *pievi* in these two para-
graphs comes from a very helpful book: Luigi Nanni, *La Parrocchia
studiata nei documenti lucchesi dei secoli VIII-XIII*, Analecta Gregor-
iana, XLVII (Rome, 1948). For the *libellus* of 1260, Nanni, 188; for the
new position of the *pievi* and a summary of remaining rights, Nanni,
155, 182-190, and particularly 182-188; for the problem of chaplains free
to baptize but not outside of the *pieve* font, Nanni, 185-186; for the
twelfth- and thirteenth-century disputes, Nanni, 145-158, and for a
valuable list, 147-149; for 1127 and 1223, Nanni, 155-157; for elective
pievi, Nanni, 159-171; for Fibbialla, Ciciana, and Picciorano, Nanni,
160-161, 198-199; for installation, Nanni, 174, 199-201; for the Padule
election, Nanni, 172. Nanni's discussion of the decline of the *pieve*
at Lucca can be compared with the slight discussion of the change at
Brescia in Paolo Guerrini, "Per la storia dell'organizzazione ecclesiastica
della diocesi di Brescia nel medio-evo," *Brixia Sacra*, XIII (1922), 3-12,
25-31, 11.

and that the archpriest's house and the adjoining land, with its figs, vines, and olives, were held of the archbishopric.[15]

In 1221, Andrea, archbishop of Bari, after an inquest, confirmed the rights and privileges of Umfredo, archpriest of Acquaviva, and of his archpresbytery. The archbishop, or his clerk, described more clearly and extendedly than the archpriest of Nervi something of what it meant to be an archpriest in the thirteenth century, this time in the south—or at least what it meant in Acquaviva. That which Umfredo had confirmed to him as inseparable from his archpresbytery was a conglomerate of lands, gardens, vineyards, houses, *villani*, and religious and quasi-religious rights: the house which was called Sant'Eustachio's before the gate of that church, the church of San Martino with its *casale* called Ventauro, a house with a *palazziolo*, three vineyards, a garden, land, uncultivated plots, two *villani*, the right to appoint *primicerii* in the church of Sant'Eustachio, to choose sacristans, to himself direct—or choose who should—the school for teaching boys, to direct the spiritualities, to suspend clerks and make them conform to the dictates of justice, to celebrate the divine office on feast days or to commit the singing to whom he would, to hear confessions and give license for hearing them. A curious figure emerges with his houses, his vineyards with their jangle of saints' names, his *villani*, and his school, a figure to whom the archbishop's wax seal and his subscription and that of Palmerio, canon of Bari and archpriest (the other, cathedral, kind) of Giovinazzo, bore witness—a man who sang before, confessed, and taught some of his parishioners, and held two of them in villeinage.[16]

Archpriests appear fairly frequently in records from the south of Italy, but except in specific places, and in specific con-

[15] L. T. Belgrano, *Il secondo registro della curia arcivescovile di Genova*, Atti della società ligure di storia patria, xviii (Genoa, 1887), 391-392 no. 351.

[16] *C.d.b.*, i; "Le Pergamene del Duomo di Bari (952-1264)," ed. G. B. Nitto de Rossi and Francesco Nitti di Vito, 165-166, no. 88; for an exempt archpresbytery, Altamura, see *C.d.b.*, vi: "Le Pergamene di S. Nicola Bari (1195-1266)," ed. Francesco Nitti di Vito, 89-91, no. 57.

nections, the nature of their jurisdiction is generally unclear. There is occasional evidence of the priests of an area acting as a corporate unit, as if they considered themselves members of some sort of territorial archpresbytery. In a case of tithe disputed between Nicola archbishop of Salerno and the priests of Eboli, which the curia of Honorius III delegated to be heard by the archbishop of Amalfi (Giovanni) and the bishop of Sarno (Giovanni III), the priests acted together. Their *universitas* was represented by two of its members, one called a *primicerius*. There is no reference to an archpriest. The Eboli case was variously deflected. The bishop of Sarno found it impossible to get to Amalfi and committed his powers to the archbishop. The priests themselves thought better of their action and withdrew from the case sometime between December 1218, when their papal mandate was procured, and February 1219, when the archbishop issued his terminating statement. In this general atmosphere of incompleteness the corporation of priests seems properly unformed. They had no seal of their own and used that of the abbot of San Pietro of Eboli.[17] The Eboli priests' evidence argues in two directions. In Eboli in 1218 the concerted action of a group of priests from the sort of area which could be expected to form an archpresbytery was conceivable, but if the priests had any institutional connection it was certainly very fragile.

The office of archpriest was important in the Italian system. At the very least its holders were convenient recipients of mandates, representatives of the establishment, in the absence of rural archdeacons. But the figure of the thirteenth-century rural archpriest, except in specific cases and areas, remains insubstantial and shadowy. Perhaps he (surrounded by his collegiate clergy) can best be visualized by looking at a place like Minturno, an archpriest's town, on a mountain's side, isolated by aridity, within the diocese of Gaeta. Perhaps he is best seen in ceremonial, as is the archpriest of Fratte in the "register" of Berard I, abbot of Cassino (an unusually rich source of information about an unusually well and fully run quasi-diocese). In mid-October 1272 Cassino's rector at Fratte,

[17] Giuseppe Paesano, *Memorie per servire alla storia della chiesa salernitana* (Salerno, 1846-1857), II, 309-311.

Giacomo of Pontecorvo, received and published a letter from the dean of Cassino under the dean's seal of black wax. The dean's letter incorporated another from the archbishop of Naples to the dean (in the address of which the dean's name precedes the archbishop's). The archbishop wrote that the bearer of his letter, Pietro of Fratte, had presented to the archbishop the included letter from the dean—formal medieval letters are often built like onions or boxes within boxes. The dean's letter to the archbishop stated that Pietro had been properly elected and confirmed as archpriest of Fratte and that Pietro, a faithful vassal to the monastery of Cassino, sought to be installed by the archbishop. The archbishop in Sant' Angelo in Formis on October 12, approved the installation and ordered that it be effected by the dean. The rector, Giacomo, acting upon this composite letter's authorization, proceeded to the actual installation. On Sunday, 16 October, at the hour of Mass, he installed Pietro first in the marble throne where archpriests of Fratte celebrated high feasts in the church—and the white marble of all those throned, dark apses in archpriestly Italian churches flashes through one's mind—and then in his regular choir stall.[18] This high formality, for all its elaboration and evocative picturesqueness, ended badly. In December 1273 Abbot Berard, having summoned Pietro to appear and show by what right he held his office, deprived Pietro, who had not appeared, and enjoined silence upon him. Berard found Pietro guilty of fraud, deceit, and perjury in his occupying the office of archpriest and involving himself in its administration.[19]

Abbot Berard's register contains another set of documents, including a long composition sealed with the abbot's lead seal and dating from April 1275, which deals in an unusually revealing way with the difficult, flimsy business of local Italian ecclesiastical administration. The documents do something toward defining the rights and responsibilities of various named officials, and specifically of archpriest and archdeacon, as always in one place at one time; but the fact that a composi-

[18] Caplet, 131-132 no. 309; the archbishop acted from Sant'Angelo in Formis.
[19] Caplet, 177 no. 419.

tion was necessary clearly argues, at least, previous and perhaps continuing uncertainty. The composition was made between the abbot and the archpriest, archdeacon, and chapter of San Germano, the central archpresbytery of Cassino's area of jurisdiction in spiritualities. The church and chapter of San Germano were to admit full subjection to Cassino, San Germano's mother church and lady. Disputes between the subject and mother church, specifically those in progress at the Roman curia, were to be abandoned. These were disputes over the making of first tonsures, over presentation of San Germano clerks to orders, over the hearing of marriage cases, the enjoining of penitents, and the correction of clerks. The archpriest had claimed these rights as pertaining to him and the church of San Germano. The abbot had claimed them as ordinary with jurisdiction over San Germano.

The 1275 definition of jurisdictions states first that when the archpresbytery should be vacant, according to ancient and approved custom, the archdeacon and chapter would seek license to elect from the abbot, or, during a vacancy, the convent. The election would be made by the chapter; and, according to custom, the elect would be presented to the abbot or convent for confirmation or rejection. Having been confirmed, the elect should be installed by someone sent by the abbot or convent, and then come to the convent to swear liege homage, fealty, and obedience. First tonsures should be given by the abbot or a bishop under his mandate, not by the archpriest. The correction of clerks' minor offenses belonged to the archpriest. With the consent of the archdeacon he should correct them and establish penances. He might suspend clerks, except the archdeacon and *primicerii*, from their offices and benefices, and excommunicate them; but he might not seize their persons to imprison them or deprive them of their benefices. Graver offenses were reserved to the abbot, his successors, and their vicars. For clarity, some graver offenses were named: notorious concubinage or usury, wandering about at night for no good reason, carrying arms, drinking publicly in the taverns of San Germano or the neighborhood, striking with malice a clerk or a layman with or without a knife, publicly playing at dice. Cases involving real or personal property were reserved to the abbot or his vicar. The abbot, however, made the archpriest perpetual penitentiary, in certain types of cases, for the parish of San Germano and the subject churches, and made him vicegerent for examining candidates to minor orders, and made him perpetual official in the parish with the power to hear all marriage cases to the point of definitive sentence, and, after consultation with the abbot or his vicar, power to proclaim definitive sentence with appeal to abbot or pope. The abbot reserved correction of the major persons of the chapter to himself—"ita tamen quod ipse archidyaconus archipresbytero honorem impendat et ipse archipresbyter honorem impendat eidem archidyacono." The abbot reserved to himself the right to visit and correct as an ordinary ought. He also reserved for himself the right to interpret the compromise.[20]

The fragments of evidence that can be thus collected from the corners of the Italian church do not strikingly deny the continued existence of something at least weakly resembling the ideal *plebanus* system with its archpriest ruling over a collegiate baptismal church, from which the clergy moved to the parish chapels to say Masses for and administer the popular sacraments (except Baptism) to the people, and to which the people came for high holiday and burial, and the clergy (and sometimes the laity) came for elections (in elective *pievi*). In this ideal constellation the archpriest moved about to celebrate the *pieve*'s local feasts, and from it he collected tithe. The baptismal parish really was in some ways a sort of subdiocese, a unit that gathered a group of Christian men and their holdings and tied them to the higher rungs of hierarchy. It may have done this more sharply and differently when the parochial clergy was elected by the laity.[21]

The archpriests were fitted into their dioceses. In 1207 the archbishop of Salerno had procured from Innocent III spe-

[20] Caplet, 193-197 nos. 442-445.
[21] Forchielli, viii-x and *passim*; Catherine E. Boyd, *Tithes and Parishes in Medieval Italy* (Ithaca, New York, 1952), 55, 101 n. 30, 155-162; see the fiscal divisions within the diocese in the volumes of the *Rationes decimarum Italiae*. For elected clergy see, too, John Larner, *The Lords of Romagna* (London, 1965), 193-194.

cific confirmation of his episcopal rights over the twelve named archpriests of his diocese.[22] Bari held Acquaviva, Genoa Nervi, Cassino San Germano to themselves. Certainly the baptismal parish continued to have a fiscal reality; both the archpriest and the parishioners felt from their different sides the *pieve* tithe.[23] Except in response to tithing and taxing, however, and the weakening defense of old privilege and in election, the thirteenth-century *pieve* system showed little real sign of vitality. It was a relic that continued to exist perhaps only because nothing (except its subaltern rival) was around to push it aside and because nothing much was demanded of it. It laxly recalled the ideals of eleventh-century Italian collegiate reform. It had little positive connection with reforming ideas that seemed new, with intensified diocesan administration, in the thirteenth century.

Episcopal administration within the thirteenth-century diocese did not in either England or Italy require the bishop's physical presence. When the bishop was present he was not expected to act alone. By about 1210 every bishop in England had an administrative assistant, an "official," an officer increasingly connected with judicial activities as he presided over the bishop's consistory court.[24] By the time of the friar archbishop John Pecham (1279-1292), in Canterbury, a diocese of which the administration was probably the most highly articulated in England, a complicated establishment of courts was apparent. The actual place of meeting for Canterbury's consistory was Bow Church, the church of Blessed Mary of the Arches, in a deanery of thirteen churches, the deanery of the Arches, a Canterbury peculiar in London. The dean of the Arches was the commissary general of the official of Canterbury. The court was physically established. The sophistication and effectiveness of the court of Canterbury under Pecham—for which there is ample and various evidence far from the Arches in local ecclesiastical archives as far north as Durham and in the rich contemporary registers of Pecham's suffragan bishops—

[22] Paesano, II, 301-303.
[23] Boyd, *Tithes and Parishes*, 161.
[24] C. R. Cheney, *From Becket to Langton, English Church Government 1170-1213* (Manchester, 1956), 147.

are indicated in one striking instance in the recommended
exact regulations of 1282, which would restrict the action of
the official of the court of Canterbury in appeals from the subjects of suffragan bishops. The proposed regulations were
based upon the recommendations of an appointed archiepiscopal commission of five men, all experienced in the law,
and the local law, and aware of the problems of the court of
Canterbury.[25] Pecham's commission and their regulations are
well known, and they are generally thought of, and reasonably, as aiming at restricting the powers of the archbishop's
court; but here they ought to be kept in mind constantly as an
indication of the serious and intricate elaboration of that court.
The Bow Church stands for physical permanence when Canterbury is seen against the unconstructed impermanence of
Italian episcopal activity.

Canterbury's definition of judicial offices and courts was
more advanced than that of other English sees, but they followed, insofar as it was pertinent for them, the same general
direction. In York the official's office was growing at the end
of the thirteenth century. During the episcopate of John
Romeyn (1285-1296) a commissary general seems to have
been a regular member of the office.[26] This sort of sureness
and proliferation was the pattern of thirteenth-century English diocesan development. By the end of the thirteenth century
another representative of bishop or archbishop was intermittently present. He was an officer less limited and less judicial
in his competence and also less permanent than the official.
He, the vicar general, might act for the bishop in his absence
in all matters that did not require episcopal orders or that were
not specifically reserved in his commission.[27]

[25] Churchill, I, 425-432; II, 686; see, too, Brentano, *York Metropolitan
Jurisdiction*, 184-195, but compare Michael M. Sheehan, *The Will in
Medieval England* (Toronto, 1963), 200-205.

[26] Brentano, *York Metropolitan Jurisdiction*, 72-77; for the official
see Paul Fournier, *Les Officialités au moyen-âge* (Paris, 1880).

[27] Churchill, I, 25-35; Edouard Fournier, *Le Vicaire-général au
moyen-âge* (Paris, 1923); Brentano, "Late Medieval Changes in the
Administration of Vacant Suffragan Dioceses: Province of York,"
The Yorkshire Archaeological Journal, XXXVIII (1955), 496-503 (where
Bekingham is mistakenly credited with Syreton's notarial work).

During vacancies of English episcopal sees, except for the two metropolitan sees of Canterbury and York, the metropolitan archbishop appointed officials as keepers of the spiritualities of the vacant sees—the temporalities went to the king. The metropolitan archbishops were not unopposed in their exercising this right in the thirteenth century; but after a series of compositions, with four suffragan sees in the thirteenth century (Lincoln, London, Salisbury, Worcester) and one in the fourteenth (Norwich), Canterbury's rights were admitted, as were York's after a sharp and complicated fight, from 1283 to 1286, with Durham.[28] The spiritualities of the metropolitan sees themselves fell to the cathedral chapters, or rather they did in the province of York. In Canterbury the disputes of the prior and convent of Canterbury, the monastic chapter, with the archdeacon of Canterbury and with the suffragan bishops of the province constantly recurred in thirteenth-century vacancies, although Robert of Selsey (the curial proctor), the convent's official after Kilwardby's resignation, acted after the suffragans' compromise of 1278.[29] Even in York the control of the province during a vacancy was unsteady.

In England the bishop was aided by administrative and judicial assistants, and when he was out of his diocese or when he had stopped being bishop he was replaced by an administrative official. There was, in England, an assumption that administrative continuity was desirable, even necessary. In Italy things were different. The Italian bishop need not act personally, although in a large number of small dioceses with bishops too poor and too inconsequent to be of any external significance there was no reason why he should not. In these lightly administered little places a bishop was enough. But the bishop might be absent, and in the proctorial thirteenth-century church he would of course be represented.

In the thirteenth-century Italian church the bishops were represented, and also sometimes aided, by vicars. The vicar might act for a short time, for a specific business, or he might be a continuing administrative assistant. The latter sort of

[28] Churchill, I, 161-240; Brentano, *York Metropolitan Jurisdiction*, 115-174, and "Late Medieval Changes."
[29] Churchill, I, 551-556; II, 222.

vicar appears for precisely those dioceses, like Città di Castello, and those provinces, like Milan, where in general the ordinary's attitude toward his diocese, the metropolitan's toward his province, was most continuously administrative, most like the attitude of English prelates.[30]

In 1294 the vicar of the bishop of Bologna acted a role in the bishop's court close to that of an English official; and Gerardo da Cornazano was vicar to both Ottaviano degli Ubaldini and his brother and successor Schiatta, bishops of Bologna.[31] In 1293, Giordano Cagnaci, the vicar of Galfrido bishop of Torino, used, in the cloister of San Benedetto, Torino, his own seal to authenticate acts. Even more impressive is a vicar of Bishop Enrico of Lucca who bore the title: *vicarius ... episcopi ... in spiritualibus super ecclesiis ultra Arnum et populis earundem*; the geography of his title and its administrative implications recall the efficiency and nature of papal administration in a diocese with constant vicars and many records.[32] Vicars general were active in Como in 1247 and in 1268 (an archpriest), and in Mantua in 1265. The bishop of Rieti had vicars, like Pietro da Roma, in 1282, and the bishop of Camerino a vicar, Nicola da Sassoferrato, in 1301. Vicars acted for the bishops of Verona early and late in

[30] Carlo Marcora, "Serie cronologica dei vicari generali della diocesi di Milano (dal 1210 al 1930)," *Memorie storiche della diocesi di Milano*, VI (1959), 252-282; for Città di Castello, see, for example, Archivio vescovile of Città di Castello, Bishops' Book VI, fo. 242 (1279), and below.

[31] See below, Chapter II, part iii, and, for example: Bologna, Archivio di stato, conventi soppressi, Sant'Agnese Bologna, 6/5596, C 328; 7/5597, F 372, F 391.

[32] Gino Borghezio and Cesare Fasola, *Le Carte dell'archivio del Duomo di Torino*, Biblioteca della società storica subalpina, CVI (Turin, 1931), 171-174 no. 88—*sigillum sue vicarie*, for Giordano see also 120-129 no. 68, 176-179 no. 90 (if both were he, he was active as a clerical person in the diocese from 1264 to 1300); for instructions by an archbishop of York for the use of the seal of the officiality see *The Registers of John le Romeyn, Lord Archbishop of York, 1286-1296, and of Henry of Newark, Lord Archbishop of York, 1296-1299*, ed. William Brown, Surtees Society, 123, 128 (Durham, 1913-1916) [hereafter *Romeyn*], I, 30 no. 68 (Durham Seals, no. 3248). For Lucca, Nanni, 173.

the thirteenth century.[33] Episcopal vicars appear repeatedly in records for Ivrea; the Franciscan bishop Alberto Gonzaga used his archdeacons, different ones, as vicars in 1281 and 1287.[34] In 1275 the precentor, Guglielmo Biscotte, had acted as vicar general in Torino; and in 1288 the archdeacon acted as the bishop's vicar general in Vercelli, a diocese in which vicars general acted repeatedly and in which delegated visitors also acted.[35] Aygler, archbishop of Naples and supposedly brother of Berard I of Cassino, was the abbot's vicar general in 1270, and in 1274 he had as his own vicar general Ugone, abbot of San Severino Maggiore in Naples.[36] The repeated names of vicars in the diocese of Orvieto, like Nicola da Matelica, using the name of their office, even when the bishop was within the diocese, are witnesses to a sort of continuing government, but few of their recorded activities are administrative in any normal sense of the word.[37] The vicar's not being exactly an episcopal administrative substitute was so clearly true in Arezzo until 1256 that the cathedral clergy claimed the right to nominate the vicar general.[38]

An extraordinary vicar appears in Monreale after the Sicilian Vespers and the Aragonese conquest. In May 1282

[33] Fedele Savio, *Gli antichi vescovi d'Italia dalle origini al 1300*, La Lombardia, ii.i (Bergamo, 1929), 364, 370-372; ii.ii (Bergamo, 1932), 312; Rome, Archivio di stato, Fiastra, no. 2259; Rieti, Archivio capitolare, armadio ii, fasc. E, no. 5; Archivio segreto vaticano, A.C.N.V., San Giorgio in Braida, 9427, 11196. For vicars at Padua see A.C.N.V., San Giacomo di Monselice, 6063, 6097.

[34] Ferdinando Gabotto, *Archivio vescovile d'Ivrea*, Biblioteca della società storica subalpina, LVI (Pinerolo, 1900), v, 72-73 no. 53; VI, 139-173, specifically nos. 402, 404, 409.

[35] Borghezio and Fasola, 139-141, no. 75; Domenico Arnoldi, *Le Carte dello archivio arcivescovile di Vercelli*, Biblioteca della società storica subalpina, LXXXV (Pinerolo, 1917), 335-336.

[36] Caplet, 60-61 no. 120, 61-62 no. 123, 63 no. 128, 63-64 no. 130, 189-191 no. 436.

[37] Luigi Fumi, *Statuti e regesti dell'opera di Santa Maria di Orvieto*, Accademia storico-giuridica di Roma (Rome, 1891), 83-85.

[38] Corrado Lazzeri, *Guglielmino Ubertini, vescovo di Arezzo (1248-1289) e i suoi tempi* (Florence, 1920), 147-148; Guglielmino quashed the pretensions which Bishop Immone seems to have set loose in 1044; the sort of diocesan division which Immone permitted, however, does seem not unlike the sort which led to archdeaconries in the North.

Archbishop Giovanni Boccamazza, acting in his own name in Monreale, granted a twenty-nine-year lease. In June 1284, acting through proctors, he granted in *gabella* a *casale* to a Palermo judge for an annual rent to be paid on the feast of the Assumption.[39] In June 1287 Archbishop Pietro Gerra granted a *casale* to a noble Palerman for an annual Assumption rent. Archbishop Pietro's action was effected by two men (one a monk of the cathedral chapter monastery of Monreale) who were called the archbishop's proctors general in Sicily.[40] In April 1291, in a document that in its date proclaimed the reign of the Aragonese Giacomo (the opposing but effective monarch), Archbishop Pietro conceded to a Palermo judge another *casale* of the church of Monreale for five years. This concession was made by a man named Giacomo Bonaguri who was a canon of Sant'Agata in Ferentino, the Archbishop's home, and who was identified as the familiar, vicar, and proctor general of the archbishop in spiritualities and temporalities in the island of Sicily.[41] Political and ecclesiastical considerations could not sever the connections between the papal and peninsular archbishop and his Aragonese, insular holdings. Too much was involved.

Although the riches and the political involvement of the see of Monreale were both unusual, they point up common episcopal problems. The bishop of the poorest little unadministered see in the Marches or Campania had constantly to be prepared to deal with and protect the proprietary interests of his see. His poverty obviously did not make his (or his see's) property less important to him. Archbishops and bishops with heavy secular involvements—and intricate feudal business like Genoa and Ivrea—could be expected, of course, to have relatively elaborate staffs of clerks occupied with their business. Genoa did.[42] But vicars were everywhere. They were ready to represent their principals in the movement heard, and still almost heard, in that constant shuffle of instru-

[39] Garufi, 60 no. 131, 60-61 no. 133; for Archbishop Giovanni see Lello, *Descrizione*, 14-19, and below, Chapter III.
[40] Garufi, 61-62 no. 134; for Archbishop Pietro see Lello, 20-28.
[41] Garufi, 62-63 no. 135.
[42] Belgrano, e.g. 294-297, 363-366, but *passim*.

ments, the vital transfer of property and regulation of income. The jobs of the Italian vicar and the English official blend into each other and overlap—but they were created, or grew, to deal with differently conceived dioceses.

The administration of vacant dioceses in thirteenth-century England was tense with the rivalry of opposing jurisdictions even though the English sees lost their temporalities to the king during vacancies. In Italy, in observable cases, the government of vacant sees fell to the cathedral chapter. The cathedral chapters administered the vacant sees, or conducted their business, through vicars, vicars general, or proctors. In 1261 the archpriest of the metropolitan who was active in the government of the diocese when it was full was the vicar of the chapter of Milan during a vacancy. During another vacancy at Milan the vicar was a Cistercian abbot—vicars were sometimes regulars in the later thirteenth century.[43] In 1294 Oberto Beccaria, prior of San Salvatore, acted in Pavia. In the 1290's, too, the archdeacon of Cremona was proctor and defender of his see.[44] In 1277, during a vacancy of the see of Salerno, the chapter was responsible for granting the Dominicans the right to have their new church consecrated by a prelate other than the archbishop of Salerno. In Bologna, at end century, "The Archdeacon," Guido de Baysio, acted as vicar of the vacant see—and showed the unusual importance of both archdeacon and official *sede vacante* in that remarkable see.[45]

The vacancy evidence for the Umbrian see of Città di Castello is considerably more extensive than that for any other observed Italian see. In 1279 two proctors elected by the chapter resisted for the chapter the attempts of the *podestà* to interfere in the administration of the see, vacant through the death of Bishop Nicolò. More remarkable is the fact that during this vacancy canon Ranaldo da Falzano, archpriest of San Savino,

[43] Savio, I.i (Milan, 1913), 613; II.ii, 133.

[44] Savio, II.ii, 140, 477.

[45] Paesano, III (Salerno, 1855), 41-42; Bologna, Archivio di stato, conventi soppressi, Sant'Agnese Bologna, 7/5597, F 386, F 391. For a short biographical sketch of Guido de Baysio (with bibliographical references), see *Dictionnaire de droit canonique*, ed. R. Naz. v. (Paris, 1953), cols. 1007-1008 [G. Mollat].

acted as capitular vicar with the title "Ranaldus canonicus Castellanus vicarius episcopatus Civitatis Castelli constitutus a capitulo episcopali sede vacante." Ranaldo not only acted—in the cloister or cemetery of the church of Santa Maria Nuova *in loco ubi jus redditur*—but also he caused to be composed and preserved a register of his acts, an almost incredible register in its Italian context.[46]

In England the office of the official during a vacancy was quite clearly defined and, even without temporalities, important. But the source of the official's authority was disputed by contending claimants, and finally it fell to the metropolitan archbishop of the see's province, the administrative and judicial superior to the bishop, the man responsible for seeing that the bishop was effectively administering his diocese when the diocese was full, but a man who officially had no property interests within the see. (Although the vacancy jurisdiction brought the metropolitan income, he received the income from the spiritualities, income which normally went to the bishop as bishop not, essentially, as landlord or tenant.)[47] In Italy the vacancy vicar's office was poorly defined—it is hard to see—but rights during the vacancy seem normally and, in the thirteenth century, without much dispute, to have fallen to the cathedral chapter, the body with the greatest proprietary interest in the bishop's cathedral church and its cult.

The insubstantiality, the administrative unimportance, of the Italian diocese is perhaps most sharply illustrated by the

[46] Città di Castello, Archivio vescovile (chancellor's office), Bk. VIII, fos. 118-138 (intermittently); see Robert Brentano, "The Bishops' Books of Città di Castello," *Traditio*, XVI (1960), 241-254, 247; Giovanni Muzi, *Memorie ecclesiastiche e civili di Città di Castello* (Città di Castello, 1842-1844), II, 164-165, 166. In 1205 the rector of Città di Castello was vicar during a vacancy: Muzi, IV, 149. See, too, the carefully administered diocese of Lucca: Martino Giusti, "Le elezioni dei vescovi di Lucca specialmente nel secolo XIII," *Rivista di storia della chiesa in Italia*, VI (1952), 205-230, 217, 219, 222.

[47] Vacancy income might be very little: in 1325 Archbishop Melton of York got thirteen marks sterling together with five marks for the expenses of his official *sede vacante* as the profits of a vacancy at Carlisle: York Diocesan Registry, the Register of William Melton (1317-1340), York R.I. 9, fo. 466v.

creation and suppression of dioceses in the Marches. Thirteenth-century popes evidently felt that they could at will (with the counsel of their consistories) suppress these dioceses, rearrange them, reconstitute them, without violently disarranging any administrative mechanism. Evidently they felt that the diocesan dignity was an award that might be given to a loyal papal Italian city as a sort of medal, and be taken away from a treacherous, pro-imperial city.

Urban IV wrote in July 1263: "predictam civitatem Racanatensem, de fratrum nostrorum consilio, episcopali dignitate perpetuo, sine aliqua spe restitutionis, apostolica auctoritate privamus, statuentes ut nullis umquam futuris temporibus civitas eadem ad hujusmodi episcopalem dignitatem valeat reassumi."[48] The papal displeasure was particularly strong because of past papal favors to the citizens of Recanati "quibus sedes apostolica eos eorumque terram, erigendo inibi ecclesiam cathedralem ac decorando terram ipsam episcopalis titulo dignitatis, multipliciter honoravit." In October 1263, Buonagiunta da Boscoli, the Franciscan bishop of the one-time see, was preferred to Iesi.[49] The lamented decoration of Recanati, of which Urban IV, furious with Recanati's defection to Manfred, wrote, was not an ancient honor. It had come, as it had gone, from the papal war with the Hohenstaufen. On 4 July 1240 Gregory IX had informed Cardinal Sinibaldo Fieschi (the future Innocent IV), the rector of the March of Ancona, that he had taken the episcopal dignity from Osimo, because it had adhered to Frederick II, and given it to faithful Recanati, which had previously been within the diocese of Numana. Gregory wrote that the diocese of Numana should be recompensed for its loss by getting another piece of the diocese of Osimo. The citizens of Recanati would agree to invest 5,000 lire or its equivalent in the

[48] *Les Registres d'Urbain IV* (*1261-1264*), ed. Leon Dorez and Jean Guiraud, Bibliothèque des écoles françaises d'Athènes et de Rome (Paris, 1892-1929) [hereafter *Urbain IV*], II, 156-157 no. 335; for this practice see Daniel Waley, *The Papal State in the Thirteenth Century* (London, 1961), 151-152; see, too, Luigi Bartoccetti, "Serie dei vescovi delle diocesi Marchigione," *Studia Picena*, XII (1936), 109; XIV (1939), 145; XV (1940), 121-122; Ferdinando Ughelli, *Italia Sacra* (Venice, 1717-1722), I, cols. 1219-1221.
[49] *Urbain IV*, II, 199 no. 416.

establishment of the cathedral church and promise to build houses for the bishop and canons. On 17 January 1241 Gregory had ordered the once bishop of Osimo, then of Recanati, to proceed to the church of San Flaviano in Recanati, which would be his cathedral.[50]

Recanati's years of honor and Osimo's years of shame coincided. On 13 March 1264 Urban IV restored the episcopal dignity to Osimo, gave it as its bishop a papal chaplain and archdeacon of Spoleto, and rearranged again the Osimo Numana borders. On 24 May Urban ordered the bishop of Camerino to grant in perpetuity to the bishop of Numana and his *mensa* the ex-cathedral of San Flaviano in Recanati.[51] But the Roman church, the special mother and lady of these dioceses, as the curia put it, had not finished their thirteenth-century rearrangement. Nicholas IV, the pope from Ascoli (whose connection with these eastern dioceses is physically preserved in the great, gorgeous, English papal cope he gave to Ascoli), made Recanati an episcopal city again in 1289. In the first half of the fourteenth century, papal wrath again suppressed Recanati, sent its bishop to Senigallia, and connected the diocese with the newly created see of Macerata. In mid-century, papal pleasure reestablished Recanati as an episcopal name—part of a double see.[52]

The intertwined fortunes of Recanati and Osimo forceably bring forward the brute facts of political history which constantly distorted and broke the pattern of ecclesiastical administration in thirteenth-century Italy. The long, morally and governmentally debilitating wars of the papacy with the Hohenstaufen and their Aragonese successors at least had the advantage of that clearly stated animosity which can, but does

[50] *Les Registres de Grégoire IX*, ed. Lucien Auvray, Bibliothèque des écoles françaises d'Athènes et de Rome (Paris, 1896-1955) [hereafter *Grégoire IX*], III, col. 277 no. 5240, cols. 189-190 no. 5074, cols. 344-345 no. 5345.

[51] *Urbain IV*, II, 260-261 nos. 4522-4525; see Waley, *Papal State*, 170, for a threat to Cagli; for Clement IV's flurry of threats from Viterbo, including his rude letter to Federigo Visconti and his denunciations of the "good" dioceses of Pisa and Città di Castello, see *Clément IV*, 255-267.

[52] Bartoccetti, *Studia Picena*, XIV (1939), 145; XV (1940), 145.

not at all necessarily, blur and confuse decisive governmental lines. In this connection the Angevin alliance may have been more disastrous to the church. The curious interweaving of secular and ecclesiastical governments in southern peninsular Italy during the reign of Charles I could hardly have been more discouraging than it was to the reformation of orderly and separate diocesan and provincial administration.[53] Still the indecision had also been very grave in the mid-century Marches around Fiastra, where various sorts of jurisdiction from opposing parties were shuffled together in remarkable contingencies and alternations.[54]

The secular-ecclesiastical disputes and the intermingling of secular and ecclesiastical governments in thirteenth-century Italy were harsh parodies of the disputes and intermingling that existed in the rest of Europe—harsh parodies, but just that. At times the disputes in England were very sharp. John can reasonably be compared with Frederick II and the interdict with the disturbances of Frederick's reign. In isolation the Canterbury dispute looks at least as serious as the Palermo dispute, the initial incident in Frederick's alienation from the papacy.[55] Anthony Bek's position as bishop of Durham was, potentially, a very confusing one.[56] Every bishop in England was involved in the secular establishment. Edmund of Abingdon, Pecham, Romeyn, Winchelsey could not have described the relations between church and state as easy ones.[57] The dis-

[53] This at least is my opinion; there seems to me a really disorderly quality about southern Italian legatine government, in which helpful boundaries are disregarded. Some sense of this can be gotten from the Salerno case discussed below, but also from any collection of Angevin documents or discussion of Angevin government, of which the most accessible are probably E. G. Léonard, *Les Angevins de Naples* (Paris, 1954) and Steven Runciman, *The Sicilian Vespers* (Cambridge, 1958).

[54] See below, Chapter IV, and Wolfgang Hagemann, "Studien und Dokumente zur Geschichte der Marken im Zeitalter der Staufer. II. Chiaravalle di Fiastra," *Quellen und Forschungen aus italienischen Archiven und Bibliotheken*, XLI (1961), 48-136.

[55] See Ernst H. Kantorowicz, *Frederick the Second* (London, 1931), 33-34, for the Palermo dispute.

[56] His position is studied in detail in C. M. Fraser, *A History of Antony Bek, Bishop of Durham, 1283-1311* (Oxford, 1957).

[57] See C. H. Lawrence, *St. Edmund of Abingdon* (Oxford, 1960),

turbance was, of course, rougher and longer lasting in Italy than in England; but its effect was not just more serious, it was in a different direction. Again, things in Italy and England were different and were seen differently. The secular embarrassments of successive archbishops of Canterbury did not permanently effect the dissolution of Canterbury's internal administration nor the slackening of its hold on its suffragans. The boundaries of English dioceses were not, in the thirteenth century, fluid. The boundaries of the dioceses of Numana and Osimo obviously were fluid. It was the fact that Osimo was different in substance from Rochester or London (as well as the fact of the different position of towns within the two communities) that permitted the Italian wars to affect Osimo as they did. The Italian wars did not cause the church to have the shape it had in Italy. The wars grew up in the church's (and the community's) shape and aggravated its difficulties. The wars' aggravation was directly felt not only in imperial deprivation and Angevin interpenetration, but also in the presence in the Italian provincial church of overly powerful ecclesiastics acting as legates, whose power cut into the structure of "normal" ecclesiastical administration.[58]

The specialness of the attachment of the church of Rome to the neighboring dioceses was a specifically Italian problem. The hard proximity of their very special mother and lady, with her band of directly subject central Italian dioceses, was undoubtedly destructive to the integrity and cohesiveness of Italian ecclesiastical provinces. The motherhood of Cosenza and Ravenna was overwhelmed by the motherhood of Rome. The crushing quality of this Roman motherhood, in the thirteenth century, was probably most destructive in provincial Italy, beyond the areas of Rome's special jurisdiction, through

---

chs. III and V (pp. 124-138, 155-182); F. M. Powicke, *The Thirteenth Century, 1216-1307* (Oxford, 1953), particularly for Winchelsey; Brentano, *York Metropolitan Jurisdiction*, 165-174 for Romeyn, particularly, but also 115-164 for Wickwane.

[58] See Guido Levi, *Registri dei Cardinali Ugolino d'Ostia e Ottaviano degli Ubaldini*, Istituto storico italiano, Fonti per la storia d'Italia (Rome, 1890); but even more helpfully, see any narrative history or the description of any extended ecclesiastical law case.

the relatively easy access to appeal of the papal curia and through the broad powers of papal legates and rectors.[59] Although the dioceses of thirteenth-century Italy seem, to the foreign observer, distracted and administratively unformed, they look firm and conventional compared with the provinces into which some of them were arranged.

For seven hundred years—from their creation in the thirteenth century until their mutilation by a surprise Allied bombing in 1943—the great bronze doors of the cathedral of Benevento blazed out the glory of Benevento's archbishops supreme among many suffragan bishops (see Figs. 5 and 6).[60] Forty-three of the door's panels told of Christ's life and His victory over death. Next to His ascension an archbishop of Benevento sat, in full pontificals, wearing the great Beneventan tiara and receiving the submission of, probably, a newly consecrated suffragan bishop. In panels around and beneath, the archbishop's twenty-four suffragans stood blessing. This splendid bronze hierarchical, perhaps Dionysian, statement of the connection between Christ's life and his ministers, however, paid honor to a metropolitan office which effected almost no observable metropolitan administration in the thirteenth century. The Benedictine archbishop Giovanni VI refused to consecrate an elect of Avellino.[61] But did the archbishop of Benevento visit his province, or hold repeated and serious provincial synods, or regularly hear appeals from the courts of his suffragans? It seems very unlikely. It does not seem certain that anyone in the thirteenth century could have been sure exactly how many suffragan dioceses there were in the province of Benevento, or exactly what they were.[62] There were lots of them. The designer of the doors thought twenty-four.

[59] See ch. IV, "The Institutions of the Papal State," in Waley, *Papal State*.

[60] Pompeio Sarnelli, *Memorie chronologiche de' vescovi ed arcivescovi della s. chiesa di Benevento* (Naples, 1691), 106-108.

[61] Sarnelli, 116.

[62] See Alessandro Pratesi, "Note di diplomatica vescovile Beneventana. Parte II. Vescovi suffraganei (secoli x-xiii)," *Bullettino dell'"Archivio paleografico italiano,"* NS I (1955), 19-91, 20-25, particularly the very helpful list on p. 25. Pratesi, in this very learned and perceptive article, accepts a theory developed by a number of historians whom he cites

In sharp contrast with the huge province of Benevento, sprawling indeterminately through the central peninsula, was the tiny coastal province of Amalfi [Map 2 insert].[63] The diocese of Amalfi stretched along the coast from the Gulf of Salerno, from a point between Vietri and Cetara, west of Salerno, westward to a point just beyond Positano. Near the center of this coastal line the diocese stretched inward to include the hill villages around Tramonti, south of Nocera. Along the coastal line just northeast of the city of Amalfi, between Atrani and Maiori, there was inserted a tiny enclave of three towns, technically cities, each forming a minuscule diocese. Two of these dioceses, Minori and Scala, were suffragans to the enclosing Amalfi; but the third, Ravello, was an exempt diocese, not an archbishopric, but subject only to the see of Rome. Besides the two enclosed suffragan sees, two other dioceses were included within the province of Amalfi. They were the island diocese of Capri, off the point of the Surrentine peninsula, and Lettere, an inland diocese imbedded in the

(L. Duchesne, A. Groner, J. Gay, H.-W. Klewitz) that the history of the ecclesiastical organization of the province of Benevento like that of its neighbors can be divided into two distinct phases separated from each other around the end of the twelfth century. The theory proposes that only in the second phase, but in it, the province attained a normal metropolitan provincial administration—that is that metropolitan normalcy came peculiarly late to these southern Italian provinces. I think that the theory is misleading. It is mistaken in accepting a "normal" provincial organization in northern Italy, even in northern Europe, in the twelfth and immediately preceding centuries; it is, I think, equally mistaken in seeing active provincial organization in Benevento and its neighbors during the thirteenth century. It is my contention in this book that although there is a crucial division in the general history of the western European church around the year 1200, the Italian peculiarity, and particularly the peculiarity of the Italian South, is that it did not partake (at least very fully) of this change. As opposed to Pratesi, I would push a geographical rather than a chronological division in examining the province of Benevento. The chronological theory was, it should be noted, initially developed by historians working on periods before 1200.

[63] Amalfi has been particularly fortunate in its historians: Matteo Camera, *Memorie storico-diplomatiche dell'antica città e ducato di Amalfi* (Salerno, 1876-1881), and Riccardo Filangieri di Candida, *Codice diplomatico amalfitano* (Vol. 1, Naples, 1917; Vol. 2, Trani, 1951).

ITALY

DIOCESE
of
CITTÀ di CASTELLO

0   5   10 Km.
0   5 Miles

PROVINCE of · AMALFI
— Boundary of province
--- Boundary of diocese

0   100   200   300 Km.
0   50   100   150 Miles

Map 2

center of the base of the peninsula and including besides Lettere itself the towns of Gragnano and Pimonte.

Again, what did a province mean? It meant that for purposes of the Roman camera, in account and collection, the Amalfi dioceses could be considered as a group. It probably meant that, under normal conditions, it was the right of the archbishop of Amalfi to consecrate his suffragan bishops. The lack of evidence in this specific connection probably argues for the universally assumed right. In 1217 Honorius III addressed a letter to Giovanni, archbishop of Amalfi, telling him that he was permitted, according to the *constitutiones canonicas*, to visit his province when it should be necessary or useful, to take moderate procurations, and to make corrections as was the duty of his office—a morning's walk to Minori, a morning's climb to Scala, a morning's sail to Capri.[64] But that the archbishop, or any of his thirteenth-century successors, ever spent these mornings enforcing his jurisdiction, eliciting answers about the state of the dioceses, suggesting remedies, we do not know and have, beyond the Honorius letter, no reason to believe.

On Thursday, 17 May (Ascension Thursday) 1257, Donadeo de Guiczone, judge of Amalfi, in his name, caused the public notary Pietro to record and have witnessed recent acts of excommunication and revocation of excommunication issued by Gualterio, archbishop of Amalfi, against and for Gerbino, bishop of Minori.[65] The archbishop had warned the bishop that according to the *constitutiones canonicas* he must visit the doorstep of the apostle Andrew—the resident patron culled by a local Roman cardinal from defeated Constantinople —on the feast of the saint's translation in May; but the bishop had chosen "perire pocius quam parere." Because of this the archbishop, zealous for the ancient honor of his church and having taken the counsel of his chapter, solemnly had promulgated a sentence of excommunication against the bishop. The bishop, fearing lest in growing contumacy he should be more gravely punished, had sought mercy. The archbishop, fearing

---

[64] *Regesta Honorii Papae III*, ed. Pietro Pressutti (Rome, 1888), 1, 93 no. 531.

[65] Amalfi, Archivio arcivescovile, A.P., sec. XIII, no. 17.

a repetition of the bishop's laxity, had made him profess his
submission and promise of future personal visits in a clear
voice, in the presence of the archbishop, the chapter of Amalfi,
the notary Pietro, and the notary's witnesses. The archbishop
was then willing to believe, or at least to state, that the bishop
had erred not out of malice, but out of simplicity, and to recall
him, as a father his son, mercifully into the lap of the mother
church.

Archbishop Gualterio, with the counsel of his chapter, had
vindicated the metropolitan right of the church of Amalfi to
gather a suffragan to its cult center at festa, and had had the
right preserved in notarial instrument. Archbishop Giovanni
had probably provoked Honorius III's letter permitting visitation. But this is very little record of metropolitan activity in a
highly recorded area and in a metropolitan see that had at least
one serious, active diocesan in the thirteenth century (Filippo
Augustariccio, at the century's end).[66] One need only look at
the corymbose heart of the province of Amalfi to know that it
cannot have been designed to be at all the sort of province that
Canterbury was in the thirteenth century. Instead it incor-
porates the remnants of tenth- and eleventh-century greatness,
the ecclesiastical title bestowed, again, as a decoration, by a
gracious papacy to honor the rich little urban centers of the
south—to decorate with a bishop, more elaborately with an
exempt bishop, most elaborately with a metropolitan archbishop. The decorations survived in the cluster of the province
of Amalfi through many centuries and different sorts of universal church. They were strange survivals in the church of
the Fourth Lateran, Pecham, and Federigo Visconti, not so
strange in the church of Recanati and Osimo.

Far to the north, at Milan, Ottone Visconti, archbishop from
1262 to 1295, was a man of great power, power that extended
itself in every direction from him, its center, and into every
activity that he touched. Ottone had been placed in a position
to express his power by Cardinal Ottaviano degli Ubaldini,
whose chamberlain he had been. Ottaviano is a familiar figure
—he has been brilliantly exposed[67]—the prototype of the Ren-

---

[66] For Archbishop Filippo's activity see below, Chapter IV.
[67] Kantorowicz, *Frederick the Second*, 646-648.

aissance cardinal, the cardinal who sang to master Cupid and "in a very perfect sonnet he sang of what he knew." With the assurance of his Ubaldini background, Ottone Visconti moved very purposefully into the government of a province fortunately well suited, for an Italian province, to his ambitions. When Ottone died he was almost ninety, a man who had for thirty-three years ruled one of the richest and most important sees of Christendom, and ruled it from a city continuingly glorious in its constantly renewed richness, a city (of perhaps even 100,000 people) whose glory, always very materially expressed, centered around the memory of one of the Church's indisputably great and precisely remembered saints, the converter of Augustine.[68] In the twenty-sixth year of Ottone's rule Bonvecin da Riva (Bonvicinus de Rippa) wrote his *de magnalibus urbis mediolani* exalting this rose, this lily, this cedar of Lebanon, this lion, this eagle of cities, great in its site, great in its faithfulness, great in its liberty, great in its dignity, a city of shrines, relics, churches (36 in the city, 240 in the country), and of ringing bells, of colleges and hospitals, monasteries and houses of friars, of many religious men—of all these religious more than ten thousand fed upon Ambrosian or ambrosial bread, in the enduring pun.[69] Ottone, having shaped and used the force of this dynamo city, took himself in his age to die in its great Cistercian house of monks, the Chiaravalle of Milan. In Milan power and religious sentiment kept in touch with each other. In a sense Ottone's administration is an expression of their contact. His great provincial councils of Savona in 1266 and Santa Tecla in 1287, with the archbishop seated in splendor among his suffragans, were acts of power and piety and also of serious administration.[70]

The seriousness of Ottone's administration is caught not

[68] Savio, I, i, 611-648; the population of Milan has sometimes been estimated considerably more extravagantly, but see H. van Werveke, "The Rise of the Towns," in *The Cambridge Economic History of Europe*, III (Cambridge, 1963), 38.

[69] Francesco Novati, *Bonvicini de Rippa de magnalibus urbis Mediolani*, Bullettino dell'Istituto storico italiano, no. 20 (Rome, 1898), particularly 63-64, 72, 78-83, 156-170.

[70] For Santa Tecla see, too, Luigi Antonio Muratori, *Rerum italicarum scriptores* (Milan, 1723-1751), VIII, 1054.

only in the records of the metropolitan see, but also in scattered provincial archives where effectiveness is really argued, as it is in a metropolitan confirmation of an episcopal privilege granted by the bishop of Torino to the church of Oulx.[71] In this privilege, sought and granted, the metropolitan reinforced his suffragan's action. He reached through the diocesan wall and touched the individual church. But the general tone of Milanese provincial action is perhaps more exactly indicated by the behavior of the bishop of Vercelli at Santa Tecla. The bishop came as he was summoned to come, but he went away again because the bishop of Brescia and not he was to sit to the archbishop's right. In a different medium the Dionysian quality of Benevento's doors is recalled. But the medium is different; the canons of Santa Tecla found their way to Vercelli's archives.[72] Still, even in this toughest of Italian provinces in its thirteenth-century glory, the radiant energy of its high ordinary was only intermittently applied to ecclesiastical administrative problems.

Federigo Visconti's work in the province of Pisa is at least as impressive as Ottone Visconti's work in Milan, and Federigo's is more strikingly preserved in contemporary record.[73] But even this most visibly vigorous of thirteenth-century metropolitans could on occasion be remarkably casual about the definition between secular and ecclesiastical and between metropolitan and primatial. His position and attitude were, however, very different from that of any recorded thirteenth-century "count" of San Lucido, archbishop of Cosenza, hierarchically disposed above his single suffragan at Martirano.[74] The difference between Pisa and Cosenza is, in an exaggerated form, characteristic of the difference between northern and southern metropolitans and their provinces. The provinces south of the band of dioceses immediately subject to Rome

[71] Giovanni Collino, *Le Carte della prevostura d'Oulx*, Biblioteca della società storica subalpina, XLV (Pinerolo, 1908), 326-327 no. 305.

[72] Arnoldi, 324-335 no. 77 (now in copy).

[73] Florence, Biblioteca Medicea Laurenziana, Plut. 33, sin. 1, particularly; see Chapter III below. I am grateful to the Biblioteca Medicea Laurenziana for their permitting me to use this manuscript.

[74] Francesco Russo, *Storia dell'arcidiocesi di Cosenza* (Naples, 1957), 300, 86, 95; Ughelli, IX, cols. 191, 221-224.

were far less clearly organized, less caught in administrative routine, than those north of Rome, than the provinces of Milan, Pisa, and Ravenna.[75] The cliché of difference between the north and the south of Italy may make the superior organization of the north seem more obvious than it should. In very many nonecclesiastical ways there was, in fact, no part of Italy so like the north of Europe as the province of Benevento, with its conventional fees and manors, its rusticity and its Normans. If basic social and economic factors were significant in determing the nature of the ecclesiastical province, as they surely were, it is not at all obvious that Benevento should have been less like Rouen and Canterbury than Ravenna was. The political, social, and economic cage in which the Beneventan monastery of Santa Maria della Strada at Matrice existed can be described so that it could almost be read into Normandy or England.[76]

There are indications of some metropolitan activity in the south. The province of Salerno was reasonably stable, and succeeding archbishops of Salerno were aware of the province's existence. An archbishop refused, at least once in the century, to consecrate a suffragan elect, the elect of Policastro in 1211.[77] In 1255 Alexander IV granted anew the privileges of the church of Salerno.[78] Alexander's confirmation included a specific renewal of metropolitan rights over specifically named dioceses; it made mention of the archbishop's right to have his

[75] Dr. A. Vasina has had in preparation for some time a study of Bonifazio Fieschi di Lavagna, archbishop of Ravenna (1275-1294), and his governing of his province; see *Felix Ravenna*, LXIV (April 1954), 41-49 (Rassegna bibliografica: G.S., "L'Arcivescovo Ravennate Bonifacio Fieschi di Lavagna (1275-1294) e la storia della Romagna nell'ultimo duecento"); the ordered nature of Bonifazio's province is clearly suggested by the progress of the case between two Bolognese nunneries described below; the purposefulness of Bonifazio's governance and the impressiveness of his court is suggested by documents from his episcopate preserved in the archiepiscopal archives at Ravenna: Ravenna, Archivio arcivescovile, H 3402 and N 6367.

[76] Evelyn Jamison, "Notes on S. Maria della Strada at Matrice, its history and sculpture," *Papers of the British School at Rome*, XIV, NS, I (1938), 32-97.

[77] Paesano, II, 324-325; Ughelli, VII, cols. 560-562.

[78] Paesano, II, 383-385.

cross carried before him through the suffragan dioceses—and the right of the cardinal canons of the metropolitan church to wear miters. Salerno's structure was repeatedly buttressed by privileges, with a marked conflation of property rights and jurisdictional rights, all built around the body of Matthew, triple-crowned apostle, evangelist, martyr.[79] The existence of Salerno as a province was not limited to parchment description. In May 1258 Cesario d'Alagno, archbishop of Salerno, in his palazzo in Salerno, sat surrounded by his suffragans and the abbots of his major monasteries—again a Dionysian tableau, perhaps more.[80]

The metropolitan position of the archbishop of Bari was also protected by recent privilege; and in his province the bishop of Giovinazzo was jealous of the position of his seat in metropolitan councils.[81] In 1268 Trasmondo, archbishop of Monreale, got permission from Clement IV to visit his province and to have his cross carried before him.[82] At least one archbishop of Brindisi kept his suffragan of Ostuni by his side.[83] And just beyond the century in 1310, provinces like Siponto, Otranto, and Trani were, upon papal demand, able to assemble themselves into councils.[84] The province was an institution that existed in thirteenth-century Italy and that could be given some life by an unusually intense prelate; but, in general, and particularly in the south, it seems to have been an hierarchical extension, a dimension of glamor, a static sunburst, possessed by sees which at some time had been thus rewarded for their peculiar eminence.[85] In one case, in the

[79] Paesano, II, 301-303, 50.

[80] Paesano, II, 386-388.

[81] *C.d.b.*, II: "Le Pergamene del Duomo di Bari (1266-1309)," ed. G. B. Nitto de Rossi and Francesco Nitti di Vito (Bari, 1899), 172-173 (app. Giovinazzo no. 3).

[82] Garufi, 49-50 no. 109.

[83] See below, Chapter II, part ii.

[84] Vendola, *Apulia-Lucania-Calabria*, 367-368, 372-373, 368-369.

[85] Interesting and informative material from this period may still exist for Cagliari. In the *Inventario di R. archivio di stato di Cagliari e notizie delle carte conservate nei più notevoli archivi communali, vescovili e capitolari della Sardegna* (Cagliari, 1902) there is listed (p. 173) as in the curia arcivescovile (item no. 2) a book of disputes over the primacy of Sardinia between the archbishops of Cagliari and

royally favored Norman see of Monreale, the award had been recent.[86]

Unlike the shadow church of Italian provinces and even dioceses with their lax lines of administration, the cathedral chapters of thirteenth-century Italy—and the bodies that echoed and resembled them—collegiate centers of cults and holders of property, were possessed of a tough, taut reality. Their image is caught, from the pontificate of Honorius III, by the seven canons of Fano, with their bishop at the high altar of their cathedral church, living three days without food, fighting against the taxation of commune and *podestà*. It is caught, too, in the chapter of Lucca's successful insistence that their bishop consult them about an extended range of appointments.[87] The thirteenth-century province of Capua is a gray abstraction; the chapter visibly sits down.[88]

The chapter extends itself across the centuries as it arranged itself in the subscription lists of formal documents; the consistory seems reassembled—the little node of men agreeing, pretending to agree, or having it pretended about them that they are agreeing. The chapter of Amalfi under the rule of Archbishop Filippo Augustariccio was recorded participating in and being regulated by, probably, the two most serious sorts of action in which a chapter involved itself. In March 1281 the Amalfi chapter witnessed and confirmed Archbishop Filippo's elaborate regulations for the future celebration of the Feast of the Translation of Saint Andrew, the second of the two great feasts of the local patron whose body was believed to lie within

---

Torres (Sassari), and also a book (item no. 3) of materials concerning the primacy of Cagliari. Although I was permitted to rummage through certain rooms and cabinets at the curia, I was unable to find, in the time I had, either book.

[86] 1197-1198: see a recent discussion of Monreale and other areas of royal favoritism in Josef Deér, *The Dynastic Porphyry Tombs of the Norman Period in Sicily*, Dumbarton Oaks Studies, v (Cambridge, Mass., 1959).

[87] For Fano, Waley, *Papal State*, 133. For Lucca, Nanni, 201 (app. no. 5).

[88] See Jole Mazzoleni, *Le pergamene di Capua*, Università degli studi di Napoli, Istituto di paleografia e diplomatica, I-II (Naples, 1957-1958) (e.g. II, 3-5, and, too, for Caserta, II, 8-11, but see, too, I, xvi).

the church.[89] In 1292 Filippo issued, in the chapter's presence, a long set of regulations governing the stipends of the cathedral clergy, their duties, and the division of the commons.[90] The Italian chapter in the thirteenth century was constantly involved in the regulation of the worship of the cult saint, the ordering of the liturgy, the division of income.

The chapter remains a tangible institution not only as it appears on documents, in diplomatic, but also in architecture, in the lasting structure of many duomo complexes, particularly in their campanili, symbols of reformed chapters, as it has been pointed out,[91] towers that raised up their bells that they might more clearly insist upon the proper attendance of the chapter at the hours of liturgical prayer. Filippo Augustariccio built a campanile at Amalfi; the date inscribed upon it is 1276. Bishop Tommaso built a campanile at Rieti; the date inscribed upon it is 1252. In February 1266 Sibilia, daughter of Sire Maione de Amirato of Bari and widow of Lord Riccardo of Montefoscolo, lay on what she assumed was her deathbed and made her will; she left five *once d'oro* to San Nicola Bari specifically designated for the repair of the campanile.[92] Campanili were built at Benevento, at Caserta, at Osimo, at Lucca, at Parma, and magnificently at Cremona. New cathedrals were constructed around the chapters at Cagliari, Volterra, and Arezzo. One was begun at Florence; and there early in the next century was built the campanile that crowns all this visible work of chapter reform, this increasingly conservative sort of reform, stretching back through three centuries.

One particularly visible thirteenth-century chapter, that at Orvieto, involved itself in an extended argument with its bishop over the location of its new church.[93] The parties were eventually able to compose their difficulties. The funds for the fabric, for the glorification of the Virgin, were accumulated with the active support of Nicholas IV and Boniface VIII, to what glorious effect any eye may see. But also, ironically, from 1292 the commune managed the *opera*, as it came to do in

[89] Ughelli, vii, cols. 224-226.   [90] Ughelli, vii, cols. 226-228.
[91] By Emile Mâle.   [92] *C.d.b.*, vi, 177-178 no. 108.
[93] Natalini, 185-186; Fumi, viii, 85-90.

Pisa, Siena, Lucca, and Naples, an odd-looking arrangement from the vantage point of Canterbury or Worcester—but hardly odd in a land where the laity sometimes elected their *pievani*.[94]

Like the chapters, occasional individual canons and prebends preserve a sharp if fragmentary reality. From the repeated lists of the thirteenth-century canons of Cosenza, with, as in 1204, an archpriest, dean, precentor, treasurer, and six canons, one canon steps forth to defend the exact boundaries of his prebend.[95] In 1222 the canon Rufo settled his dispute with the Cistercian monastery of Sambucina over what to do with rain water and water spouts between a prebendal house of his and a house which belonged to Sambucina and which was right on Rufo's property line.[96] Rufo promised, in the compromise settlement, not to build anything or put any timber up on the Sambucina house, but rather to build a wooden gutter on his own house. Sambucina committed itself to building a gutter and spout on its own wall through which rain water would be shot out from between the houses.

Another prebendal water image comes from the chapter of Salerno and from a 1292 complaint against the *abbas* Simone Capograsso, canon and cardinal deacon of the cathedral church.[97] The elect of Cosenza, the royal chancellor, claimed that he had been conceded a house and garden near the church of San Matteo Piccolo and on the street called *alicanali* (A li Canali) in Salerno. A special conduit had brought water to the house on the *alicanali*; but Simone Capograsso to serve his own purposes had diverted the chancellor's water to a bath (*balneum*) called San Pietro ad Curiam, after the church.

[94] Fumi, viii.

[95] Alessandro Pratesi, *Carte latine di abbazie calabresi provenienti dall'Archivio Aldobrandini*, Studi e Testi, vol. 197 (Vatican City, 1958), 191-193 no. 76.

[96] Pratesi, *Carte latine*, 308-309 no. 131.

[97] Carlo Carucci, *Salerno dal 1282 al 1300, Codice diplomatico salernitano del secolo XIII*, iii (Subiaco, 1946), 127-128 no. 98; the title *abbas* was still, in the late thirteenth century, not infrequently applied to southern Italian cathedral dignitaries who may well have been connected with collegiate churches, but who have no visible or suspected monastic connections. Pratesi, 263-264 no. 109.

Farther south and east, in 1217 Guarniero, a canon of San Marco Argentano is seen carefully dealing with his property (not liquid, but caught in an interesting and described ecclesiastical complex). He sold for three *besants* a piece of land (presumably his own) in Cocchiato which lay to the east of land belonging to the bishopric of San Marco and near the land of Guarniero's prebend. Small and fluctuating incomes did not promote in individual canons a casual attitude about precise prebendal boundaries.

Diocesan bishops took their chapters, canons, and prebends very seriously. They consulted with them; and moved to reform, bishops were moved to reform their chapters. Bishop Nicolò of Città di Castello, an extraordinarily able diocesan, concentrated a considerable part of his reforming attentions, from 1271 and particularly from 1275 to 1279, on reforming the chapter of his cathedral church of San Florido, on forcing it into the regulated communal morality and administrative control that the rule of Saint Augustine implied and into an accepted division of income and observance of liturgical order.[98] A bishop of in very many ways a very different sort from Nicolò, his longer-lived contemporary at Arezzo, Guglielmino degli Ubertini in 1263 turned his attentions to the reform and regulation of his canons, to their dress, their records, their incomes, their orders, their exact performance of the liturgy, their following the Roman office.[99]

A principle familiar to Bishop Grosseteste in Lincoln helps explain capitular reform and connect it with the sort of reform that was more generally pursued during the period in which Nicolò and Guglielmino were active: for the flock that would follow him the shepherd's example is more potent than his words are.[100] The principle, only very slightly absorbed by

[98] Muzi, II, 158-160.

[99] Lazzeri, *Guglielmino Ubertini*, 151; *Documenti per la storia della Città di Arezzo*, ed. Ubaldo Pasqui (Florence, 1899—), II, 364-374 no. 623; for the spread of the Roman office in central Italian dioceses see S.J.P. van Dijk and J. Hazelden Walker, *The Origins of the Modern Roman Liturgy* (Westminster, Maryland and London, 1960), 398-399.

[100] W. A. Pantin (from Eccleston) in D. A. Callus, ed., *Robert Grosseteste* (Oxford, 1955), 195.

men like Bishop Guglielmino, suggests the pastoral reason hidden within southern approaches to reform, distant as these are from Grosseteste's own pastoral reforms with their superb articulation of act and idea. It is a principle, a sentiment, that can also make to seem more important the sort of constantly worried property arrangement and liturgical settlement that one sees at Orvieto.[101] The totem cult can be seen in a way that connects it with the missionary pastor. It could be hoped that ordered incomes supporting orderly canons might replace what was disorderly and fruitless, the scandalous squabbling, at the center of the diocese. The eyes of the Italian diocese were turned in toward its center, toward the cathedral church. That church should be serene, its energies devoted to the liturgy. The bishops' reforms like the bell towers were meant to call back to their services those wanton seculars to whom the old reforming papacy had tried to bring something of the spirit of Cluny; but bishops and bells called in Italy long after the rise to popularity of other forms of corporate religiosity and long after the conventional use for quite other purposes of incomes established for the recital of the liturgy.

A statement of the motivating sentiments of the reforming bishop is sometimes recorded. On 9 July 1276 the bishop of Vercelli, Aimone de Challont, visited Sant'Eusebio, the larger of the two houses of the split Vercelli chapter, and tried to restore the elegance of its ancient order.[102] The harangue of his recording document connected his effort with the doctrine of works and with the established belief that capitular benefices should remain connected with liturgical prayer. Bishop Aimone reorganized the twenty-four canons into a recalled hierarchy and enjoined them to proper silence in the choir, except for the sound of their office; he reminded the canons that "a church is a house of prayer and of God."[103]

Cathedral chapters and their regulation did not seem unimportant to northern bishops. In England in the decades around 1200 there was a great deal of concern among bishops

[101] Natalini, *passim.*
[102] Arnoldi, 314-320 no. 73.
[103] Arnoldi, 316.

about chapters.[104] English chapter regulations, in fact, are better known than Italian ones; and chapters in England seem to have come to be better ordered than those in Italy. But the relative isolation of capitular reform in the Italian church gives it a different tone and a different importance. Like the Italian *pieve* and archpriest, the Italian chapter is a blatantly obvious feature on the Italian ecclesiastical map.

The Italian and English chapters also look different because of their quite different conventions of residence. In England by the later thirteenth century in the nonmonastic chapters a comparatively neat little body of resident canons ran the church at home, and a larger body of nonresident canons drew its income from away.[105] In Italy, here as in almost every other phase of ecclesiastical life, there was less definition; a swarm of chapter clerks moved around the general neighborhood of the cathedral city. Many of their benefices may have seemed, in spite of all efforts, too poorly defined and too poor to help much to support a distant and important papal or royal-imperial clerk. (The Italian canon's actual, not technical, status seems frequently to approach that of the English vicar choral.) Besides, in Italy Matthew Paris's marauding Italians were at home.

Undoubtedly Italian bishops were attracted to the reformation of their chapters partly by the difficulty of definition which led the chapters into further difficulties (and also by the hope that here, if anywhere, definition was possible). There were double cathedrals and double chapters, as, of course, there were in two dioceses in England, in Bath and Wells and in Coventry and Lichfield (and as, in a way, there were to be with the later English colleges of minor clergy). Bishop Aimone of Vercelli visited the larger of his chapters separately in 1276. The cathedral clergy of Salerno's lower

---

[104] Cheney, *From Becket to Langton*, 121; Kathleen Edwards, *The English Secular Cathedrals in the Middle Ages* (Manchester, 1949), and Henry Bradshaw and Christopher Wordsworth, *Statutes of Lincoln Cathedral* (Cambridge, 1892-1897).

[105] See Brentano, *York Metropolitan Jurisdiction*, 29-33, for the chapter of York toward the end of the thirteenth century, divided, perhaps somewhat artificially, into "elements."

church who were separately organized had their stipends ordered in 1256.[106] Bishop Guglielmino of Arezzo tried to effect the union of Arezzo's chapters, the *cattedrale* and the *pieve*, under one provost in 1250.[107] Chapters might threaten, as at Naples or Rieti, to grow too large to support and regulate themselves.[108] Scandal and disorder in the choir of Bari caused Archbishop Doferio in 1205 to enact new regulations for the duomo chapter so that there would be exactly forty-eight clerks for the forty-eight stalls. He also enacted that boys aspiring to join the duomo clergy should first renounce their places in the basilica of San Nicola.[109] Chapters might, and often did, divide themselves into remarkably elaborate hierarchies—particularly those pretentious chapters whose major canons bore the title of cardinal as they still did at Amalfi, Salerno, Ravenna, and Naples.[110] The structure of the income of some Italian chapters also made stability of arrangement rather more difficult than in England. If the broad, fixed fields of York are kept in mind, the sources of income for the church of Gaeta seem mercurial, shifty. Thirteenth-century Gaeta was, at least in noticeable part, a city of flats, and part of the church's income came from flats.[111] Thirteenth-century Amalfi was a city of shops, and a large part of the church of Amalfi's

[106] Arnoldi, 314-320 no. 73; and see Vittorio Mandelli, *Il Comune di Vercelli nel medio evo* (Vercelli, 1857-1861), III, 101, 97-98; Paesano, II, 401 n. 1.

[107] Lazzeri, 50, and, more generally, 48-86.

[108] Pasquale Santamaria, *Historia collegii patrum canonicorum* (Naples, 1900), 257-259 no. 48, 261-266 nos. 51-52, 269-273 no. 55, 277-284 no. 58; for a more general history of the church of Naples see Luigi Parascandolo, *Memorie storiche-critiche-diplomatiche della chiesa di Napoli* (Naples, 1847-1854), and, particularly for capitular problems, III, 196-197 no. 34; for Rieti, see below, Chapter III.

[109] *C.d.b.*, I, 141-143 no. 73.

[110] For cardinal canons see Stephan Kuttner, "Cardinalis: the History of a Canonical Concept," *Traditio*, III (1945), 129-214, 154-155, particularly n. 9; Robert Brentano, "Sealed Documents of the Mediaeval Archbishops of Amalfi," *Mediaeval Studies*, XXIII (1961), 24.

[111] *Codex diplomaticus Cajetanus, Tabularium Casinense*, I (Montecassino, 1888), e.g. 389-390 no. 410, for the gift of part of a house, in 1262, with its description, what it is under, what over, and how to get in and out.

income came from shops.[112] The church of Cosenza's various
income included a fee which it had gotten in a trade with
Sambucina, a fee which had come from the domain of Frederick II and which included men villein and free and a mill
on the Basento.[113] Part of San Nicola Bari's income came
from the customs of the port of Bari.[114]

The variety of pattern of income, even agricultural income,
in Italy may have made it difficult for quite serious diocesans
to support papal capitular regulations. In 1266 a very serious
diocesan, Bishop Leonardo of Giovinazzo, met his chapter to
help it insure its continued welfare. He meant, as he said,
properly to arrange ecclesiastical goods as a good pastor should
in order that the *divinus cultus* should grow rather than
shrink. But Bishop Leonardo's ordering, his confirmation of
custom, was of a sort that the Decretals had called inconsonant
with reason—although in the pertinent decretal Alexander
III had permitted the archbishop of Salerno (if the identifica-
tions are correct) to tolerate the irrational custom because it
was so prevalent and because debt might press so hard.[115]
Leonardo confirmed the ancient and approved custom of the
church of Giovinazzo, enunciated by his predecessors and still
observed, that if any canon should die between the first of
March and the end of December, he might leave, alienate, all
of his olives, his rents, his income for that year—all income
due to him until the first day of January after his death—to
whomever he wished. The olive crop of the year of his death
was to be his. He could thus borrow on the crop early in the
year, and his creditors would have the assurance that his un-

---

[112] This is abundantly apparent in documents preserved within the
archbishops' archives at Amalfi (see Robert Brentano, "The Archiepiscopal Archives at Amalfi," *Manuscripta* IV [1960], 98-105).

[113] Pratesi, *Carte latine*, 220-226 nos. 87-90, 230-233 no. 93; for the
seemingly neat chapter at Cosenza, see Russo, 300.

[114] *C.d.b.*, VI, 66-68 no. 42.

[115] *C.d.b.*, II (Giovinazzo app.), 206-207 no. 23, where the order is
very noticeably hierarchical (one "priest" who does not so identify
himself is placed within the priest group); the decretal is c. 13, X,
iii,5; (the dates of its stated custom are 1 March to 1 November) and
see cc. 8, 16, X,iii,5; this prebendal problem is logically connected with
the general problem of the growing crop—which in England even a
lessee could bequeath according to Bracton: Sheehan, 285.

expected death would not in robbing him of his earthly benefice rob them of their return. Bishop Leonardo solemnly sealed
his enactment with a pendant seal; and an archpriest, two
primicerii, seven priests, four deacons, and one subdeacon, presumably Giovinazzo's resident chapter, witnessed it. These
poor Giovinazzo borrowers, given their olives that they might
not need to (or could) beg to sustain themselves in their sacred
work, managed, beyond their olives, intricate patterns for pro-
ducing little bits of income from vineyards and onion
patches.[116] The stability of York incomes, and also their relative similarity to those of Worcester and Winchester (never
forgetting Winchester's towns or any chapter's city properties)
are pointed up by the incomes of Giovinazzo, and their differences from those of, for example, Amalfi or Milan.

The church of Milan was not only richer than churches like
Giovinazzo; it was also meant to be noble, and its nobility
came to be regulated.[117] When it seemed to their advantage,
chapters like Milan's or Salerno's insisted that prebends be restricted to the local nobility or citizenry.[118] But the nobility
to which a chapter like Milan's restricted itself was of the peculiar Italian sort, urban and numerous. In neither England
nor Italy were there those high aristocratic chapters with
which French and German churches decorated themselves. In
Italy there was, though, a sort of chapter very important in the
total structure of the church, local, liturgical, sometimes poor
and straggling, a chapter truly at the center of the diocese, cap-
turing the eye of the diocesan bishop who was still often its
actual elect and who was still curiously close to it, as was its
archdeacon, who in fact had generally not been freed at all.

For any sort of conviction, for the thirteenth-century Italian

[116] See *C.d.b.*, II, 203-204 no. 21; there is an interesting analysis of
Giovinazzo chapter incomes in the tenth assessment records for 1332
(Vendola, 63ff.); it heavily emphasizes that these are olive incomes,
although it includes house rents, vineyards, etc. The inquest was made
by a Simone de Anglia, master of sacred theology, Bishop Guglielmo's
vicar general in temporalities and spiritualities; he records his own
income (64) as 1 *oncia* from olives, 8 *tari* house rents and 8 *tari* land
rents, i.e. about two-thirds from olives.

[117] Carlo Castiglioni, "Gli ordinari della Metropolitana attraverso i
secoli," *Memorie storiche della diocesi di Milano*, I (1954), 11-56, 13-14.

[118] Paesano, II, 329.

church to have any sort of recreated reality, the formal distinctions—chapters, provinces, legates, dioceses, archpriests—must
be reassembled, put back into nature and watched moving
around and against each other. Here two kinds of acts can be
watched: that of the relatively active reforming bishop trying
to build something in the Italian church; that of the paired
disputants defining in their disputes the shape of the church.

The Fourth Lateran Council of 1215 was the secular
church's official announcement of a general change in the way
that educated or enthusiastic ecclesiastics looked at their world
and more specifically at their jobs. Although the Fourth
Lateran hélped define the change and certainly advanced it,
the Council did not cause the change. It was a change in the
general psychology, in the will and in the perception, that
turned men, in contemporary image, from Euphrates to
Tigris, from Mary to Martha, from Cistercian to Franciscan.
It was a change that is perfectly clearly visible in the chroniclers of character and act, in the difference between William
of Malmesbury and Matthew Paris or between Otto of Freising and Salimbene; it is visible in the changes within secular
government, in the attitudes of political theorists, in the movement from Salisbury to Aquinas, in the growth of the universities, in the taste for Aristotle's political animal.[119] Faces as
well as minds were freshly described, acts as well as intentions
freshly valued.

It was a change that was preached by Peter the Chanter in
Paris, and Francis in Umbria (and the world), as well as by
Innocent.[120] Paris, the friars, the Lateran all told a waiting
audience that enthusiasm should be turned to outward act, to
reasoned governance, to pastoral care. The praised bishop no
longer turned his diocese into another Egypt, a replica of
eremitic Thebes full of sacred uncommunicating cells and
islands; instead, like Grosseteste, he turned his diocese into

[119] These historians are discussed in Chapter V.
[120] John W. Baldwin, *Masters, Princes and Merchants* (Princeton,
1970); cf. Waley, *Papal State*, 171.

a mission field, blew down the walls and made all men communicants with God and with each other.[121]

The bishops of Italy were not completely insensible to the new enthusiasm. Into the unlikely consistency of the Italian church, incompletely aware of their peculiar difficulties, some Italian bishops, touched by the pastoral enthusiasm which Innocent defined, tried to act out the thirteenth-century plan of reform. In the most stagnant dioceses the mud was occasionally stirred and an embedded bishop was aroused enough to try to crack the immunity of some local, rich and corrupt monastery. Too frequently, in fact, the episcopal mind was able to save itself from comprehending the full pain of the call to action and was able to deflect the pastoral persuasion into a simple war against monastic peculiars. These wars were more sublimation than expression, perhaps, but they were at least a deflection of the papal plan. There were other Italian bishops who tried through visitation (the most vigorous method of episcopal reform) to do what Paris and the Lateran papacy would have them do.[122] Graziadio Berlinghieri visited the diocese of Pistoia during his "twenty-seven years of glorious governance" ending in 1250.[123] Giovanni de Advocatis visited Como in 1277.[124] Filippo, archbishop of Salerno, visited the clergy and people of Nocera in 1293.[125] Federigo Visconti visited spectacularly; and successive bishops of Città di Castello visited carefully.[126]

Bartolomeo, archbishop of the frail diocese of Santa Severina, reserved the duty of coming to an annual synod in his metropolitan church in his grant of monastic properties to Cistercians in 1202, and in this showed at least some residual sense of diocesan organization.[127] In relatively well organized parts

[121] Pantin (in Callus), 179.

[122] For enthusiasm and visitation see C. R. Cheney, *Episcopal Visitations of Monasteries in the Thirteenth Century* (Manchester, 1931), and see Cheney's Florence, Vercelli, and Cosenza references (p. 28).

[123] Antonio Rosati, *Memorie per servire alla storia de' vescovi di Pistoia* (Pistoia, 1761), 93-94.

[124] Savio, La Lombardia, ii.i, 374.

[125] Paesano, iii, 89-91.

[126] For Città di Castello see below, this section; for Federigo Visconti, see Chapter III.

[127] Pratesi, *Carte latine*, 172-175 no. 68.

of the church, in the provinces of Ravenna and Milan, there were even appeals from provincial subjects to the metropolitan archbishop; there was a real sense of an administered church. But in general, as a fairly close examination of some of its parts can indicate, the Italian church was not prepared to hear and understand the papal-conciliar message at all literally.

The diocese of Rieti lay very close to Rome.[128] Its neighbor to the west was the diocese of Sabina, one of the six dioceses with cardinal bishops and in the closest sense a member of the province of Rome.[129] In 1252 Innocent IV, a pope insufficiently recognized as an ecclesiastical reformer, sent a prominent member of his curia, the corrector Tommaso, to be Rieti's new bishop.[130] Tommaso, rather surprisingly on the face of it, turned out to be a serious diocesan. The substance of the letters Tommaso had corrected, or perhaps something earlier and more important, had swept him into the movement of thirteenth-century reform. His campanile in Rieti, which in itself celebrates the older sort of reform, carries, on its side, verses that celebrate his involvement:

> concilium celebrans mox ritu pontificali
> visitat ecclesias tua cura sub ordine tali. . . .[131]

Records of his performing his job as episcopal judge-arbiter

[128] For Rieti, see Giuseppe Mazzatinti, *Gli archivi della storia d'Italia*, IV (Rocca S. Casciano, 1906), 208-268; Michele Michaeli, *Memorie storiche di Rieti* (Rieti, 1898-1899); Francesco Palmegiani, *La Cattedrale Basilica di Rieti con cenni storici sulle altre chiese della città* (Rome, 1926); Paolo Desanctis, *Notizie storiche di S. Salvator Maggiore e del seminario di Rieti* (Rieti, 1884); I should like to thank Monsignor Emidio de Sanctis for granting me access to the archives.

[129] For a sense of the old province, before Silva Candida was united to Porto (c. 1120-1124), see Kuttner, "Cardinalis," 148, 151 (the *septem* as distinguished from the *forenses episcopi*), 173, and Kuttner's references.

[130] Peter Herde, *Beiträge zum päpstlichen Kanzlei- und Urkundenwesen im 13. Jahrhundert* (Kallmünz, 1961), 19, 21-22, and *Innocent IV*, III, 34 no. 5614; and see below, Chapter III.

[131] For various transcriptions of these verses see Palmegiani, *La Cattedrale*, 17; Ughelli, I, col. 1204; Michaeli, III, 37; Desanctis, 41; for the entire inscription none is really, but Ughelli and Michaeli are relatively, exact.

remain in Rieti.[132] Tommaso tried to make a disciplined territorial unit of, to give some sort of real diocesan validity to, a diocese long distracted by war and unformed through neglect.

An important part of Tommaso's plan was the subjection to his authority of the local abbey of San Salvatore and its subject churches.[133] The dispute which this attempt at subjection caused brought a case before a court of auditors delegated by Pietro Capocci, cardinal deacon of San Giorgio in Velabro. The cardinal's auditors were canons of two Rieti churches, Filippo of San Ruffo and Bartolomeo of San Giovanni Evangelista. Before these auditors on 7 March 1254, the bishop, or his proctor, presented his positions against the abbot and the rectors of the subject churches. Witnesses were prepared to substantiate each position; and to each position the abbot replied.[134] The positions and replies, but particularly the positions, reveal a great deal. Taken together they are a glass clearly reflecting the Italian prelate's effort to bring the common thirteenth-century enthusiasm to the church's difficult Roman center. In detail they elaborate that difficulty. Less clearly, perhaps, they imply the distortion of the ideal itself.

The bishop's first point was that the abbey and its churches were within the diocese of Rieti. The abbot would not believe it. The bishop proceeded to describe the extent of the diocese, and the abbot to deny its border points. The bishop claimed that the abbey was located inside of the diocesan borders, and the abbot said that it was not. The bishop said that the subject churches were within the diocese; among the churches the abbot made judicious discrimination in his denial. The bishop claimed that the abbey was called San Salvatore of Rieti in

[132] Rieti, Archivio capitolare, armadio II, fasc. D, nos. 2, 3, 5, 6.
[133] Rieti, Archivio capitolare, armadio IV, fasc. P, no. I; Desanctis, app., xv-xix no. 2.
[134] For Capocci, see particularly Waley, *Papal State*, and most particularly 149-150, 153-154, and "Constitutions of the Cardinal-legate Peter Capocci, July 1249," *English Historical Review*, LXXV (1960), 660-664; for the Rieti churches from which the delegates came, see Palmegiani, *La Cattedrale*, 88-91, 117-120; for the abbot's replies see particularly, archivio capitolare, armadio IV, fasc. P, no. I, "5"; and for the schedule of witnesses (what they were to swear to, how they knew, a fascinating document), armadio IV, fasc. P, no. I, "4."

common usage, and—an interesting claim from a papal corrector—that the abbot and convent had impetrated papal letters that called the monastery (in the oblique case) San Salvatore *Reatini*; and the abbot admitted both. The bishop further claimed that the abbey and its vassals went to arms at the
will of the *podestà* and council of Rieti, to form what was
called in common speech the *hostem et parliamentum* of
Rieti; and the abbot admitted it. The bishop claimed that the
abbey had contributed to the fortifying and walling of the city
in time of need, but the abbot replied that, although this had
been sought of them by the *podestà*, they had paid a sum of
money and their liberty had been recognized.

The bishop's positions then turned to ecclesiastical history.
The bishop claimed that Adinolfo, bishop of Rieti, had been
received in procession and given fit procurations many times
in the monastery of San Salvatore.[135] The abbot admitted that
Adinolfo had been twice received, but not in formal procession. To further points the abbot admitted that Rainaldo de
Labro was received, but without a formal procession, and that
Bishop Giovanni de Nepi was received many times, but not as
lord. The bishop said that at Bishop Giovanni's mandate the
monastery had received as monk the bishop's familiar Dom
Leone; but the abbot said that Dom Leone was received at
the bishop's request (*ad preces*), not at his order (*ad mandatum*). The bishop then claimed that Innocent III had ordered a papal chaplain to place all of the churches and chapels

[135] For Adinolfo and his brothers and their family, see Angelo
Sacchetti Sassetti, "Rieti e gli Urslingen," *Archivio della società romana
di storia patria*, ser. III, XVI-XVII (1962-1963), 1-24, particularly p. 3
and nn. 9 and 13; Sacchetti Sassetti's dates for Adinolfo's pontificate
are 1189-1212, and he dates the ten years of strife as 1200-1209; see,
too, Sacchetti Sassetti for Rinaldo and Bertoldo, particularly pp. 1-2;
for the Urslingen in connection with the more general disturbance
see Kantorowicz, *Frederick the Second*, under Berthold and Reginald;
for the Urslingen and the papal state, see Waley, *Papal State*, 126-127,
and under Bertold and Rainald; for the application of the general
struggle to Rieti, see Michaeli, III, 5-35. The dates and the actual
succession of thirteenth-century bishops of Rieti have not, I think,
been satisfactorily established, but some of Michaeli's dates may prove
helpful here (Michaeli, II, 237, and IV, 225): Adinolfo, 1188; Rainaldo
(de Labro), 1215; Giovanni, 1236.

of the monastery in subjection to the church of Rieti; the abbot admitted this, but said that the mandate was provoked by the monastery's contumacy and was afterward revoked except with regard to Santa Cecilia, which had been conferred on the son of Sinibaldo Crescenzi, and that later Honorius III had revoked even its subjection. The bishop claimed that his predecessors had solemnly celebrated divine services, had preached and exercised their episcopal rights in the church of Santa Cecilia. The abbot admitted the services and the sermons. The bishop claimed that each year the church paid a *census* of bread and meat to the church of Rieti on the feast of Saint Cecilia; but the abbot said that he thought that this was due to the services celebrated there on the feast day. The bishop then claimed and the abbot denied that the bishop's predecessors had visited four specific churches as they had the monastery, and that his predecessors had heard marriage cases, and granted commissions concerning them, within the abbey's territory. The bishop claimed that his predecessors had ordained clerks of the abbey, but the abbot said the bishops had acted under license, not as diocesans.

The bishop claimed that the monastery had been cited in these matters in the time of Gregory IX; the abbot admitted a commission, but no citation. The bishop said that the cardinal deacon of Sant'Angelo was given as auditor in the case; the abbot replied that he believed that the cardinal had been made auditor, but that the abbey had not been cited. The bishop again proposed and the abbot denied that the abbot had been cited at the petition of Giovanni, bishop of Rieti, and that the citation had reached the abbot.

The bishop then turned to another sort of history, the evils of war and the tears of Italy, the interruption of normal government. The bishop asserted—and the abbot to each point demurred—that it had been fifty years since the consecration of [Adinolfo] bishop of Rieti, that because of the war between the citizens and city of Rieti on the one side and the noblemen, the Marquess Abeamondo, Matteo, and Berardo de Lavareta [di Rinaldo di Barete], the bishop's brothers, on the other, the bishop was driven for ten years and more, by fear, from his see; the abbot believed that the bishop left his see—nothing more. Tommaso claimed that because of this war and schism the bishop was unable through this whole time to exercise his episcopal jurisdiction in his see. Bishop Tommaso claimed, and the abbot agreed, that after the resignation of Adinolfo a year elapsed before the election of Gentile de Pretorio, canon of Capua, who held the see as an unconsecrated elect for two years and then resigned it, and that a year—but the abbot queried the time—after the resignation of Gentile, Rainaldo de Labro was elected. Bishop Tommaso claimed, although the abbot said that he did not believe it, that after the consecration of bishop Rainaldo (on account of the badness of the times and the wars then waged by the Emperor Frederick and the brothers Duke Rinaldo and Bertoldo against the Reatine and Roman churches) Bishop Rainaldo was unable to exercise his episcopal jurisdiction for ten years and more. The abbot admitted the bishop's contention that after the death of Bishop Rainaldo over half a year elapsed before the election of Bishop Giovanni, but the abbot refused to admit that for the three years that Giovanni lived he was unable to exercise episcopal jurisdiction on account of the wars and schism that arose between him and the chapter of Rieti. The abbot further refused to admit that after Giovanni's death more than four years elapsed before the consecration of Bishop Rainaldo Benencelli or that for the four years that he lived he was infirm and unable to exercise episcopal jurisdiction because of the wars. The bishop claimed that after the death of Rainaldo Benencelli the church was vacant for a year, that it was then held another year by Rainaldo of Arezzo, and then resigned by him; this the abbot accepted except for the length of the vacancy.[136] Bishop Tommaso further claimed that the abbot and convent of San Salvatore harried and molested the bishop and kept him from exercising his jurisdiction over them. The abbot said that this was not true because the bishop had no jurisdiction over them. The abbot replied similarly to the bishop's claim that the abbey denied the bishop his episcopal rights; the bishop had no rights over the abbey, the abbot said. Similar claims and similar denials were made for the subject churches.

[136] For Salimbene and Rainaldo of Arezzo see below, Chapter III.

Bishop Tommaso then turned his attack a final time. The bishop said that during the papal-imperial wars, the monks had taken the emperor's side against the Roman church. The abbot admitted that the then abbot, Giacomo, had. But the body of the monks, he said, had not supported the emperor, and Giacomo himself had been deposed. To an elliptically recorded question about the emperor's nuncios, the abbot replied that they had in fact confiscated the abbey land. He himself had fled away, he said, but the body of the monks remained and received their victuals from the emperor's factors.

The parties met again on 1 April. The bishop presented his positions against individual churches and heard the response of their rectors. The bishop claimed that his predecessors had consecrated churches, altars, chalices, and ornaments, and that the churches were within the diocese. The rectors denied the claims in general, although they admitted fragments of them. The rector of San Giovanni in Pratojanni admitted that Dodone, once bishop, had consecrated an altar, that another bishop had consecrated a chalice, and that, at the mandate of the abbot of San Salvatore, he had received priest's orders from Rainaldo de Labro. The rector of San Salvatore Vecchio admitted similarly receiving his deacon's orders; and other rectors made admissions of the same sort.

The general position of the abbot for the defense was that although San Salvatore and its churches might be within the physical confines of the diocese, they were not really, jurisdictionally, within the diocese. The abbey had been exempt from its foundation and immediately subject to the pope. Popes had instituted, blessed, and removed abbots; and there had been a legatine visit of reform by a cardinal during the reign of Gregory IX. The abbot said that the abbey actually had quasi-episcopal jurisdiction with the right to visit, reform, excommunicate, absolve, hear inquiries in marriage cases, receive procurations, synodals, see-dues (*cathedratica*), to install archpriests, provosts, and parish priests, to remove or suspend them, and generally to exercise those rights that a diocesan exercised. The abbot said that bishops often came to the monastery of San Salvatore, but that they were received with informal hospitality. The abbot said that the diocesan acts which the bishops had performed were done not *de jure* but *de mandato* of the abbot. The abbot said that all papal acts that had seemed to deprive the abbot and abbey of their immunity—the sort of action suggested by the 1211 Innocent III document preserved with the records of the case—had been temporary and had been revoked.

The points of the bishop's positions and his opponents' replies prick out the pattern of ecclesiastical administration. The church of Rieti is the church of Italy in microcosm. The problems that vexed the bishops of Italy, the curious contours of Italian ecclesiastical topography are drawn within the tight, close confines of the Rieti testimony. The method of the Rieti disputation is as characteristic as its matter, but less peculiarly Italian.

The common thirteenth-century diocesan impulse touched even the least likely Italian province, the province of Rome, whose cardinal bishops occupied the most obviously eccentric Italian sees and had the most obvious other spheres of activity.[137] Successive cardinal bishops of Sabina tried to establish the jurisdictional integrity of their strange central diocese. Early in the century Bishop Giovanni da San Paolo tried to restrain the ebullient exemption of the ancient monastery of Farfa in so far as it affected his diocese.[138] The result of the struggle between the curiously titan figures, the cardinal bishop and the venerable, propertied, old central Italian house of Benedictines was the sort of hard, realistic, but noncommittal compromise with which arms were stilled all through the world of the thirteenth-century church militant. Farfa's Sabina churches were, in 1208, divided between the clearly exempt and the episcopally dependent. The shape of the compromise which Giovanni's successor, Pierre du Douai, arranged with the abbey of Santa Maria di Pozzaglia, through the mediation

[137] For "the alarming disintegration of diocesan unity in the very city of Rome" in the first half of the eleventh century, see Kuttner, "Cardinalis," 196 and nn. 91-93; in 1018 Benedict VIII granted the cardinal bishop of Porto the island of San Bartolomeo in the Tiber, and powers of ordination in Trastevere; Kuttner is a convenient, and attractive, introduction to the Roman Church.

[138] G. Tomassetti and G. Biasiotti, *La diocesi di Sabina* (Rome, 1909), 96-99.

of Leone Brancaleone, cardinal priest of Santa Croce in Gerusalemme, was vertical rather than horizontal, jurisdictional rather than territorial. Episcopal right lay with the cardinal bishop, but the abbot might be his vicar.[139] In 1294 a copy was made of a 1235 convention through which the bishop obtained a limited jurisdiction over the house of San Salvatore di Scandriglia, even over its appurtenances within the abbatial area of Farfa should the abbot of Farfa fail to act; the cardinal bishop who had pressed Gregory IX's curia to this definition was Goffredo Castiglione who was later, in 1241, elected Pope Celestine IV.[140] In 1219 Honorius III had confirmed a concord in a dispute over property between Bishop Pierre and the archpriest and canons of his cathedral church.[141] The acts of a diocesan synod in 1312 were recorded, and an episcopal vicar visited in 1343.[142] In that year, 1343, there was compiled a register of Sabina episcopal jurisdiction.[143]

Taken all together this does not make the diocese of Sabina sound very much like Grosseteste's Lincoln. The evidence of episcopal effort is, in the end, slight and fragmentary. It stays very close to disputes over income. In Sabina, as elsewhere, it is often hard to distinguish between episcopal greed and episcopal reform. What the cardinal bishops' efforts do show is that even in Sabina there occasionally blew odd breezes which connected the diocese with the centers of ecclesiastical and episcopal reform like Innocent III's great Lateran Council a few miles away. Cardinals sometimes tried to be bishops and establish ordered dioceses.

In the diocese of Tivoli, Sabina's neighbor, built around its papal town, there was some episcopal activity in the thirteenth century. Giacomo Antonio Colonna (1210-1219) was able, in the last years of Innocent III and the first of Honorius III, to hold the pretensions to diocesan spiritual jurisdiction which the abbot of Subiaco pressed against him within a compromise

[139] Tomassetti and Biasiotti, 100-101.
[140] Tomassetti and Biasiotti, 101-102.
[141] Pressutti, 1, 362 no. 2179; in 1343 there were seven canons besides the archpriest (Tomassetti and Biasiotti, 63).
[142] Tomassetti and Biasiotti, 58, 104.
[143] Tomassetti and Biasiotti, 63-95.

resolution suggested by the papal curia.[144] In the second half of the century Bishop Giacomo (1265-1282) was active in getting confirmation to jurisdiction in specific diocesan areas. In 1280 the bishop held a synod for the reformation of the clergy.[145]

Pagano, bishop of Volterra, responded to the prevailing sentiment and attacked the jurisdictional pretensions of the ancient house of San Pietro in Palazzuolo (Monteverdi) in the early years of the century—an attack overshadowed by the flaming end of the house, with a single surviving monk cringing in the woods, on that "tragic night" in 1252.[146] The bishop of Monteverde, close neighbor and suffragan of Conza in the South, in Campagna, was building or rebuilding his spiritual and temporal hegemony in the eighties and nineties. In 1286 Sinibaldo, bishop of Salpi, acting under the authority of the legate Gerardo, bishop of Sabina, held an inquest concerning the claimed seignorial rights of the bishop of Monteverde, in which the archdeacon and archpriest of the cathedral church were active. In 1292 Sarraceno, archdeacon of Capua and canon of Melfi, the arbiter elected in a controversy over episcopal jurisdiction between Bishop Gauberto of Monteverde and the prior of San Leonardo di Carbonara, decided that, as the bishop claimed, the church of San Leonardo was within the diocese, in spiritualities, and ought to be subject to the bishop in spite of the prior's alleged exemption. The bishop was declared to have matrimonial cases and episcopal penances with the power of excommunication and interdict over parishioners. The prior should institute as chaplain a secular clerk whose correction, visitation, and deposition pertained to the bishop. The decision was notarized in the archdeacon's residence by a Venosa notary in the presence of dignitaries from neighboring dioceses. It was an important decision for

[144] Giuseppe Cascioli, "Nuova serie dei vescovi Tivoli," *Atti e memorie della società tiburtina di storia e d'arte*, IV (1924), 160-162.
[145] Cascioli, 195-196.
[146] Elena Galletti, "La Badia di San Pietro in Palazzuolo (Monteverdi)," *Maremma*, Bolletino della società storica maremmana, VI (1931), fascs. 2-3, pp. 71-78, 74.

Monteverde; without Carbonara it would have become half
the little diocese it already was.[147]

The diocese of Sabina was disturbed by the presence within
its borders of the abbey of Farfa, and the diocese of Tivoli was
cursed with Subiaco. Volterra had Palazzuolo, and Monteverde had Carbonara. But not all of the encumbering and dis-
tracting monasteries were the relics of ancient foundations
that had accumulated their immunities through the centuries;
in the thirteenth century prelates were still releasing the tension of their transitory religious enthusiasm by granting immunities to monasteries. In 1300 Brother Giovanni di Roc-
cataone, the proctor of the Celestini, appealed to Rome on
their behalf because the bishop of the new Lucera had tried to
visit and correct their monastery of San Giovanni in Piano,
and to exercise his episcopal office over it, to the injury of the
abbatial rights of Santo Spirito del Morrone.[148] The difficulties
of the bishop of the new see were the result of a quite recent
grant. In 1294 (the year of Peter Celestine's papacy) the archbishop of Benevento, Brother Giovanni, a Cassinese monk
whom Martin IV had confirmed in his see and who much admired Peter Celestine, had given up his rights over San Giovanni and handed them over to Morrone. But in Lucera new
bishop and new immunity arranged themselves in the familiar
pattern of opposition.

From the diocese of Vercelli within the province of Milan
there is evidence of episcopal effort to establish diocesan order
in the thirteenth century. The pattern of the reforming, administrative bishop fought by representatives of privilege and
convention recurs; but episcopal activity in Vercelli was more
considerable and more persistent than it was in places like
Sabina, Tivoli, and Lucera. Vercelli, lucky in its bishops and a
lively member of an unusually vigorous province, was a diocese in which ecclesiastical government seems to have been
unusually effective and also in which records seem, for Italy,

[147] Salvatore Santeramo, *Codice diplomatico barlettano*, i (Barletta,
1924), 133-138 no. 45, 191-194 no. 69.

[148] T. Leccisotti, "Documenti di Capitanata fra le carte di S. Spirito
del Morrone a Montecassino," *Japigia*, xi (1940), 27-44, 28-29, 39-40.

to have been unusually fully written. Certainly Vercelli records—as no one who hears an echo in its name can be completely surprised to discover—have been unusually well preserved. The survival raises one of the recurring problems of thirteenth-century Italian history: to what extent does there seem unusual activity only because there is unusual survival; to what extent is unusual survival an indication of unusual activity? The problem is not totally insoluble; there is certainly reason to believe that in a system of conventional government in which the value of written evidence was recognized, active and provident governors were particularly careful about the production and preservation for the future of their own written governmental records.

Activity at Vercelli can be watched in the bishops' attempts to bring the monastery of San Nazario of Biandrate within the jurisdictional diocese. Biandrate was one fragment of the material which Vercelli bishops were trying to mold into something with real diocesan coherence. On Tuesday, 24 October 1228, in the chapter house at Novara before three judges delegated by Gregory IX (the archdeacon Giacomo, Odemario the provost of San Gaudenzio, and Abbate de Castello, a canon of Novara), Guido, provost of Sant'Agata, the proctor of Ugo, bishop of Vercelli, and Buongiovanni de Ungaris, the syndic of San Nazario, met to contest the conflicting claims of the diocesan bishop and the privileged monastery in the local version of a constantly repeated conflict.[149] The judges acted under a papal mandate which had been sought by the bishop, who had complained that the abbot and convent together with certain other religious of his diocese refused to show him the obedience and respect due him. The episcopal proctor, as plaintiff, presented his *libellus* to the Novara court and offered witnesses. The monastic proctor joined the con-

---

[149] Arnoldi, 274-276 no. 46; at mid-century Buongiovanni was still acting as clerk: G. B. Morandi, *Le carte del museo civico di Novara*, Biblioteca della società storica subalpina, LXXVII(2) (Pinerolo, 1913), 80-82 no. 51; see another San Nazario dispute, with a clerk of the diocese of Novara, before a canon of Santa Tecla, Milan, and his monk deputy, in 1230: Morandi, 75-77 no. 46.

test and said that San Nazario should not in fact be considered part of the diocese of Vercelli. He claimed that San Nazario had witnesses and could produce documents that would prove that it had enjoyed its liberties for over forty years.

The judges, having heard and seen and, with the consent of the parties, having taken counsel with those learned in the law in the city of Novara, gave sentence. The monastery was to show due obedience and reverence to the bishop with regard to consecrations, synods, orders, and the jurisdiction generally exerted over a nonexempt monastery. The monastery was not to be considered exempt from the bishop in whose diocese it was located. The outlines of hearing and decision, together with the fact that a notarial instrument drawn up by the notary Anselmo established Guido as the bishop's proctor, were preserved in the instruments of another notary, Pietro, and survive.

There is an air of truth, of convincing detail, about the action of the Novara delegates in 1228. San Nazario would seem to have been settled within the diocese of Vercelli. But in 1248 the heirs of the contestants were active again. On Saturday, 1 August of that year, the contest was in progress in Novara, in the *canonica* of San Gaudenzio, before Guala Brusato, the provost of Novara, acting as delegate for Gregory of Montelongo, the papal legate. Vercelli in the person of its bishop-elect Martino was represented by the proctor Guidotto, *custos* of Santa Maria of Novara, and San Nazario by Dom Filippo de Bocca, monk and proctor. The judge acted under a mandate of the legate that was sealed in wax and dated from Milan. The mandate incorporated the complaint of the bishop elect. The elect had been summoned to the general council of Lyons. He had sought a reasonable subsidy for his expenses from the houses of his diocese, but the monks of San Nazario, "unfeeling sons to their spiritual father," had shown no compassion.

The legate ordered the delegate to find out if San Nazario was in fact immediately subject to Vercelli and its elect. If it turned out to be, the delegate should make them pay. The libellus presented by the bishop's proctor had demanded ten lire of Pavia from the monastery for Lyons expenses and had stated that the monastery was within the diocese of Vercelli and subject to Vercelli. It had further claimed that the bishop had been bound to go to Lyons since he had been summoned by the pope through the archbishop of Milan; both papal and archiepiscopal letters were displayed. The proctor of San Nazario replied that even if it should be true that the monastery was locally within the diocese of Vercelli it was not subject to Vercelli because the pope had made it exempt from all episcopal jurisdiction. He said that the abbot and convent had stood in and enjoyed their freedom and had shown no subjection to the church and bishop of Vercelli for the space of ten, twenty, thirty, forty, fifty, sixty, seventy, eighty years, and more, to a time to which memory did not run. This, the proctor said, he could prove with a written privilege. The legate's judge, like his papally delegated predecessors, took counsel with the wise of Novara. They gave him their opinion in an instrument sealed with three wax seals. The delegate judge read his decision in the presence of the provost and a number of canons of San Gaudenzio. The house of San Nazario was again declared to be within the diocese of Vercelli and subject to its bishop. It was said to be responsible for common subsidies.

The proctor of San Nazario alleged that the sentence was *male pronunciatam*; he appealed to the pope and sought letters dimissory. The court granted the letters and gave the appellant until the feast of the Nativity of the Virgin (8 September) to appear at the papal curia to prove his appeal. The fish were again out of the net and swimming, at least temporarily, free. How could 1228 permit 1248? It is a question that might even have occurred to the Novara notary of 1248 if he were, as seems possible, the son of the 1228 notary. The exaggeration of legal language, running beyond the memory of man, seems not enough of an explanation. The diocese of Vercelli, for all its unusual qualities, must have been so little active as a diocese that a monastery caught within its jurisdiction in 1228 could in 1248 pretend never to have been caught. It was caught enough (even if it appealed in 1228) for the legate's judge, with his Novara advisers (who may have had reason to oppose monastic rebellion in their own diocese), to find again the same answer.[150]

The sporadic energy of Vercelli diocesan government, with the curiously vacant, untenanted quality of the interstices between individual governmental acts and with the lack of local governmental memory, which is seen in the evasions of Biandrate, is seen again, but this time from the other direction, in the repeated entanglements of Santa Maria di Vezzolano. Vezzolano, of which there are considerable medieval remains, was a small exempt house of Augustinian canons locally within the diocese of Vercelli. Its exemption was tested by a particularly able and active bishop of Vercelli, Aimone de Challont of Aosta.[151] Aimone ruled the diocese from his translation in 1272 until 1303; his episcopal behavior, his name, and his career all suggest transalpine influences. In 1287 or 1288 Bishop Aimone demanded, on pain of interdict and excommunication, that reluctant houses within the diocese pay, within eight days, their share of the expenses that the bishop had incurred at the recent provincial council of Milan, presumably Ottone Visconti's Santa Tecla council of September 1287. The money was to be paid at the *tabulam* of Emanuele Borromeo. In April the bishop's vicar general, Raynerio Avvocato, archdeacon of Vercelli, acting with a panel composed of Alessio, archpriest of Vercelli, Nicolò, prior of Bugella, and Giuliano of Cremona, and acting upon the advice of the same Giuliano and of Antonio Preapano, men learned in the law, declared that the house of Vezzolano had established its exemption and need not pay its subsidy.[152]

In 1298 Archdeacon Raynerio Avvocato was, as vicar general, again active on a panel whose job it was to examine claims of exemption from diocesan jurisdiction. His associates were Nicolà, archpriest of Vercelli, and Guglielmo de Stipulis. Bishop Aimone had held a full synod in his palazzo in Vercelli in which he had demanded that all exempt monasteries prove their exemption within forty days. On 16 May it was

---

[150] Arnoldi, 294-298 no. 60 (Antonio "Faxolus" son of Pietro "Faxolus"; Pietro "Varolus").

[151] Mandelli, iii, 97-98.

[152] Arnoldi, 335-336 no. 78.

admitted that Oddone, provost of Vezzolano, had established Vezzolano's exemption before the panel by means of a privilege from Pope Alexander. But on 1 June, a fortnight later, two visitors delegated by the bishop arrived to visit and correct the canons of the house and to exercise in the bishop's name the visitorial rights of the Vercelli mother church of Sant'-Eusebio. They sought to establish the inclusion of the house within the jurisdictional diocese (and within the controlling influence of the diocese's cult center). This the canons could not permit. Provost Oddone said that he did not want to receive or admit the men as visitors or to give them procurations; but he said that he was willing to receive them in his monastery as the bishop's messengers and special friends, and as the special friends of Vezzolano. The visitors accepted the distinction and admitted that they stayed at Vezzolano as friends and not visitors.[153]

The problem of Vezzolano's exemption was again raised in the early fourteenth century. On Wednesday, 28 March 1319, the Provost Nicolò and eight canons of Vezzolano, acting in their cloister, made one of their co-canons their proctor. He was to protest before Eusebio da Tronzano, Bishop Uberto's vicar general (as he had been Bishop Aimone's vicar general in 1303 and vicar general during the succeeding vacancy) against a proposed visitation.[154] Two months later, on 16 May, the canons, still anxious to protect their immunity, got Oddone Silo, the archdeacon of Turin, "tenens locum episcopi ecclesie Taurinensis vacantis," to authorize a transcription of their bull of exemption from Pope Nicholas.[155] The history of Vezzolano and Vercelli is a queer congeries—the efficiency of set days, examining panels, *quo warranto* proceedings, synods, visitors delegate, the continuing ordered government of a vicar gen-

---

[153] Arnoldi, 343-345 nos. 83-84.

[154] Arnoldi, 350-351 no. 89; Vercelli documents emphasize the rights of the church of the saint, Eusebio (see too Arnoldi, 353 no. 91); for vicar general Eusebio see Mandelli, III, 97-98.

[155] Arnoldi, 351-353 no. 90; Arnoldi assumes the bull, dated 10 Kalends March, first year, from Saint Peter's, was from Nicholas IV, but it seems more probable that it was from Nicholas III, who was dating from Saint Peter's at about this point in his pontificate; Nicholas IV was dating from Santa Maria Maggiore.

eral, together with the strange lack of official memory and the implied limitation of governance to periods of spasmodic activity.

In the distant Italian South, at Brindisi, the heavy, decorated splendor of Archbishop Pietro III Paparone's conception of pastoral duty reflected itself in those waters in which, according to legend, the body of Saint Theodore had worked its miracle and proved its love for Brindisi (see Fig. 4). Pietro Paparone, accompanied by his worthy band and his constant (but perhaps not voluntary) Oliver, Pietro II, bishop of Ostuni, his only suffragan, was borne across the harbor to the island monastery of Sant'Andrea in January 1245. The archbishop was in process of carrying out his relatively vigorous and imaginative, and ornate, campaign for the regulation and subjection of the corporate bodies of clerics and religious within his diocese. His campaign stretched at least through the decade from 1239 to 1249. In 1239, delayed in his action, he said, by debilitating sickness earlier in the year, he arranged a reforming concord with the clergy of his cathedral church. The concord purportedly returned the chapter to its historical position, that which it had held under Pietro II of Bisignano (1225-1239) and which had been arranged by earlier archbishops like Gerardo (1196) and Pellegrino (1216-1224). This piece of historically minded reform was recorded, encased, in an elaborate and archaic document, redolent, with its heavy harangue, of ancient archbishops.[156] At the end of this reforming decade, in 1249, the Dominicans of Brindisi were finding Pietro III's rigor oppressive. In that year the pope, an official noticeably absent from many of Pietro's affairs, delegated the archbishop of Bari and the bishop of Bitetto to hear a dispute between the archbishop and the friars, some of whom may be presumed to have been former co-voyagers.[157]

On 6 June 1244 Abbot Nicola and the monks of the monastery of Sant'Andrea in the harbor recognized the archbishop as their father, the church of Brindisi as their mother, and re-

---

[156] Gennaro Maria Monti, *Codice diplomatico brindisino*, 1 (492-1299) (Trani, 1940), 84-88 no. 53. For the Theodore legend, Ughelli, IX, cols. 5-6, 7.

[157] Monti, 121-122 no. 68.

turned to their old subjection. The archbishop had vindicated his rights as "metropolitan and diocesan," a combination of titles he constantly used in diocesan affairs, in the imperial *curia magna*—a strange twist in the distorting winds of southern Italian politics. Pietro III had the act recorded before many witnesses, including the prior of the Hospitallers as well as the bishop of Ostuni and important local friars, in a magnificent document with forty-five subscribing witnesses and at least an intended lead seal.[158] The abbey's subjection was witnessed on June 6. On the following 12 January, in 1245, the archbishop rode over the water from Brindisi to the island in a bark filled with a remarkably impressive court—a "ship of the church"—that included nine canons of Brindisi, the bishop and a canon of Ostuni, Dominicans from Brindisi, Franciscans, two knights from Naples, three Bolognesi, two Spoletans, and Matteo, abbot of Santa Maria di Ferorelle (who subscribed the descriptive document in Greek).

When the bark reached the island, the water gate of the island and both of the monastery gates were open. When the boat made its landing the archbishop stood in it with his chapter; and the abbot and monks came and kissed his hand and made obeisance to him, and then, taking him by his arms and sides, helped him onto the shore. There they placed him, seated, on a rock near the water's edge. They went back to the monastery and returned in procession to the seated archbishop; and they bore with them cross, censer, and holy water. The abbot at the archbishop's command took the holy water and sprinkled it upon him. The archbishop rose. The monk, Andrea, began in high voice to sing a responsory which the notary called "In columpne specie" (actually "In columbe specie / Spiritus Sanctus visus est"—Pietro may more readily have provoked the image of ungrammatical "column" than that of "dove"). The monks led the archbishop through the monastery gate and gave him a silk cope and a *cauda* and excused themselves for not having a miter on the island that they could give him. They then, with incense smoking, candles blazing, and water sprinkling, took the archbishop into the

---

[158] Monti, 97-99 no. 61; the editor found only a wax seal.

church and to the high altar. There the archbishop prayed. Rising, he went to the church's throne and gave his blessing. The monks came and subjected themselves to him. Then Mass was said, and when it was finished the archbishop went into the chapter house and preached a sermon. Then he formally visited the monks and corrected them. Next, still marking the monks' subjection, he went and ate of their procurations; and again he took a formal oath of subjection from the abbot and nine monks. All this was described in a notarial instrument that it might serve as a lasting reminder of what had been accomplished. Besides being notarized, the document was subscribed by nineteen witnesses, and sealed with the wax elliptical seals of the bishop of Ostuni, with its chasubled and mitered bishop, and of the abbot of Santa Maria di Ferorelle, with its mitered abbot and liliated staff and his name in "epigraphia latina." The visitation was a gaudy triumph for the archbishop's hierarchic principle.[159]

The Greeks of Santa Maria di Ferorelle, who through their then abbot had contributed to the subjection of Sant'Andrea, were, on 27 May 1246, forced to place their Greek subscriptions on one of Pietro III's elaborate documents, to swear their fealty to the Virgin and San Leucio of Brindisi, to admit that the archbishop was their metropolitan and diocesan bishop. Their abbot, Nicodemus, swore to avoid conspiracies against the archbishop, to oppose them, and to denounce them, to keep the archbishop's counsel and defend his rights (saving the rights of the lord emperor and of the abbot's order), to receive the archbishop's nuncios, attend his synods, and not to alienate or re-enfeoff (*inpheudabo de novo*) without his license or mandate. The abbot swore that each year on its feast of San Leucio in January he would visit the mother church of Brindisi or, if he were sick, send a brother. The oath was taken before Pietro of Ostuni, Nicola abbot of Sant'Andrea, Benedetto abbot of Santa Maria di Parvoponte, Brindisi, and a mass of witnesses, forty-seven signatories.[160]

In the midst of what comes to seem the pattern of Italian dioceses, Città di Castello is a surprise. Città di Castello was

[159] Monti, 100-104 no. 62.
[160] Monti, 116-118 no. 66.

directly subject to Rome, so that it was not at all involved in relations with a metropolitan. In every other way it would have seemed a fully, conscientiously, and continuously administered diocese in any part of western Europe in the thirteenth century. The reality of Città di Castello administration is unavoidable. The bishop and his administrators acted, and the bishops' notaries carefully recorded the acts, in the piazza of and under the arch of the bishops' palazzo in Città di Castello, in its cloister, in the cloisters of monasteries, and in *pievi*. The bishops sat in judgment over diocesan disputes, they held reforming diocesan synods, and they moved around and around the diocese in careful visitation. The ideal, potential thirteenth-century diocese is here in act, alive.

The period of Città di Castello's most obvious activity is in the later thirteenth century, during the pontificates of three remarkable and heavily recorded bishops: Pietro V d'Anagni (1252-1265), Nicolò, former abbot of San Severino, Orvieto (1265-1279), and Giacomo d'Enrico Cavalcanti (1280-1301).[161] But the unusual quality of the diocese's administration is apparent for a considerably earlier period, before similarly expressed vigor became conventional in northern European dioceses. Bishop Matteo (1229-1234) visited the clergy in *pieve* after *pieve*; he asked questions, took oaths, tried to reform and correct.[162] By the time, then, of Bishop Nicolò's great visitations of 1270 and 1272 there was no novelty about the general practice. From 12 October to 26 November 1270 Bishop Nicolò visited. He stopped twenty-two times, at churches, *pievi*, hospitals, Benedictine monasteries, from the far north of the diocese in Corliano to the far south in Comunaglia [Map 2, insert]. In April 1271 he visited again, on succeeding days, the *pievi* of Uppiano and Tiberina, west of Città di Castello, and again in November, as far north as Sucastelli. In November 1272, the bishop was involved in another more extended visitation. He moved quickly from Montone, Ronti, and Morra, in the south and west, to Sovara and San Cassiano, in the northwest; and he visited Benedictine

---

[161] Muzi, ii, 132-142, 147-160, 165-177.

[162] Muzi, ii, 122-125; it seems odd that Forchielli was hesitant about Umbrian *pievi*: Forchielli, 28.

monasteries as well as the secular clergy of the *pievi*. In January and February 1273 Nicolò was again visiting in the northwest from Corliano to Borgo Sansepolcro, and in April and May in the central part of the diocese. The bishop visited, and the bishop's notary, Guido di Giovanni, recorded; and the records survive, at least in part, in the neat visitation *quaterni* in the fifth of the books of episcopal records in the episcopal chancery at Città di Castello.[163]

Bishop Nicolò was not easily put off by suspect monastic resistance to visitation. In 1268, Tedelgardo and his Benedictine house of Sant'Angelo, Arduino e Tedaldo (Badia Tedalda), in the north near the borders of the diocese of Montefeltro, resisted. The abbey claimed exemption and privilege but offered, in October, to receive the bishop if he would come as a friend rather than as a visitor. He would be received as courteously as their very dearest friend. The bishop refused, and had his refusal recorded. He demanded to see Sant'Angelo's privileges. They were not produced. In spite of Abbot Tedelgardo's repeated conferences with the bishop, as the bishop visited about the diocese, the abbey reduced itself to contumacy after it declined to respond with proper representations to a formal summons to appear before the bishop in Borgo Sansepolcro. Nicolò's efforts may not have been effective immediately, but eventually Sant'Angelo was caught within the diocese.[164]

Nicolò's concern with the fringes of diocese did not distract his attention from the *canonica* at its center within the cathedral church of San Florido. Like other Italian bishops he tried to press capitular reform, particularly, it has been thought, after he returned, spiritually refreshed, from Gregory X's ecumenical council at Lyons.[165]

[163] Città di Castello, Archivio vescovile, Bk. v, fos. 9v-15v, 38v-41.
[164] Città di Castello, Archivio vescovile, Bk. iii, fo. 77; for the abbey see Muzi, iv, 148-151—it was visited in 1489.
[165] Thought by Muzi. Difficulties with the chapter continued, in the last year of the century, in October 1299, Salimbene of San Severino, a papal (Boniface VIII) *cursor* brought to Prior Deodatus, auditor of the sacred palace (surrounded by his notaries), a commission in a case instigated by an appeal of Martino who held a benefice in the great church at Città di Castello and who acted as the chapter's

In November 1269 Bishop Nicolò celebrated a diocesan synod in the cathedral church of San Florido. The synod was clearly planned to express diocesan unity as well as to effect diocesan reform. The difficulty of winter weather had been considered in planning the synod, and ample time for the arrival of participants granted, but a general not a particular synod was demanded. All abbots (presuming nonexemption), archpriests, "prelates," and rectors of churches were summoned. Present and witnessing the synod's *acta* were the provost and archdeacon of the church of Città di Castello and four canons of Città di Castello. The enacted canons of the council concerned themselves with a variety of conventional ecclesiastical problems: with the administration of the sacraments (leavened bread should not, after the Greek manner, be used for the Eucharist, for example); with clerks who should avoid carrying arms, playing at dice, frequenting taverns, practicing the craft of surgery, and keeping concubines; with the problems of pluralism and nonresidence; with the use of unblessed vessels and vestments, with profaned churches and with altars damaged, moved, or defiled and in need of reconciliation; with usurers; with the required office, the required orders, and with the selling of church land—canons that were like shot, broadcast at the problems of the clerical order.

The council also made pronouncement against those who broke the peace and did not fulfill their duties to the bishop, who made conspiracies and eluded diocesan jurisdiction, and against those who called themselves exempt, but who could or would not within three months of the synod produce and show the bishop sufficient privileges. Specifically, the bishop attacked the monasteries of Pianezzolo (Camaldolese, in the territory of Arezzo), Marzano, Tedaldo, Lamole, Scalocchio, Giove (Olivetani), Galliano, and Oselle (Vallombrosan). Episcopal research in documentary sources, papal and imperial, had, it was said, shown the monasteries to be of the diocese, but they had not come to the diocesan synod. The monasteries were to produce their written privileges within

proctor; the chapter's dispute was with Bishop Giacomo: Città di Castello, *Canonica*, II, 53.

term, prove their exemption, or suffer excommunication. The bishop also attacked the abbot of Petroja and the prior of Cella di Castagneto for not coming to the synod, and placed under interdict and suspended those ultramontane clerics particularly from the *pievi* of Borgo San Sepolcro and San Cipriano who had not attended.

In council as in his visitations Bishop Nicolò was walling and patching and sticking together his diocese, keeping it in actual working existence. He was also attacking those clerical abuses which the most harshly analytical of his near contemporaries had found at the very root of ecclesiastical "decay"— the casual use of sacred office, object, and income, and particularly the twin evils of pluralism and nonresidence. The bishop also demanded his synodals, two *soldi* from each chaplain and rector; and he in the tradition of his see, with its continuous awareness of the value of recorded, remembered government, had the synod's acts recorded and saved.[166]

Thirteenth-century bishops of Città di Castello mimicked contemporary popes in their ideas about pastoral care. They mimicked them in the language of their documents. They also mimicked their techniques of governing as in their use of judges delegate. (With a nice sense of definition and in a document with a nice ear for papal language, in January 1279, Bishop Pietro, approaching his final infirmity, commissioned his vicar general to hear and decide a case of appeal between a widow and her son on one side and the archpriest of Monte Santa Maria and a member of his *pieve* on the other.)[167] The bishops of Città di Castello governed with principles, language, and techniques that could hardly have seemed strange to their contemporaries in Lincoln or Canterbury or Carlisle; and they governed in a way and with an intensity that most of their English contemporaries would have admired, and perhaps even envied. But the peculiarly intense and effective (for Italy) government of Città di Castello was not completely or always dependent on its bishops. In the 1279-1280 vacancy between the pontificates of Bishop Nicolò and his successor, Bishop Giacomo d'Enrico Cavalcanti, the canon Ranaldo da

---

[166] Muzi, II, 154-157.
[167] Città di Castello, Archivio vescovile, Bk. VI, fo. 242.

Falzano, acted as capitular vicar.[168] The record of his acts shows him to have been not just a guardian of the see's property, but also of its administrative and judicial activity—as in his trial of the dicing clerk, Picolello di Pietro, who had played and lost at *codarone*, across the Tiber on Saint Lucy's Eve, a diversion from Picolello's trip to Colonnata di Ronti, where he went to serve at Mass.[169] Ranaldo clearly saw the see as a good deal more than a mere aggregate of property.

The vision of the bishops' notaries was, for their place and time, peculiar, too. From the time of Bishop Matteo's notary Urso, who constructed a visitation book in 1230, at least, a series of these men constructed an orderly, defined, consistent, continuing official memory for the see. They gave their bishops' acts, and so the diocese, an extra dimension in time. Among the notaries, Pietro da Canoscio, active in the 1250's and 1260's during the pontificate of Bishop Pietro V d'Anagni, seems to have been particularly effective in organizing chancery technique; but Guido di Giovanni, Rainaldo Armanni, Guido di Bonaventura, a number of others, are impressive, too. They recorded the acts of men representing an entity more than and different from a group of estates clustered around a cult center and a collegiate church.[170]

It is not easy to understand what Città di Castello means. Extraordinarily active prelates in other Italian dioceses with unusually well-kept records display at best the echoing forgetfulness of Vercelli or the grandiloquent masque of Brindisi, the suggestion of real order at Bologna, the Herculean efforts of the Visconti, the fragments of Tommaso of Rieti, or Fra Bonifazio Fieschi at Ravenna. Why is Città di Castello so different—as if Worcester or Hereford or even Lincoln had been given notaries and *pievi*, deprived of a metropolitan, and set down in the middle of Umbria? Can it

---

[168] Città di Castello, Archivio vescovile, Bk. viii, fos. 118-138, intermittently; see, too, Muzi, ii, 164-165, 166.

[169] Città di Castello, Archivio vescovile, Bk. viii, fo. 133v.

[170] Brentano, "Bishops' Books," particularly 244-247; for a statement of the distance between Città di Castello and Rome, see Waley, *Papal State*, 180: "Città di Castello, a border territory and one always more amenable to Tuscan pressure than papal claims . . ."—talking of Città di Castello's support of Conradin.

mean that all other Italian dioceses, except perhaps Bologna and Lucca, are improperly seen, that only this diocese reveals itself as the others would if accident had not robbed them of a crucial set of books like the Bishops' Books of Città di Castello? It is hard to believe—could there be so many accidents? The combination of effort and emptiness in Vercelli is very compelling; it seems so clearly to describe rather unusual action placed in a normal void.

If Città di Castello is unique, or at least very unusual, a seemingly insoluble problem remains. Why did the thirteenth-century seed find this ground good? A single positive reason cannot be found. A number of rather intriguing negative reasons, permissive conditions, present themselves. Although Città di Castello was close to papal centers and presumably relatively susceptible to papal influence, it was not a papal residential city, disturbed and distracted by the curia's presence. Although the diocese had a cult saint, his cult was not very powerful—not distorting or inhibiting. Although the diocese was organized around a central city of unique importance, its city was not involved in very significant widespread commercial activity, and it had not produced an overwhelmingly powerful commercial class. Although there were a number of resisting monasteries in the diocese, none was of the first importance—none was a Farfa or a Subiaco. Although the diocese was disturbed by the thirteenth-century wars, and by the rivalry between Città di Castello and Borgo San Sepolcro, it was not shredded by disputes, as Rieti was. The diocese was not cursed, in the thirteenth century, with a bishop like Guglielmino Ubertini of the neighboring diocese of Arezzo—a man whose secular power was enough to crush the structure of ecclesiastical government. Although the see was not particularly poor, it was not rich enough to whet the greed of the distant and powerful. It was a middle-sized see of middling importance in a rather isolated part of the papal middle of Italy, at some distance from most vigorous thirteenth-century political action. In this situation its (locally) unusual tradition was allowed to develop itself. Each notary could build upon the work of his predecessor. The bishops from their various backgrounds could build themselves into the continuing pattern.

Still it is easy here to ask the wrong, the impertinent, question—why did only Città di Castello understand the papal appeal and the nature of the thirteenth-century diocese, rather than why did Città di Castello alone fail to understand, or at least express, the nature of the thirteenth-century Italian church.

The Italian bishops pushing at the shape of their dioceses make much of the consistency of their church clear—chapter, *pieve*, and a memory pretty much restricted to cult and property. The sharp difference of Città di Castello points from inside at the peculiarity of the Italian church.

Records of diocesan government are rare in Italy. Records of law cases are not. The universal church was universally litigious, and evidence of its litigiousness is preserved, in bulk or in fragment, from Bologna, Perugia, Florence, Siena, Naples, Salerno, Amalfi, Ravello, Bari, from all parts of the peninsula. The cases generally centered themselves around disputed property or disputed jurisdiction, but they might touch almost any phase of life, as they might glance through almost any court.

A bright reminder of this variety comes from Capri in the early fourteenth century. It was an old Anacapri custom on Palm Sunday for laymen of Anacapri to walk in procession, sing Psalms, and carry images of the crucified Christ and of the Virgin to the shrine of San Costanzo. The custom was displeasing to Fra Nicolò, the bishop of Capri, and his clergy and they forbade its continuance. The men of Anacapri sought a remedy against this restriction from King Robert. In October 1335 Robert delegated the decision of the insular dispute to his familiar, Fra Landolfo Caracciolo, archbishop of Amalfi. Fra Landolfo heard the claims of the men of Anacapri and the opposing claims of the men of Capri in his court and found for the Anacapritani. In 1338 they again had their procession. Along their way they were stopped by a band of ruffians, clerics and laymen from Capri, who shouted insults and threw stones that broke the sacred images. Another letter was sent from the king to the archbishop, and the secular arm was in-

voked against the offenders so that in future the men of Anacapri could sing unmolested on their country Palm Sunday
roads.[171] The bishop of Capri was pressed to a broader view of
Christian worship, and the men of Capri town to a narrower
view of civic rivalry.

The description of normal, less obviously colorful, cases,
about resisted visitations and contested rents, tells a lot about
the church in which the cases happened. The disputants are
like people in a maze, pushing its sides, feeling its height, determining for us its structure, that is the structure of the
church. They, the disputants, point out matters of constant
concern, what, in a way, the church is about. They also make
clear the ladder (a misleadingly linear figure) of appeal from
court to court. Appeals sometimes moved into secular courts,
as in the case of Anacapri against Capri, but in fact they usually aimed themselves directly or indirectly at Rome. As the
proctor for an appellant, the provost of Città di Castello, said,
before a canon of Anagni who had been delegated by the
bishop of Città di Castello, in 1263, a papal tribunal is superior
to that of any ordinary, and no ordinary can or ought to interfere with its jurisdiction.[172] To announce and implement
this persuasion at some time in the proceedings appeared ad-
vantageous to almost every disputant in every recorded case.
Fragmentary thirteenth-century cases which do not specifically
describe the Romeward movement, can still be assumed to
have been (from analogy with cases that were) in fact or in
intention involved in it.

The only way to understand what these law cases are really
like is to look at some of them, at quite a number of them
brought together from various places, to pick them up out of
a box and turn them over in your hand. Some are small, their
essential points quickly perceived (or so they can be made to
look in stylized narration); they can be glanced at and tossed

[171] Camera, II, 678.
[172] Città di Castello, Archivio vescovile, Bk. III, fo. 22v. One pope's
(Innocent IV's) thoughtful, extended consideration of the problem
of appeals and their reception can be seen, for example, in his commentaries on *de rescriptis* (X,i,3), *de officio et potestate iudicis delegati*
(X,i,29), and *de appellationibus* (X,ii,28).

aside. Some are extended and intricate in themselves, as are the Bologna and Rossano-Matina cases here. Some are (or all are, and some ought thus to be seen) inextricably caught in the ecclesiastical (at the very least) politics of their neighborhoods, as are the Bari cases here. Cases like this cannot be reduced to statistics. If they are, if their connecting tendrils are sheared off and their interiors are painfully disentangled, they lose their individuality, their life, and their power to demonstrate. Still, in going through them, it is possible to carry a guide, a sort of form, which points out those things that ought particularly to be observed and noted, those questions that should always be asked. The most important points and questions are obvious enough, but it is perhaps convenient to mention some of them: What in each case is the matter in dispute, what sort of substance is it? Who are the disputants, what sort of men or corporations, with what obvious and what suspected affiliations? What is the source of the court's power (immediate as well as ultimate), to whom have the local disputants moved their appeal? What sort of men, how many, of what rank, from where, are the judges? Where do they hold their courts, whom do they find as witnesses? What are the words and acts and tricks that in repetition become the cliché of the court and courts? How, and after how long, does the case end, or not end? On what principles, if the word seems apposite, is decision made? What sort of power does the decision express, and on what sort of power does the hope for its enforcement seem to be based? What sort of mechanism is used to implement the decision? And through all of this, what sort of church (and how segmented), what sort of view of church, and what sort of hope for church are implied?

In late thirteenth-century Bologna a litigious and acquisitive Dominican nunnery, Sant'Agnese, struggled in a series of courts for what it called its share, probably a fourth, of a considerable Lambertazzi (Ghibelline) inheritance.[173] Sant'Agnese's opponents, lay and ecclesiastical, seem to have been competent and interested combatants, but none of them

[173] For the Lambertazzi see Vito Vitale, *Il dominio della parte Guelfa in Bologna, 1280-1327* (Bologna, 1901), particularly chs. I and II, pp. 13-74.

can be known so well as Sant'Agnese because none saved so successfully the neat codices and notarial instruments recording activities day after day in court after court. Fibers from Sant'Agnese's cases against the other heirs of Enrighetto de Baysio reached into a good deal of the recent history of Bologna and its contemporary society. The cases involved themselves with the Lambertazzi party's rebellions, its expulsions from the city and its readmissions, the confiscation and regranting of Lambertazzi goods, the commune's keepers of the goods.[174] They involved themselves with the peculiar, privileged position of the new orders, of the Dominicans' exemption from excommunication and taxation, and with the structure of inheritance and wardship in a difficult family.[175]

Sant'Agnese's interest in the Enrighetto de Baysio inheritance came to it with two of its nuns, Agnese and Beatrice, daughters of Adelaxia and of Federigo, Enrighetto's son. The convent was engaged in dispute with Cecilia, wife of Bonacurso de Predacolora and daughter of Enrighetto, who claimed that the convent held goods that formerly belonged to her mother, Benvenuta, and that now rightfully belonged to her. The convent was also engaged in a dispute with Agnese's and Beatrice's three cousins, Enrighetto, Francesco, and Pietro, brothers and sons of Ymelda and of Pietro, son of Enrighetto. After the older Pietro's death in 1270 (before the Lambertazzi expulsion) the three boys had become (in 1271) wards of Federigo, the girls' father and their (the boys') uncle, and also of Maio, another uncle and Federigo's brother. Maio had predeceased Federigo before the boys' majority. After Federigo had died, the boys (now, in the late 1290's, matured) asserted that some of Pietro's quite impressive inheritance—valuable

[174] Bologna, Archivio di stato, conventi soppressi, Sant'Agnese Bologna, 5/5595, D 268, D 272, D 300(2); for Sant'Agnese see Cesare Monari, *Storia di Bologna divisa in libri otto* (Bologna, 1862), 722. (Sant'Agnese is the Caserma M. Minghetti on Via Castelfidardo.) An Inquisition transcription from 1732 of twelve papal letters for Sant' Agnese, of which nine are thirteenth-century, is preserved in the Vatican: Archivio segreto vaticano, fondo Domenicani, 298.

[175] Bologna, Archivio di stato, conventi soppressi, Sant'Agnese Bologna, 5/5595, D 284 (and see Guido de Baysio's intrusion in the case: 7/5597, F 391).

horses, arms, and lawbooks, as well as land and household goods and clothes—had been confused with the goods of their intestate guardian. This case of the cousins spelled itself out at length into an impressively elaborate set of documents. The nuns of Sant'Agnese also engaged themselves in dispute with the older Enrighetto's son, Federigo's brother, the cleric Francesco.[176] Protected by their Dominican connections, represented by their male proctors, particularly Tiberto and Enrico, and led by a succession of prioresses, the forty (or approximately forty) nuns of Sant'Agnese were everywhere active in securing their possessions.[177]

Most immediately interesting, for the ecclesiastical historian, of Sant'Agnese's de Baysio disputes is its struggle with another Bolognese nunnery, also eager to defend its possessions, Santa Maria Maddalena, Val di Pietra.[178] The two convents—one, Sant'Agnese, now a *caserma*, the other, now noteworthy because near the site of an ecclesiastical cinema, for their pains—represented two generations of de Baysio women. As Agnese and Beatrice, Federigo's daughters, had betaken themselves to Sant'Agnese, their mother, Federigo's wife, Adelaxia, had betaken herself to Santa Maria Maddalena. Religious action was not uncommon in the family, obviously, but also convents probably seemed suitable havens in time of danger for Lambertazzi widows and daughters who carried with them a chance, in other times, of some inheritance.[179] Not very surprisingly the confused possessions of the two generations of women brought dispute to the two houses of religion.

[176] Bologna, Archivio di stato, conventi soppressi, Sant'Agnese Bologna, 7/5597, F 364(1), F 384, F 390, F395(2); 5/5595, D 269, D270; 7/5597, F372.

[177] This guess at the number of nuns is based on recurring and changing witness lists, e.g. Sant'Agnese Bologna, 6/5596, C 314 (in 1287).

[178] Maria Maddalena was outside the Porta Saragozza; it later became San Giuseppe: for Bolognese topographical information, see Luigi Breventani, *Supplemento alle Cose notabili di Bologna . . . di Giuseppe Guidicini* (Bologna, 1908), and Celso Faleoni, *Memorie historiche della chiesa Bolognese e suoi pastori* (Bologna, 1649).

[179] In 1304 Fra Francesco, son of Enrighetto de Baysio, was attached to the chapel of San Mamus and lived in "Borgo S. Mami" (?Borgo San Mamolo); Sant'Agnese Bologna, 8/5598, G 432, G 433.

The dispute was brought to court at Bologna, where episcopal jurisdiction seems to have been, quite unsurprisingly,
unusually articulate and continuously well organized. The
case was heard by Gerardo da Cornazano, canon of Tournai,
then vicar of Ottaviano, bishop of Bologna. By 11 February
1294 the nuns of Sant'Agnese had decided to move the case to
another court.[180] On that day their proctor, Fra Tiberto, met
Santa Maria Maddalena's proctor, Bonaventura de Varis, in
the episcopal palace in the place where justice was rendered
and sought letters dimissory from the vicar's court. Fra Tiberto appealed to the Archbishop of Ravenna. He complained
that in a case of debt brought by the convent against Maria
Maddalena, Maria Maddalena had hindered the case by claim-
ing that Sant'Agnese was suffering under a sentence of excommunication pronounced by papal legates or nuncios. But,
claimed Fra Tiberto, that was quite impossible because Sant'
Agnese belonged to the order of Friars Preacher and was by
privilege specifically exempt from this sort of excommunication. Fra Tiberto objected that the vicar should have ignored
the Maria Maddalena contentions and proceeded to the matter
of the case.

On 2 May 1294 Fra Tiberto went to the convent of Santa
Maria Maddalena to deliver a citation, dated 30 April from
Argenta (the archbishop's castle in the archpriest's town in the
northwestern part of the diocese of Ravenna).[181] The citation
was sent from the Archbishop of Ravenna's court, from the
court of his auditor. The auditor to Archbishop Fra Bonifazio
Fieschi (a Dominican, but archbishop because a Parmesan
Fieschi, according to Salimbene) was then Guardino, the archbishop's chamberlain and a canon, a cardinal subdeacon, of the
church of Ravenna. The citation, sealed with the auditor
canon's seal, found Santa Maria Maddalena already contumacious; it demanded Maria Maddalena's presence before the
court at Argenta on the tenth day after the receipt of the citation, in order that Maria Maddalena's contumacy might not
grow. But on 11 May its contumacy was considered to have
grown sufficiently for Guardino, under the portico next to the

180 Sant'Agnese Bologna, 7/5597, F 345.
181 Sant'Agnese Bologna, 7/5597, F 347.

piazza communale in Argenta, to act. He pronounced the prior, prioress, sisters, and convent of Maria Maddalena contumacious, and made an executor to place the syndic of Sant'-Agnese in possession of a vineyard in Bologna—that Maria Maddalena might not glory in its contumacy.[182] Two days later in Bologna, Guardino's executor, Bartolomeo di Fra Antonio, a notary of Bologna, put Fra Tiberto, Sant'Agnese's syndic, in corporeal possession and tenure of the vineyard in a ceremony performed at the vineyard's site near Maria Maddalena.[183] On 19 May Fra Tiberto brought a further letter to Maria Maddalena; it, dated the previous day from Argenta, proceeded toward the excommunication of Maria Maddalena which Sant'Agnese urged that Maria Maddalena's contumacy demanded.[184]

Guardino's letter of 18 May was issued, it said, notwithstanding any inhibition that Maria Maddalena might have procured from Ildebrandino, bishop of Arezzo, the papal rector in spiritualities and temporalities in Bologna and the Romagna. By the time of Guardino's letter the convent of Maria Maddalena was, quite patently, trying to move its case with Sant'Agnese to the court of the papal rector. The rector's response to their case was, as they must have hoped and perhaps expected, more favorable than the archbishop's. The rector's court of audience presided over by himself and by his auditor, an archpriest, found the decisions of the archbishop's court null and void.[185] The audience's decision was based on the advice (embodied within a written statement) of legal counsel, specifically of the local legist Deotecherio of Castrocaro, at Castrocaro in the diocese of Forlì. The rector's court in Castrocaro—in which the two proctors, the notary Giovanni di Damiano da Bologna for Maria Maddalena and Ser Tantobene da Castrocaro, substituting for Ser Bartolino di Maestro Jacopino da Imola for Sant'Agnese, heard the rector's sentence —held a various company of witnessing dignitaries including Aghinolfo de Romena, count palatine in Tuscany, Cambio, the

[182] Sant'Agnese Bologna, 7/5597, F 348.
[183] Sant'Agnese Bologna, 7/5597, F 349.
[184] Sant'Agnese Bologna, 7/5597, F 350.
[185] Sant'Agnese Bologna, 7/5597, F 344.

precentor of Ravenna, and Deoteguardo, archpriest of the *pieve* of San Damiano in the diocese of Sarsena. The heart of Deotecherio's statement of advice and of the rector's sentence was that the nuns of Maria Maddalena could not have been found contumacious legally by the archbishop's court—and they had been there condemned for their contumacy—because they were not properly cited, and that sentence could not have been pronounced against them legally because they were neither present nor contumacious.

The problem of Maria Maddalena's contumacy is explored at some length in their appeal from Ravenna to the "legate of the apostolic see in the province of Romagna and to the apostolic see itself."[186] The Maria Maddalena syndic, Fra Petrigolo, proposed the appeal before Gerardo da Cornazano, still vicar of Ottaviano, bishop of Bologna, *tanquam coram publica et honesta persona*. When Fra Petrigolo had taken his exceptions against the archbishop's court's jurisdiction to the archbishop's court, he was expelled and abused by the Dominican archbishop. The archbishop, Fra Bonifazio Fieschi, spoke roughly, "It was bad of you to come. Get out immediately, and worse luck to you, all of you. Don't dare to show up again." Fra Bonifazio's behavior still manages to suggest, as it did to Deotecherio, improper citation. Fra Petrigolo said that he really feared physical violence should he have persisted in trying to present his exceptions.

Fra Petrigolo's appeal is preserved within a document recording Fra Giacomo Martello's action of 29 October 1294. Fra Giacomo, then syndic and proctor for Sant'Agnese, on that day presented to the prior of Maria Maddalena a letter of Fra Bonifazio's (sealed with the archbishop's seal of red wax on which was sculpted his image) in which the archbishop announced to the prior, the prioress, the nuns, and the convent his denial of their allegations about his behavior, his demand that they prove the validity of their appeal within eight days, his determination, otherwise, to proceed as was just in the case. His letter was sent from Forlì on 27 October.[187]

On 24 June 1294 Fra Tiberto, as proctor of Sant'Agnese, had

delivered letters from the rector, bishop of Arezzo, to the abbots of San Felice and San Procolo, both in their cloisters (one Gratian-haunted) in Bologna. The rector, Bishop Ildebrandino, recalled from the abbots Maria Maddalena's case, which he had delegated to them; he recalled it to his own court of audience and inhibited the delegates from proceeding further, in his letters dated 17 June, from Modigliana in the diocese of Faenza.

In early 1295 the dispute between Sant'Agnese and Santa Maria Maddalena moved to a new phase. On 7 January proctors of the two convents, Fra Giacomo and Fra Tiberto for Sant'Agnese and Fra Petrigolo for Maria Maddalena, met in Bologna under the portico of the house of Albertino *quondam domini Thomasii Ughetti* and recorded their selection of arbiters to make compromise and find decision in the related disputes that had arisen out of the confusion of Adelixia's, Agnese's, and Beatrice's properties, and of the decisions emanating from the bishop's, the archbishop's, and the rector's courts. The arbiters they chose were the Dominican Fra Pagano and that Albertino, a doctor of laws, by whose house they stood. Both convents agreed to stand by the arbiters' decisions, and they had their agreement recorded in the *Libri memoriales* of the commune of Bologna.[188]

The arbitration (with its communally recorded agreement) brought at least to temporary end a case that had moved quickly through a series of vertically adjacent courts. The courts, those of bishop, metropolitan archbishop, and papal rector, had in fact proved the spokesmen of the two disputants, and they (at the law's Bolognese center) had based their decisions on adjectival technicalities. They left the decision on substance to the eventual arbiters.

In the south of Italy, in Bisignano, sixteen years earlier, on Saturday, 20 August 1278, in the morning, two papal judges delegate, the archdeacon and precentor of Bisignano, con-

[188] Sant'Agnese Bologna, 7/5597, F 352(2); Commune of Bologna, Lib. Mem., 1295, 1, "88," fo. 262v. For an interesting parallel see an appeal from the vicar of the bishop of Padua, with a request for the bishop of Adria as auditor, by the abbess of San Giacomo di Monselice: Archivio segreto vaticano, A.C.N.V., San Giacomo di Monselice, 6097.

vened their court to give interlocutory sentence in a dispute between the Cistercian abbey of Matina and the archbishop of Rossano.[189] Their decision questioned, they returned the case, appealed, to Nicholas III's curia. "We have set the term for prosecuting the appeal through the whole month of November," they wrote, "from which point your Holiness can make whatever future provisions may seem pleasing to you." They wrote a report of the case ninety-eight lines long in contemporary transcript and filled with legalistic maneuvering and citation from the two laws.[190] In returning the case the judges at least temporarily removed it from the immediate area of the rights and properties in dispute. Matina, Bisignano, and Rossano stretch across Calabria in a band, north of La Sila, between the Tyrrhenian and the Ionian seas, just south of the Gulf of Taranto. It was rough country in the thirteenth century, and Greek as well as Latin.[191] This case, in fact, recalls the adventures of Romania—with Matina Cistercians facing the Greek archbishop across the rules of the Roman church.[192]

[189] The documents for this case are among those calendared in the "Documenti non pubblicati" of Pratesi, *Carte latine*, 447-449 nos. 205, 206, 207, 210, 211, 212, 213, 214, 215, 216.

[190] Archivio segreto vaticano, Archivio Aldobrandini, documenti storici, abbadie, 4 no. 47—the composite document. The Archivio Aldobrandini has been moved back and forth between the Vatican library and the Vatican archives; if it is not in one, it should be sought in the other.

[191] For recent discussions of the Greekness of southern Italy see: Roberto Weiss, "The Greek Culture of South Italy in the Later Middle Ages," *Proceedings of the British Academy*, xxxvii (1951), 23-50; Ciro Giannelli, "L'Ultimo ellenismo nell'Italia meridionale," and Paul Goubert, "Quelques aspects de l'hellénisme en Italie méridionale au moyen-âge," both in *Atti del terzo congresso internazionale di studi sull'alto medioevo* (Spoleto, 1959), 275-298, 299-312; for continuing Greek archbishops of Rossano, to 1364, see Weiss, 30, and Goubert, 310.

[192] For the Cistercians in the East: Elisabeth A. R. Brown, "The Cistercians in the Latin Empire of Constantinople and Greece, 1204-1276," *Traditio*, xiv (1958), 63-120. For some reference to Angelo the Greek, and for mention of the Rossano family of Mezzabarba (Mediobarba, Mediabarba), see Alfredo Gradilone, *Storia di Rossano* (Rome, 1926), 302-303, 594. For both Archbishop Angelo and Paolo Mezzabarba, see M.-H. Laurent, "Contributo alla storia dei vescovi del regno di Sicilia (1274-1280)," *Rivista di storia della chiesa in Italia*, ii (1948), 371-381, 378; and for Goffredo, bishop of Bisignano, *ibid.*, 373-374.

The case, in its recorded phase, had been initiated by a May 1278 mandate of Nicholas III (which included a conventional clause restricting appeal). The mandate, addressed to the bishop, archdeacon, and precentor of Bisignano, ordered them to act as papal judges delegate in the dispute. The mandate had been provoked by an appeal from the abbot and convent of Matina, who complained that the archbishop of Rossano (Angelo the Greek) had descended upon Matina granges, San Pietro and others, within the diocese of Rossano. The archbishop had, they said, raided the granges and occupied them with force of arms and taken away animals and grain to the injury of the monastery. The panel of judges was narrowed to two by the withdrawal of the bishop of Bisignano, who, according to the archdeacon and the precentor, delegated his powers in the case, even to sentencing, to them.

The two judges cited the parties to appear, themselves or through proctors, before them; and they set the term through twenty-five days (from Thursday, 14 July) to early August, to Monday, the eighth. On that day there appeared before them a representative of the archbishop, his clerk, P. (Paolo) Mezzabarba (Mediabarba), the *primicerius* of Rossano (and almost certainly the archbishop's own successor). Mezzabarba brought a letter (in which the papal judges' names preceded the archbishop's) in which the archbishop excused himself from appearing. The archbishop could not appear within the set term, he said, because he was sick, suffering severely with double tertian fever. He did not, however, want the case to proceed when he was not personally present because it was a difficult case and it involved a significant segment of the fruits of the church of Rossano. For this reason Mezzabarba had been sent not as a proctor who might plead the archbishop's defense, but only as a bearer of letters, the letter excusatory and also the written testimony to the incapacitating gravity of the archbishop's illness. But Mezzabarba did come with sufficient powers to make appeal to the apostolic see and to seek letters dimissory should that be necessary.

The testimony to the archbishop's illness (dated the previous day, 7 August) was the result of the collaboration of a royal judge of Rossano (G. da Nicastro), two notaries (Leocefalo da Rossano and J. da Bisignano), and a physician (Master A. da Scala—by Amalfi, near Salerno). The archbishop had been observed lying in bed in his chamber as he had lain for five days, certainly too ill to take himself to Bisignano without grave danger. Because of this, Mezzabarba sought an extension of the term for the archbishop.

The judges, that they might consider the archbishop's request, postponed decision in their court until the following day, Tuesday, 9 August. On that day Mezzabarba appeared with other archiepiscopal letters. These letters made Mezzabarba proctor sufficient to offer exceptions in the case, which he did. His exceptions showed the results of investigations into the judges' connections and, through elaborate citation, into the pertinent regulations of the two laws. It was perilous, according to the Rossano exceptions, to permit a case to be tried before suspect judges. The Bisignano judges were suspect, it was claimed in the exceptions, because of their connections with Matina. Mezzabarba said that the precentor of Bisignano was the friend and familiar of the abbot of Matina, that the precentor had many gifts from the convent, and that he was bound to help it. Mezzabarba said that G., the advocate of the Matina party, was the precentor's blood-kin, the son of his brother. He cited legal texts which he felt should make it clear that these allegations, if true, invalidated the precentor's delegation. Mezzabarba asked that the delegation be revoked and that the matter of the revocation be decided not by the delegates themselves but by special arbiters, as the (cited) law specified. He proposed the bishop of Cerenzia, to the south of Rossano, as the archbishop's arbiter.

The Matina party said that the Rossano exceptions should not be entertained because they were proposed only after the term had elapsed. Moreover, their case was strengthened and the Rossano case weakened, on the same day, through the testimony of the Rossano judge, G. da Nicastro. The judge was sworn in and questioned before the delegates concerning the instrument validating and describing the archbishop's illness. The judge confessed that he was not actually present to take the physician's sworn testimony, but rather that he had commissioned a notary to take it.

In order that they might deliberate further, the delegates postponed decision until Thursday, 18 August, for which day both parties were cited. The proctor of the archbishop then made exception to the contention that the judicial term for the archbishop's appearance had closed on 8 August; he objected to the court's way of numbering the days of the term. He repeated an objection to a suspect letter with erasure and difficult script and ink. Mezzabarba said, too, that if, and the erasure raised doubt, the Rossano proctor in the Roman curia had in fact chosen the archdeacon of Bisignano to be the Rossano judge delegate, he had exceeded his powers. The Matina proctor (Brother P.) insisted again upon the Rossano side's contumacy, upon their only having appeared before the court out of term. Both sides cited specific legal texts to support their positions. The judges delegate summoned both sides to appear again on the Saturday following, 20 August, in the morning at the hour of terce, to hear interlocutory sentence.

It seemed to the delegates, on 20 August, that the Rossano exceptions were not valid and that the Rossano judge, the archdeacon, had been properly chosen at the Roman curia. Mezzabarba immediately appealed to Rome and sought letters dimissory. The appeal did not seem compelling to the delegates, but they returned the appeal to the pope and set the term through November.

To the report of the case at Bisignano are appended two letters issued by Giacomo, canon of Bologna and auditor of contradictory letters. The first of the auditor's letters, dated Saint Peter's, Rome, 15 May 1278, is in the form of the *littere* (or *littera*) *conveniencie*. The letter tells which proctors chose which judges in the *audientia*. The abbot of Matina chose the precentor of Bisignano. The archbishop of Rossano's proctor (L. de ?Grava, Guerra, Guā), chose the archdeacon of Bisignano. The bishop of Bisignano was the common, third judge, granted by the auditor. The second letter from the auditor, dated Saint Peter's, 14 May 1278, is an *inspeximus* enclosing a letter from Giacomo's predecessor, G., master of the schools of Parma and auditor of contradictory letters; the enclosed letter is dated Viterbo, 4 November 1276. Giacomo said that he had examined the earlier letter, from the papacy of John XXI, in

which his predecessor declared that in his presence the archbishop of Rossano (Angelo) had made the clerk L. his proctor
in the curia for impetrating letters and for electing and revok-
ing judges.

In fact, the struggle between Rossano (archbishop and chapter) and Matina over the grange of San Pietro de Guidel-
magno was still being pursued in 1314. In that year there was
an effort to implement an arbitration made by Roberto, archdeacon of Cassano all'Ionio, and Andrea da Cervicati, precentor of San Marco Argentano (the two dioceses to the north
and west of Rossano and Bisignano—Cervicati, like Matina,
was locally within San Marco, and they were close to each
other). The arbitration which seems to have been strongly
backed by the local secular establishment—Roger of Sanginero,
Elizabeth of Cantanzaro—gave the grange to Matina and im-
posed silence upon Rossano.[193]

The Rossano-Matina case is a good example of the sort of
dalliance that was carried on between a partisan court and the
party to which it was not partisan. The case has particular flair
because of the archbishop's directing his party's movements
from his improperly validated sickbed, in a stew, one is led to
believe, of malaria and law books. In the Rossano-Matina case
the selection of legal texts by both sides (but particularly by
the Rossano, side, which needed the law more because it did
not have the court) is impressively specific in citation, extensive, and various.[194] At some points, from Rossano, the citation

---

[193] Archivio segreto vaticano, Archivio Aldobrandini, documenti
storici, abbadie, 4 no. 83; there is a Greek signatory.

[194] The Rossano party cited first: C., III, 1,18; C., III, 1,16; c. 41, X,
ii,28; c. 61, X,ii,28; c. 39, X,i,29; c. 2, VI,ii,15 (i.e., Innocent IV, Lyons,
canon 11: Hefele-Leclercq, v:2, 1646-1647); then next: c. 25, X,i,29; c.
2, X,ii,6; c. 50, X,ii,28; then: D. L,16,223; and, again, c. 50, X,ii,28; then:
c. 1, VI,ii,12 (i.e., Innocent IV, Lyons, extra-canons, no. 5: Hefele-
Leclercq, v:2, 1665-1666); D. II,11,1; D. IV,8,23; c. 24, X,i,29; finally: c.
4, X,ii,25. The Matina party cited: c. 4, X,ii,25; then: c. 51, X,ii,20; c.
39, X,ii,20; then: C 29, C II, q.6, arguing to this (?)c. 9, X,iv,1; then:
c. 7, X,ii,12; finally: cc. 1, 2, X,ii,15. (I should like to thank Professor
Gerard Caspary for having helped me to identify several of these citations, and also for discussing some of the problems of the case with
me.) For Innocent IV on c. 4, X,ii,25, see *Commentaria* (Venice, 1578),
fos. 120-120v. For Hostiensis on *de exceptionibus*, see *Summa Aurea*

(as of c. 50, X, ii, 28) is also impressively apt. This all may be due in part to the availability to the Rossano side of some compilation like the *de exceptionibus* section of Hostiensis's *Summa Aurea* (although memory, wit, and the *glossa ordinaria* might produce much the same effect). The Rossano side used Codex, Digest, Decretals, and post-Decretal Innocent IV decretals. The Matina side used Decretum and Decretals. One decretal (c. 4, X, ii, 25: *Pastoralis* from *de exceptionibus*) was used by both sides against both sides. This specific decretal as it is elucidated by Innocent IV, an authoritative commentator, seems reasonably susceptible to complicated interpretation; but canon law at its best was not neatly conclusive. Presumably it was not meant to be; had it been it would certainly have wrecked the working judicial system.

The Rossano-Matina case was given an interesting turn by the questioning of the powers of the Rossano proctor in the *audientia*; judicial administrative mechanism, and particularly the selection of judges, is exposed as much as is the mind of the law. In the Rossano-Matina case, too, the alternatives, but not at all necessarily mutually exclusive alternatives, of appeal and arbitration were both suggested; but only the appeal was, initially, implemented. Final arbitration (if in fact it was final) fell, much later, to arbiters encouraged by local secular powers. The whole (visible) complicated legal action of the Rossano-Matina case took place within a noticeably close neighborhood, and one poor enough so that a single grange could be of real significance. The Rossano-Matina case was, also, a case of Latin against Greek.

The intermingling of Greek and Latin in the Calabrian

(Lyons, 1568), fos. 160v-163v. Writing to *pia consideratione* (c. 1, VI,ii,12) a quarter of a century after the Rossano-Matina case, Joannes Andreae said in his *glossa ordinaria* to the Sext: *Haec est notabilis decretalis et quotidie practicabilis: Liber Sextus* (Rome, 1584), 245. The aptness of c. 50, X,ii,28, which I have in mind, has to do with the similarity between the suspect advocate in the decretal and the suspect advocate in the case; but of course it is possible that the decretal gave the Rossano party the idea for their accusation—the accusation did not have to be substantiated, at least in the part of the case that survives in the document.

church is effectively and visually recorded in the preserved sentence of another bench of delegates who acted in January 1279 at Santa Severina, the city of the Sibarite see stretching south from Cerenzia to the Gulf of Squillace.[195] The plaintiffs were two laymen, brothers, of whom one acted as the other's proctor. They claimed a piece of land that was held by the Cistercian abbot and convent of Sant'Angelo di Frigillo within the diocese of Santa Severina. The disputed land was adjoined by some land of the church of Matina held by Sant'Angelo and near a Sant'Angelo grange. The action was brought under a mandate of Nicholas III dated from Saint Peter's, Rome, on 1 June 1278. It was a mandate of the common form *super terris, debitis, possessionibus, et rebus aliis*.[196] The proctor plaintiff brought the papal letters to the judges designate, Nicolò, archpriest, Basilio, treasurer, and Stefano Pullello, canon of the church of Santa Severina. A copy of the rescript was given to "Frater Petrus, monacus, yconomus, sindicus, procurator, seu actor" of the monastery, a proctor with powers to reply in the case.

On 21 November 1278 the plaintiff offered his *libellus*. The proctor of the monastery admitted that the monastery did hold the land, but he pleaded that he did not know further circumstances. Given a set day to produce his exceptions, he was able to produce witnesses and evidence sufficient to satisfy the court that the monastery had held the lands through thirty and forty years and longer. The plaintiff failed to establish his rightful tenure. On Tuesday, 10 January 1279, sentence was given and the monastery and its proctor were pronounced finally absolved. From this sentence the plaintiff appealed to the pope, and the bench of delegates offered him letters dimissory. They set the term of the plaintiff's appeal through the next thirty days. But at this point the case was halted through intervention of "common friends" who helped the parties to a compromise. The monastery agreed to help pay for the travel and expenses of the plaintiffs with a bull, a cow, a hog, and other

[195] Archivio segreto vaticano, Archivio Aldobrandini, documenti storici, abbadie, 4 no. 55. I should like to thank Monsignor P. Canart for helping me with the Greek script of this document.

[196] With conventional clause restricting appeal.

things; and the plaintiffs renounced all their rights and claims, all actions and appeals, and they promised that they would never bring the monastery to court over these things again— all under penalty of twenty-five *once* of gold.

To ensure the memory of all this, a public instrument was drawn up and signed by many witnesses. The signatories form an interesting group. They include: Nicolò Marri, royal judge of Santa Severina, who was statedly ignorant of letters, but who affixed his wobbly holograph cross; the plaintiff; a man called Richard of Jerusalem and another called Pietro of Policastro; a canon of Santa Severina; the precentor of Strongoli, Santa Severina's small neighboring diocese to the northeast. These men, and three others, are subscribed in Latin. But there are also four Greek subscriptions; and of these, three are the subscriptions of the judges delegate themselves. One sees, then, as one looks at the witness list of this document two uneven columns of subscription, mixed Greek and Latin, but in which three judges of the Roman pontiff sign in Greek, in spite of the facts that the plaintiff's subscription is in Latin and that the defendant was a house of Cistercian monks.

Arbitration was regular, but of course it was not always successful. Arbiters' courts, like delegates' courts, could be, or be considered, partisan. In November 1296, in his chamber in the hospice of the monastery of San Pietro ad Aram in Naples, where according to legend Saint Peter had converted Saints Candida and Aspreno (Naples' first bishop), the legate, Landulfo cardinal deacon of Sant'Angelo, sat as an arbiter in a dispute from the diocese of Benevento.[197] As he acted, Landulfo was surrounded by ecclesiastical dignitaries: Fra Azone, the bishop of Caserta; Bartolomeo, bishop of Vico Equense; Tizio, archpriest of Calvi (?Calle, Celle) and papal chaplain; Masters Alessandro da Castroveteri, canon of Capua, and Cristoforo, canon of Benevento; Master Gualterio Cutzinello, the physician; and the notary Hugolino. In the cardinal legate's presence stood Jaquinto, abbot of the great Benedictine monastery of Santa Sophia in Benevento and a party to the dispute in

[197] Archivio segreto vaticano, Archivio Aldobrandini, documenti storici, abbadie, 4 no. 69.

question. The dispute had arisen between Santa Sophia and Amerigo the younger, son of Amerigo de Sus, and Amerigo the younger's wife, over certain territories or their boundaries, in the diocese of Benevento, of which one tenement was held of the monastery of Santa Sophia, and the other of the Benedictine monastery of Monteverde in the diocese of Boiano.

The dispute had reached the Sicilian royal curia, and King Charles had ordered his officials to make an inquisition over the boundaries of the tenements. The official determinations of the inquisition had been embodied in a notarial instrument made by a Boiano notary. But, as Landulfo's instrument complained, the determination did not cause the discord to cease or even diminish. Instead, provoked, the discord grew. So the abbot for his monastery and Amerigo for his son and daughter-in-law asked the cardinal to act as arbiter in the case and help them to arrive at some amicable composition to which they both would hold. The abbot of Monteverde, who was present, approved.

The cardinal ordered local investigation and inquisition. The pertinent testimony was returned to him under the seals of his inquisitors. He showed it to the proctors of both parties. He then cited them both to appear to hear his award. He said that he had examined evidence and privileges, and consulted the learned in the law, and that he had come to the conclusion that the division and determination recently made by the royal officials should be put into effect. But Saint Peter's success at San Pietro had been greater. Although the abbot of Santa Sophia was present to hear the award, no one was present for the family of Amerigo de Sus. Since they had been properly cited, they were contumacious. The cardinal ordered the notary Giovanni da Cosenza to draw up the recording instrument, and he had his seal appended to it.

East of Naples, north of Rossano and Bisignano, at Bari on the Adriatic, the thirteenth-century archbishops ruled over a diocese rich in interest for us and in difficulties for them. The archbishops had significant disputes with three of the religious corporations within their diocese in the thirteenth century. They fought with the Benedictine monastery of Ognissanti in the suburb of Cuti, with the cathedral chapter, and most seriously and exhaustingly with the great cult center and secular chapter of San Nicola. The archbishops attempted to repress the swelling pretensions of independencies. They also tried, and under considerable political disadvantage, to catch potential rebels more securely within the net of their jurisdiction. In 1255, for example, Enrico, bishop elect of Bari, had Bartolomeo, archdeacon of Salpi, extract from the archpriest of Cerignola and ten members of his chapter an oath of obedience to the archbishop.[198] The Cerignola group thus tied their diocese of Canosa anew to the archbishop, its bishop, and they did it in the presence of the bishop elect of Minervino.

In Rome, in April 1234, Stefano, cardinal priest of Santa Maria in Trastevere, caused to be written and sealed with his seal a report of what had happened so far in his hearing of the case between Ognissanti and Marino, archbishop of Bari.[199] The cardinal had the record made, he said, so that if the hearing were interrupted nothing should be forgotten. The cardinal auditor's hearing had grown out of an appeal from Ognissanti. Ognissanti had, at last, found intolerable an earlier arbiters' compromise. That compromise had temporarily ended a dispute over whether Ognissanti was an exempt house or whether it was bound to pay the archbishop tithes and a fourth of its mortuary fees. According to Grifo, Ognissanti's prior and its proctor in Rome in 1234, the archbishop had brought the Benedictines to trial on a writ of common form, *super obedientia et reverentia*; and then, in a way that Ognissanti's *libellus* made to sound legally dubious, the archbishop had managed to get the delegates, the archbishop of Trani and the bishop of Giovinazzo, converted to a board of arbiters, and he had extracted from them an interested award. The award was a compromise according to which Ognissanti was to pay five *once* of gold a year instead of tithes and mortuaries. According to Grifo the monastery had paid its five *once* for five years.[200] This money, with the monastery's various expenses, like sending proctors to Rome, keeping them there, and bringing them

---

[198] *C.d.b.*, I, 194-195 no. 104.

[199] *C.d.b.*, I, 177-182 no. 96.

[200] *C.d.b.*, VI, 92 no. 58 makes the *oncia* equivalent to 47 *soldi*, prov. sen., in 1232.

home, which Grifo estimated at 100 *once*, added up to 125 *once* (and the contrast between the two parts of the sum is startling). Grifo asked the cardinal auditor to force the archbishop of Bari to repay the convent 125 *once*. Grifo also asked the cardinal to confirm the convent's independence.

The opposed positions of the Ognissanti and Bari proctors—the latter, Rainaldo, a monk of San Benedetto, Bari—expose the earlier action more clearly. Rainaldo sought the confirmation of the earlier arbitration and also asked for the 100-*once* penalty that had been set against either party if it broke the compromise agreement (and one notes the repetition of the conventional sum). He stated the recurring initial position in cases of this sort, that the convent was in the diocese; and Grifo responded equally conventionally that the convent was in it, but not of it, "in diocesi sed non de diocesi." Grifo admitted, at this point, that the earlier arbiters had been chosen by both sides, but he insisted that they were chosen not only for determining whether or not the tithes and mortuaries were owed, but also "super obedientia et reverentia et subjectione monasterii." He refused to permit himself to believe the business of the 100-*once* penalty. Rainaldo put it that the *libellus* before the arbiters had demanded tithes and the archbishop's portion of mortuaries from the possessions of the monastery within the diocese, and particularly those possessions acquired since the "second" Lateran Council.[201] The *libellus* had sought tithes and mortuaries for the fifteen previous years, and these were estimated at ninety-five *once*. The abbot of Ognissanti had replied to this earlier *libellus* saying that these things were not, he believed, of right demanded of his convent. For the sake of peace, Rainaldo contended, both sides had accepted a compromise. Grifo admitted that he thought compromise had been made but that the abbot and convent had not subscribed the instrument which embodied it.

At this point, unfortunately, the dialogue between Grifo and Rainaldo ends, and Stefano's decision does not appear. Fortunately, the earlier arbiters' award, dated 23 August 1228, is appended to the 1234 report. In it prelates Giacomo of Trani and

[201] The Council of 1123, perhaps; see Boyd, *Tithes and Parishes*, 126 n. 68.

Palmerio of Giovinazzo, having taken the counsel of Artusio, bishop of Canne, and Masters Goffrido and Ruggero, canons of Trani, state their compromise and have it redacted by Filippo the notary, in the presence of Bartolomeo, archdeacon of Trani, Pintulo, canon of Trani, abbot Malconsiglio and Lazzariccio, canons of Bari and of Grifo, then called monk and priest of Ognissanti. Ognissanti is to pay its five *once* yearly in three terms, on the feasts of the Assumption, Christmas, and Easter. The archbishop is enjoined to silence. The archbishop of Trani and the two bishops subscribe their names.

Although the cardinal auditor's action, except for its recording, becomes mute in March 1234, a record remains of Ognissanti's November activity in the south.[202] In Foggia on 18 November a local judge authorized a local notary to write an authentic copy of five Ognissanti privileges, two archiepiscopal and three papal ones, one from the late eleventh and the others from the first half of the twelfth century. The papal privileges confirmed the archbishops' earlier grants of exemption. The notarization took place, it says, because the abbot of Ognissanti wanted to send the privileges to his proctor in Rome. "Because the time was winter and the place was distant," there was "threat of uncountable accidents." The copies were made "lest through these accidents the documents be lost, and through their loss the liberties of the monastery be lost." It was, in a way, a convenient winter's distance for the abbot, because his first two, and crucial, privileges are forgeries.

Whatever the outcome between Cuti and the archbishops of Bari, a residue of potent ill feeling evidently remained as late as 1274. In that year the abbey brought a complaint before the papal curia.[203] In a dispute over a debt, the abbey complained, the Romans Bonifazio di Paolo di Bonifazio and Constanzia the widow of Pietro Rigi had gotten, to the abbey's prejudice, a common form writ issued to the Archbishop of Bari as sole judge delegate. In order that the case might proceed without prejudice, if it had not yet actually reached the *litis contestatio*, the *audientia* added two other judges. One was Giacomo, canon of San Nicola Bari, selected at the instance of Ognissanti (a

[202] *C.d.b.*, VI, 97-98 no. 62.
[203] *C.d.b.*, XIII, 37 no. 21.

connection to be noted), and the other the bishop of Bitonto, given as the third judge by the *audientia*.

The recurring animosity between the archbishops of Bari and the collegiate church of San Nicola was an enlivening thread of thirteenth-century Bari history.[204] San Nicola's strength was based directly and indirectly upon its holding the body of its great saint. The relic had been culled from the east at the end of the eleventh century—an event so brilliant in hagiographic history that the transporting sailors were still remembered in the tenement and privilege their descendants held in thirteenth-century Bari.[205] In the thirteenth century San Nicola still attracted devotion and the riches that devotion brings. A man like Giovanni, notary of Trani, not only named his son Nicola but in 1235 also made offering to the canons of San Nicola that the office for the dead would be said and the bells rung at San Nicola on the anniversary of his Nicola's death.[206] In 1262 a canon of San Nicola named Agralisto could look back upon a lifetime spent, since boyhood, in the service of the church; he could testify to its prescriptive privileges.[207] The church was a splendid but, for the archbishops, difficult, physical part of the diocese.

The church also had internal difficulties, disputes for its stalls. In 1207 at Trani, Bartolomeo archbishop of Trani, acting as a papal judge delegate, heard a case between San Nicola, represented by Biandemiro, its prior, and Stefano de Consilio, priest of Ognissanti Trani, over Stefano's place and stall in San Nicola. The participants were surrounded by the clerical establishment of Trani, the archdeacon (named Peter Abelard), the *primicerius*, and other clerks.[208] Sixty years later, Master Giovanni da Cortona, archdeacon of Messina, as auditor general of the legate cardinal bishop of Albano, heard the case of the clerk, Melitiacca Peregrini, who had been, he claimed, violently ejected from his stall in San Nicola and who

---

[204] For a recent introduction to the cult of Saint Nicholas see Charles W. Jones, *The Saint Nicholas Liturgy*, University of California English Studies, 27 (Berkeley, 1963), 1-6, or Virginia Wylie Egbert, "St. Nicholas: the Fasting Child," *Art Bulletin*, XLVI (1964), 69-70.

[205] *C.d.b.*, VI, 34-35 no. 20.   [206] *C.d.b.*, VI, 99 no. 63.

[207] *C.d.b.*, VI, 168 in no. 105.   [208] *C.d.b.*, VI, 35-36 no. 21.

had appealed to the pope.[209] Obviously the richness of the shrine church and its relative security tempted those men who were stirred to recurring hopes of advancement, stirred perhaps too by the same vacillations in the Guelf-Ghibelline struggle that seem to have adjusted the sometimes opposing fortunes of the two great churches of Bari, San Nicola and the Duomo.[210]

From the continuing debate between the archbishops and San Nicola (which kept proctors moving through the south and, like Nicola di Manuele, borrowing at Rome), record of incidents of particular interest survives.[211] The braid of dispute was complicated by the strand of Guelf against Ghibelline and of Prior Biandemiro, rejected aspirant, against Marino Filangieri, successful nominee (nominated by the pope, but pleasing also to the emperor) to the archbishopric in 1227. From this braid the record picks out illuminating procedural detail.[212]

In October 1234 Nicola de Sifando, clerk and proctor of San Nicola, was active in Benevento. He was there trying to persuade Pietro, the timorous *primicerius* of Benevento, one of three papal judges delegate in a case between San Nicola and Marino, archbishop of Bari, to come to Bari. He acted before a number of Beneventans, including a notary and a judge, and the *primicerius*'s two co-delegates, Fra Pelegrino of the house of Hermits in Eboli and Giovanni di Franco, canon of Capua. The proctor asked that, since he would give Pietro his expenses for coming to Bari, as he would Fra Pelegrino, Pietro should come to Bari with his co-judges to hear the case. Pietro replied that he was ready to come to Bari if he could have a safe conduct from the emperor or his justiciar, because the emperor had recently put Benevento under interdict and Pietro feared for both his person and his goods. He said he really was afraid to come without safe conduct, but that he did not intend to disobey the injunction of the papal mandate to go to Bari if he could go with safe conduct. The proctor told

[209] *C.d.b.*, XIII, 14-15 no. 6.
[210] *C.d.b.*, VI, 118.
[211] *C.d.b.*, VI, 87-88, 91-94 nos. 56, 58, 59.
[212] See *C.d.b.*, VI, 118-119.

Pietro that he offered him safe conduct under bond of 100 *once* from the church of San Nicola and that was surely safety enough. But Pietro replied that that was no safety at all. The proctor offered to go to the imperial court and ask for a safe conduct for Pietro. He asked the two co-judges to wait for Pietro until he, the proctor, should return from court, since there was plenty of time remaining during which the papal commission would be valid. The judges refused. The proctor appealed to the pope in case the two judges should proceed, the third being absent, since the hesitant Pietro was the judge that San Nicola's proctor at Rome had gotten for their side.[213]

Late in 1241 the continual dispute between San Nicola and the archbishop burst into a flurry of physical activity. Rainerio, the cardinal deacon of Santa Maria in Cosmedin, had commissioned, as auditors for the reception of witnesses in a phase of the dispute, Bartolomeo, abbot of Santo Stefano of Monopoli, the archdeacon of Benevento, and Matteo de Duce; and for Matteo de Duce the archdeacon of Capua was then substituted. The abbot of Santo Stefano, who was staying in and around Bari, took the initiative in organizing the arrangements for the process and wrote accounts of its difficulties back to the cardinal. With the consent of the canons of San Nicola, he said, term for their production of witnesses before the auditors, who would come to Bari, was set from the Feast of Saint Andrew (30 November) until Christmas.

The archdeacon of Benevento arrived in Bari on Friday evening, the night before Saint Andrew's Day; and two clerks (one of the archdeacon's and one of San Nicola's) were sent off to tell the abbot, who was in a place of his obedience, San Giorgio "de loco rotundo." Immediately, on Saturday night, the abbot rushed off to Bari. On Tuesday the abbot received the letters from the cardinal and the archdeacon of Capua about his, the archdeacon's, substitution for Matteo de Duce. On Wednesday the abbot came to look for the archdeacon of Benevento, but he could not find him. Neither archdeacon was present.

The abbot waited for the archdeacon of Capua, who arrived

[213] *C.d.b.*, VI, 96-97 no. 61; for an example of an action actually affected by lapse of time, see Harvey, *Walter de Wenlok*, 166n.

on Friday, the feast of Saint Nicholas (6 December) at the hour of Mass. On the same day at vespers the abbot and archdeacon sent the judge Guglielmo and the notary Leone to San Nicola to cite the canons of San Nicola to present witnesses the following day at the hour of Mass at the monastery of San Benedetto. But when the summoners arrived at San Nicola, the canons, fearing to hear their citation, fled before their coming, slipping away to hide and gather in groups in the corners of the church, like fish swimming, frightened, in some elaborate fishbowl (see Fig. 8).[214]

The following day at prime the abbot and archdeacon met at San Benedetto to await the canons; and summoners were again sent to cite the canons. When the summoners got to San Nicola the canons saw them and immediately fled—except for the prior, Biandemiro, who did not have the use of his legs and could not get away. The summoners cited the prior and told him to tell the canons that the abbot and archdeacon awaited them at San Benedetto and were prepared to receive their witnesses according to the cardinal's mandate. From the prior the summoners received this answer, that the prior was infirm—to which his being caught (as well as his death the following year) lends credence—and that he did not wish to come, and that the other canons were not present. The auditors also sent to Angelo the so-called proctor of San Nicola, but he said that he was infirm, that he renounced his commission, gave it back to the canons, and wanted to have nothing more to do with the case. The auditors, convinced of San Nicola's malice, sent the summoners to San Nicola again. This time the canons were at Mass, so they could not flee and had to listen.[215] But they said that they wished to make no re-

---

[214] C.d.b., vi, 123-126 no. 80A; the editor dates the event and document "verso il 1250," but the correspondence of day and date, and the fact that Biandemiro was alive, but incapacitated, make the date, almost surely, 1241; by August 1242 Biandemiro had been succeeded as prior by Salvo: C.d.b., vi, 110-112 no. 74.

[215] Mass seems to have been a clever time to deliver summonses: see the case of Prior Claxton of Durham, caught as he was vested for the high Mass on Saint Cuthbert's Day, at the hour of terce, 20 March 1281; he was given a mandate from his metropolitan archbishop: Brentano, York Metropolitan Jurisdiction, 117.

ply, that the summoners should go to the prior, and that his response should be the response of all. The summoners found the prior lying in bed. He said, "We will not come to the auditors' presence or send anyone, because we have appealed from them and sent our messenger off to the lord pope, because the two auditors cannot proceed, the third having retired."[216] ("—Meaning to say, he did not choose / to leave the oyster-bed.")

Of one of the letters to Rainerio from his auditors, presumably that returning their commission, only a lacework of phrases survives. Some of the phrases are very nice ones: they include the most graphic description of the canons' flight— "fugientes accessum," "veluti timentes aliquid audire mandatum diversosque se colligantes in omnes per angulos ecclesie." But the more formal phrases, bare and scattered, are as revealing as narrative. They suggest a conventional pattern of subterfuge and frustration heightened by the curious track-and-field quality of the Bari case; "labors without profit"; "a colleague being absent"; "deceit"; "and on the following day he (or it) was not found"; "under his seal"; "more fully to you"; things of that sort—visually expressing the nature of delegate justice. A final conventional sentence is fully preserved: "May your eyes see justice (equitatem)."[217]

The canons of San Nicola were able to see, or at least to write of, the whole encounter very differently from the auditors.[218] The great saint (for in their document their church is their saint, strongly personified) is vexed by unnecessary and inexcusable expenses and annoyances. The auditors had complained that San Nicola was unwilling to pay their expenses for their stay in Bari; San Nicola complains that the archbishop will not pay his share of the expenses. The auditors had mentioned a slight extension in term sought by the archbishop; San Nicola (in a legal mood different from that in which it fled the summoners) complained of the difficulty of delay in a case in which their witnesses had from day to day to go out and sail the seas, and in which frail ancient witnesses to old

[216] *C.d.b.*, vi, 125-126, 123-125 in no. 80A.
[217] *C.d.b.*, vi, 126.
[218] *C.d.b.*, vi, 126-128 no. 80B.

prescription might die at any time. San Nicola particularly objected to the way in which the archbishop demanded that they produce their privileges; the saint had two great defenses, they said, privilege and prescription. Delaying the case by prescription was dangerous to the saint.

San Nicola's century of trials, inquisitions, and constant acquisitions ended well. In 1300 Romoaldo, archbishop of Bari, that he might not, without charity, be a tinkling cymbal, his "chancery" said, solemnly confirmed San Nicola's immunity.[219] San Nicola had returned to a position as favorable as that it had held in 1218 when Archbishop Andrea had promised to seek nothing from pope or king against its immunity. Andrea had made his promise (if the document is in fact authentic, and truthful) out of his devotion to Saint Nicholas, and the clerks of San Nicola, and, significantly, the king.[220]

In 1270 the archbishop of Bari and his cathedral church had settled their dispute, buried it in compromise. One of the terminating documents, embellished with thirty-five subscriptions in all, was subscribed by twenty-six clerks and canons of the cathedral chapter, a majority, presumably, of that body.[221] The Duomo dispute has left fewer known rewarding documents than the other two major Bari archiepiscopal disputes, but it has its own peculiar taste. It was a dispute over the division between archbishop and chapter of the church's newly restored properties—after the Angevin-papal government had thrown the meat into the cage.

In the Bari cases there is a continued suggestion of alliances between Cuti and San Nicola and less surely between San Benedetto, Santo Stefano Monopoli, and the archiepiscopal see.[222] The Bari cases seem to have been closely involved with the specific personalities and connections of Prior Biandemiro

[219] *C.d.b.*, XIII, 138-139 no. 89.

[220] *C.d.b.*, VI, 57-58 no. 35.

[221] *C.d.b.*, II, 34-39 nos. 16-17 (the subscriptions are in no. 16).

[222] See, e.g., *C.d.b.*, VI, 155 no. 97: Santo Stefano opposed to Cuti in 1257 and the case given over to Guglielmino, canon of San Nicolà, "propter malitiam temporis"; for the possible connection through Grifo, see *C.d.b.*, VI, 66-68 no. 42.

(from his capture by Germans in 1201 until his death in 1242) and Archbishop Marino Filangieri.[223] The cases were certainly involved with the political and geographical-commercial peculiarities of thirteenth-century Bari, with local customs and local animosities. This local attachment and shaping by particular circumstance was, of course, true of every set of ecclesiastical cases. Each is only really understandable in its local context. It has local roots buried deeply and tangled around in the particular circumstances from which it grew. But each also contains some of the common elements which come to seem characteristic of Italian cases as one examines large numbers of them from various parts of the peninsula. At Bari one notices particularly the way in which the parties to disputes organize and pay their judges. The mechanism becomes visible as in bad times it fails to work properly, as a Bari proctor finds that the judges he tries to manage are a reluctant and clownish road company. The Bari cases also repeatedly explore the use of the third and dissident judge, of delay, appeal, and the partisan court. They show the use of preserved documents.

Much more concisely a Tuscan case from the 1280's shows the value to both sides of one side's contumacy: one gets a favorable sentence; the other gets rid of an unfavorable court. Both thus prepare for arbitration. In 1287 and 1288 the Benedictine Badia in Florence and the men of Signa (between Florence and Empoli) were involved in a dispute over tithes owed to the Badia's hospice. Records of the Badia-Signa case, reporting acts in the Duomo at Florence and in the cloisters of the Badia, and including two pieces of *processus*, survive in the very neatly notarized instruments of the imperial notary, Gianni di Piero.[224] A mandate of Honorius IV, dated from Santa Sabina on 31 January 1286, delegated the hearing of the case to Ruggero, *plebanus* of the *pieve* of Sant'Andrea of

[223] See *C.d.b.*, VI, 24-25 no. 12; prior by March 1207: *C.d.b.*, VI, 34-35 no. 20; perhaps by September 1206: *C.d.b.*, VI, 31-33 no. 19.

[224] Florence, Archivio di stato, conventi soppressi, Badia di Firenze, "15 Apr. 1287," 2 instruments, actually dating through 16 August 1286 and 16 May 1287. I have tried to describe the relation between the *processus* and other documents produced by delegates' courts in *York Metropolitan Jurisdiction*, 239.

Empoli. By 1 April 1286 Ruggero had convened his court in the Duomo at Florence, and the opposing proctors, Martino, hospitaller of the Badia's hospice, and Ridolfo, syndic for Signa, were before him. By 16 August 1286 Martino was accusing the Signa party of contumacy and asking Ruggero to excommunicate them and to order them to pay Badia expenses.

Ruggero's court was again active on 15, 23, 24, 26, and 28 April and 2 and 16 May 1287. During most of this time both parties were represented: the Badia by Martino and Signa by the notary Cione Uberti. By 26 April Ruggero was citing Cione peremptorily to appear between none and vespers on the following Friday with three florins for his counsel and, with his counselors, to proceed to the allegations. On 2 May Martino accused the opposing party of contumacy. On 16 May both Martino and Cione were summoned before terce on the morrow for sentencing. On 17 May, sitting as a tribunal in the Duomo, Ruggero gave sentence. His award appeared to Signa too much to favor the Badia, so the men of Signa appealed to the Roman curia.[225] But in process of the Signa appeal both sides agreed to accept a friendly arbiter; and Rainerio Ghiberti, canon of Florence and papal chaplain, was chosen for this purpose. The period of arbitration was set between 13 September 1288 and 1 January 1289. A compromise award was granted, in Rainerio's lodgings at the Duomo, on 31 December 1288—over ten months after the consecration of Nicholas IV, the successor to Honorius IV, the pope whose mandate had initiated the delegated judicial act, but less than three years from the date of Honorius's mandate.[226]

In the episcopal palace at Ravello on Monday, 30 October 1290, Tolomeo, bishop of Ravello, sat as judge and pronounced sentence in a case about olive oil.[227] His sentence was written

[225] Florence, Archivio de stato, conventi soppressi, Badia di Firenze, 17 Mag. 1287.

[226] Florence, Archivio di stato, conventi soppressi, Badia di Firenze, 13 Sett. 1288.

[227] Carucci, *Salerno dal 1282 al 1300*, 95-107 no. 79; Luigi Enrico Pennacchini, *Pergamene Salernitane (1008-1784)* (Salerno, 1941), 172-179 nos. 30, 31; Antonio Balducci, *L'archivio della curia arcivescovile di Salerno*, Biblioteca della *Rassegna storica salernitana*, I: *Regesto delle pergamene* (Salerno, 1945), 49 nos. 159, 160 (in *arca terza*), and II: *Chartularium ecclesiae salernitanae* (Salerno, 1951), 60-61, nos. 112, 113.

by Master Bartolomeo Baraiolo, canon of Ravello and notary of
the church of Ravello and of the *acta* of the bishop's curia;
and he was surrounded by a group of witnesses that included
Sergio del Giudice, doctor of canon law and canon of Salerno
and Amalfi, Nicolà Capudscrofa of Salerno, doctor of civil
law, and the *primicerius* and three canons of Ravello. Tolomeo
was acting as delegate for Berardo, cardinal bishop of Palestrina and papal legate. The case, in which Tolomeo's decision
marked the end of one stage, was a sharp, material, and complicated dispute between the archbishop of Salerno and his
men (*vassalli*) of the fee of Olevano sul Tusciano.

The archbishops claimed, among other privileges, the right
to control the pressing of olive oil in mills within the fee. Archbishop Cesario d'Alagno had returned to his diocese to carry
on a sharp destructive war against adulterine mills in the
1240's. Archbishop Filippo in his turn complained that when
he had been out of the diocese, cited and away at the Roman
curia, before 1290, the men of Olevano had illegally set up
mills, in Matteo Vitelli's house in the casale of Salitto, in Gilio
de Floresio's house in the casale of Ariano, perhaps in other
places. The legate had ordered the bishop to inquire into supposed infringements of Salerno rights and if they were in fact
being violated to have the mills destroyed. The Salerno side
duly presented its allegations to the bishop of Ravello, alleging
long custom, through eighty years, and citing the actions of
Archbishop Cesario. The men of Olevano made it clear to
the bishop, he said, that they did not wish to appear before his
court; they said it openly. And the urging of the archbishop
as well as the advice of the court's counselors pressed the
bishop to declare the men of Olevano contumacious. The
bishop judge gave the archbishop a term for proceeding to
present his case.

A Salerno proctor, Assaldo Tirara of Scala, appeared before
the judge and again pressed him to acknowledge the contumacy of the Olevano side which refused to answer the Salerno allegations. But a proctor, Matteo de Carabella (whose
proctorial powers the Salerno side questioned), appeared and
sought a term. He planned, he said, to discredit the Salerno
proofs and witnesses. In a series of legal maneuvers before the
judge bishop, the Salerno party pressed for action in the case

and a sentence including a declaration of contumacy against Olevano, and the Olevano party pressed for continuing terms and recognition of their contention that their absences and seeming vagaries had not in fact been contumacious. Eventually the court had set the next to the last day of October for pronouncing definitive sentence. Matteo, the Olevano proctor, however, appealed; and on 28 October Nicola Rufulo of Ravello, a doctor of civil law and Matteo's advocate, brought a schedule of appeal to chambers in Naples where the bishop of Ravello then was. On 30 October in Ravello the judge finally pronounced his sentence to both parties. The adulterine mills were to be destroyed. For *molitura* the men of Olevano were to give Salerno one part in seven of their oil. They were to pay expenses of trial.

The process before Tolomeo of Ravello was a complicated one. It revolved through the legalistic turns of succeeding judicial terms during which Salerno seemed constantly within sight of victory and Olevano maintained only a halting connection (but did maintain it) with a court probably always hostile in spite of a surface pretence of impartiality. (Could, in fact, a bishop of Ravello really sympathize with rebellious Salerno *vassalli*?) But this complex process was only a small part of the total case, which wound its way to a compromise conclusion, to which the then archbishop of Salerno, Berardo, and the inhabitants of Olevano agreed, in 1306.[228] Since, in spite of Tolomeo's decision, Olevano continued to resist Salerno's right, the archbishop turned to the royal court of Charles II in 1292 and asked for the aid of the secular arm. Until 1295 Charles was involved in the case. He wrote to his *strategos* of Salerno and to his justiciar in the principate variously instructing them to try to settle peacefully, to enforce, investigate, reprimand, the disobedient tenants, the insistent archbishop who disregarded appeal and even (as the king complained to him) once summoned three men of Olevano to treat with him and then had them thrown in prison.[229] In April 1295 the king wrote from Rome to the *strategos* to sus-

[228] Balducci, I, 50 no. 166 (*arca terza*); Paesano, III, 130.
[229] Carucci, *Salerno dal 1282 al 1300*, 257-258 no. 221.

pend all proceedings because an appeal concerning the case was pending in the Roman curia.[230]

In 1292 Stefano, dean of Nola, brought to definitive sentence a case about a Campanian shop rather than Campanian oil, a case which had originally been delegated by Nicholas IV to the legate cardinal bishop of Palestrina and heard before the auditor of the causes of his court, a case which again sings of partisan court, contumacy, appeal, and compromise. The legate had died in the middle of the case, and it had been re-delegated to the Bishop of Ravello. The bishop had subdele-gated to the dean. The disputed shop was in Naples in a place called Sant'Arcangelo de Porta Monachorum; the dispute was between a Neapolitan clerk, Landolfo Siginolfo (represented by his father Riccardo, a knight, and also by a substitute proc-tor), and the abbot and monastery of Cava (represented by a monk, Bartolomeo da Gragnano).[231] On 9 July 1292, the dean, acting under the portico of the house in which he lived in Nola, found against Landolfo who was considered contuma-cious, although Landolfo's proctor stated, in appeal, that he had not been admitted to the court. Giovanni de Raymo, canon of Sant'Agata, as the court's executor was ordered to put Cava in physical possession of the shop.[232] Giovanni, desiring the aid of the secular arm, brought his mandate before a notary and judge in Naples; he was further strengthened by a sentence of excommunication against anyone who should try to impede the judgment. Giovanni was active in Naples in January 1293. But, in fact, the case was settled in February 1293 when Landolfo officially accepted the subdelegate's sen-tence, renounced his claim to the shop, and promised to harass Cava no more. The renunciation was given to Filippo, arch-bishop of Naples. It was procured by Cava by their granting Landolfo ten *once* of gold.[233]

---

[230] Carucci, *Salerno dal 1282 al 1300*, 269-270 no. 236. The case is dis-cussed in Carlo Carucci, *Un feudo ecclesiastico nell'Italia meridionale, Olevano sul Tusciano* (24-29), a pleasant, historiographically interest-ing little work in which Carucci examines Olevano with more than an historian's love.

[231] Cava, Archivio di Badia, arca LIX, no. 114.

[232] Cava, arca LIX, no. 99.

[233] Cava, arca LX, no. 2.

On 4 February 1287 Filippo, archbishop of Salerno, in Salerno, sealed and subscribed (and Musco Pisano, clerk of
Amalfi, and the priest, Pietro, the archbishop's chaplain, also
subscribed) a document which would insure Cava's secure
tenure of another disputed holding, and which concluded a
case that argues the importance of legates and documents.[234]
The abbot of Sant'Andrea de Apio, a Benedictine monastery
in the diocese of Capaccio near Roscigno, had appealed
against Cava's continued holding of the church of Santa Vennere and its rights and appurtenances. Santa Vennere was located next to the abbey of Sant'Andrea de Apio, within the
diocese of Capaccio, and it had been held, according to Abbot
Matteo of Sant'Andrea, by his predecessors. The case was delegated by the legate Gerardo, cardinal bishop of Sabina, to be
heard by the archbishop of Salerno. At the instance of the
Sant'Andrea party the archbishop summoned the abbot of
Cava to appear on Saturday, 1 February 1287; Cava was represented by its proctor, the notary Damiano. Sant'Andrea
asked restitution and also fifteen *once* of gold. But the monastery of Cava, great keeper of archives, was able to produce an
earlier instrument of sentence, and with it to convince the
archbishop to impose silence on Sant'Andrea.

In a different part of Italy, a case in which a different sort
of substance was disputed tells again of contumacy. On 4 April
1261 in the Lateran palace in the presence of two papal scrip-
tors (Francesco da Rieti and Napoleone da Rieti), a clerk of
Chieti, and the clerk and proctor of the dean of Besançon,
sentence was pronounced in a Camaldolese case by the papal
auditor and chaplain, Master Matteo de Alperino.[235] The case
was concerned with a contested abbatial election at the Camaldolese house of San Michele of Castal de'Britti in the diocese
of Bologna. The replaced elect, the monk Geremia, appealed
to pope Alexander IV. Alexander selected Matteo as his auditor; and Geremia selected Tostoveni, plebanus of Camaggiore
(diocese of Florence), as his proctor. Matteo summoned Ger-

---

[234] Cava, arca LVIII, no. 114.

[235] Florence, Archivio di stato, conventi soppressi, Camaldoli, 4 Apr.
1261.

emia's opponent repeatedly and properly in the *audientia publica*. He did not appear and was found contumacious. Having consulted John of Toledo, cardinal priest of San Lorenzo in Lucina, Matteo pronounced sentence in favor of Geremia.

Just a little over a half-century earlier, on 16 November 1205, in the episcopal curia at Ascoli, two delegates of Innocent III, Pietro, the bishop, and Goffredo, the archdeacon of Ascoli, stated their decision in a case over land claimed both by the abbot of Santa Sofia in Benevento and Santissima Trinità in Venosa.[236] The abbot of Santissima Trinità had not appeared as cited, but sent excuses, considered frivolous by the judges, through his messenger. The Venosa messenger objected to the appointment of the archdeacon as judge, appealed from the court, and retired. The judges, concerned about the fatiguing expenses of the abbot of Santa Sofia, summoned the abbot of Santissima Trinità peremptorily. Since he did not appear, the judges, having taken the counsel of the chapter of the church of Ascoli, the judges of the city of Ascoli, and others, pronounced him contumacious. The judges found for the abbot of Santa Sofia.

In 1220 the abbot of Santa Sofia (Matteo) and the archdeacon of Benevento (Pietro) were acting as papal judges delegate in a dispute over the church of San Giovanni in Marmorata, on the coast between Atrani and Minori and within the diocese of Ravello.[237] The disputants in the case were a priest named Giovanni de Turano and Sergio Capuano, a canon of Amalfi. The dispute had previously been decided in favor of Giovanni by two other papal delegates, the bishop and archdeacon of Scala. Honorius III's mandate to the Beneventan judges, dated 22 July 1220, asked them to confirm the

[236] Pratesi, *Note di diplomatica*, 81-82 no. 14.

[237] Ravello, ex-cattedrale, bolle, Perg. 9 (old number 80); R. Brentano, "A Ravello Document," *Traditio*, xv (1959), 401-404; the Beneventan judges examined the sealed Scalese document, but only subscribed their own notary's instrument. For an authoritative discussion of actions of confirmation, see Innocent IV's *Commentaria* on c. 1, X,ii,30. See aslo Peter Herde, *Marinus von Eboli: "Super Revocatoriis" und "De Confirmationibus"* (Tübingen, 1964) [extract from *Quellen und Forschungen*, XLII-XLIII], particularly 230-233, 239-248.

Scalese sentence if they found it just and correct. Giovanni brought his mandate to the Beneventan judges. They cited Sergio four times to appear personally or through a proctor. Sergio did not appear. He did, the Beneventans wrote, send someone in response to the first summons to ask for an extension of time. This Capuano representative perhaps tested the sentiment of the court and found it clearly hostile; his retiring from the court retired the Capuano side into hopeless (or hopeful) contumacy. The judges perused the older sentence and found it just and canonical. They confirmed it, enjoined Sergio Capuano to silence, and had a Beneventan notary write a copy for Giovanni's security. It is not immediately clear why the case was moved from a pro-Giovanni Scala court to a pro-Giovanni Benevento court. It removed the case from the actual area of the tangle of coastal dioceses—Scala, Ravello, Amalfi—where Capuano interests were particularly strong. Amalfi had recently acquired the body of Saint Andrew through Capuano generosity—if that is the right word. Perhaps from Benevento it was easier to contemplate the possible eventual necessity of excommunicating a Capuano.

Of these two small cases from Ascoli and Benevento, one emphasizes counsel, and the other neighborhood. Each quickly makes its point about contumacy. Both of these little cases show, as most of their predecessors here do, the creative use that could be made, by interested parties, of the deficiencies of a basically inefficient sort of government.

The documents in Italian cases constantly make clear the connection between the mandate and its beneficiary rather than its addressee or the officials of the government that issued it. Just as Giovanni brought his mandate to Benevento, Pagano, rector of Sant'Egidio in Latignano, brought his mandates in 1292, addressed to the delegate bishop of Città di Castello, to the bishop's house in Città di Castello.[238] (Pagano's were dated at Rome, Santa Maria Maggiore, 15 June; and they were delivered on 30 June.) Mandates are frequently preserved in the archives not of their addressees, but of the insti-

---

[238] Brentano, "Bishops' Books," 249: Città di Castello, Archivio vescovile Bk. vi, fos. 228v-229.

tution that the action they initiated eventually benefited.[239]
A 1286 Honorius IV mandate to the Augustinian prior of San
Frediano in Lucca and to the *plebanus* of the church of San
Pietro, Montecatini, to investigate the claimed overpayment
of procurations by the Badia in Florence, is found of course in
the Badia's archives.[240] A 1291 Nicholas IV mandate directs
the delegate *plebanus* of the *pieve* of Sant'Andrea Pistoia to
hear a case between the Servite prior and convent of Santa
Maria and certain citizens of Florence. It is preserved in the
archives of Santa Maria (Santissima Annunziata), and so is a
similar 1291 Nicholas IV mandate to another delegate,
Monaco, archdeacon of Siena.[241] Similarly a Martin IV mandate to investigate abuses against the Cistercians of Settimo is
found in the archives of the Cestello (Settimo's heir) of
Florence.[242]

The sort of men who were delegated, their sort of office, is
also clear: a canon of Chiusi in a case between the archdeacon
of Siena (Monaco) and laymen of the diocese of Siena; the
abbot of the Badia of Poggibonsi, the *plebanus* of the *pieve* of
San Pancrazio in the diocese of Fiesole, and the archdeacon
of Siena in a case, four years earlier in 1291, between the Cistercians of San Galgano and the prior of San Felice and lay
associates.[243] These men of the middle in the Italian church—

[239] For an example in which the peculiar significance of the archives
of deposit is unusually clear, a case in which Durham manipulated
Carlisle affairs to its own advantage, see Brentano, *York Metropolitan
Jurisdiction*, 90-92, 199-207.

[240] Florence, Archivio di stato, conventi soppressi, Badia di Firenze,
18 Febb. 1286.

[241] Florence, Archivio di stato, conventi soppressi, Annunziata, "28
Ag. 1291" (both).

[242] Florence, Archivio di stato, Cestello, 18 Genn. 1282.

[243] Florence, Archivio di stato, Monte Commune, 1 Sett. 1291, and
Montepulciano, 21 Marz. 1295. For canonical and chancery regulations
about suitable delegates (and for negotiations in the *audientia*), see
Peter Herde, "Papal Formularies for Letters of Justice (13th-16th
Centuries)," *Proceedings of the Second International Congress of
Medieval Canon Law*: Monumenta Iuris Canonici, Series C, Subsidia,
vol. 1 (Vatican City, 1965), 321-345, 339 and notes; and George G.
Pavloff, *Papal Judge Delegates at the Time of the Corpus Iuris
Canonici* (Washington, 1963), 9-11. Mr. Gero Dolezalek has now in

the caste of the *plebanus*, the abbot, and the archpriest—were joined by their superiors, bishops and archbishops, on boards and benches of delegates; but their's seems the dominant caste. They did not, of course, always hear their cases themselves. In a rather unusual survival from 1258, a document of subdelegation, the provost of the church of Santa Maria, Poggibonsi, subdelegates the abbot of the Badia of Capolona (Arezzo diocese) in a Camaldolese dispute.[244] (The commission was made in the provost's *area* in the old city, with one of his household present.) A number of subdelegates are seen in action; but subdelegation does not seem to have been a major force in shaping Italian cases, except perhaps in removing a disinterested judge. Subdelegates were of essentially the same caste as delegates, often they were merely the delegate's co-delegates.

Delegated cases themselves seem, however, to have been very important in shaping the structure of Italian ecclesiastical jurisdiction. Their carefully preserved records, in sharp contrast with the vague records of the ordinary church, urge their reality and importance—the carefully observed acts in the canons' cloisters at the great church of Siena, in San Nicola in Bari with its scurrying canons.[245] In 1291 the convent of Santa Maria di Valdiponte appealed against the aggression of its bishop, Bulgaro of Perugia. It saved its appeal and copied it in the seventeenth century. In the strange late hand, a usual action, against a usual grievance, argues a usual technicality—whether or not the appeal was made in proper term.[246]

When in November 1269 Leonardo the Cistercian bishop of Anglona sat, the center of his diocese, to confirm the privileges

preparation a valuable edition of Pisan formulary material from the first half of the thirteenth century for a dissertation for the law faculty at Frankfurt; it is certainly to be hoped that it will be published in the not too distant future.

[244] Florence, Archivio di stato, conventi soppressi, Camaldoli, 15 Giugno 1258—"habati capoleoni."

[245] Siena, Archivio di stato, Sant'Agostino, 17 Genn. 1288.

[246] Perugia, Archivio di stato, Santa Maria di Valdiponte, no. 21.

of the Cistercian house of Convento Sagittario, he was surrounded by a court of witnesses, the canons of his cathedral church, some of whom were also archpriests in his diocese.[247] Brother Leonardo's tableau is the characteristic gesture of the church ordinary in Italy, with its dioceses puckered to their central churches, its liturgical and monastic memories, its slight territorial organization half-absorbed in, or unfreed from, its colleges of clergy. And as disjointed as is the pattern of ordinary administration is the ordinary church's appearance in history. It appears in occasional ceremonial act, in grant, in dispute, in notarial photograph, and quickly disappears: a man of the church ordinary, Don Lando, archpriest of Mercogliano, bobs up in 1203 to give his bastard son Lando a chestnut grove and a garden, disappears for three years, reappears briefly, and is gone; he is characteristically fragmentary.[248] The rare continuous exposition of Città di Castello points up the normal fragmentation.

Against this pattern of ordinary brokenness one sees the relative clarity, strength, and continuity—the conventionality in northern European terms—of the church delegate, the papal *ad hoc*, as opposed to the local ordinary, administrative, and judicial church. One sees this in the nice records of the Badia in Florence. But the Badia's record-keeping is peculiar as well as nice. Gianni di Piero's single, small sheets of notarized *processus* themselves suggest the unnaturalness of continuous record-keeping in the episodic Italian church. When only the naturally episodic government of delegates becomes continuous and demands official memory, something seems askew.

A pattern of Italian delegate procedure does seem to appear in the various detail of many cases. The pattern is built about the same common forms (and technically it follows much the same process) as delegate procedure in the north of Europe. There is here the same use of the technicalities of procedure to inhibit and in the end defeat what would seem, superficially, to be the course of justice. Appeals, frivolous exceptions, par-

[247] Ughelli, viii, col. 85.

[248] Giovanni Mongelli, *Abbazia di Montevergine, Regesto delle pergamene*, ii (Rome, 1957), 35 no. 1184; the older Lando appears again in October 1206 (Mongelli, 45-46, nos. 1236, 1238).

tisan judges, and claimed excommunications abound. Contumacy is the word that rules the courts.

In Italy as in England the taste for clean, reasoned disputation, but distorted—the distant, crazed (or conventionalized) echo of Aquinas and Scotus—is sensed in the courts, filled as they were with the products of the schools. One can see that taste helping to shape the arguments at Rieti. But in Italian courts as in English ones the real tone is Quintilian's, not Aristotle's. The courts were luxurious winter gardens in which rhetorical *dubitatio* (the pretense of uncertainty through initial hesitation which gives an air of truth to statements) flourished.[249] In almost every case there are indications that by the time a court met to begin its elaborate ritual of setting terms and hearing evidence its decision was made—and not by the controlling clarity of the law, but by the court's personal composition.

Courts seem generally to have been partisan. But their partisanship fits into a set of assumptions about practical canonical justice in the thirteenth century (perhaps only partly conscious) which gives it, court partisanship, a rather special function. Since the almost universal end of cases in which there was serious dispute between powerful, respectable parties (and right and long custom were elements of power) was compromise, partisan judicial decision became like an advocate's presentation. It presented powerfully its side's case.

The partisan court and the eventual decision by arbitration seem quite natural segments of the sort of government that really existed most of the time in most places in both State and Church in the thirteenth century. (However, it should be kept in mind that the change of the president of a court from judge to arbiter, particularly when the same man remained president, might merely mean that he and the contestants in the case found it more convenient to work under rules more relaxed than those of a formal Romano-canonical judge's court; arbitration could mean something like the committee of the whole court, as it seems clearly to have done in such a conversion by a cardinal auditor in a 1239 case over water-mills

[249] Quintilian's *Institutio oratoria*, ix,ii,19.

between Santa Maria Nuova and San Sebastiano in Rome.)[250] In the case before papal delegates the disputant helped choose the judges; he paid them their expenses; he protected them; and he brought them documents that he had had made for them—documents that he stored in his archives when the case was over. In the final compromise, as in a marriage, the real celebrants were the coupled disputants, although a guarding authority might guide them to the altar and help them with the formulae. Cases before delegates' courts implemented a government of self-help and good compromise. This government defined the reality of local power and, in defining it, avoided disorder.[251] The disputed endings of cases before delegates were not really inane; they were part of a workable, although elaborate, expensive, and intermittent system. They, in fact, used effectively the necessary deflection between stated purpose and act that inefficient official government made universal in thirteenth-century Europe.

Although much of the Italian pattern of procedure before judges delegate seems exactly the same as the English pattern, some parts of it seem to have been shaped by local conditions. It is natural, of course, that a general sort of government which tries to define local reality should change its techniques from place to place. Legates were, quite naturally, prominent in Italy. They separated the church from the pope, in a way; but they also drew litigation up a ladder of appeal. Single dele-

[250] For the use of arbitration see, for example, Brentano, *York Metropolitan Jurisdiction*, 142-145; and for arbitration in the important Lucca *pieve* disputes, see Nanni, 145-150. The general run of the documents in the San Giacomo di Monselice collection (Archivio segreto vaticano, A.C.N.V.) for the thirteenth century seems to me very much to confirm this pattern. For the water-mill case: Rieti, Archivio di stato, fondo comunale, pergamene 4, 5.

[251] Definition through local inquest was conventional, and perhaps particularly conventional in the south of Italy; see Eduard Sthamer, *Bruchstücke mittelalterlicher Enqueten aus Unteritalien*, Abhandlungen der preuss. Akademie der Wissenschaften, 1933, phil. hist. Klasse, 2 (Berlin, 1933); see, too, Dieter Girgensohn and Norbert Kamp, "Urkunden und Inquisitionen der Stauferzeit aus Tarent," *Quellen und Forschungen aus italienischen Archiven und Bibliotheken*, XLI (1961), 137-234. On papal confirmation of arbitration, see Herde, *Marinus von Eboli*, 236-239.

gates and arguments about set terms seem peculiarly noticeable; the prevalence of both probably has to do with the relative quickness of movement of Italian appeals—appeals which
often did not need to dally with the *audientia*'s three judges
but which did have to worry with the exact time of actions.

In general, appeals in Italy do seem to have moved up
quickly from court to court toward legate or curia; they do
not seem to have broken horizontally into fragmented courts
of opposing delegates, into an endless diversionary proliferation of subdelegates. Actions in Bologna and Durham seem
thus to have differed: in Bologna, with pope and university
close, they climbed promptly toward Rome; in Durham (at
least sometimes) they broke and dallied to indecision through
country towns. In both North and South the complications of
delegate procedure led to compromise.

Papal reform of the ordinary church in the thirteenth century—the creation of an ordered, administrative, pastoral
church—seems to have been reform of a sort particularly inappropriate, or unacceptable, to the Italian church. Certainly
the specific reforms of the thirteenth century cannot have been
provoked by the positive example of the church in Italy with
its decaying *pievi* and antique dioceses. It was very probably
provoked by the thought of distant universities, most specifically by the Paris of Peter the Chanter, Robert Curzon, and
Stephen Langton. (Possibly, too, thirteenth-century popes
were persuaded that the northern sort of organization, toward
which their legislation seemed to be pushing, produced a more
heartily taxable church or at least facilitated tax collection.)[252]
But in spite of the fact that ordinary ecclesiastical reform was
peculiarly inapplicable to Italy, the system of delegation seems
to have worked relatively well there. The curia thought ordinary reform, and saw delegated action (and saw that action
where it often dealt with the important substance of real
property).

The Italianness of the Italian church—named lawyers, diag-
nosing doctors, towns in north and south, its difference from
the English church—must not disguise the sharp regional dif-

[252] Consideration of this problem should begin with William E.
Lunt, *Papal Revenues in the Middle Ages*, 1 (New York, 1934).

2. Salisbury Cathedral

1. Cremona, façade of the Duomo

3. Martyrdom of Thomas Becket, reliquary of Thomas Becket at Anagni

4. *Above right*—Relief (almost surely thirteenth century) of the harbor and city of Brindisi: the legend of the arrival of Saint Theodore, in laminated silver on the Arca di San Teodoro in Brindisi

5. Detail of the Benevento doors

6. The thirteenth-century bronze doors at Benevento; the archbishop and his suffragans are in the lower panels

7. The cloister of Santa Maria di Valdiponte. 8. *Below left*—San Nicola Bari, in the corners of which the canons hid on Saint Nicholas's Day, 1241. 9. *Below right*—A thirteenth-century Italian painting of a bishop from the crypt frescoes at Anagni

10: The apse of the cathedral of Santa Giusta in Sardinia

11. *Above right*—An Italian sculpted bishop, thought to be thirteenth century, in the parish church at Bardone near Parma

12. The interior of the cathedral of Santa Giusta in Sardinia

13. San Pietro in Ferentillo. 14. *Above right*—The ruin of San Giuliano over Spoleto

15. Fiastra, the farmyard and flank of the church

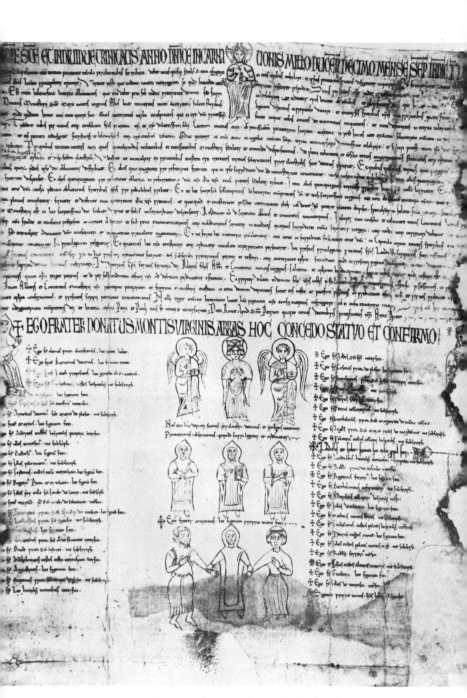

16. A Montevergine document (No. 1297) on which the donors are drawn making their gift through the abbey to Christ the Redeemer

17. *Left*—Santa Croce del Chienti, façade and chickens
18. *Right*—The gate of San Cosimato from the piazza

19. Detail of Pietro Lorenzetti's predella painting of Honorius IV approving the rule of the Carmelites

ferences in a very local church, local even to its benches of delegates. The south was partly Greek; the north was a motley collection of city-states. The ecclesiastical south was generally less well organized administratively than the north. But even the lack of a generally controlling positive pattern, in a church that considered itself a sort of unity, argues a characteristic incoherence. It is administrative incoherence that most sharply distinguishes the church of Gaeta, Naples, Sorrento, Amalfi, and Salerno from the church of the Cinque Ports.

III · BISHOPS AND SAINTS

S AINT Philip Benizi, flaming with love, wanted not to be
a bishop. Scenes of his rejecting the authority that
might corrupt him are verbally and visually familiar.
In story he flees from the popularity of Florence. In sculpture
he rejects the honor that has failed to tempt him, in dramatic
movement admirably suited to the Baroque, as on the façade
of San Marcello on the Corso in Rome. Philip was a man devoted to holy places and sacred images, Mass at Carfaggio, the
crucifix at Fiesole. As he lay mortally ill, he cried to his followers, "Bring me my book! Bring me my book!" They came
with book after book, but he rejected them all. Finally, the
most sympathetic of the friars, understanding, brought him his
crucifix; and Philip said, "This is my book." Philip believed,
as his experience had encouraged him to, in the power of emotion, in healing presences. In 1285, as he lay dying, his fervent
plea to his encircling Servites was "Love one another."[1]

Robert Grosseteste, bishop of Lincoln, whose canonization
was never in fact effected, was, in 1250, trying, at Lyons, to
reconstruct Innocent IV into the sort of pope whom he could,
as he desperately wanted to, obey. Grosseteste wrote of the
pastor-needing souls, constantly endangered, "for the life of
each one of whom the Son of God was willing to die a shame-
ful death."[2] Grosseteste saw the world divided into dioceses
that were divided into parishes that were full of men with
souls. He "felt about the diocese of Lincoln as a great missionary would feel about the peoples of Asia and Africa."[3] He

[1] For Saint Philip see the *Acta Sanctorum* for August 23 (August,
IV, 655-719), particularly 693 for the flight from Florence, and 706 for
the "book" story and Philip's preparation for death; see too *Vies des
Saints et des Bienheureux* (by the Benedictines of Paris), VIII (1950),
439-443; Philip was canonized in 1671.
[2] Quoted by W. A. Pantin in D. A. Callus, ed., *Robert Grosseteste*
(Oxford, 1955), 179; for Grosseteste see Callus, and in this connection
particularly the Pantin essay ("Grosseteste's Relations with the Papacy
and the Crown"), including the discussion of the "schoolman-bishop,"
178.
[3] Pantin, "Grosseteste's Relations" (in Callus), 179.

felt, in effect, that salvation could be administered, that it did not move as an incomprehensible expression of grace and love jumping like an unpredictable brush fire from passionate response to passionate response, hopelessly beyond control. He felt that a decent and intelligible (at least in act) pastor could do a lot. His key to everything lay in the cure of souls. It was part of a profound order that possessed his mind: music, mathematics, logic, political man in society. Aristotle, Gregory I, and something of the reason of Francis combined themselves in the figure of the bishop. His was a different and broader segment of Christ than Benizi's.

The bishop and the friar—perhaps with a fellow, the scholar —sometimes separate, sometimes combined, were the ecclesiastical heroes of the active thirteenth century. They were heroes interested in touching in a number of ways, on a variety of levels, the newly provoked and visible community of Christendom. These preachers and wanderers and rulers were really displacing, to a significant degree, the Josephs in Egypt, the Daniels in Babylon, the Lots in Sodom, of the old island monasteries.[4] The displacement was neither uniform nor universal, but it was given something approaching universality by the great universities which the friars found irresistible and which could even woo houses of Benedictines and a house of Cistercians to Oxford if not to Bologna.[5] The bishop and the friar were in both Italy and England, but not in equal proportions. Filippo Benizi is a national phenomenon, the flaming saint caught only tenuously within the framework of the governmental church. He was, essentially, a friar, like Francis, in the century between those two exotic monks, Joachim and Peter Celestine. In spite of England's own Franciscanism, the bishop is English, the friar Italian.

Grosseteste's diocese, Lincoln, entered the chronological thirteenth century with the death of its saint bishop, Hugh of

---

[4] I have borrowed the conventional cluster of monastic figures from Walter Daniel: *The Life of Ailred of Rievaulx*, ed. F. M. Powicke (Edinburgh, 1950), 9.

[5] See David Knowles, *The Religious Orders in England*, 1 (Cambridge, 1956), 25-27; Frank Barlow, *Durham Annals and Documents of the Thirteenth Century*, Surtees Society, 155 (Durham, 1945), 129-130.

Avalon, in the year 1200. Hugh's life describes with misleading precision the change from one sort of prevailing religious sentiment to another, from the hair shirt to the shepherd's crook, from the twelfth to the thirteenth century.[6] It also describes a trip to the North.

Hugh went as a child of eight with his widowed father, a Burgundian knight, to a house of Austin canons. When Hugh was about twenty-five he looked for a stronger religious experience and went to the Grande Chartreuse, the purest center of twelfth-century religious withdrawal from general society. When he was probably almost forty Hugh came to England as prior of the English Carthusian house of Witham (a house that seems to have been founded as part of Henry II's penance for Becket's murder). When he was about forty-five, in 1186, Hugh was chosen, because of his "exceptional goodness," bishop of Lincoln.[7]

The see for which Hugh was chosen was, as his own biographer, Adam of Eynsham, pointed out, remarkable, huge, with its eight archdeaconries extending into nine counties, its cities, its innumerable parishes. It would have been hard to find a diocese bigger or more populous, Adam wrote.[8] Hugh's reaction to his election—after some hesitation about its validity and its motivation—was one of complete acceptance. He became fully and imaginatively and indefatigably a pastoral bishop. He moved about his diocese; he took a special interest in the confirmation of children (an act he refused to perform, in symbol that seemed important to him and contemporaries, without dismounting from his horse).[9] Hugh was interested in the proper use of clerical incomes and their connection with

[6] For Hugh, see *The Life of St. Hugh of Lincoln*, ed. Decima L. Douie and Hugh Farmer (Edinburgh, 1961-1962), particularly in the "Introduction," I, vii-xlix. I have borrowed the contrast of hair shirt with shepherd's crook from an unpublished essay by Susan Millinger Smith, in which she is comparing the Richard Wych of the Dominican Ralph Bocking with the Richard Wych of the Benedictine Matthew Paris; the shirt is Benedictine, the crook Dominican—both thirteenth century.

[7] *The Life of St. Hugh*, I, 94.

[8] *The Life of St. Hugh*, I, 93.

[9] *The Life of St. Hugh*, I, 127-128.

the proper performance of pastoral duty; and he emphasized the connection by quoting from Saint Paul on the profits of altar and temple.[10]

Hugh was, in the thirteenth-century sense, both practical and active, but he did not completely renounce his Carthusian past. For a month each year he retired to Witham, to the old life of contemplation, to a life of simple chores. He particularly liked washing dishes; and in this small, incidental way, as in the larger pattern of his later life, he chose the role of Martha. His life was not torn cleanly away from the continuing devotion of past times. He wore a hair shirt. His presence had a miraculous effect upon the disposition and behavior of the huge and once peculiarly vicious swan that lived at one of his manors. The change in the direction of his life as he matured remains clear, however; and it was both prophetic and influential.

Oliver Sutton, with a name that recalls the romance of Francis, was a late thirteenth-century successor of Hugh and of Grosseteste at Lincoln. He was consciously a successor: he tried to have Grosseteste canonized, as Hugh (who was translated at the beginning of Sutton's episcopate) had been canonized long before, in 1220.[11] As the century had begun with Hugh's death, it ended, in 1299, with Sutton's death. Sutton was "prudent in directing things both spiritual and temporal" as John de Schalby wrote; and Schalby knew.[12] He was Sutton's registrar, who, for nineteen years, moved through the diocese with Sutton, carting documents and recording acts.

[10] *The Life of St. Hugh*, I, 115, 120 (I Cor. 9:13; I Cor. 9:18; II Thess. 3:10).

[11] Eric Waldram Kemp, *Canonization and Authority in the Western Church* (London, 1948), 118-120, 176.

[12] *The Rolls and Register of Bishop Oliver Sutton, 1280-1299*, ed. Rosalind M. T. Hill, Lincoln Record Society, 39, 43, 48, 52, 60 (Hereford, 1948-1965) [hereafter *Sutton*], III, xxiii; Oliver Sutton is one of the most visible of English bishops largely because of Miss Hill's beautiful edition of his register, but also because of her short, brilliant essays —her *Oliver Sutton, Dean of Lincoln, Later Bishop of Lincoln (1280-1299)*, Lincoln Minster Pamphlets, 4 (Lincoln, 1959) exposes, unpretentiously, exactly, and attractively, the sort of life a late thirteenth-century English bishop lived.

He watched the bishop with the strained but heightened perception produced by the "intimate contact of two men who must often have been tired, worried and over-worked."[13]

Look at Sutton through Schalby's register and you must see a mind about to burst, a conscience almost swamped. The months from June 1292 through December 1293 were not extraordinary months for Sutton; but, like many others, they could have convinced him that no man's mind or conscience could bear the intensity or the multiplicity of the bishop's job. Thomas Chapel, the rector of Bletchingdon, was wandering about the diocese (or beyond it) out of his mind, and had to be found and cared for (as did Bletchingdon have to be cared for). The dean of Rothwell had to be asked to sequester the goods of the late Master Michael, rector of a mediety of Isham, until the rector's executors made good the defects he had left in church and manse. The royal government had to be asked to arrest a number of men forty days excommunicate and still obdurate. The abbot and convent of Bardney had to be protected from a hostile party that kept them from collecting their tithes. Since while William chaplain of Ecton was pronouncing a sentence of excommunication certain malefactors had assaulted him, snatched the list from his hands and the candles from his assistants, those who could be found had to be brought before the bishop's official. John Garland of Dunstable, a clerk, could be absolved from the excommunication he had brought upon himself for fornication with Cecily Drayton, a nun of Markyate; John had to go to Rome by the coming feast of the Circumcision. A woman named Petronilla, whom the bishop had baptized and who had been a Jewess in her youth, had to be commended to the *custos* of the converts in London. The bishop granted, in December, the lord of a Hertfordshire manor the right to have a private chapel because his lady when pregnant could not get over the rough, muddy road to the parish church. Those men had to be excommunicated who had attacked Henry of Donnington and another clerk in the manse of Stenigot, had made one of them kiss the rear end of a horse, and also had kept him from get-

[13] *Sutton*, III, xxiii; see too J. H. Srawley, *The Book of John de Schalby*, Lincoln Minster Pamphlets, 2 (Lincoln, 1949).

ting his wounds attended to. Thomas Isaac of Grantham, though he was properly ordained, was hazy about the words of a number of common Masses and had to be kept from the cure of souls. The bishop had to try to help recover the breviary that the chaplain Robert of Wootton had dropped from his saddle and the copy of the second part of Gregory's *Moralia* on Job that had been stolen from the Dominican house at Northampton. The prior and convent of Kyme had had money extorted from them for the return of a horse lent to ecclesiastical superiors. The rector of Dalderby had leprosy. A priest ignored his excommunication for striking a clerk in a churchyard. The goods of a paralytic had been stolen. Someone had stolen Sir Ralph Paynel's swans. A merchant had pulled John Chaplain of Boston by his hood. Poaching, intestacy, a priest ordained abroad, a chancellor for Oxford, a belfry to be built, the Austin Hermits of Huntingdon, Balliol chapel, masters on Catte Street, the two dead oxen that belonged to Alan and Emmicena of Holland, a collector for alms for Sant'Assencio at Anagni, the indulgenced cross erected in honor of All Saints at Easingwold, a superstitious blood-rite that may have been performed on Easter eve—an intricate array of details, some common form, recurred with different names at different places, but all demanded action from the bishop. They interrupted his planned routine of confirming, ordaining, visiting, dealing with sick or inadequate pastors, and pricked it out to a bursting reality.[14]

But Sutton's mind, although details extended it, did not burst. For nineteen years, day after day, he worked and made decisions. He supervised dependent institutions, dealt with disputed elections, guarded the circumference of the important, troublesome university of Oxford, and supervised a corps of archdeacons as well as the members of his own household and administrative staff. Nor did he—he is so far from Cuthbert or Bruno, from Eangyth and Heaburg—write "in tear-stained letter under what a load of misery and under what a crushing burden of wordly distractions" he was "weighed

14 *Sutton*, IV, 42 (and 70); 42, 40, 42; 35-36, 40; 43, 156; 15-16; 73-74, 157; 120-121; 144-145, 115-116; 17-19, 8-9; 76, 82; 44; 140-143; 75; 145; 132; 54; 149; 65; 81, 78.

down."[15] Instead he wrote, through Schalby, one great codex and six rolls of episcopal register.[16] The register recorded the detail of Sutton's conscientious, governing, pastoral life, in the pattern of the map of his archdeaconried diocese. Sutton's life was expressed at length in time and place; and it expressed constantly an optimistic attitude about the possibility of reforming men through rational governmental process.

It would be dazzling to think of three hundred Italian bishops simultaneously bursting with Sutton's governmental enthusiasm. It is a thought that the available evidence does not make necessary. In April 1227, at Benevento, Manasses, bishop of Volturara, for the length of one transaction, for the making of one document, emerges from obscurity.[17] There was nothing particularly episcopal about Manasses's action. He acted as the *custos* of the church of San Matteo *a porta aurea* (that is, at the Golden Gate, as it was customary to call that gate of Trajan that still adds beauty to Benevento). The bishop as *custos* granted a house belonging to the church to a man, his wife, and their legitimate sons born and unborn, for twenty-nine years, in return for an annual rent to be paid on the church's festa, the Feast of Saint Matthew. The bishop received an initial payment, a third of which went for a bell for the church, the rest to be kept by the bishop for other "hutilitatibus" of the church. If the man should die before the twenty-nine years were over, the house would fall to his wife and his sons. If they should all die, it would revert to the church. At the end of twenty-nine years the house with all its improvements would revert to the church. The house, which

[15] Words are borrowed from Ephraim Emerton's translation of Eangyth and Heaburg to Boniface: *Letters of Saint Boniface* (New York, 1940), 36 (Tangl, 14); the sentiment, however, was not unknown in Sutton's diocese, as Miss Hill has pointed out (*Oliver Sutton*, 13); a prioress of Fosse, whom Sutton tried to dissuade from resigning, "declared, 'weeping so much that it was amazing to see,' that the cares of her position had become intolerable."

[16] *Sutton*, I, xiii and ff.

[17] Archivio segreto vaticano, Archivio Aldobrandini, Documenti storici, Abbadie, 4 no. 3; Ughelli, who did not mention Manasses, gave five lines of one column to his two thirteenth-century bishops of Volturara (VIII, col. 392).

had previously been held by a widow, was located near the church and by the piazza leading to the gate and the gate itself.

There is nothing very startling about Manasses's action, or about its tendrilled notarial document with its judge's subscription, or even about a poor diocese's bishop's being involved, beyond his diocese's borders, in an affair without any episcopal significance—except that it was probably connected with supplementing inadequate episcopal income.[18] It is startling to cast this single document (of 17½ x 36½ cms) against the codex and six rolls of Sutton's register. Asked to define the word "bishop," at least to define it functionally, Oliver Sutton and Manasses of Volturara must have given different answers.

The men of Molassano could look at Ottone, archbishop of Genoa, as the cherry tree under which they swore fealty to him, as the men of Saint Albans in England could their abbot (through their cellarer) as the ash tree of his court, a twist of vegetation and power rather than God's vicar, their pastor.[19] Throughout the church militant, for centuries, the men who prayed in society had been obscured by the gross material things with which they protected and supported their prayers. It was an almost universal condition, assumed, conventional.

To some men, significant ones, in each generation's stratum of reform, it seemed a repulsive perversion of Christian leadership. They fought to free religion from the filth of wealth

[18] The evidence from tenth assessments is hard to interpret exactly, but its general import is almost always clear. In the case of Volturara the assessment for the episcopal *mensa* in 1328 supports what one would assume of its poverty: Vendola, *Apulia-Lucania-Calabria*; the income from this single San Matteo *a porta aurea* house in 1227 is one-fifth of the total assessment for the episcopal *mensa* of Volturara in 1328.

[19] Luigi Tommaso Belgrano, *Il Registro della curia arcivescovile di Genova*, Atti della società Ligure di storia patria, ii, 2 (Genoa, 1862), 467-468—at Molissana on 2 May 1204, between terce and nones; Ada Elizabeth Levett, *Studies in Manorial History*, ed. H. M. Cam, M. Coate, L. S. Sutherland (Oxford, 1938), iii. There is an extended analysis of the declining feudal position of the bishops of Pistoia in Sabatino Ferrali, "La Temporalità del Vescovado nei rapporti col Commune a Pistoia nei secoli XII e XIII," in "Vescovi e diocesi in Italia nel medioevo": *Italia Sacra V* (Padua, 1964), 365-408.

without at the same time making it, religion, impotent or shrilly proud. Some of these men were extremists like the Brettini friars, followers of the naked Christ;[20] but more conventional Franciscans and Dominicans, like Pecham and Aquinas, constantly worried the problem of poverty, fought about its implications against the remembered picture of Christ and his apostles, and did what they could, at least, to free themselves from the prison of property. Inspired by the purity and beauty of the reformers' poverty, their own generations, in the shadow of the Magi, heaped upon the reformers presents of gold—or land and silver. As the donors hoped they bought for themselves a bit of poverty, they buried poverty in wealth. Franciscans succeeded Cistercians.

Some men in regular orders, perhaps the majority of them even in the thirteenth century when the discussion of poverty was particularly excited, were completely unaware of, or had completely repressed, the difficulty and distastefulness of the man of God's being rich and entangled in mundane affairs. Matthew Paris was such a monk. One hears him in his *Chronica Majora* talking with Richard, earl of Cornwall, about the great expense of the buildings at Richard's new foundation of Cistercians at Hayles. Matthew wanted, he said, to put nothing false in his chronicle, so he asked Richard about cost. He found that the church had cost 10,000 marks. Then Earl Richard added to his answer something which Matthew called *quoddam verbum memorabile*. "Were it pleasing to God that I had spent everything in my castle at Wallingford," Earl Richard said, "I would have spent it wisely and to my advantage." Richard's and Matthew's God, although perhaps not very neatly defined, is far from the naked Christ.[21]

[20] Francis Roth, "Cardinal Richard Annibaldi, First Protector of the Augustinian Order, 1243-1276," *Augustiniana*, II (1952), 26-60, 108-149, 230-247; III (1953), 21-34, 283-313; IV (1954), 5-24; II, 134. For Francis as a follower of the naked Christ, see M. D. Lambert, *Franciscan Poverty* (London, 1961), 31-67, especially 62—and see Lambert generally for the first declining century of Franciscan poverty sympathetically interpreted.

[21] Matthew Paris, *Chronica Majora*, v, 262; see, too, Knowles, *Religious Orders*, I, 6, for an exquisite description of the founder's

The Bishop of Volturara appearing out of the mists to rent his house by the arch of Trajan was, thus, not engaged in a surprising sort of transaction. It is the isolation of his act that is peculiar. The reforming bishops of thirteenth-century England were caught in the universal muddle of property and power, but they were caught in it, very many of them, as they did lots of specifically pastoral things. The pastoral activities of the great majority of Italian bishops are hidden, if in fact they ever existed.

The secularism of these mundane Italian bishops was both petty and grand. Manasses represents petty secularism clearly enough. Grand secularism has many famous representatives. Their names are written all over the history of Italy. Bartolomeo Pignatelli, Dante's "il Pastor di Cosenza," the noble Neapolitan whose movement from archbishopric to archbishopric, from Amalfi through Cosenza to Messina, did not dull his sword, seems to have performed his most signal service to the church by casting the dead Manfred from his grave.[22] Two successive archbishops of late thirteenth-century Monreale burlesqued their type of important office holder. Giovanni Boccamazza, a Savelli relative, passed through his tenure of the see, actually spending some time in Sicily before the Vespers, on his way to the cardinalate. Pietro Gerra moved from Sora to Rieti to Monreale to Capua on his way to the patriarchate of Aquileia; Monreale was of course not physically available to him. Both Giovanni and Pietro were politicians, diplomats, extra-diocesan administrators. There seems nothing to indicate that either of them was troubled by the thought of pastoral care.[23]

bringing the relic of the Sacred Blood to Hayles and the consecration of the new church.

[22] Francesco Russo, *Storia dell'arcidiocesi di Cosenza* (Naples, 1957), 391; Bartolomeo is talked of in the third canto of the *Purgatorio*.

[23] See G. L. Lello, *Descrizione del Real Tempio e Monasterio di Santa Maria Nuova di Morreale* . . . (Palermo, 1702), 14-28; *Cronica Fratris Salimbene de Adam ordinis minorum*, ed. O. Holder-Egger, *M.G.H., SS.,* xxxii (Hanover and Leipzig 1905-1913) [hereafter Salimbene], 608; E. Traversa, *Quellenkritik zur Geschichte des Patriarchen Peter II Gerra (1299-1301)* (Görz, 1906) [Separatabdruck aus dem 56. Jahresbericht des k.k. Staatsgymnasiums in Görz], 34; it

The rejection of the pastoral function in thirteenth-century Italy was not always a matter of the consecrated bishop's allowing it, quite casually, to be absorbed into the material aspects of his office, or of his never realizing that he as bishop ought in fact to be an administrative pastor. He might, like Philip Benizi, spurn the episcopacy and let the spurning be an incident in his quest for saintly purity—no cherry tree for him, no house by a Roman arch, no collection of rich offices and swords. Through a section of Salimbene's chronicle Rainaldo d'Arezzo plays this spurning part fully and articulately.[24]

As Franciscan lector at Rieti, Rainaldo had so impressed the canons of the cathedral church that they honored him by electing him bishop. He, to be free of their honor, sought Innocent IV at Lyons. Innocent, having heard of Rainaldo's learning and sanctity, and having taken the counsel of his cardinals, ordered Rainaldo to be a bishop, and made him one, while Salimbene himself was present at Lyons. Leaving Lyons, Rainaldo started back toward Italy. On the Feast of the Ascension he preached to the people and celebrated a pontifical Mass and wore his miter in the friars' church in Genoa. Salimbene himself, already a priest, served for Rainaldo at Mass. Afterward, with the Genoese friars, they had a first-rate seafish dinner in the refectory.

The next night, Stephen the Englishman (the lector at Genoa who had joined the order as a little boy and who had come out from England a handsome man, spiritual and literate and wise in counsel, full of the readiness to preach) preached a beautiful sermon. Stephen recalled what a saintly man, a Franciscan lay brother back in England, used to say about the Paschal candle. When the candle was lighted in the

would be wrong to imply that Pietro took no interest in his dioceses; see e.g. Rieti, Archivio capitolare, armadio II, fasc. E, no. 3 (Mazzatinti, 213-214); and Trasmondo, their predecessor at Monreale, took enough interest in his province to get papal permission to visit it with his cross carried before him, in 1268: Carlo Alberto Garufi, *Catalogo illustrato del tabulario di Santa Maria Nuova in Monreale* (Palermo, 1902), 49-50 no. 109.

[24] Salimbene, 322-329; my description of Rainaldo hovers between a translation and a paraphrase in the hope that Salimbene as well as Rainaldo can be captured.

church it glittered and shone as it flamed; but when the horn of the snuffer was placed on it the candle darkened and went out. Thus it was with a Franciscan: when in the order he flamed and glowed with divine love and made light the way of others through good example. Then, fixing his point, Stephen said, "But remember yesterday at dinner how our bishop behaved. He allowed the friars to genuflect before him when they served him dishes at table. It is what the lay brother used to say of the Paschal candle." Hearing all this, poor Bishop Rainaldo groaned and begged permission to speak. He said that he had once been a flaming candle burning in the Franciscan order, giving good example to all those who observed him; and he said that Friar Salimbene, who had lived with him two years in the house at Siena, could testify to his old behavior. Rainaldo said that the friars of Tuscany and the house that had sent him to Paris to study would bear witness to his past life. If the friars had genuflected to him at dinner it was certainly not because he had wanted them to; but he could not beat them back with his staff. He begged not to be thought vainglorious. He knew his Ecclesiasticus: "Be not exalted in the day of thy honour"; and "He shall entertain and feed and give drink to the unthankful, and moreover he shall hear bitter words."[25] Then on bended knees Rainaldo said— and Salimbene heard and saw it—that it was a fault if he had given bad example and that as soon as he could he would tear the bishop's horns, the miter, from his head.

Rainaldo bade the Genoese friars farewell. He went to a monastery of white monks near Genoa where there was an old man (? Ugone) who had voluntarily renounced the bishopric of Turin and retired to the Cistercian cloister. The old man had heard that Rainaldo was a great clerk and newly a bishop. He sighed and said, "I am surprised that a prudent man should do anything so stupid, that you should become a bishop. Think. You were in the noblest order, the order of Saint Francis, the order of the friars minor, the order of extreme perfection, in which he 'who perseveres even to the end' without doubt 'shall be saved.'" The old man quoted Proverbs and Paul to the Hebrews and talked of himself as having been

[25] From Ecclus 11:4 and 29:31.

a bishop. He had tried to reform his clergy, but he could not. Rather than sacrifice his own soul he had resigned. He thought of Saint Benedict as his model.

In response to the old man Rainaldo said nothing, for he knew the old man spoke the truth and he remembered the warning of Ecclesiasticus not to contradict the truth or be ashamed to say it (4:25). But Salimbene thought somewhat differently and he said to the ex-bishop of Turin, "Look, father, you sent your clerks away; but think if you did well," and he quoted Zachariah and Jeremiah and Innocent III and many others. He quoted at length, or so he reports, from Innocent III in the titulus *de renunciatione* from the Decretals. Innocent said, and Salimbene quoted, "Do not think that Martha chose a bad part"; and he spoke of the security with fruitfulness, the pleasantness with usefulness, of combining the active with the comtemplative life, of going "now up to the mountain, now down to the field." He went on to warn against desertion of the pastoral rule lest Christ might not deign to receive the postulant at his feet with Mary.[26] Salimbene talked, and the bishops listened. Friar Rainaldo said nothing. He intended to rid himself of episcopal office.

Rainaldo traveled on in the direction of Rieti. When he got there his canons came to see him. They said that one of their co-canons was young and wanton and that he behaved more like a layman than a clerk. He wore his hair to his shoulders. Rainaldo dragged the wanton by his hair and boxed him on the ear. He called the canon's relatives, who were rich and noble, and told them that the boy must be clerk or lay, that his present compromise was insupportable. The relatives said that the canon should be a clerk, and that the bishop was free to make him one. The bishop cut the canon's hair and made him wear an enormous tonsure to compensate for his past negligence. The canon himself seemed penitent.

The bishop was, however, convinced that he could not really reform his clergy because they did not want to live as they should. Rainaldo had in fact given his canons constitutions, in 1250, with set fines and punishments. One of Rainaldo's documents survives in Rieti; it is still sealed with his pointed oval

[26] c. 10, X,i,9.

white wax seal on a strip of parchment.[27] Rainaldo forbade
the canons to hit each other, to insult each other, to alienate
or exchange the church's property. It is clear that the thirteenth-century Rieti chapter was really a difficult one. There
were repeated inhibitions against its unconstitutional growth
in numbers, as well as repeated reorganizations of its income.
Urban IV, in a sharp mandate to the bishop and chapter,
quashed the appointment of sixteen canons, nephews and
cousins, illiterates and boys; this occurred just ten years after
the cardinal bishop of Ostia, acting under a commission of
Innocent IV, had quashed appointments because by then, in
1253, the chapter had fifty members—its constitutional number came to be twenty-one, but in 1249 it was only twenty.[28]
(But a pope, Nicholas IV, from Rieti in 1290, created a canon
non obstante the constitutional restriction on number.)[29]

Rainaldo left Rieti and its continually inflated chapter to
look again for Innocent IV. Innocent was in Genoa (in late
May and June 1251). Rainaldo tried again to resign his
bishopric. Innocent saw that Rainaldo's purpose was fixed.
Innocent promised Rainaldo that he would absolve him of the
bishopric when he came into Tuscany. Rainaldo went to Bologna because he hoped the pope would pass through it (as he
finally did in mid-October) on his way to Tuscany. When the
pope was actually in Perugia (from November 1251) Rainaldo went to him. There, before the cardinals in consistory,
Rainaldo resigned office and benefice. He laid his *pontificalia,*
staff, miter, and ring, before the pope's feet. The cardinals and
the pope—but according to Salimbene particularly the pope
who had consecrated him—were disturbed by Rainaldo's
action. The pope had felt him a good bishop for Rieti; everyone had; and, Salimbene said, he was. They all, pope and cardinals, begged Rainaldo that, for the love of God and to honor

[27] Rieti, Archivio capitolare, armadio II, fasc. B, no. 1: "Frater
Rainaldus permissione divina Reatinus episcopus . . ."; dated Rieti, 9
March 1250 (Mazzatinti, 214).

[28] Rieti, Archivio capitolare, armadio IV, fasc. F, nos. 1-4. (Ostia is
no. 2; the Urban bull is no. 3; no. 4 is from 1313, a constitution of
Bishop Giovanni) (Mazzatinti, 221); for the twenty of 1249: armadio
IV, fasc. D, no. 3.

[29] Rieti, Archivio capitolare, armadio VII, fasc. E, no. 7.

them, for the utility of the church and the salvation of souls, he not resign. But Rainaldo said all entreaties were useless. The cardinals asked, "What? Even if an angel spoke to him? If God revealed what we have said to him?" The pope, seeing how fixed Rainaldo's intention was, tried to persuade him by telling him that, although he might give up the responsibilities of pastoral care, the order of bishop and the power of ordaining would remain to him. Rainaldo said, "I will have nothing at all."

Absolved, Rainaldo went back to the friars. He took a little sack, or wallet, or basket; and he begged bread for the day. As he went through Perugia begging, he met one of the cardinals come from consistory. The cardinal said to Rainaldo, "Now wouldn't it be better for you to be a bishop than to go about this way begging? Didn't our lord say that it is more blessed to give than to receive?" But, according to Salimbene, quickly the cardinal might have wished to have left Scripture alone. With a wealth of quotation Rainaldo overwhelmed him. Rainaldo and his quotations pressed the spiritual over the material in giving and receiving, praised poverty, and derided the wisdom of this world. The cardinal knew that God spoke in His saint. He went back to consistory next day and told the pope and the other cardinals what he had learned from a begging bishop. They were, according to Salimbene, struck with wonder.

Rainaldo asked the Franciscan minister general, John of Parma, to send him where he would. John sent him to the house at Siena where many knew him. He was there from the Feast of All Saints, at the beginning of November, until after Christmas, when he died and "went to God"; and going, he or his merits, sent back a cure for a canon of Siena who had been paralyzed for six years. Friends and co-canons took word of the miracle to the friars. As they went out of the gates of Siena they heard the chanting friars carrying Rainaldo to the church. The messengers and their news made a happy funeral. Salimbene, considering the life and death of this man with whom he had lived for two years in Siena, and whom he had often seen in Lyons and Genoa, found him very learned, a great lector in theology, a man of magnificent heart. For

Salimbene to believe that there was another such man in Tuscany he would certainly have to see him with his own eyes. Salimbene was impressed too by the fact that Rainaldo had a saintly brother, a Vallombrosan, good and literate and a friend to the friars. Meanwhile on 5 February 1252 Innocent IV replaced Rainaldo with his corrector Thomas, a curialist, who proved a serious diocesan.[30]

Italy was not, of course, completely without any bishops who took their jobs seriously. The mysteriously conventional (from a northern point of view) and hard-working bishops of Città di Castello make this glaringly clear, even if it can never be clear why the former abbot of a Premonstratensian house (San Severino under Orvieto) Nicolò, bishop from 1265 to 1279, for instance, should have behaved so (locally) peculiarly, why he should have been such a persistently orderly pastoral diocesan, involved in visitation, synod, and record-keeping. (Clement IV's letter of provision does sound more than mere formula when it speaks of the fame Nicolò had won because of the magnificent growth, spiritual and temporal, of San Severino under his rule.) A proximate cause for Nicolò's behavior, but only a proximate one, exists in the behavior of his provided predecessor, Bishop Pietro V Rossi d'Anagni (1252-1265). Nicolò's own behavior undoubtedly influenced that of his elected successor, Bishop Giacomo d'Enrico Cavalcanti (1280-1301), formerly a canon of Orvieto.[31] A continuing tra-

---

[30] Rieti, Archivio capitolare, armadio II, fasc. D, no. I (two original copies of Innocent's letter to the chapter announcing his provision) (Mazzatinti, 212); for Innocent's itinerary, see *Innocent IV*, IV, 543-572.

[31] For the appointments and elections of the three bishops, see: *Innocent IV*, III, 97 no. 5903; *Clément IV*, 37 no. 151; *Nicholas III*, 288 no. 648; and Giovanni Muzi, *Memorie ecclesiastiche e civili di Città di Castello* (Città di Castello, 1842-1844), II, 134-135, 147, 165. For Nicolò, see N. Backmund, *Monasticon Praemonstratense*, III (Straubing, 1956), 608; and for San Severino in general, see Lorenzo Fiocca, "Chiesa e abbazia dei Santi Severo e Martirio (fuori di Orvieto)," *Bollettino d'Arte*, IX (1915), 193-208. Catalogue references (e.g. Leopoldo Sandri, *Gli Archivi dell'Umbria*, Ministero dell'Interno, pubb. XXX, 1957, p. 138) would seem to indicate a valuable source for Nicolò's rule at his abbey: Orvieto, Archivio di stato, archivi vari, Abbazia dei SS. Severo e Martirio, "Sexternus libellariorum Monasterii

dition was applied by a continuing staff. The bishops of Città di Castello lie isolated at a little distance at one edge of the thirteenth-century Italian spectrum. But surviving fragments from the episcopates of a number of bishops, men like Luca of Cosenza, Leonardo of Giovinazzo, Graziadio of Pistoia, Guercio Tebalducci of Lucca, argue that one could form and populate a category of relatively interested diocesans, some even in the first half of the century.[32]

Some relatively conscientious Italian bishops and arch-bishops revealed themselves in synods. At both Ravenna and Milan provincial synods were provoked by Gregory X's Second Council of Lyons. In some ways this council seems to have been more effective in catching and holding the attention of the Italian church than was Innocent III's Fourth Lateran Council. Second Lyons was clearly an important council: its thirty-one canons as well as the action around it show a serious concern for significant moral and more general, ecumenical, problems. Some of its proposed remedies for current difficulties may sound a little more practical than they seem in fact to have been; but they were never vacantly verbose. Gregory X's summons were effective: the records of diocese after diocese still retain evidence of local reaction. Gregory X was a man in some ways even more imposing than his great predecessor; he was less morally and spiritually indecisive than Innocent III. As Salimbene said of Gregory, "He was a good man, just and honest and God-fearing."[33] Probably one of the most potent reasons for Second Lyons's attracting attention was that its

Sancti Sever', 1256-1297" (Matricola 830, no. 1). Actually the twenty-four documents extend only from September 1295 to February 1297. The Sexternus is interesting on one count; it shows careful record-keeping at Nicolò's abbey thirty years after his departure, and record-keeping that in some ways recalls Città di Castello: the alternating pairs of written and vacant folios, the clear organization around an ecclesiastical institution—fifteen notaries wrote the twenty-four acts.

[32] Russo, 366, and Alessandro Pratesi, *Carte latine . . . dall'Archivio Aldobrandini* (Vatican City, 1958), xxviii, xxix, xxxi, xxxiv-xxxv; *C.d.b.*, II (Giovinazzo), 172-173 no. 3, 197-207 nos. 18-23; Antonio Rosati, *Memorie per servire alla storia de' vescovi di Pistoia* (Pistoia, 1761), 90-94.

[33] Salimbene, 493.

audience was prepared for it. The sixty years since the fourth Lateran had taught prelates to know the importance of general councils; and, as in the text for its opening sermon, Second Lyons was specifically made to recall the Fourth Lateran, to evoke a response that could seem traditional.[34]

In any event the two great northern Italian provinces echoed the council-holding of Lyons at home; but they did not echo it in quite the same way. The thirty canons of Ottone Visconti's council in Santa Tecla, Milan in 1287 were particularly concerned with clerical discipline, clerical immunity, the enforcement of excommunication, and the protection of the clerical orders.[35] The nine canons of Bonifazio Fieschi's council in San Mercuriale, Forlì (for Ravenna) in 1286 followed more carefully the words of Second Lyons (e.g. Forlì, IV; Lyons, XIII). The Ravenna canons were homelier and more physically detailed. But there were also similarities: both carried the conventional injunction against clerical gaming.[36] Fra Bonifazio moved in a different direction from Ottone Visconti in his enjoining his clergy to physical charity to Christ's poor.[37] This may argue a sort of Christian sentiment in Bonifazio that was lacking in Ottone; it may merely argue that the two archbishops were working in different synodal traditions. The fact that the twenty-seven canons of Nicolò of Città di Castello's council of 1269 (which also forbids clerical gaming), before Nicolò had gone to second Lyons, are even more full of physical detail (bloodshed, concubines, burned roofs) than the Fieschi council may point to the fact that Fieschi was just more old-fashioned than Visconti.[38]

[34] Hefele-Leclercq, VI, 169 (Luke 22:15).

[35] Luigi Antonio Muratori, *Rerum italicarum scriptores* (Milan, 1723-1751), VIII, 1054ff.; Domenico Arnoldi, *Le Carte dello archivio arcivescovile di Vercelli* (Pinerolo, 1917), 324-335 no. 77.

[36] Gerolamo Rossi (Rubeus), *Historiarum Ravennatum libri decem* (hac altera editione libro undecimo) (Venice, 1589): "Concilia provincialia Ravenn. antiqua quattuor: concilium primum," 830-836.

[37] Canon II.

[38] Muzi, II, 154-157. The detail of the in some ways conservative Luccan synod of 1253 seems to strengthen this suggestion: Paolino Dinelli, "Dei sinodi diocesi di Lucca dissertazioni: IV" in *Memorie e documenti per servire all'istoria del Ducato di Lucca*, VII (Lucca, 1834), 53-141, 53-58, and Mansi, XXIII, cols. 821-824.

Federigo Visconti, archbishop of Pisa, held at least four great councils.[39] His council of 1258, when the church of Pisa was being reassembled after the confusion caused by its adherence to the imperial side, in the Staufen wars, tried something that the councils of Ravenna and Milan did not.[40] It pressed hard for the liturgical consistency and the liturgical distinctness of Pisa. It tried to make the provincial church, in this sense, an organism. Its canon III says that since—in a dominant and repeated thirteenth-century cliché—members ought not to be at discord with their head, all Pisan secular churches should follow the Use of the great church of Pisa. (In this Visconti, against the borders of Rome, sounds like William Wickwane of York, more than two decades later and against the borders of Canterbury, trying to insure the Use of York and to protect it against the Use of Sarum.)[41] In his canon XXXIX, Visconti ordered that in Pisa on Holy Saturday no one was to sing a Mass or sound a bell before the ringing of the bells at the great church of Pisa. Repeated liturgical injunctions were connected with the demand that every *plebanus* with his clerks, except one left to serve the religious needs of the people, should be present for the celebration of two great Pisan days of consecration, those of Santa Maria and San Pietro *a grade*. The blessing of Palm Sunday olive leaves and popular processions were to be controlled. Clerks should not carry arms, involve themselves in the practice of medicine unless they knew something about it, keep women, or (as elsewhere) play at dice or gamble. There were canons regulating clerical dress which shaded into very serious considerations of the reception and administration of the sacraments, in the direct tradition of the Fourth Lateran: insistence upon penance in serious illness, on weekly Mass-going, yearly confession and

[39] Dora Lucciardi, "Federico Visconti arcivescovo di Pisa," *Bollettino storico pisano*, I:2 (1932), 7-48, II:1 (1933), 7-37, II, 16; see, too, Celestino Piana, "I Sermoni di Federico Visconti, Arcivescovo di Pisa," *Rivista di storia della chiesa in Italia*, VI (1952), 231-248.

[40] Antonio Felice Mattei (Matthaejus), *Ecclesiae pisanae historia*, II (Lucca, 1772), app., 1-8; for the in some ways, related, and close, 1253 council of Bishop Guercio of Lucca, see Mansi, XXIII, cols. 821-824, and Dinelli, 53-58.

[41] See Brentano, *York Metropolitan Jurisdiction*, 25 n.9.

communion, the careful preservation of the Eucharist and sacred oil, the proper limitation of the daily saying of Mass. No clerk should sit in church when the Body of Christ was elevated or from that time until after the "per omnia secula seculorum" was said. Any priest hearing of the death of a pope should within eight days say a Mass for his soul. Federigo Visconti's church tried to be a centralized, liturgical, and also, unfortunately rather surprisingly, at least in part a religious thing.[42]

In isolation the quality of Federigo Visconti's synodal constitutions might seem again merely due to their coming from a specific synodal tradition, accidentally, or almost accidentally, current in Pisa. But the constitutions are not isolated. In the whole thirteenth-century Italian church, outside the pages of Salimbene, no other provincial prelate lives as Federigo Visconti does. He talks and remembers, and waves his hands —not just his arms and his pontificalia. Federigo's action is not merely the scattering of many informative documents from a busy pontificate, although it is that too.[43] It is above all action caught in a single manuscript kept by the Franciscans of Santa Croce in Florence, his book of sermons.[44] Sermons can be as formal and stiffly inarticulate as synods are; this is true even, perhaps even particularly, in the century from which Paul's Cross comes, which sent the friars out to preach, and which built *amboni* in Federigo's Pisa.[45] Conventional *exempla*

[42] Canons XXIX, XXXVII, XL; XXI, XXXI, XIX, IX; e.g. XXXIII and XXXIV, XXX, XVI, XV, XXIII, XXIV, XII, XXXII.

[43] See Mattei, II, 1-45, and Niccola Zucchelli, *Cronotassi dei vescovi e arcivescovi di Pisa*, Pisana 2 (Pisa, 1907), 94-102.

[44] Florence, Biblioteca Medicea Laurenziana, Plut. 33, sin. 1. The manuscript identifies itself as being from Santa Croce; for the library of Santa Croce, see Charles T. Davis, "The Early Collection of Books of S. Croce in Florence," *Proceedings of the American Philosophical Society*, CVII:5 (1963), 399-414.

[45] See G. R. Owst, *Preaching in Medieval England: an Introduction to Sermon Manuscripts of the Period c.1350-1450* (Cambridge, 1926), 198 (there is documentary evidence of Paul's Cross's existing from 1241, of preaching there from 1330); Owst noted the conjunction of *amboni* and famous preaching at Pisa (page 160), but I do not believe there has been any study of the connection between the iconography of the *amboni* and that of Federigo's sermons.

(sounding deceptively fresh), heavy texts, and rigid patterning make sermons mute. Federigo Visconti's texts are heavy; he loved his learning. His composition was far from casually revealing of the pattern of his mind; he loved the formality of the text's returning. But he himself keeps bursting through. The memory, the personal memory of his own life, is pushed hard against the text he has learned at school or in his chamber, against Augustine, Bernard, Isidore, and Bede. Like some early Thomas More, Federigo must talk of the moment in Bologna, the days in Paris, the Pantheon or the *candelora* in Rome.[46]

Federigo Visconti came from one of the major families of Pisa. The Visconti had long been important in the city, and they had recently been active in Sardinia. Federigo was born about the year 1200, probably. He remembered being a schoolboy at San Siro, and then Bologna. He became a domestic chaplain to Innocent IV—here again an unusually distinguished bishop is connected with Innocent and his household. Federigo was with Innocent when Innocent made Peter Martyr a "saint." He went with Innocent to Lyons and then went on to Paris and its learning. In Paris he watched with interest, and remembered, later to talk of it, the high esteem in which the Franciscans were held at the royal court. He came back to Pisa a canon and *plebanus* of Vico.

From 1241 Pisa's relations with the papacy, when they had existed at all, had been extremely difficult. The Pisan capture of the prelates in the Genoese galleys seemed a more startling sort of attack than the papacy could bear. Imperial Pisa was cut off from the church. After Federigo was elected Pisa's archbishop, he went, in 1255, to Anagni to try to heal the wounds; but in spite of his having old friends at the curia he remained "electus" of a disfavored see from 1254 until 1257. Pisa was received back into the church's favor in 1257. The bull of absolution was read by a Franciscan in Pisa's San Francesco; and Pisa gave itself over to three days of solemn procession. Federigo marked the return to the church by celebrating the foundation of the great hospital of Pisa (great too in

[46] Laurenziana, fos. 25, 35, 42v, 82, 85, 91v-92; Lucciardi, I, 9-11; II, 32-37.

its indulgences) in a large convocation of distinguished prelates. Federigo then convoked his first synod. He spent the ensuing years visiting, correcting, encouraging, preaching, following—in thirteenth-century episcopal idiom—the steps of Christ. Federigo was also a builder and began the Camposanto.

In the late 1260's, however, Pisans, and seemingly Federigo among them, were unable to resist the attraction of Frederick II's Staufen heirs or to find in themselves any attraction to Charles of Anjou. The city welcomed Conradin in 1268. It fell again into papal disfavor and became again the object of papal threats. Gregory X, upon his election in September 1271, turned sharply on Pisa, which, ironically, had received the end of the papal vacancy with much rejoicing. Gregory threatened (as Clement IV had) to rip away the last vestiges of episcopal dignity that remained to condemned Pisa, as if it were another Recanati or Osimo. The Pisans treated with Charles. In 1273, again with much rejoicing, they rejoined the church, in time for Federigo to be summoned again to Lyons in 1274. Three years of peace preceded Federigo's death in October 1277.[47] But Federigo's death, unlike that of almost every other thirteenth-century Italian archbishop, did not silence him. The live voice is still heard, as it is, wonderfully clearly, in the moment of fire in his sermons when he speaks of Francis:

> Truly blessed are those who actually saw the blessed Francis himself, as I did, through God's grace. I saw him, and with my own hand I touched him, in a heavy press of people in the great piazza at Bologna.[48]

One March morning in 1263 Federigo Visconti took a little bark from San Pietro to San Rossore, where he celebrated a sailors' Mass. He then boarded a magnificent and well-stocked

[47] See particularly Lucciardi, i, 7-19; ii, 7-28; also: Laurenziana, fos. 8v, 24, 30, 68, 97, 110, 134v, 136, 127v; Zucchelli, 98-102; David Herlihy, *Pisa in the Early Renaissance* (Yale, 1958), 39, i. (Archbishop Federigo is not written of at length in Herlihy's book but he is very much alive there.)

[48] Laurenziana, fo. 85; I have changed the number ("we" to "I") in translating, because the plural seems to hide from modern eyes the very personal quality of the statement; but it is worth noting that Federigo did speak of himself as "we."

Pisan galley, painted red, decorated with miter and pastoral cross, fore, aft, and midship, with a great red cloth over its prow. He sailed to an Easter visitation of Sardinia, that he might move from white Pisan church to white Pisan church in a path through the exquisite green of the Sardinian spring-tide.[49] Federigo had planned, and explained, his proposed visitation carefully. He had finished a meticulous visitation of his chapter and diocese; and he had then turned to the visitation of his province, according, as he said, to the provisions of Innocent IV's constitution *Romana ecclesia*.[50] He had begun his provincial visitation with the neighboring diocese of Massa Marittima. The bishop of Massa had at first offered to receive his metropolitan. Then, after consulting his chapter, he had decided to refuse and to appeal to Rome. The appeal came to nothing. While Federigo was in Sardinia, his relative Enrico de Abbate, a canon of Massa, acting as proctor for the bishop and chapter of Massa, swore, before Federigo's delegates in this matter, to accept Federigo's visitation.[51]

Characteristically Federigo's preparations for his metropolitan, primatial, and legatine visitation of Sardinia were not merely physical and legal; they were also scriptural. As he preached, Federigo saw himself as another Judith. In the historical sense Judith was a woman who exposed herself to grave danger for the safety of her city. Allegorically he, Federigo, was a Judith in his going into Sardinia; and he asked the priests of Pisa to pray to God in His high throne in heaven to send, as He had to Judith, an angel out of heaven to guard him in his going and in his staying in Sardinia and in his coming back. In the allegory he saw not only himself as Judith, but Pisa (*civitas nostra Pisana*), the city or the see or both combined, as Bethulia, Judith's city. Considerably more startlingly he saw Sardinia as Holofernes. Federigo himself was not completely satisfied with the last analogy. Although he undoubtedly liked the scriptural figure, he could not be un-

[49] Laurenziana, fo. 141; see, too, Emilio Cristiani, "I diritti di primazia e legazia in Sardegna degli arcivescovi pisani al tempo di Federico Visconti (1254-1277)" in "Vescovi e diocesi in Italia nel medioevo": *Italia Sacra*, V (Padua, 1964), 419-427.

[50] c. 1, VI, iii, 20.   [51] Laurenziana, fo. 140.

aware of the fact that only rarely, and then to replace it, did the careful visitor remove the head of the visited, even the abstracted, collective visited. Federigo did not deny the analogy, but he added to it: "Holofernes stands for Sardinia or for Prospero, archbishop of Torres (Sassari)." Prospero of Reggio, the Cistercian archbishop of the great northern Sardinian see, was already identified as the ecclesiastical leader of the opposition to Pisa in an island torn into various divisions (which from the distance seem most importantly the division between Pisa and Genoa). Prospero was, in Federigo's sermon, the named member of the Sardinian conspiracy against the primatial and legatine powers of Pisa, the city-see which was (through Bethulia reinterpreted) "indeed a virgin of the Lord."[52]

Federigo set out on the Friday of Passion Week, 23 March 1263.[53] Besides his great galley he had with him a small twelve-oared baggage ship. His company was a distinguished one. It included two canons of Pisa, the *plebanus* of Cascina, Pietro da Ceprano (who was Federigo's "chamberlain and scribe or notary"), Federigo's cross-bearer Orlando, and thirty-five laymen and servants. There were the archbishop's officials and familiars, but also two ambassadors of the commune of Pisa, who were the archbishop's brother and his nephew-in-law, and two knights, who were the archbishop's nephews. The sailors, who were commanded by Alberto Follario, came from the archbishop's maritime fees of Vada and Piombino. The sailors of Livorno had chosen to send money rather than themselves. They sent forty lire to replace twenty sailors. With this money twenty more sailors were procured from Vada and Piombino, to add to Vada's twenty and Piombino's sixty, to make the full complement of one hundred.[54]

Federigo sailed to Vada and got there the same day. The next day, on a favorable wind, he sailed to Piombino, where he

[52] Laurenziana, fo. 134v.

[53] A detailed account of the visitation is preserved in Laurenziana, fos. 141-143; I have followed it closely, as has Lucciardi (1, 28-35), whose account I have found very helpful, particularly for the identification of place names.

[54] For these fees see Lucciardi, II, 9; and see II, 9-14, for the archbishop's feudal and judicial rights and responsibilities.

spent Palm Sunday, said Mass in the *pieve,* and confirmed
many children, in the afternoon, at Santa Maria, the church of
the Franciscan nuns. He reboarded the galley and sailed to
Longone. Then having sailed by the coasts of Elba and Cor-
sica, having moved from port to port, on Good Friday he
finally arrived in Sardinia. He spent Easter at Terranova
(Olbia) in the northern judgeship of Gallura and was received with much honor by bishop and judge. The day after
Easter, 2 April, he went to the port of Santa Lucia in the diocese of Galtelli, where he was met by the judge and also the
bishop of Galtelli. Embarking again, he sailed on to Cagliari
on the southern coast of Sardinia. He arrived in Cagliari on
the octave of Easter.

Since it was evening when the archbishop landed, he did not
immediately enter the city. He waited so that the entry could
be, as the people of Cagliari wished, more solemn. The archbishop spent the night with the Franciscans in the suburbs.
In the morning, on Monday, 9 April, he went up to the city.
His procession included a great many people, Franciscans,
clerks, laymen and women from Cagliari and Stampace. Honored by nobles and merchants, flashing with silver, red and
scarlet, furs and peacock feathers, thus ablaze from head to toe
and blazing with his sacred vessels, Federigo rode mounted
on a horse whose saddle was covered with scarlet and whose
bit and pectoral were silver, as were the archbishop's spurs.
Federigo's description relishes the luxury: some of the scarlet
was really of the very best, it notes, ten lire and eight *soldi,*
Pisan, the *canna.* "Thus," the account concludes this episode,
"we solemnly entered Cagliari, and at the church of Santa
Maria we made a sermon to the people."[55]

Federigo stayed in a house near Santa Maria because the
archbishop of Cagliari's house was not big enough.[56] The
archbishop of Cagliari himself was in Rome, but his suffragans
presented themselves to Federigo, honored him, and gave him
gifts of bread, wine, meat, and cheese. The bishop of Suelli,
the vicar of the archbishopric gave Federigo money for expenses: twelve lire of Suelli, fifteen lire of Dolia, and fifteen

[55] Laurenziana, fo. 141v.
[56] Laurenziana, fo. 141v: "quia domus archiepiscopi non erat capax."

lire of Genoa. From that time, too, the bishop of Suelli became Federigo's constant companion. While the prelates were
still waiting in Cagliari for horses, on 25 April the local
churches celebrated the Feast of Saint Mark. The archbishop
and the bishop made a solemn procession and sang the litany
from church to church in the area—and granted indulgence,
and read the Gospel, and heard confessions, and returned
home to Santa Maria. There Federigo said solemn Mass and
preached to the people. He ordered that the litany be sung
every year as, it seems, it had not been.

Meanwhile that old enemy, Cistercian by order, Lombard
by nation, Prospero of Reggio was busy at the curia. He tried
to impede Federigo's action by establishing the fact that he
was no longer legate because of a deprivation connected with
past excommunication of the Pisans.[57] Prospero impetrated
papal letters that would invalidate Federigo's legateship and
order the bishops of Sardinia not to obey him. The messengers
carrying the letters did not reach Federigo. They were captured by the people of Cagliari and only later released at the
request of the judge of Arborea and the archbishop of Oristano. Hearing something of the matter, Federigo said that if
he really were deprived of his legateship it would not matter,
because he still ought to be admitted to the island's sees as
primate and patriarch of all Sardinia.[58]

Horses finally arrived for the archbishop's party, but not
from the judge of Arborea or the archbishop of Oristano or
his suffragan bishops. For this they apologized but said that
they were caught in a long siege, to Pisan interests, which occupied an army of 1,000 horsemen and 3,000 foot.[59] At last on
6 May Federigo started inland. On the first day he got to Terralba where he made the litany of the Ascension and where
the archbishop of Oristano came to lunch with him. On the
following morning, the Feast of the Ascension, he was received
in solemn procession by the people of Oristano, archbishop,

[57] Laurenziana, fos. 141v-142.
[58] Laurenziana, fo. 142. For Prospero, see Angelo Mercati, "Per la
storia letteraria di Reggio Emilia," *Saggi di storia e letteratura*, 1
(Rome, 1951), 41-114, 65-66.
[59] Laurenziana, fo. 142.

clergy, and laity. The merchants and the Pisans of the city had
carried over his head a cloth of gold, from his entering the territory of Oristano until his arrival at the cathedral church.
There Federigo celebrated solemn Mass; he was assisted at the
altar by the archbishop of Oristano and the bishop of Suelli.

Federigo waited for eight days in Oristano. He hoped that
the judge of Arborea might be free of his siege and come to
him. On the eighth day Federigo rode on to the monastery of
Bonarcado, locally within the diocese of Oristano. On the following Friday, 25 May, the archbishop rode on. On Saturday
he was within the bishopric of Ottana in the province of Torres (Sassari). He had thus entered the third province of Sardinia—or the fourth if the northeastern dioceses within the
province of Pisa count as one. In Ottana the judge of Arborea,
with two hundred knights on horseback, rode to the archbishop's presence. They all dismounted and came up to the
archbishop on foot to do him honor. The judge kissed the
archbishop's hand before he remounted. The judge was present at the archbishop's solemn Mass, as were the bishop of
Suelli, and the bishops of Terralba and Santa Giusta of Oristano province, and the bishop of Bosa of Torres province, and
also many nobles and knights. After Mass they all—the archbishop of Pisa, the bishops of the three Sardinian provinces,
and the representatives of Pisan military power—ate together
a joyous banquet. Afterward the judge and his men rode back
to their siege, and the judge said in parting that he hoped he
would see the archbishop again in Oristano. The archbishop
remained three days in Ottana; and the whole countryside
flocked to see him. Because the bishopric was vacant, the archbishop collected together all the clergy of the place and visited
them. He made commissions to hear many matrimonial
cases.[60]

Because of the war between the judges of Arborea and Sassari, it was not safe for the archbishop to travel on to Sassari,
so he turned back to Oristano. There he and his household
were given presents. He himself was given by the archbishop
of Oristano a beautiful white palfrey with a valuable Sardinian
saddle, which saddle and palfrey Federigo later sent on to the

[60] Laurenziana, fos. 142-142v.

Roman curia as a present for Cardinal Ottobuono. At Oristano, Archbishop Federigo visited the bishop and chapter of Santa Giusta. They were brought before him in the judge's palace, dug like some sort of shellfish out of their exquisite little cathedral (see Figs. 10 and 12).[61]

Federigo left Oristano and rode back to Terralba. The next day he rode to Ales. At Ales he said Mass, preached, confirmed a large number of children, and visited the chapter; he stayed two days. Then he rode to Frussia and to Suelli where he celebrated Mass, preached, confirmed lots of boys and girls, and again stayed for two days. Then he rode on to the see of Dolia and acted similarly; but he stayed only a day because a messenger came to him at Dolia to say that the galley was ready to go back to Pisa. Federigo rode to Cagliari and said Mass at Santa Maria and preached a sermon in which he thanked the people of Sardinia, clergy and laity, for their graciousness to him and his household. Then on the Feast of Saint Rainerius, on June 18, in the afternoon, he again boarded the galley. He sailed to Santa Lucia in the diocese of Galtelli where, since the old bishop of Galtelli had recently died, he confirmed the new elect. Because he was leaving Sardinia he gave commission to three Sardinian bishops, the bishop of Terranova and two suffragans of Sassari, to consecrate the elect.[62] He then set sail for Portoferraio in Elba, and, the day after, for Populonia and then Vada. Finally, on Wednesday after the Feast of Saint John, on 27 June, he reentered Pisa. And, making account with his chamberlain, he found that beyond the gifts and offerings he had gotten, which amounted to 500 lire, he had spent 800 lire from his own *camera*.[63]

It has seemed wise to tell at length Federigo's expensive visitation; it is the longest journey into ecclesiastical administration in the thirteenth-century provincial Italian church. It is a bright story of boats bobbing, scarlets flashing, horses being ridden. Its hero is an extraordinary man, eccentric, intensely interested in his own sermons, busy confirming and saying litanies, always with the memory of his once having touched

[61] Laurenziana, fo. 142v.
[62] Laurenziana, fo. 142v.
[63] Laurenziana, fo. 143v.

Saint Francis burning in his mind. The memory of Saint Francis seems to be at the center of the man pushing him to action, coaxing him to notice the Franciscans in a crowd, to go to Franciscan churches, to stay at their houses—at the very least one must say that the Bologna incident was part of the equipment that he carried to Sardinia. But, although this Franciscan-encouraged journey is one of the most impressive pieces of ecclesiastical action in the whole Italian thirteenth century, although it tempts one to compare Federigo with the most literarily familiar of all Italian archbishops, the great Federigo Borromeo, it was at the same time both a very secular and a very ecclesiastically ill-defined visitation.[64] The whole action was clearly connected with traditional Visconti family interests. It was an action encouraged by, and partly supported by, the commune of Pisa. Its entourage included Pisan, and Visconti, ambassadors. It gathered the church of Sardinia to the Pisan side. The definitions of and distinctions between Federigo's roles as archbishop, metropolitan, primate, patriarch, and legate are unclear; and his attitude toward Rome was one which may well have made it seem wise to send off the white palfrey with its Sardinian saddle to a Fieschi cardinal. It is odd, too, with Francis in one's mind—although perhaps conventional always in ecclesiastics—to follow in the footprints of Christ with peacock feathers on; they were singularly lacking from Christ's life—even admitting the alabaster box of ointment. And there is the analogy with Judith. The visitation was a curiously mixed affair.

In fact, there is something about this best of all Italian visitations (always excluding those of the bishops of Città di Castello) that, if it is turned to the right angle and shaken a little, seems to tug at some memory of English visitation, one in which a sudden movement reveals something surprising. When the memory is clear, it is a shock to put the two visitations together. Matthew Paris tells the English story of how Boniface of Savoy, archbishop of Canterbury, came to visit the canons of Saint Bartholomew's in London, and of the sub-

[64] Federigo Visconti called Federigo Borromeo to my mind before I had read Lucciardi's similar reaction; but this may only indicate Manzoni's power.

prior's receiving him because the prior was not at home.[65] The canons made procession and rang bells and lighted candles and dressed themselves in rich choir copes; but the archbishop cared little for this and said he had come to make a visitation. One of the canons said, and he spoke for all, that they had a learned and diligent bishop who visited them when they needed it, and that they did not wish to be visited by anyone else. Then the archbishop flew into a rage and "unmindful of the sanctity of his predecessors" struck the old subprior and pulled him about and cried, "This is the way to deal with English traitors." A horrible scene followed, with the archbishop swearing and rushing upon the poor old subprior and crushing him against the choirstalls and ripping his gorgeous cloak so that its precious metals and jewels fell to the floor. As the enraged archbishop moved, his vestments flew back; and many of those present saw clearly that he was armed. They were, Matthew Paris says, filled with horror to see an archbishop armed. The scene of Becket's death, as Matthew may have meant, is grotesquely parodied—hair shirt to armor, martyrdom to bullying, defense of the church to its destruction. At the sight of the armor Matthew makes his scene rip open, the texture of normal human behavior has burst.

Although Matthew seems to lack any appreciation at all of Boniface's admirable plan of visitation, he was not always completely unsympathetic with the man. When Boniface defended the whole clerical order, Matthew could see him moving in the footsteps of Becket.[66] But, in general, Boniface was to Matthew a man more suited by training and inclination to being a knight than a bishop—an illiterate, inexpert foreigner.[67] Although Matthew was rather taken by the idea of civil servants becoming good bishops in the tradition of his name-saint, he seems not to have been similarly persuaded by the related and more familiar military tradition.[68] There is no

---

[65] Matthew Paris, *Chronica Majora*, v, 121-123.

[66] Matthew Paris, *Chronica Majora*, v, 632.

[67] Matthew Paris, *Chronica Majora*, v, 120.

[68] Bishop William Raleigh of Norwich was hoped to be a Matthew: *Chronica Majora*, iii, 618; this attitude in Matthew Paris was observed in Marion Gibbs and Jane Lang, *Bishops and Reform, 1215-1272* (Oxford, 1934), 17.

doubt about what Matthew thought about the flashing of armor beneath a vestment. It is clearly meant to be a stunning revelation, a high moment of ugliness in Matthew's history.

If a breeze had, on the field of Ottana, disarranged Federigo Visconti's vestments to reveal him protected by armor, it could in its context hardly have produced any surprise at all. A man who was in many ways a very good Italian bishop might spend a great deal of time at the business of war. A striking example of this sort of bishop is Guglielmino Ubertini of Arezzo. Guglielmino held synods, visited his diocese, corrected indiscipline in his clerks, tried to regulate the life of his chapter, encouraged religious orders (some, the Franciscans rather than the Camaldolese) and charitable organizations; but his life was in large part given up to war and bloodshed, to the battling of factions and orders and communes. In 1289, thirty-four years after his consecration, he died in battle. His helmet and sword were carried away by his enemies, the Florentines, to hang as trophies in their baptistery.[69] Boniface of Savoy in his armor was perhaps only a southerner who had not adjusted to the ways of the north.

Mixed bishops, with their knightly qualities, were examined by Salimbene. He practiced a description of one in describing Nicola of Reggio and then reworked it for one of his major characters, Innocent IV's nephew, Bishop Obizzo of Parma (Salimbene's native city):

> He was a military sort of man, and I can describe him as I have already described Bishop Nicola of Reggio. For with clerks he was a clerk, with men in regular orders he was a regular, with laymen a layman, with knights a knight, with barons a baron. . . . He was a great dealer and he alienated the goods of his see . . . , but he got back what he alienated and made much for the see. He was a literate man learned in canon law and expert in ecclesiastical office. He knew the game of chess, and he held secular clerks tightly under his rule.[70]

[69] Corrado Lazzeri, *Guglielmino Ubertini vescovo di Arezzo (1248-1289) e i suoi tempi* (Florence, 1920), *passim*, but more particularly, 50-56, 117, 122, 139, 151-152, 160-164, 234.

[70] Salimbene, 62.

This mixed or segmented, checkered man as cleric is not
surprising in a century that opened with Aleaumes of Clari
(fighting as if he were another Turpin and described with
pride in his brother's book) and closed with the pontificate of
Anthony Bek, a century in which Urban IV was seen by a
Sienese merchant as "more like a temporal lord than a pope."[71]
There was no country in western Europe in which the type
was unknown, and his description describes a condition and a
problem in the whole church. But in the constant presence of
the mixture, the awareness of the different modes of behavior
appropriate to the two orders was not lost. It sometimes appears rather surprisingly, as in Salimbene's description of
Anselmo di Guarino: that pretty man was "inept at arms.
He had been raised too much at the curia with the cardinals
and had learned priestly manners"—one might not have
thought the cardinals could teach them.[72] But in spite of both
presence and awareness, the bishop as checkered cleric was
shocking, and is surprising, in England but not in Italy. The
difference in his position and reception indicates a real difference between the church in Italy and the church in England.
Grosseteste's desire, written to the king of England in 1245 or
1246, "that spiritual things be dealt with by ecclesiastical and
spiritual men, secular things by secular men," could hardly
have been understood, as Grosseteste meant it, by an Italian.[73]

Italian bishops fall then into various overlapping categories.
There are those, the great majority, who did not move enough
in any direction to leave a decipherable trace in history. There
are those men, like Manasses of Volturara, who have left no
sign of any episcopal involvement, but who emerged occasionally to perform some ordinary secular act. There are those,
like Bartolomeo Pignatelli or Giovanni Boccamazza, who are
quite visible, not as diocesans but as warriors or politicians or

[71] The document is partly translated in Daniel Waley, *The Papal
State in the Thirteenth Century* (London, 1961), 165.

[72] Salimbene, 62.

[73] W. A. Pantin (in D. A. Callus, *Robert Grosseteste* [Oxford, 1955]),
199. One must of course always keep in mind the English bishops from
whom there is little record of taste for purely pastoral activity; a good
example is Merton at Rochester: J.R.L. Highfield, *The Early Rolls
of Merton* (Oxford, 1964), 30-34.

civil servants. There are the saints, like Rainaldo, who turned in disgust from a job that they saw as an empty honor rather than a duty. There are the quiet bishops of Città di Castello, and a very few others perhaps, who seem essentially to have been responsible diocesans. Finally there are those men, ranging from Federigo Visconti to Guglielmino Ubertini and Obizzo of Parma, who reflect their communities variously and are divided into segments like their communities'. None of these bishop types suggests itself as an inevitable source or mold for the great central leaders of an enthusiastic national church.

These are of course not the only sorts of categories into which the Italian bishops can be divided. This is not the conventional way of describing bishops; and some conventional descriptions should prove helpful in understanding what sort of men Italian bishops were. Above all it is always necessary to remember that there were very many more of them than there were English bishops and that they are and can be a great deal less well known.[74] It is safe to say that there were a great many more of every conceivable category, except saints and scholars, among Italian bishops.

Many Italian bishops were local to the town and *contado* of their sees. This phenomenon, the really local bishop, fairly rare in England, common in Italy, is a measure of the difference between the structure of the two societies and of their attitudes toward themselves. In England aristocratic west-country families like the Giffards and the Cantilupes provided bishops for west-country sees in the general area of family dominance (but not only there); in Italy the Fieschi, the Capuani, the Visconti turn up at home (but not only there). There were of course very great differences among Italian sees. Sees more or less in the hands of patrons who were not bound by local interests (Naples, Monreale, Sora, Rieti) had episcopates less local than freer sees (Amalfi) or ones in towns with tougher local interests (Pisa, Genoa, Milan). But, in spite of diocesan differences, one of the clear general characteristics of the Italian church was its very specific localness; and this localness is noticeable in, to choose examples, Salerno, Amalfi, Sessa

[74] See Ernst H. Kantorowicz, *Frederick the Second* (London, 1931), 143.

Aurunca, Bologna, Florence, Pistoia, Pisa, Potenza, Milan, Arezzo, Lucca, Volterra, Genoa, Squillace, and even Rome.[75]

Unfortunately it is impossible to reduce Italian episcopal backgrounds to any sort of reliable statistics. There is little to suggest whether or not the bishops who can be at all known form a representative sample; the famous bishops, known because of their appearance in extra-diocesan records, are presumably atypical, but not necessarily unrepresentative in terms of background. More disturbing to statistical analysis is the fact that there is the broadest possible variation in the depth, security, and detail of possible knowledge of the backgrounds of the bishops about whom something can be known. Some of the bishops are genealogically fixed members of familiar, visible, and important families: Federigo Visconti, Ottone Visconti. Some are clearly members of families whose position in society is visible but not in such detail or in such a clearly defined way: Filippo Augustariccio. Some are connected with their supposed backgrounds only by suggestive names, single acts, shady local traditions, or hints in unreliable sources. The reduction to figures would make their backgrounds seem unduly, misleadingly secure; but the possible significance of their backgrounds must not on that account be discarded. The contrast with English bishops, about whom a great deal more can be said but sometimes very perilously, is revealing. To put it very crudely, there is a striking difference between the English landed-gentry bishop (men like Langton and Sutton) and the Italian urban-patriciate bishop. Neither is at all exclusively the type of its country, but each clearly represents its and not the other's country. In both countries investments were varied and the sources of income of both types of family were impure. But clearly the preponderant landed investments of the Eng-

[75] For Sessa Aurunca, see Giovanni Diamare, *Memorie critico-storiche della chiesa di Sessa Aurunca* (Naples, 1906), 178 (particularly for Roberto II de Asprello); for Pistoia, Rosati, 80-87, 94 (Buono, Soffredo Soffredi, Guidaloste Vergiolesi); for Potenza, see Ferdinando Ughelli, *Italia Sacra* (Venice, 1717-1722), VII, col. 139 (Oberto, who translated the bones of Saint Gerard); for Squillace, Ughelli, IX, col. 435 (Ricardo, archdeacon of Squillace); for Lucca, see Martino Giusti, "Le Elezioni dei vescovi di Lucca specialmente nel secolo XIII," *Rivista di storia della chiesa in Italia*, VI (1952), 205-230, 218, 220, 223.

lish gentry were more stable than were the significantly mercantile and banking investments of the patriciate. Directly and indirectly this difference may well be even causally connected with different episcopal attitudes toward slow, relatively permanent ecclesiastical constitutional reform on the one hand and the frenetic expression of religious enthusiasm on the other. At the very least this difference helps define the more general Anglo-Italian difference.

There was a noticeably higher proportion of regulars, monks and friars, in the Italian than in the English church. Italian Dominicans seem to have been particularly prominent. Against poor Kilwardby alone at Canterbury can be cast a large group which includes bishops and archbishops of Cosenza, Lucca, Lipari, Syracuse, Gravina, Acerenza, Taranto, Naples, Potenza, Genoa, Terni, and Bologna.[76] There were also Franciscans as, for example, at Anglona, Tricarico, Reggio Calabria, Cosenza, Gubbio, Terni, and of course Rieti (and Rome).[77] There were Austin hermits at Naples and Terni; and there were Cistercians, as at Anglona, Cosenza, Torres, and Tertiveri, and Benedictines, as at Benevento, Gravina, and Nicastro—a large and general sprinkling of regulars of which this is only a small sample. At Benevento, in the vacancy after Capoferro's death, between 1280 and 1282 (after one candidate declined), four opposing capitular parties

[76] For Gravina, Ughelli, vii, col. 118; for Acerenza, Ughelli, vii, col. 36; Taranto, Ughelli, ix, col. 137; Ughelli is certainly not completely trustworthy (although I have sometimes found him more trustworthy than his successors—he was sometimes closer to his sources); but I think he is a safe source, and probably still the best source for this sort of general impression; for Lucca, Giusti, 220; for Lipari and Syracuse: M.-H. Laurent, "I Vescovi di Sicilia e la decima pontificia del 1274-1280," *Rivista di storia della chiesa in Italia*, v (1951), 75-90, 87-88; for Cosenza, see *Dictionnaire d'histoire et de géographie ecclésiastiques*, ed. A. Baudrillart, A. de Meyer, and E. Van Cauwenbergh, xiii (Paris, 1956), cols. 928-930: article by R. van Doren; for Terni, see Conrad Eubel, *Hierarchia catholica medii aevi*, i (Münster, 1913), i, 285.

[77] For Anglona, Ughelli, vii, col. 84; for Tricarico, Ughelli, vii, col. 150; for Reggio Calabria, Guarna Lagoteta, "Cronaca dei vescovi ed arcivescovi di Reggio di Calabria," *Rivista storica calabrese*, vii (1899), 169-184, 182; for Gubbio, Ughelli, i, col. 645.

elected four potential archbishops: a canon of Benevento, a corrector of apostolic letters, a Franciscan, and a Benedictine. The Benedictine (admittedly an unusual one—a prominent Cassino monk and Neapolitan politician bound for a dubious cardinalate under Celestine V) won; he defeated, with the support of the "wiser" part of the chapter and the investigating cardinals (one was Hugh of Evesham) and Martin IV, representatives of three lively elements in Italian ecclesiastical life. (The successful candidate's political sympathy for the regular life may have come to seem excessive when in the 1290's he granted away episcopal rights to the Celestini.) At Terni in the later part of the century three orders of friars succeeded each other to the episcopal see. At Nocera Umbra, a diocese with a peculiarly saintly thirteenth-century history, in 1222 after a short pontificate, the regular bishop, Saint Rainaldo, died.[78]

The outlines of Rainaldo's life are blurred by a particularly difficult hagiographical tradition as well as by the difficulties inherent in all conventional hagiography. As a young man the aristocratic Rainaldo was led by his ascetic piety to the hermitage of Santa Croce at Fonte Avellana. There his administrative abilities as well as his asceticism were noticeable. Chosen bishop of Nocera, he at first declined, but then accepted God's will, and tried, in the tradition of ancient saint

[78] For Tertiveri, Ughelli, viii, col. 390; for Nicastro, Ughelli, ix, col. 405; for Benevento, Ughelli, viii, cols. 140-141, and *Les Registres de Martin IV*, ed. F. Olivier-Martin and others, Bibliothèque des écoles françaises d'Athènes de Rome (Paris, 1935) hereafter *Martin IV*, 65 no. 175; for Giovanni of Benevento and the Celestini, see above, Chapter II. Giovanni of Benevento is dealt with at some length in Otto Vehse, "Benevent und die Kurie unter Nicolaus IV," *Quellen und Forschungen aus italienischen Archiven und Bibliotheken*, xx (1928/9), 57-90. The difficult evidence from Nocera Umbra (the "Legenda Minor" and the "Legenda Maior" of Rainaldus) is carefully examined and criticized in an interesting and valuable article: Gino Sigismondi, "La 'Legenda Beati Raynaldi,' le sue fonti e il suo valore storico," *Bollettino della deputazione di storia patria per l'Umbria*, lvi (1960), 5-111—for the matter of Rainaldo's life, see particularly 31 and 41-44; the form "Rainaldo" rather than the more conventional, for Nocera Umbra, "Rinaldo," is used here in order to avoid the implication that the medieval Latin form is different from that for the name of Rainaldo of Rieti.

bishops from Martin of Tours through Wulfstan of Worcester, to live the contemplative life as he acted the active life. As
a bishop, the recorded Rainaldo gave himself over to fasts,
vigils, prayers, and sleeping on floors. He also indulged in a
personal sort of charity by adopting a local orphan boy, whom
he taught to come to him and to his lay and clerical guests
before dinner every day and to say, "For the love of God and
of the Blessed Virgin Mary give alms to me a poor little creature"; and thus the bishop reminded all present (except perhaps
the child) of Christ in His poor. But Rainaldo did not restrict
himself to the grooming of his own soul and those of his immediate guests. He was also remembered and admired (and
the admiration is as important as the dubious fact) for having
been something of an active diocesan. He went about his diocese, it is said, correcting and reforming. A specific instance
is recalled, his excommunication of the spoilers of a church
dedicated to Saint Peter in the neighborhood of Gualdo
Tadino. Rainaldo's being a religious was not thought to have
interfered with his being a bishop; instead, in a rather pale
way, it encouraged him to episcopal act.

Regulars were evidently not considered unsuitable candidates for the episcopacy as it was understood in Italy (except
perhaps in Benedictine but royal Monreale). The presence of
regulars (except in saintly cases like those of the Rainaldos of
Rieti and Nocera and in an excessive case like that of Giovanni of Benevento who gave things away) seems to have
caused almost no variation in the pattern of episcopal action
or apathy.

In Italy as in England civil servants and curialists were
given episcopal sees, as were representatives of great feudal
families like the Filangieri. There were Staufen favorites at
the beginning of the century, Angevin ones at the end, and
papal favorites throughout. Some of these men, like those from
the curia of Innocent IV (who "too much loved his own") or
like the Angevin Aygler of Naples or Gregory IX's Guercio
Tebalducci at Lucca, proved unusually capable bishops.[79]

[79] Salimbene, 62; "Multum enim dilexit propinquos suos papa In-
nocentius quartus"; and it seems to have applied to his own clerks as
well as his own nephews.

Some remained attached to their old preoccupations. There is, however, probably some real significance in the contrast between men like Berard of Messina and Peter of Ravello, persistently royal Italian bishops, on the one hand, and, on the other, Richard Marsh of Durham and Walter Gray of York, great English civil servants who became very serious diocesan administrators.[80]

The Italian episcopacy was not quite completely devoid of scholars. There were men like Marino of Eboli, archbishop of Capua, Palmerio, bishop of Tricarico, Nicola, bishop of Crotone (Innocent IV's clerk, learned in Greek), Ardingo da Pavia of Florence, and, in one of his guises, Federigo Visconti.[81] They were, however, a very inconspicuous group. Their insignificance makes a sharp contrast with the prominence of the brilliant scholar bishops of thirteenth-century England.

The English bishops of the reign of Henry III have been divided into four categories: monks; administrators and magnates; university graduates and teachers; diocesan and cathedral clergy.[82] Italy, for the longer period of the entire century, demands an adjustment of these categories: monks must be changed to monks and friars; and magnates, in so far as they are local magnates, are better joined to diocesan and cathedral clergy than to administrators. These changes made, the difference between the English pattern and the pattern of observable Italian bishops seems clear: significantly more religious and more local clergy and magnates in Italy; significantly fewer scholars; probably fewer administrators except in insular

[80] See: Kantorowicz, *Frederick the Second*, 297; Walther Holtzmann, "Berard, Erzbischof von Messina (1196-cr.1233)," *Quellen und Forschungen*, XXXIX (1959), 221; F. M. Powicke, *King Henry III and the Lord Edward*, I, 2; *The Register, or Rolls, of Walter Gray, Lord Archbishop of York*, ed. James Raine, Surtees Society, LVI (Durham, 1872).

[81] For Crotone, Ughelli, IX, col. 385. For Marino, see Fritz Schillman, *Die Formularsammlung des Marinus von Eboli* (Rome, 1929); and Peter Herde, *Marinus von Eboli* (Tübingen, 1964); for Ardingo, see R. Davidsohn, *Storia di Firenze*, II (Florence, 1956), 255.

[82] In Gibbs and Lang.

Sicily; but not fewer magnates of more than local importance
—like the Filangieri (out of Naples) or the Fieschi (out of
Genoa) or Boccamazza of the Savelli (out of Rome). The
Italian church was weak in exactly that category which gave
the English thirteenth-century church its distinction: the
category of Langton, Poore, Edmund of Abingdon, Grosseteste, Wych, Sutton, Wickwane, Winchelsey, and (except in
their being friars) Kilwardby and Pecham.

The way in which English bishops became bishops during
the reign of Henry III has been carefully analyzed.[83] There
were seventy-six successful elections between November 1214
and 1273. Of these, fifteen were really free capitular elections
of the sort that became most highly developed in thirteenth-
century Europe (and in thirteen of these cases the elect was a
learned secular clerk). At the other extreme six bishops were
directly appointed by the pope without an election. At center
twenty-five disputed elections were referred to the papal curia,
and the disputes were variously patched and decided. Of the six
direct papal appointments only that of Kilwardby, the learned
Dominican, was after the date of the general reservation of
1265, although Kilwardby's successor Pecham, the learned
Franciscan, was also a papal nominee (after 1273). Both Kilwardby and Pecham were selected in the tradition of the selection of Stephen Langton, a learned secular clerk, whose appointment was at least the incidental cause of the long dispute
between John and Innocent III in the early part of the century.[84] Of the eight prelates of the province of York in the
period from 1279 to 1296 (four secular clerks, three Austin
canons, and a Benedictine), five were elected by their chapters
(not without external pressures); two were elected and then
provided by a pope interested in the validity of the procedure
and perhaps in extra fees; and one was reelected by capitular
representatives at Rome.[85] The thirteenth was a century in
which capitular election was clearly recognized as the normal
way of selecting bishops, but in which inappropriate elections

[83] Gibbs and Lang, 69-93.
[84] Decima L. Douie, *Archbishop Pecham* (Oxford, 1952), 47-49; F.
M. Powicke, *Stephen Langton* (Oxford, 1928), 75-101.
[85] Brentano, *York Metropolitan Jurisdiction*, 60-61.

and capitular disputes easily took the election to the pope's hands. Partly in response to at least implied local demand, the curia developed a law and a technique for provision, in special cases, and then from 1265 in general.[86] The movement was not a direct and continuous one from free election to provision; and it seems difficult to doubt the sincerity of the electoral legislation of Gregory X at Lyons, after 1265 and also after a barrage of appeals.

In Italy as in England, the thirteenth century was one of mixed capitular election and papal provision; and in Italy as in England disputed elections provoked papal action. In Italy more than in England the papacy found it necessary to press the nomination of bishops sympathetic to its own pretensions, particularly against the Staufen.[87] A number of early century papal-imperial difficulties centered around the control of episcopal elections or episcopal nominations. In disputed elections the opposed parties, generally two or three, within the local electorate were thus sometimes attached to more general interests; but whether they were or not, their opposition practically forced the papacy to act. It could adjudicate at a higher and more generally perceptive level the local conflict of interests, secular or ecclesiastical; it could keep the chapter from falling into squalid and destructive squabbling.

In the first decade of the century there was a disputed election in the see of Cerenzia.[88] There had been various parties early in the process of election—one of them supporting the

[86] For episcopal elections see Geoffrey Barraclough, "The Making of a Bishop in the Middle Ages," *Catholic Historical Review*, xix (1933), 275-319; for the development of provision see Geoffrey Barraclough, *Papal Provisions* (Oxford, 1935), and Ann Deeley, "Papal Provision and Royal Rights of Patronage in the Early Fourteenth Century," *English Historical Review*, xliii (1928), 495-527. Innocent IV's serious and lengthy (for Innocent) consideration of the problems of provision and election is apparent in his commentaries on *de postulatione praelatorum* and *de electione et potestate electi* (X, i, 5, 6).

[87] See Kantorowicz, *Frederick the Second*, *passim*, but particularly 141-145.

[88] Pratesi, *Carte latine*, 214-220 no. 86; for Giovanni, bishop of Belcastro, see M.-H. Laurent, "Contributo alla storia dei vescovi del regno di Sicilia," *Rivista di storia della chiesa in Italia*, ii (1948), 373.

archdeacon of Cerenzia; but eventually all, it was said, chose as a compromise candidate a cleric named Madio, chaplain of the count of Crotone. The chapter had sought license to elect from the legate Gerardo, cardinal deacon of Sant'Adriano, at Palermo. The chapter announced their selection to the legate at Catania. The legate Gerardo, although he found the election valid, did not, he wrote, want to derogate from the rights of the metropolitan archbishop of Santa Severina; the legate wrote to the archbishop ordering him to confirm the election if he found the elect suitable and the election valid. The archdeacon, treasurer, and canon Pietro of Cerenzia, however, came to the legate and told him that the dispute between the count of Crotone and one of his enemies (P. Guiscard) made it impossible for them to go to their metropolitan or for him to come to them safely. They said too that it would be hard to collect three bishops for a consecration at Cerenzia. The legate himself then carefully examined elect and election, consulted with the wise and learned, and confirmed the election. Since it was difficult to collect bishops in Calabria, he chose three bishops present in his court to consecrate the elect of Cerenzia.

At the last minute, when all was prepared for consecration, however, there arrived Guglielmo de Nereto with letters from the archbishop of Santa Severina and other prelates saying that since the election at Cerenzia had by default fallen to its metropolitan, the archbishop of Santa Severina, he had chosen Guglielmo as bishop of Cerenzia. The legate explained to Guglielmo that the chapter of Cerenzia had not lost its election by default and that it had in Madio selected a suitable bishop. Guglielmo appealed to the pope. The legate granted letters explanatory to take to the pope, but on the way, at Taormina, Madio was intercepted and robbed of his letters, evidently by Guglielmo or an accomplice.[89] Madio sent a messenger back to the legate to ask for similar letters. Hearing nothing from Guglielmo in due time, the legate sent a mandate to the archbishop of Santa Severina to have Madio consecrated. The

---

[89] Bearing letters could be a dangerous business in the south of Italy in various ways; see Kantorowicz, *Frederick the Second*, 479-480, for the maltreatment of a poor man from Caserta "carrying a perfectly harmless letter from the pope about a benefice for his son."

archbishop hesitated, consented, and then, with violence, re-
neged. After a long time, the legate said, the clergy and people of Cerenzia begged that they no longer be deprived of a
bishop, and they showed letters testimonial from the archbishop of Messina, a bishop, a chapter, an abbot, the count of
Crotone, his son or brother, other magnates of Calabria, asking the legate to have Madio consecrated immediately. The
legate wrote more sharply to the archbishop of Santa Severina;
but he found that the elect had been summoned to Cosenza
by three judges delegate procured by Guglielmo from the
Roman curia. The judges were Luca, archbishop of Cosenza,
and the bishops of Bisignano and Belcastro. The legate wrote
of this that he believed that Guglielmo had acted fraudulently
and that no one might be canonically cited to a place where
it was unsafe for him to go (as it would be for Madio to go to
Cosenza because of the hatred men felt for the count of
Crotone). The legate wrote, too, that Guglielmo was actually
closely connected with one of the delegates and in fact that the
whole thing was preposterous. The legate referred the whole
case—the whole violent local stew of disputing magnates secular and ecclesiastical, Latin and Greek—back to the pope (*ut
de vultu suo prodeat iudicium equitatis*).

A document at Amalfi gives the 1293 Amalfi electoral dispute after the death of Archbishop Filippo Augustariccio a
physical setting.[90] As was its custom, the chapter congregated
on the appointed day in the Duomo to proceed to election.
But the canons did not meet together: one party went into the
choir of the church and one into the crypt. The party in the
choir sent to the party in the crypt and told it to come up and
elect; but the party in the crypt refused and maintained its
dissident integrity. Similarly, but not in such visible parts,
parties of canons throughout the Italian church, from nearby
Salerno and Policastro to distant Ravenna and Lucca, dis-
agreed with each other and fought for their candidates.[91] The
easiest solution to their disputes was direct papal action; and

[90] Amalfi, Archivio arcivescovile, A.P. sec. XIII, no. 56a. For the
fascinating Lucca elections of 1256 and 1269, see Giusti, "Le Elezioni,"
218-219, 220-222.
[91] For Policastro, see Paesano, II, 324-328, for Lucca, Giusti, 213.

the constant disputes must have suggested that it would be expeditious to eliminate the capitular procedure altogether.

Not all thirteenth-century popes were eager, as Gregory X's papacy makes clear, to accept a suggestion, however convenient, that would admit the defeat of a cardinal principle in recent ecclesiastical reform—a principle that had, in a minority of cases perhaps, in some parts of the church, like England, worked to such stunning effect a real ecclesiastical reformation. Besides the disputes did not always work out badly. In Bari—to take an example equally devoid of shame and glory—on 19 August 1280 Archbishop Giovanni died. Early in the morning of the "following Tuesday" his body was buried. The canons of the church gathered at vespers on that Tuesday to fix a day for the election of the new archbishop. They chose the following Wednesday. Of those who ought to be and could be present for the election there were forty. They proceeded to the election by the method of scrutiny. Ballots were cast. Then the three scrutators questioned the voters individually and then published the results. Thirty canons voted for their fellow the legist Romoaldo, a chaplain to the cardinal bishop of Ostia; nine voted for the Roman Pietro Sarraceno; Romoaldo voted for Perceval of Milan. All were converted without public controversy to the Romoaldo party. On 14 September, within the month, the elect gave his assent; and four days later on 18 September the canons chose two proctors, who made their way to the curia to seek papal approval for the election.[92] It was a conservative and expeditious election; and it chose exactly the sort of man who might have been provided—just as did the Reggio Calabria election in choosing a chaplain of Innocent IV's in about 1252.[93] This was the sort of man whom local chapters often found it wise to select even when the elect chose not to accept—as the papal curialist and auditor of contradictory letters, Giffrido of Anagni, chose, for whatever reasons, not to accept the see of Todi in 1282.[94]

Elections at Ravenna have been examined with unusual

[92] *C.d.b.*, ii, 62-64 nos. 29-30.
[93] Lagoteta, 181.
[94] *Martin IV*, 50-51 no. 134.

care.[95] Because suffragan bishops participated in the metropolitan election, Ravenna elections maintained in the thirteenth century an archaic quality peculiarly appropriate in this
province, unusually coherent, but also curiously unresponsive
to contemporary ecclesiastical practice. Their participation permitted toughly determined suffragans like Obizzo of Parma
to arrive for election with a persuasively large body of followers who gave a sort of physical strength to his vote unavailable
generally for the vote of even the richest canons.[96] These suffragans were the successful candidates in Ravenna elections
and provisions with unusual frequency from the translation of
the Bolognese Egidio de' Garzoni from Modena in 1207 to the
translation of Obizzo himself from Parma in 1295. The process
of election at Ravenna has seemed to show a definite change,
centering around the general papal reservation of 1265, from
local elections at the beginning of the century to papal provision at the end. This has in turn suggested a fundamental
change in the nature of the episcopacy itself from its representing the local aristocracy at the beginning of the century to its
being an arm of the papacy at the end. This in its turn has suggested the creation of a new world with a real split between laity
and clergy and with a new self-awareness for the laity.[97] In fact
something did happen in Ravenna to the way in which an
archbishop was made. The machinery changed in the thirteenth century, although papal intervention of a less rigorously
theoretical sort than that to come was perfectly apparent in
the first election of the century after the death of Archbishop
Guglielmo in 1201. Then Innocent III rejected the candidates

[95] Augusto Vasina, "L'elezione degli arcivescovi ravennati del sec.
XIII nei rapporti con la Santa Sede," *Rivista di storia della chiesa in
Italia*, x (1956), 49-89; see, too, Augusto Vasina, "Un arcivescovo ravennate del Duecento: Filippo da Pistoia (1250-1270)," *Rivista di storia
della chiesa in Italia*, xv (1961), 81-100.

[96] Vasina, "L'elezione," 74.

[97] These are Vasina's ideas, "L'elezione," 52, 87; although they seem,
at least in part, mistaken to me, they are (at least with Giusti's) the
most interesting ideas that I have read about thirteenth-century
Italian episcopal elections. Lazzeri's view of Arezzo elections is very
different; he believes elections continued until the fifteenth century
(p. 12); in Lucca elections changed in 1300 and after: Giusti, 224-229.

of both of two parties of electors and insisted upon a new election. Furthermore it is possible, even probable, that over a longer period of time than the century there was a very real change in the sort of man who became archbishop of Ravenna; but it is hard to support this change in the thirteenth century itself: what is the difference between Obizzo and Egidio, or Egidio's successor Ubaldo, translated from Faenza in 1208, or Simeone, unanimously elected and translated from Cervia in 1217?

It would certainly be hard to establish over the whole Italian church much real change in the sort of bishop chosen between the beginning and the end of the thirteenth century. The mechanism of provision did become tighter (as it clearly did, for example, at Lucca in 1300 and after), but it was far from universally applied. In Città di Castello the good bishops of 1252 and 1265 were provided, but their successor, the good bishop of 1280, was elected; none was local. When the mechanism of provision was applied it frequently advanced "holy men," particularly friars, rather than papal tools. It still responded to almost the same combination of pressures from local potentates, southern royalty, the curia, and religious enthusiasm. The figures themselves—papal nephews, merchants' sons, Angevin instead of Staufen favorites and civil servants, religious, curialists, lawyers—may have changed somewhat within their categories, particularly in that they may have been better or at least more professionally educated. But certainly over much of the church local potentates were not displaced. Amalfi remained essentially local throughout the middle ages.[98] There does not seem to have been a clear change from the local, as the thirteenth century passed, in, to take a fairly random sample of observable sees, Bologna, Orvieto, Arezzo, Ascoli, Florence, Volterra, Taranto, Genoa, or Siena —although, after the death of Ottone Visconti, it could be argued for Milan. There is nothing to suggest that the change was greater or papal intervention more pressing in the smaller and more obscure, the invisible, sees.

The continuing localness of Italian bishops is connected with

[98] Robert Brentano, "Sealed Documents of the Mediaeval Archbishops of Amalfi," *Mediaeval Studies*, XXIII (1961), 23-24.

another peculiarity. They were, after their elections, city and chapter bishops, unlike the manor bishops of England. By the late thirteenth century, archbishops of York, for example, did not spend much of their time in their chapter's town of York. They spent their time on their own manors, places like Cawood, Bishop Thorpe, and Laneham. The church of Saint Peter in York was essentially the chapter's. The archbishops moved around like the itinerant English landed nobles that they in part were. Oliver Sutton moved from manor to manor in Lincoln, and Richard Swinfield twisted about the diocese of Hereford.[99] The bishops of Italy, on the other hand, when resident seem frequently, even generally, to have been stationary, sedentary. The archbishop of Ravenna moved about. The archbishop of Benevento went to the country, and the bishop of Fermo stayed in San Claudio. But the bishops of Bologna and Città di Castello when they were at home were at home in Bologna and Città di Castello.

As their society encouraged them to be, the archbishops of Salerno and Amalfi, the Visconti of Milan and Pisa, were city men, of the cities of their sees. The Dominican Pietro II in speaking of his Naples as Parthenope, the virgin city, was speaking of the city in which he lived, his home if not his birthplace.[100] The bishop, too, was at home in his church, part of its liturgy, the old-fashioned head of his chapter. What else should he be in Bitetto, for instance, with its single parish, its

[99] Brentano, *York Metropolitan Jurisdiction*, 29-30 and *passim*; Hill, *Oliver Sutton*, 7 (Sutton's manor-houses within the diocese were at Stow Park, Liddington, Nettleham, Sleaford, Louth, Newark, Buckden, Fingest, Banbury, Thame, Dorchester-on-Thames, Wooburn, and Spaldwick; he also had houses at the Old Temple just outside the City of London and at Theydon Mount in Essex—a Sutton family, not a Lincoln, manor); John R. H. Moorman, *Church Life in England in the Thirteenth Century* (Cambridge, 1946), 187-191, from Richard Swinfield's Household Roll, essentially a visitation of the diocese, within Moorman, a map, "a vivid picture"; a nice example of Fermo's San Claudio diplomatic is: Rome, Archivio di stato, Fiastra, no. 1207 (1259).

[100] Pasquale Santamaria, *Historia collegii patrum canonicorum* (Naples, 1900), 257.

church with fourteen canons and four dignitaries.[101]   The
bishop was still *capo* of this little establishment. The constant
biting poverty of the poor little sees of Italy, and the financial
worries of even greater sees like Cefalù (worried about its
mensa), kept bishops at home, rather than, as it might have in
England, sending them to their farms. The bishop of Fano,
finally locked with seven canons starving in his church rather
than allowing his clergy to be taxed, ought constantly to be
kept in mind.[102]

The Italian bishops' incomes were, too, frequently city incomes. The difference between English and Italian chapters
holds. The English bishops were rich country cousins. But the
difference must not be made too sharp. Much Italian episcopal
income did come from country rents. The bishop of Winchester was an entrepreneur in new towns.[103] By the end of the
thirteenth century much of the bishop of Ely's income was
nonagricultural: half was from rent; and the work of his men
on his demesne lands brought only 40 percent of his total income.[104] Still the difference is very noticeable; and the different patterns were each assumed in their own societies. In Italy,
why, even if he could afford to do as he wanted, should the
bishop be eccentric and go into the country? Italy's being
socially precocious retarded its episcopal and capitular
development.

One can never be sure what an individual bishop was really
like. Turned to a slightly unaccustomed position he can look
quite different from his accepted caricature. From the point of
view of Tavistock Abbey, Walter Bronescombe, the good,
efficient, long-pontificated (1257-1280) bishop of Exeter, can
look "arbitrary" and his policies can seem to have been formed

[101] See the article of F. Bonnard in *Dictionnaire d'histoire et de
géographie ecclésiastiques*, ed. A. Baudrillart, A. de Meyer, and E. Van
Cauwenbergh (Paris, 1912—), IX, cols. 18-19.

[102] See Palermo, Archivio di stato, Cefalù, no. 73, a papal letter
from 1306; for Fano, Waley, 133.

[103] Maurice Beresford, "The Six New Towns of the Bishops of
Winchester, 1200-55," *Medieval Archaeology*, III (1959), 187-215.

[104] Edward Miller, *The Abbey and Bishopric of Ely* (Cambridge,
1951), 93-94, 101.

by acquisitive subordinates.[105] On the other hand, Hubert Walter, that old model of secular prelacy, looked at hard and freshly, can be shown to be "genuinely zealous for the welfare of the Church," with even the suggestion "of a deeper conviction";[106] and, as a matter of fact, he has always looked rather good from Witham.[107] Boniface of Savoy is always changing.[108] Any single Italian bishop could, perhaps, if there were sufficient evidence, be moved in our perception, and his character completely changed. There are also exceptions to the general pattern. But the pattern is strikingly clear. It was the century which in England (as in Rome) produced a remarkable episcopate, men, at various distances, of the Grosseteste pattern—Langton, Gray, Hugh of Wells, the Giffards, Edmund of Abingdon, Cantilupe, Sutton, Swinfield, Kilwardby, Pecham, Winchelsey, Wickwane, Romeyn, John Halton, Simon of Ghent, John of Pontoise; but in Italy the bishops, as bishops, were nothing, inert. Since the Italian church, or at least Italian religion, was anything but inert in the thirteenth century, the action was obviously elsewhere.

In England the saint governed and wore a miter; he was driven by his sanctity to accept the terrible burden.[109] Langton and the Parisian school from which he had come had obviously formed the pattern; but Becket, too, who perhaps knew nothing of how a pastoral bishop should live, had, in dying, given the English church vigor and freedom, an heroic pattern, had (perhaps with the help of the memory of Anselm)

[105] H.P.R. Finberg, *Tavistock Abbey, A Study in the Social and Economic History of Devon* (Cambridge, 1951), 23.

[106] C. R. Cheney, *From Becket to Langton* (Manchester, 1956), 32-41, particularly 36, 39: this seems to me a remarkable revelation; Cheney seems to change Hubert Walter as one watches.

[107] See James Bulloch, *Adam of Dryburgh* (London, 1958), 27-28.

[108] See, for example, Gibbs and Lang, 22.

[109] Cf. Cheney, *From Becket to Langton*, 28: "Saints are rare in the annals of the English episcopate . . ."; saints, of course, are always rare, that is how one notices them; but compared with Italian episcopal saints, I am arguing, English saints are not rare, and, more than that, the English pattern of sanctity is episcopal rather than anti-episcopal. It is true that Walter Mauclerc resigned from the see of Carlisle to become a Dominican, but his resignation is an exception and even its purpose is clouded by doubts about Mauclerc's motives.

made it a good thing to be an English bishop. And it was not just theoretical; thirteenth-century English saints were in fact bishops.[110] In Italy (with the rare and difficult Nocera Umbra sort of exception) the bishop and the saint were different things. The saint was a saint partly because he had refused to be ensnared by the house by the arch, the men swearing fealty under the cherry tree, the friars genuflecting at dinner, because he was not what a bishop seemed to be in Italy. England was Martha, and Italy was Mary.

At the center of the movement of the Italian church was Francis, risen "like the sun out of Ganges" from Assisi. He was, of course, not only Italian, but he was very Italian. He was surrounded and preceded by a host of minor religious enthusiasts lacking his perfection; and he was followed by a troop of friars and hermits each reflecting a little of his completeness.[111] As Grosseteste is the model of English sanctity, Francis is of Italian sanctity. Although Grosseteste's sanctity could be built into institutions, made to do an orderly job, as Francis's, it turned out, could not, next to Francis Grosseteste must always look pale. In Francis himself the high romantic rejection of reason achieved its own reason—his love had no need for university or chancery. And he set Italy aflame. What in the thirteenth century happened in Rieti? Francis preached there and made its valley sing, and the Nera's, "awake with a thousand voices."[112] What happened in Federigo Visconti's life? He saw and touched Francis at Bologna. What excited Salimbene? The old friar at Città di Castello, who convinced

[110] Kemp, 176-177.

[111] See Rudolph Arbesmann, "The Three Earliest Vitae of St. Galganus," *Didascaliae, Essays in Honor of Anselm M. Albareda*, ed. Sesto Prete (New York, 1961), 1-38; it is interesting to compare the generations of Francis's followers with the generations of his "portraits": see Sister M. Anthony Brown, "Early Portraiture of Saint Francis," *Franciscan Studies*, xxi (1961), 94-97. See the generations change the interpretation of poverty in Lambert, *Franciscan Poverty*.

[112] The description of the Nera valley comes from a lyrical passage in Paul Sabatier: *Life of St. Francis of Assisi*, tr. L. S. Houghton (New York, 1912), 106.

Salimbene to change his name and reject its pride, had been received, the very last, into the order by Francis himself.[113]

Francis's Franciscans managed to maintain something of his quality. Consider the figure of Filippo da Pistoia, archbishop of Ravenna (drawn in detail and at length by Salimbene) loving his bastard son like another Absalom, rough in his manners and hard in his talk, surrounded by his terrible and ferocious household.[114] In the presence of Franciscans he and they turned gentle. The violent bishops of Italy—one may, in a way, even include Innocent IV—were like the wolf of Gubbio to Francis and his followers, except that most of them returned to their old ravening ways when Francis or his Franciscans were gone. Grosseteste was pale, but what he built could be kept a while by lesser men.

Less important than Francis, but more typical of Italian enthusiasm, and Italian rejection of the world's reason, was Margaret of Cortona.[115] She was a woman and therefore, for the thirteenth century, almost inescapably a vessel of emotion, uneducated, capable only of a lower or a higher reason than that of the secular clerk who knew the schools. Margaret, having left her cruel stepmother and lost her knightly paramour, with his dog and her child, was a grotesque echo of Francis. In her long war with the physical part of herself, tearing at her flesh, calling her body her enemy, she could have been a thousand years from the reasoned metaphysic of Aquinas. Her soul no more had the shape of her body than Italian Christianity had the shape of its dioceses.

Just as Margaret rejected her body, the hermits of Monte Siepi around the shrine of Galgano rejected the world, and so did the other various fringes of almost lunatic (if beautifully lunatic) extremists whom cardinal Ricardo Annibaldi molded,

[113] Salimbene, 38-39; Francis's death looms large in the little *cronichetta* of Rieti with its only fourteen entries for the thirteenth century: Biblioteca Apostolica Vaticana, Vat. lat. 5994 fos. 87v-88 (Pietro A. Galletti, *Memorie di tre antiche chiese di Rieti* [Rome, 1765], 127).

[114] Salimbene, 399.

[115] For Margaret see the *Acta Sanctorum* for February 22 (February, III, 302-363).

at Santa Maria del Popolo in 1256, into the order of Austin Hermits.[116] And even in the fourteenth century, when world-rejecting mystics could have felt at home in England, Austin Hermits like William Flete, in gestures of extreme rejection, turned to Italy.[117] But of course even in England in the thirteenth century the dominance of what seems reason was frail and partial. Part of Edmund of Abingdon's gear at the university of Paris, sent by a loving mother, was a hair shirt.[118]

Above articulate Italians in the thirteenth century there constantly hovers the figure of Joachim of Flora. Luca of Cosenza was his secretary. Salimbene was overwhelmed by him. He appears everywhere. He was not, perhaps, a personal mystic; but his "illuminated" view of history and life, the unfolding revelation, rejected the common scholastic view of reason. "He was," as it has been said, "a lyrical, not a systematic thinker."[119] For Joachim, as for Francis, Philip Benizi, Margaret of Cortona, and Peter Celestine, the flight to the irrational was available and desirable—and the flight to the truth or the virtue that avoided the logic of schools and the details of government.

In Italy, unlike England, thirteenth-century enthusiasm also expressed itself in heresy. ". . . The slumbering souls were awakened . . . [and the] dumb, untutored minds. . . ."[120] Through the century heretics worried kings in the south and bishops in the north of Italy. Heretics could, and did, prove financially rewarding to the involved orthodox: an inquisition banker in Viterbo could pick up a quick five lire on property exchange.[121] But the more important economic connection

---

[116] Roth, "Cardinal Richard Annibaldi," *Augustiniana*, II (1952), 230-235.

[117] Aubrey Gwynn, *The English Austin Friars in the Time of Wyclif* (Oxford, 1940), 107, 139-210; W. A. Pantin, *The English Church in the Fourteenth Century* (Cambridge, 1955), 246-247.

[118] C. H. Lawrence, *St. Edmund of Abingdon* (Oxford, 1960), 83, 223.

[119] See Morton W. Bloomfield, "Joachim of Flora," *Traditio*, XIII (1957), 249-311, for a clear summing up of Joachimite problems; the quotation is from page 261.

[120] Henry Charles Lea, *A History of the Inquisition of the Middle Ages* (New York, 1955), I, 268—out of context.

[121] Rome, Archivio di stato, Santa Rosa di Viterbo (Cass. 87), no. 5 (Matharotio di Giovanni buying in 1285 for forty lire and selling in

with Italian heresy was a different one, and not merely economic. The cities of Italy, probably particularly as they were
swollen by the immigration of newly rootless country laborers
and crowded with paupers, were ideal arenas for acts of sensa-
tional religious enthusiasm, for quasi-heretical sects and
brotherhoods.[122]

Explosive enthusiasm, sometimes hidden beneath the surface, sometimes open and active, was a major ingredient in
Italian thirteenth-century religious and ecclesiastical life. It had
various connections which are, and have proved, very hard to
disentangle and evaluate: an intellectual connection with mil-
lenarian Joachimism; an heretical connection with dualistic
Manicheanism; a political connection with Staufen Ghibel-
linism; a social connection with the propertyless zealot branch
of Franciscanism. Enthusiasm burst forth in the year of the
Alleluia and in the great processions of flagellants in 1260. It
expressed itself in the activity of clusters of heretics in Rimini,
Florence, Prato, San Gemignano, Ferrara, Verona, Genoa,
Orvieto, in many other Italian towns (although it is often hard
to isolate the doctrines of those whom their enemies called
heretics). Enthusiasm moved the magnificent but sometimes
shrill brilliance of the Spiritual Franciscans in the direction
of their Fraticelli end. In a gaudy combination of seeming
contradictions it produced a martyr saint—Peter of Verona,
Peter Martyr, Bolognese, friar preacher, master inquisitor,
hammer and victim of heretics, enthusiast killed by enthusiasts, officially recognized as a saint, by Innocent IV, almost
instantly, within a year of his death, not after lingering and
disjointed processes like those even of Margaret of Cortona
and Philip Benizi. Most important to see and remember, this

1289 for forty-five lire—two documents stitched together), no. 6
(Matharotio as the Inquisition's banker in 1287); see, too, Giuseppe
Signorelli, *Viterbo nella storia della chiesa* (Viterbo, 1907-1938).

[122] For this class of country laborers see Gino Luzzatto, "L'Inurba-
mento delle popolazioni rurali in Italia nei sec. XII e XIII," in *Studi
di storia e diritto in onore di Enrico Besta*, II (Milan, 1939), 184-203;
for the crowds of paupers: David Herlihy, *Medieval and Renaissance
Pistoia* (New Haven, Conn., 1967), 114; and William M. Bowsky,
"The Impact of the Black Death upon Sienese Government and
Society," *Speculum*, XXXIX (1964), 1-34, 7.

Italian enthusiasm was not merely an occasional or an eccentric thing, but a pervasive and overwhelming fact in a church in which conventional institutions like archdeaconries, diocesan boundaries, and even bishops seem, where they exist, external and lifeless. The Italian church was, at least relatively, a church of "preaching," not of "pastoral care."[123]

The tone of Italian enthusiastic diversity and eccentricity was further heightened by the presence of Greeks (with the monks of their eremitical tradition) and Saracens in the south. Both in their different ways troubled the Roman church.[124]

[123] In this connection I am borrowing "preaching" and "pastoral care" from Max Weber (in translation): *The Sociology of Religion* (Boston, 1964), 74-75. For a general discussion of the problems of enthusiasm, see Gioacchino Volpe, *Movimenti religiosi e sette ereticali nella società medievale italiana, secoli XI-XIV* (Florence, 1961), particularly 87-99 on heretical sects. For the Spiritual Franciscans see Decima L. Douie, *The Nature and Effect of the Heresy of the Fraticelli* (Manchester, 1932), particularly for the early period, 1-21 and for the influence of Joachim, 22-48, and for Ubertino da Casale, 120-152, and for the historians who had worried the problem, 259-279. For the Alleluia of 1233 and the flagellants of 1260, see Salimbene, 70-72, 465-466; a group of essays in *Il Movimento dei Disciplinati nel settimo centenario dal suo inizio (Perugia, 1260): Deputazione di storia patria per l'Umbria*, Appendice al Bollettino 9: Raoul Manselli, "L'Anno 1260 fu anno Gioachimito?" 99-108; Candido Mesini, "I Disciplinati a Parma," 305-316; Emilio Ardu, "Frater Raynerius Faxanus de Perusio," 84-98; Jean Leclercq, "La Flagellazione volontaria nella tradizione spirituale dell'occidente," 73-83. For a different interpretation, see Norman Cohn, *The Pursuit of the Millennium* (New York, 1961), 124-127. For cathars in thirteenth-century Italy, see Steven Runciman, *The Medieval Manichee* (New York, 1961), 128-129. For the connection of bishops with this enthusiasm, see Raoul Manselli, "I Vescovi italiani, gli ordini religiosi e i movimenti popolari religiosi nel secolo XIII," in *Vescovi e diocesi*, v, 315-335. For an analysis of enthusiastic medieval heresy, see R. A. Knox, *Enthusiasm* (Oxford, 1950), 92-116. For Peter Martyr, see the *Acta Sanctorum* for April 29 (April, III, 678-719), or the *Vies des Saints et des Bienheureux* (by the Benedictines of Paris), IV (1946), 735-742.

[124] For the Saracens see *Codice diplomatico dei Saraceni di Lucera (1285-1343)*, ed. Pietro Egidi, Società napoletana di storia patria (Naples, 1917), and Kantorowicz, *Frederick the Second*; for the Greeks, see: Ercole Pennetta, "Spiritualità bizantina nel Salento medievale," *Studi Medievali*, ser. 3, II:2 (1961), 480-483; Germano Giovanelli, "I fondatori di Grottaferrata ed il bizantino dell'alto medioevo nell'Italia

Presumably in a different context this diversity could have pressed secular and ecclesiastical rulers to a more systematic and rigorously defined sort of government. In thirteenth-century Italy it did not.

It would be hard to find princes more eccentrically enthusiastic than the sons of Charles II of Anjou, king of peninsular Sicily. Louis (of Toulouse), whose renunciation of his heritage —rejection of rule—is familiar in the version of Simone Martini, came under Franciscan influence as a youth and never freed himself from it.[125] After being allowed to give up Naples to his brother Robert, Louis was further allowed to retire from the circle of the royal family at Castel Nuovo, to move to the white, sea-bound solitude of the Castel dell'Ovo. There in quiet he made himself ready to become a priest—with a copy of the *Summa Theologica* that his father had bought for him. Charles, Louis's father, wanted Louis, if a cleric, a respectable bishop, of Toulouse. Louis wanted only Franciscan humility. On 5 February 1297, in a great assembly at Rome, at the Ara Coeli, high on the Capitoline, before two cardinals and a huge crowd, Louis dramatically removed his bishop's vestments and showed beneath them his Franciscan habit.

Louis's father was enraged. Louis himself moved north toward France. He stayed at Siena and left the friars there a Bible which he had supposedly written with his own hand. He stayed at Santa Croce in Florence. He was to have little time to devote to his diocese and seems in fact to have been bent upon resigning it. He died on pilgrimage to a cult center

---

meridionale," *Studi Medievali*, ser. 3, 11:2 (1961), 423-424; Illuminato Peri, "Resistenza e decadenza dei 'Greci' di Sicilia," *Studi Medievali*, ser. 3, 11:2 (1961), 492-494. Readers may wish to consult the essays pertinent to the problem of the Greek church in Italy in *L'eremitismo in Occidente nei secoli XI e XII* (Pubblicazioni dell'Università Cattolica del Sacro Cuore, Contributi, 3rd ser.: Miscellanea del Centro di Studi medioevali, iv) (Milan, 1965); they were not, however, available to me when I wrote this chapter.

[125] Margaret R. Toynbee, *S. Louis of Toulouse and the Process of Canonization in the Fourteenth Century* (Manchester, 1929), 51; it would, as Miss Toynbee makes clear, be wrong to press Louis's being an Italian too far—he can just as well be called Provençal.

of the Magadalen on 19 August 1297. He was only twenty-three.[126]

The peculiarities of Louis's brother Robert, who actually succeeded to the Neapolitan throne in 1309, were in a different direction. Even as children Louis had been "contemplative" and Robert "active": one a player of chess, the other a thrower of stones.[127] Robert, "the Wise," became a serious king, a source of justice, a patron of the arts.[128] He also became a lay preacher. His sermons survive in great bulk. They were preached before clergy as well as laity. They are surprisingly liturgical and ecclesiastical. Robert preached on the text "I am the Good Shepherd," on "Gold and Silver are not for me"; he preached sermons about his brother.[129] Robert was as mixed a creature (although moving from the other direction) as Federigo Visconti or Obizzo of Parma. He refused to see as reserved to the cleric a peculiarly clerical office. He concluded a bizarre century for the royal houses of Naples, from the eccentricities of Frederick II to his own.

Superficially, but only superficially, there may seem a sort of contradictory opposition between the exotic spirituality of live saints and the crushingly physical presence of dead saints in thirteenth-century Italy—with its increasing pile of prelatical corpses dead through unnatural causes: Arezzo; Tortona; in Santa Prassede. Certainly the most noticeable difference between the cults of saints and the hoards of relics in Italy and those in England was the presence of so many, or so many parts of, the great saints of the universal church in Italy. Many of the distantly past events that the whole church celebrated had happened in Italy; and, particularly after the fall of Con-

[126] Toynbee, 100-127.

[127] Toynbee, 48-49.

[128] See: Romolo Caggese, *Roberto d'Angio e i suoi tempi* (Florence, 1922-1930); Émile G. Léonard, *Les Angevins de Naples* (Paris, 1954), 270-294.

[129] Walter Goetz, *König Robert von Neapel (1309-1343)* (Tübingen, 1910), 29-34, 46-70: 47-68 (list of sermons); 69-70 (an example); in list: no. 9, "Good Shepherd"; no. 10, "Silver and gold" (Acts 3:61); no. 93, "Martha, Martha" (Luke 10:41); nos. 98 and 112, Louis bishop and brother (translation, 112—Hebrews 11:5); no. 276, Louis king.

stantinople at the beginning of the thirteenth century, many major saints (or, again, parts of them) who had died elsewhere were brought to Italy. The triumphant crusaders furnished Italy with relics as Napoleon did France with paintings. In consequence there was a major difference between Saint Andrew's in Amalfi and Saint Andrew's in Rochester: Saint Andrew himself was, or was believed to be, at Amalfi. Saint Paul's and Saint Peter's in Rome were full of the echoes of the saints themselves as their namesakes in London and York were not. Rome, although in fact richer, was not relatively so attractive as a cult center as it had been before the rediscovery of Jerusalem (and perhaps of Christ), but it was still heaped high with the bones of saints that men wanted to be near. And although the thirteenth century was not the golden age of the relic, Thomas Aquinas, lying on his deathbed at Fossanova, thinking his last syllogism, can hardly have been unaware of eyes contemplating his body, minds thinking what a splendid relic he was about to become.[130] Jocelin of Brakelond, writing at the beginning of the century, could produce only one moment of religious enthusiasm in his book, the great scene of the nocturnal exposure of the body of Saint Edmund.

Saint Edmund was not the only important saint in England; and some English saints were well known outside of England. Becket was major as, among other things, the accounts of his Canterbury shrine show. Much money came in, and much money went out.[131] But, except for Becket's, England's cults

---

[130] See Giuseppe Paesano, *Memorie per servire alla storia della chiesa Salernitana* (Salerno, 1846-1857), III, 19-22, where the relish for Aquinas relics is wonderfully and probably unself-consciously recreated: "le sue sacre spoglie."

[131] C. Eveleigh Woodruff, "The Financial Aspect of the Cult of St. Thomas of Canterbury," *Archaeologia Cantiana*, XLIV (1932), 18-32: see the chart of receipts and expenditures on p. 19; Woodruff emphasizes (pp. 18, 27) that an important shrine cost its owners a great deal as well as, generally (cf. 1233-1242) bringing them even more money. See, too, Raymonde Foreville, *Le Jubilé de Saint Thomas Becket du XIIIe au XVe siècle* (Paris, 1958). For the strange sort of trip that a local cult might make, see E. P. Baker, "The Cult of St. Oswald in Northern Italy," *Archaeologia*, XCIV (1951), 167-194.

were clearly secondary and provincial. Italy was a hoard of really great relics; and in the thirteenth century it remained distinctly a land of cult centers. The impressive looking *acta* of the thirteenth-century archbishops of Milan and bishops of Bologna are, for example, rather surprisingly essentially a series of indulgences supporting these centers (and sometimes, admittedly, their useful connections, like hospitals).[132] Innocent V's short pontificate (the earlier half of 1276) was disturbed by a relic raid in the south of Italy, or so the bishop of Canne complained. Armed clerics from Barletta had come to Canne and stolen the relics of the high altar of the major church (where the body of the Blessed Ruggero was) and taken it back to their own church. The archpriest of Barletta had another story. According to him the relics had been taken from Canne according to an agreement made with the archpriest of Canne, to protect the relics while work was being done on the church. Either way the importance of the relics is unmistakable.[133]

The shape of medieval religious enthusiasm is, in some part, outlined by church dedications.[134] In great part this sort of enthusiasm was not determined by national boundaries: dedications to the virgin heavily outrank all others in both Italy and England. Furthermore the number of church dedications does not necessarily indicate the local strength of a saint's cult: Peter was a relatively unpopular (in numbers) dedication in

---

[132] Giacomo C. Bascapè, *Antichi diplomi degli arcivescovi di Milano e note di diplomatica episcopale*, Fontes Ambrosiani 18 (Florence, 1937), 82-97; Giorgio Cencetti, "Note di diplomatica vescovile bolognese dei secoli xi-xiii," in *Scritti di paleografia e diplomatica in onore di Vincenzo Federici* (Florence, 1944), 157-223; note particularly, 175-178; of course, these are precisely the documents that would be most carefully preserved.

[133] Salvatore Santeramo, *Codice diplomatico barlettano*, 1 (Barletta, 1924), 86-90 no. 32; cf. Laurent, "Contributo," 377-378, and his citations.

[134] The following information about Italian dedications outside of the city of Rome comes from the appropriate volumes of the *Rationes decimarum Italiae*. They (the *Rationes*) do not of course date dedications, except terminally; they are not complete; they give only a rough description of dedications and should not be thought of as exhaustive and precise.

thirteenth and early fourteenth-century Rome; Matthew, a saint to whom churches seem not to have been much dedicated in either country, had more churches than usual, but not at all an impressive number, in his diocese of Salerno, where his cult, as every other indication including personal names shows, was very strong. Saint Florido, the local saint of Città di Castello, was perhaps too shadowy a saint to press far beyond his cathedral; there were several churches dedicated to him in the diocese, perhaps a fifth as many as to Saint Blaise. Of the twenty-nine churches around Bobbio, three were dedicated to Saint Columban: there was some pressure from the local cult.

The easiest way to grasp the pattern of dedications in the two countries (although one that of course may be misleading) is to look at the list of most popular dedications, in order, in an area (a diocese and a county) from each country. In the diocese of Bologna in the year 1300 the order would seem to be: the Virgin Mary (with about eighty-five, more than three times as many as the two Johns together); the two Johns (generally indistinguishable, although the Baptist was usually more popular); Michael (whose dedications match the Johns if a plain "archangel" is added); Peter; Martin; James (excluding dedications to Philip and James); Andrew; Blaise; Lawrence; Nicholas (all to this point with fifteen or more dedications); Bartholomew (nine dedications); Christopher; George (with six, like Christopher); Benedict. In the county of Norfolk the dedications run: Mary; All Saints; Andrew; Peter; Margaret; Michael; the Johns (thirty-three, with only three for the Evangelist); Nicholas; Edmund; Martin; Botolph; Lawrence; George; "Holy Trinity and Saint James the Greater"; Ethelbert.[135] There is more similarity than difference, although Edmund, Botolph, and Ethelbert are locally English (as too are Bologna dedications to Tecla, Donnino, Gemignano, and many others locally Italian). The Norfolk

---

[135] All the information about Norfolk comes from C.L.S. Linnell, *Norfolk Church Dedications*, St. Anthony's Hall Publications, 21 (York, 1962); unlike the *Rationes*'s, its terminal dates are not fixed, so that popular modern dedications like All Saints may give a false impression about the thirteenth-century pattern. Linnell includes a discussion of "cluster dedications," pp. 8-9.

dedications to Margaret of Antioch represent a cult particularly strong in Norfolk, and stronger in England it would seem than in Italy, as Blaise was stronger in Italy. There are differences that the list does not make immediately apparent. The distance between Mary and other dedications is much sharper in Bologna; the number of saints with only one or two dedications, sometimes almost unidentifiable, is much greater in Bologna. The English pattern is much more orderly: there is a relatively high proportion of dedications to great saints with relatively (but only relatively) strong personalities.

If one turns from Bologna to the city of Rome, the difference from Norfolk is more noticeable.[136] Here again dedications to the Virgin were heavily preponderant: there were almost seventy of them. Here again appear universally popular saints with no particular local connection (except that they were the names of popes, as of all other kinds of people): over twenty dedications to Nicholas, almost ten to Martin. In Rome there were almost thirty direct dedications to the Savior, which seems a local peculiarity; there were nine in all England. There were twenty Roman dedications to Saint Lawrence—an extraordinary number, although Lawrence was a popular medieval saint. The really peculiar thing about Roman dedications—predictable but important—was the great number of churches built about the bones and houses of local saints of the distant, imperfectly remembered past: Cecilia, Susanna, Prassede, Pudenziana, Sabina, Prisca, John and Paul, and the rest —and the early popes. That quality perhaps inherent in all saints' cults, the devotion to a sort of *genius loci* devoid of personal characteristics—geographical rather than personal, not particularly Christian, and certainly not particularly thirteenth century—is especially apparent in Rome. In this Rome is quintessentially Italian.

The two great Italian miracles which supposedly occurred (were later said to have occurred) during the second half of the thirteenth century are also, in a way, curiously appropriate.

---

[136] Roman dedications are taken from G. Falco, "Il catalogo di Torino," *Archivio della società romana di storia patria*, xxxii (1909), 411-443; the catalogue was probably composed between 1313 and 1337.

Mary's house, it was piously believed, flew indirectly from Nazareth to Loreto. The doubting Hungarian priest at Bolsena saw Christ's blood run from the Host and stain the stone. The miracles were connected with Christian beliefs which were not local; but they were caught and made into local shrines, each buried in a place, although Bolsena's treasure was half-captured by Orvieto.

Miracles still graced both countrysides, although the official church was at least intermittently cautious about them. The anonymous compiler of the *Libellus quatuor ancillarum*, a collection of depositions made to procure the canonization of Elizabeth of Hungary (in the process of 1233) wrote:

> . . . at the Curia they look for evidence of blameless life and excellence of conduct, rather than miracles, which are, as often as not, feigned by human craft or diabolical deceit.[137]

(One is forced to recall the grand assize and the disappearance of ordeal.)[138] It was a world from which magic was disappearing; but plenty of people were unaware of the disappearance. Saintliness continued to provoke, as it always does, magic and the irrational. As late as the late nineteenth century it was still remembered that on each year on 14 April, the local feast of Saint Richard Wych (that scholarly, good-living, thirteenth-century bishop of Chichester) in Heathfield, Sussex "an old woman used to bring in to some public place in the village a covered basket from which she let fly a cuckoo."[139] (The day, moreover, was not that which Urban IV had given Richard in 1260—22 January, but an Old Style version of his generally observed English feast—3 April.)[140] When Grosseteste died,

[137] Quoted in Lawrence, 26, in connection with Edmund of Abingdon's process; Lawrence stresses the fact that both "inquiries were conducted in Italy by Italians" and so were relatively legally refined.

[138] See John W. Baldwin, "The Intellectual Preparation for the Canon of 1215 against Ordeals," *Speculum*, xxxvi (1961), 613-636.

[139] Frances Arnold-Forster, *Studies in Church Dedications or England's Patron Saints* (London, 1899), i, 432: I do not believe that Arnold-Forster is really very trustworthy; see Wych in A. B. Emden, *Biographical Register* (Oxford, 1957-1959), and in Gibbs and Lang, 44-45.

[140] *Urbain IV*, i, 20 no. 59.

bells rang in the woods at night. At Wych's funeral, music mixed mysteriously with the mourning—"the nightingale and the turtledove."[141]

In both the Italian and English churches devotion penetrated at least at times beyond the fraternities and gilds of merchants in towns, the "colonies of pious laymen, widows, and spinsters" around Santa Croce, to the almost inarticulate and invisible people who formed the crowds in parishes, the soldiers in armies, the peasants on the land. In 1275 or 1276 Richard Burton, a villein on the lands of Isabella de Forz at Sevenhampton, paid thirteen shillings and four pence for license to sell his chattels and go off to the Holy Land.[142] Court records make it clear that he was not at all singular.[143] In Bologna even the Lambertazzi became priests.[144] In 1259 a girl named Margherita, in the Marches, gave herself and her land to a monastery of her name-saint (Santa Margherita de Cretaccio).[145] In Italy the flagellants beat themselves. The silent community occasionally reveals its reactions.

In April 1281, Peter the Lombard, in fact a Lombard living in Rome, contemplated his death, although he was sound in

[141] For Grosseteste: Matthew Paris, *Chronica Majora*, v, 407, 408; for Wych: E. F. Jacob, "St. Richard of Chichester," *Journal of Ecclesiastical History*, vii (1956), 174-188, 188 (translating Ralph Bocking).

[142] *Accounts and Surveys of the Wiltshire Lands of Adam de Stratton*, ed. M. W. Farr, Wiltshire Archaeological and Natural History Society, Records Branch, xiv (Devizes, 1959), 71; for confraternities, see Gennaro Maria Monti, *Le Confraternite medievali dell'alta e media Italia* (Venice, 1927), particularly: i, 85-88, 91-92, 94-95, 105-107, 125, 127, 134, 137-138, 150-153, 155, 157-164, 223, and ii, 144-158; for Santa Croce and the Santa Croce quotation used in this paragraph, see Charles T. Davis, "Education in Dante's Florence," *Speculum*, xl (1965), 415-435, 422.

[143] See for example the *Rolls for the Justices in Eyre for Yorkshire, 1218-1219*, ed. D. M. Stenton, Selden Society, 56 (London, 1937), 88, 183, 215: by 1218-1219 "going off to Jerusalem" is not an uncommon way of describing a lower-class disappearance.

[144] Pietro Sella, "La diocesi di Bologna nel 1300," *Atti e memorie della R. deputazione di storia patria per le provincie di Romagna*, ser. 4, xviii (1928), 97-155, 104.

[145] Rome, Archivio di stato, Fiastra no. 1215.

body, and made a will.[146] In it he, perhaps not consciously (and of course only in part), defined the pattern of his religion. Much of his will provided for the paying of debts and for bequests: to his brother, his sisters-in-law, his sisters (for whose housing he provided), his nephews and his nieces (legitimate and illegitimate), his doctor, and Ricka, his foster daughter. But the will also devoted itself to pious purposes. Fifty pounds were to be invested in an olive grove in Tivoli for the use of the churches of San Salvatore de Termis and San Benedetto de Termis (where, as the will says, the Lombards were accustomed to gather), which were once near the present sites of the Piazza and Palazzo Madama and of San Luigi dei Francesi.[147] The income was to be used for lights for Peter's soul and the souls of his relatives; the income's source was not to be alienated. Peter left money to subsidize a pilgrimage to the Holy Land (forty *soldi*) or Gargano (twenty *soldi*) or Farfa (five *soldi*), to the last of which the Termis churches were or had been connected. He willed five *soldi* to the recluse of San Salvatore de Termis and five *soldi* to the church of Sant'Eustachio for a silver pyx in which to keep the sacred Host. He also left money for a pyx at San Lorenzo in Damaso. (Sant'Eustachio and San Lorenzo had in 1231 been engaged in a dispute over San Benedetto; San Lorenzo seems to have had the better claim.) He left money for restoring the image of Saint Gregory on the wall of Santa Maria della Rotonda (the Pantheon) opposite the house of Compagio di Giovanni Lucidi. If he died in the city, Peter asked to be buried before the altar of San Benedetto de Termis.

This is the not unconventional will of a Roman Lombard, which, in its pious bequests, outlined a neighborhood in Rome

[146] Rome, Archivio di stato, Santi Cosma e Damiano in Trastevere (San Cosimato), (Cass. 5) no. 311.

[147] Christian Carl Friedrich Huelsen, *Le Chiese di Roma nel medio evo* (Florence, 1927), 212; for Lombard holdings beyond the Milvian: Rome, Archivio di stato, Santi Cosma e Damiano in Trastevere (San Cosimato), (Cass. 5) no. 271. For Compagio's sale of a vineyard on the Vatican for 60 li. prov. sen., in June 1278, and for his wife Bartolomea and his daughter-in-law Aldruda (approving at home), see *Liber Censuum de l'Église Romaine*, ed. Paul Fabre, L. Duchesne, G. Mollat (Paris, 1910-1952), II, 53-54.

from the Pantheon and Sant'Eustachio to San Benedetto and
San Salvatore, a little neighborhood (with outriders perhaps in
Tivoli and beyond the Milvian, in Farfa and San Lorenzo,
establishments tied to the Termis churches). It is a will that
speaks devotion to the Host tied to a place. But in the Marches,
not far from Loreto, a man from Montolmo (Corridonia)
wrote his will thinking of Christ. His legatee nephews must
build a portico for Christ's poor, where these poor could rest
and be guests and warm themselves at a fire and cover themselves with bedclothes; and in 1278 an Amalfi nobleman, too,
among his ecclesiastical benefactions remembered to leave
bedding to the local hospice for the poor.[148] Sacred and personal place did not have a monopoly on Italian piety.

Celestine V's place was the Abruzzi. Celestine was a holy
man of the mountains, withdrawn from society, from reason,
and from rule—pure even of thought and efficiency. His choice
as pope was perhaps an effort to bring Francis's sort of fire to
the rotting institution at the church's heart (the actual Franciscan remedy had failed). It was also a denial of the papacy's
function and a submission to the darkness of royal domination.
As, in September 1294, the elected Celestine drew out his inefficient delay in his home province, he met the archbishop
elect of Canterbury.[149] Robert Winchelsey, a serious and vir-
tuous man and a distinguished scholar, had spent a year and a
second exasperating Italian summer worrying about the expenses that he incurred for his church and waiting for a pope
to be elected and then for himself to be confirmed and conse-

[148] Rome, Archivio di stato, Fiastra no. 758: the will of Rainaldo di
Pietro di Riccoccio da Montolmo, from 1233; Riccardo Filangieri di
Candida, *Codice diplomatico amalfitano*, II (Trani, 1951), 167-169 no.
424. Pietro's concern for eucharist and pyx ought to be seen not only
against Bolsena and the Fourth Lateran but also provincial enactments
like canon IV of the Luccan synod of 1253: Dinelli, 54.

[149] Rose Graham, "Archbishop Winchelsey: from his Election to his
Enthronement," *Church Quarterly Review*, CXLVIII (1949), 161-175;
F. M. Powicke, *The Thirteenth Century* (Oxford, 1953), 673, 678,
717-718; *Registrum Roberti Winchelsey, Cantuariensis Archiepiscopi
(1294-1313)*, Canterbury and York Society, LI (Oxford, 1952-1956),
particularly 1285-1287; Robert Brentano, "'Consolatio defuncte caritatis': a Celestine V letter at Cava,".*English Historical Review*, LXXVI
(1961), 298-303.

crated. In Celestine and Winchelsey the two churches met—
their two sorts of bishops and their two sorts of saints, with
their very different blameless lives and excellent conducts.
Characteristically Celestine waited less than four months after
his own consecration to resign his ugly office. Winchelsey went
home to years of intricate and intense pastoral care, to the difficult and sensitive representation of the ecclesiastical order in
society, to a life of brave and thoughtful action, even to exile,
but never to the complete resignation of his trying responsibility. When in January 1295 Winchelsey arrived at Norwich
on his way home (having sailed from Dordrecht to Yarmouth
in order to avoid French territory), he was met by Prior Eastry
of Canterbury. Eastry brought Winchelsey the ecclesiastical
ornaments that Pecham had used.[150] Among the ornaments
were three gold pins to hold the archbishop's pallium in place
—gaudy trinkets, but they locked Winchelsey as they had
Pecham to a life of duty.

By the end of the thirteenth century the church of Padre
Pio and the Torlonia and the church of William Gladstone
were, in many ways, already formed. Formed too, or in process of forming, was the tragic chasm between the movement
and gossip churning around the Easter Sacrament at Santa
Maria in Trastevere and the verger's guarding the center aisle
against anyone's crossing it at dead Vespers in Durham. The
division between the churches is seen when Winchelsey is
cast against Celestine; it is seen equally clearly if Winchelsey
is cast against Celestine's successor, Boniface VIII, ensconced
in Gaetani fortresses like the Torre delle Milizie or the Cecilia
Metella. It is seen too if Winchelsey is cast against the memory
of Giovanni Buono of the Bonites, the actor (if tradition
holds) who turned his talents to religion.[151]

[150] Rose Graham, "Archbishop Winchelsey," 173.
[151] See Roth, "Cardinal Richard Annibaldi," *Augustiniana*, ii (1952),
123-124, and particularly 131 n. 223.

IV · FORTRESSES OF PRAYER

 Y THE beginning of the thirteenth century western
monasticism had, for the most part, ended that recent flight into enthusiasm which is its glory. The
age of Anselm, Bernard, and Ailred was clearly past. Its English and Italian lingerers at end-century—Hugh of Avalon,
escaped to his great diocese, and Joachim of Flora, to his apoc-
alyptic Sila—seem more to prophesy future nonmonastic than
to remember past monastic greatness. The monasteries themselves seem to have been trying to find again their old place in
society, to be again, as Orderic's Conqueror had called them,
fortresses of prayer. Ancient gifts paid for the recurring, remembering liturgy, sung around the collected relics. The cults
went on. New wills brought some new gifts. But the monasteries came back to their old purposes and limitations in a society that found those purposes less compelling. Enthusiasm
for monasteries may have dwindled less than enthusiasm in
monasteries, but it had dwindled. The monasteries' spiritual
place, in so far as it was left to be filled at all, was filled, after
the first few years of the century, by the new and initially very
different orders of friars.

Even by the end of the thirteenth century the old orders had
not reached Katharine Bulkeley's state of terrible and now
familiar confusion. In 1538 that well-born abbess of Godstow
would write to Thomas Cromwell, in defense of her old nunnery, "Be assured there is neither Pope, Purgatory, image nor
pilgrimage nor praying to dead Saints used amongst us."[1] But
the confusion was great enough by the decade between 1160
and 1170, when a German Cistercian wrote his contribution
to the continual quarreling dialogue between his order and the
Cluniacs. In his piece of the dialogue, the German Cistercian had his fictitious Cluniac claim that the Cluniacs were
Marys and that the Cistercians were Marthas, the dull parti-

[1] *Letters and Papers Foreign and Domestic of the Reign of Henry
VIII*, ed. James Gairdner, xiii:2 (London, 1893), 911.

sans of the active life.[2] By the 1230's a bad English Benedictine prior was punished by being made to become a Carthusian.[3]

The confusion about purpose was, in the thirteenth century, matched by shabby monastic behavior in society—the undistinguished procession of monks who move through the records of English eyres. The Worcestershire eyre of 1221 revealed that the abbot of Bordesly had come with his monks to the church at Stone and there taken off William Brasey, charged with the death of Philip of Harvington and in sanctuary, in the cowl of one of the Bordesly monks.[4] The Yorkshire eyre of 1218-1219 found that Jeremiah of Ecclesfield, who had cut off three of Maurice of Askern's fingers, had given himself up to religion at Fountains.[5] These unsavory entries to convents are not unrelieved. There is, for example, an innocuous exit from a convent revealed by the same Yorkshire eyre: a brother of Meaux was found drowned in the Ribble, and no one was suspected.[6] What is lacking in the thirteenth century is the answer of spiritual brilliance which had made seem relatively unimportant the tawdry and insignificant monks who were also present in the time of monasticism's greatness. Ailred of Rievaulx had his Jeremiahs (his most singular distinction came from dealing with them); but there is no suggestion that Jeremiah of Ecclesfield had an Ailred.

The friars broke in every place, as Matthew Paris, bitterly Benedictine, wrote.[7] As the old orders watched, the sacred walls of the world went down—and bishops and wolves were more easily placated than the old orders were. Occasionally

[2] David Knowles, "Cistercians and Cluniacs, the Controversy between St. Bernard and Peter the Venerable," *The Historian and Character and Other Essays* (Cambridge, 1963) 74-75: "a retort which throws no little light on the general confusion of thought prevailing in the author's circle."

[3] C. H. Lawrence, *St. Edmund of Abingdon* (Oxford, 1960), 163.

[4] *Select Pleas of the Crown I (1200-1225)*, ed. F. W. Maitland, Selden Society, 1 (London, 1887), 86 no. 135.

[5] *Rolls of the Justices in Eyre for Yorkshire (1218-1219)*, ed. D. M. Stenton (London, 1937), 215-216.

[6] *Rolls of the Justices in Eyre for Yorkshire (1218-1219)*, 249.

[7] Matthew Paris, *Chronica Majora*, III, 332-334.

bishops, as at Salerno, distrusted the Franciscans.[8] Paris and
parish priests were prepared to fight the friars particularly
when incomes were threatened.[9] Kings, as at Naples, and
nobles, as of Aquino, hated the friars' stealing their sons.[10]
But generally the friars swept all before them. They moved,
around the ancient saints, into the mosaics of Maria Maggiore.
They surrounded and influenced great men, like Grosseteste,
Wych, and Louis IX, who had not actually joined one of the
orders, as had Aquinas, Bacon, Marsh, and Kilwardby.[11] The
thirteenth century is the century of the mercurial friar; and in
Italy, at least, it is the mildly Gothic San Francesco of the
cities that still visually recalls the thirteenth century. The friars
blind us to the monks. But, in a way, what the friars have to
tell us seems too brilliantly obvious to be very helpful. The
subtler, bumbling response of the monks to those impulses
that first created and then destroyed the friars seems more informative (although far less edifying, and terrifying) than the
often-told story of the friars themselves. In particular, deca-
dence seems more revealing of local differences than does international enthusiasm.

By the end of the thirteenth century the two great groups of
orders had turned themselves toward each other. The bulk of
the friars had become conventional and respectable. Even the
Franciscans had produced their undistinguished pope and
lived, propertied, in houses. The monks, in spite of their bitter
complaints, had also changed. They had become surprisingly
mobile. The Italian Cistercians of Fiastra and the English

[8] Giuseppe Paesano, *Memorie per servire alla storia della chiesa
salernitana* (Salerno, 1846-1857), II, 341-342.

[9] For a recent discussion of the dispute between the secular masters
and the friars at Paris, see Decima L. Douie, *Archbishop Pecham* (Oxford, 1952), 26-35.

[10] For Charles II's reaction to the loss of Louis, see Margaret R.
Toynbee, *St. Louis of Toulouse* (Manchester, 1929), 112.

[11] For the governmental organization of the two greater orders of
friars see: G. R. Galbraith, *The Constitution of the Dominican Order,
1216-1360* (Manchester, 1925); Rosalind B. Brooke, *Early Franciscan
Government* (Cambridge, 1959). For a recent investigation of the intellectual and educational activities of later thirteenth-century friars
in one Italian city, see Charles T. Davis, "Education in Dante's Florence," *Speculum*, XL (1965), 415-435.

Benedictines of Durham moved quickly and often from their cloisters. By the end of the century the English Benedictines were admitting a changed world and cooperating with it enough to establish themselves formally at the university in Oxford, although this development seems not to have occurred in the slower air, in this connection, of Italy.

The change from reflective, contemplative, spiritual Euphrates to active Tigris, which seems the most significant change in religious sentiment from the twelfth century to the thirteenth, the change in fact from monk to friar, can be seen quite early, actually, in the monasteries themselves. It is apparent in the brightest of early thirteenth-century monastic histories. In the chronicle of Jocelin of Brakelond, withdrawn, claustral, inefficient Hugh of Bury Saint Edmunds, regretted but despised, is (in the late twelfth century) succeeded by Samson, efficient, external, preaching in the vernacular, guarding his estates. Samson was the sort of man who came to typify the great thirteenth-century prior, abbot, or abbot bishop, like Henry of Eastry at Canterbury, Robert Champeaux at Tavistock, Hugh of Northwold at Ely, Berard at Cassino, efficient farmers in a big way, alive to the world.[12] These men were almost as extroverted as Francis or Anthony of Padua, but in a different way.

From the distance, the thirteenth-century monastery can be seen as a pathetic creature, a deserted dinosaur, a ruin. Seen from within, as much as that is possible, the successful monasteries, the ones that survived, look very different. Much of their brittle fragility disappears. Great ones like Bury and Saint Albans are huge, heavily propertied corporations fighting angrily and absorbedly against taxation and loss of revenue. Smaller ones like Santa Maria di Valdiponte are careful housekeepers intent upon the endless job of balancing their budgets. Bury and Saint Albans are quite visible. One can,

[12] For Henry of Eastry see R.A.L. Smith, *Canterbury Cathedral Priory* (Cambridge, 1943), and David Knowles, *Religious Orders in England*, 1 (Cambridge, 1956), 49-54; for Robert Champeaux see H.P.R. Finberg, *Tavistock Abbey* (Cambridge, 1951), 260-261; for Hugh of Northwold see Edward Miller, *The Abbey and Bishopric of Ely* (Cambridge, 1951), 77-78, 279.

in different ways, almost go inside each of them. Jocelin has kept the monks of Bury and their attributes, except, one trusts, spirituality, alive. In Matthew Paris the institutions of Saint Albans, its walls and fields seem to speak. There is nothing like either Jocelin or Matthew from Italy. But the detailed accounts of Santa Maria di Valdiponte keep that monastery alive in a different way.

Santa Maria di Valdiponte was a Benedictine monastery (see Fig. 7). It was, by the thirteenth century, already several hundred years old.[13] It was locally within the diocese of Perugia, not far from the Tiber, about a third of the way, going up, from Perugia to Umbertide. Its churches and sources of income stretched out toward Trasimeno and Gualdo and Gubbio and even, in isolation to the south, to the diocese of Civita Castellana. It had possessions in the city of Perugia, around San Gregorio in the Porta Santa Susanna. Valdiponte was, in numbers, a small monastery. In late September 1265, for instance, there seem to have been resident only seven monks and two *conversi*.[14] These religious were surrounded by a household of servants; and their number was continually augmented by day laborers, like the men hired to gather olives, the artisans who mended parts from the mills, or shoed the horses and asses, or worked on the belfry and choir, or helped build an occasional house, and by notaries. In spite of its smallness the abbey had both abbot and prior, a regular chamber-

[13] Lorenzo Fiocca, "Chiesa e abbazia di S. Maria di Valdiponte detta di Montelabate" *Bollettino d'Arte*, VII (1912), 361-378; E. Ricci, "Santa Maria di Valdiponte," *Bollettino della regia deputazione di storia patria per l'Umbria*, XXXIII (1935), 249-324. Vittorio de Donato, *Le più antiche carte dell'abbazia di S. Maria Val di Ponte (Montelabbate) I (969-1170)*, Regesta chartarum Italiae (Rome, 1962), vii-xxiv. For a general introduction to Italian monasticism, see Gregorio Penco, *Storia del monachesimo in Italia* (Rome, 1961). In Ricci's essay, which is based on transcripts made by Alberico Amatori (d. 1875), there are lists of Valdiponte churches, possessions, dependent clergy sometimes assembled, and books (see particularly pages 274-275, 292-303, 305-324). For San Gregorio in Perugia, see particularly Angelo Pantoni, "Chiese Perugine dipendenti da monasteri," *Benedictina*, XI (1957), 177-218, 193.

[14] Perugia, Archivio di stato, conventi soppressi, Santa Maria di Valdiponte, no. 25, fo. 2.

lain, and at least an occasional sacristan; and on important occasions the few residents could be joined by the clergy of dependent churches. The monastery recruited new members in the later thirteenth century; the names change, and the numbers do not fall. These men had books to read: sermons, Epistles, the rule, Gospels and commentaries, lives of the fathers, acts of the martyrs, Bruno and the Decretum, Gregory— a fair little library.

Valdiponte was not poor. It drew considerable profit from its woods, its mills, its grain, its vines and olives, and sometimes from its fruit and nut trees, its livestock, and its wool.[15] But its budget was close. The budget's balance could be endangered by heavy necessary repairs at one of the mills (particularly the mill on the Tiber which seems, not unreasonably, to have been considerably more important than the mill on the Ventia). The budget could be temporarily swamped by two great connected expenses, the death of an old abbot and the election of a new one, with doctors' bills, expensive ceremonies, clothes, trips to Rome. These were expenses that made necessary the borrowing of a sum of money equal to the total income for several months.[16]

The detailed notarized accounts in which the chamberlain reported all income and all expense from the time of the last account were rendered by the chamberlain to the abbot, or in vacancy to the prior and monks, in cloister or dormitory, about the abbey, at irregular intervals of several months: August, January, March, June, August, December, January, June, July. The accounts (of which the first sixty-two folios are now lost or strayed) cover the period from 1265 through 1288, from the last year of Abbot Ercolano, through the whole abbacy of Trasmondo, through the first two years of Abbot Deodato.

[15] See, for example, Valdiponte, no. 25, fos. 2, 2v, 3v, 5, 6, 14, 16, 20v, 22v, 67, 82v, 103v, 104, 104v, 106; see Ricci for Valdiponte churches and possessions; for a general introduction to monastic economy and its position in the general economy, see Gino Luzzatto, *An Economic History of Italy*, tr. Philip Jones (London, 1961); for a specific and exact examination of ecclesiastical estates in the neighborhood of Lucca, see P. J. [Philip] Jones, "An Italian Estate, 900-1200," *Economic History Review*, VII (1954), 18-32.

[16] For example Valdiponte, no. 25, fos. 2v, 10, 10v, 110.

When the first of the surviving accounts was written the monk
Mafeo was chamberlain. He was replaced in 1267 by the prior
Mauro, who was replaced as prior by the monk Buono. Mauro
remained chamberlain for twenty years until in 1287 he was
replaced by the monk Angelo.[17]

Although a notary was imported for redacting the accounts,
the chamberlain himself is very much present in them: "I
paid," "I bought," "when I went to Perugia," "fifteen florins
of gold for a horse I sold."[18] Around him are collected the detailed and vivid, but ordinary, household expenses: the repeated expense of buying and repairing footwear (the wise
economy of the discalced orders becomes apparent); money
spent for bread, for cheese and eggs, for pepper (three *soldi* a
half-pound in 1265, five *soldi* and three *denari* a pound in
1266, and seven *soldi* a pound in 1267, eight *soldi* six *denari*
in 1268, fourteen *soldi* for two pounds for the Christmas of
1285), for cloth for the abbot, for paper for a letter "we sent"
—twelve *soldi* for repairing the mole beneath the bridge, three

[17] For the papal confirmation of the election of Trasmondo, who
had been rector of the Valdiponte church of San Gregorio Perugia, see
Édouard Jordan, *Clément IV*, 100-101 no. 368; a misprint in Jordan
(which Pantoni follows) dates the confirmation 20 October 1268, instead of 20 October 1266. The Valdiponte accounts are more revealing if they are compared with other roughly contemporary price lists
and accounts: like the household accounts for the minor Ammannati
heirs in Florence, for the period just following that of the Valdiponte
account and published by Armando Sapori in "Un Bilancio domestico
a Firenze alla fine del Dugento," *Studi di storia economica medievale*
(Florence, 1940), 75-93, 82-93; or like the sort of price list sometimes
attached to the records of litigation or the proving of wills, as for
example the 1297 estimate of the value of the goods claimed rightfully to belong to the heirs of Pietro de Baysio of Bologna (who had
died twenty-seven years earlier)—a list which includes valuable
horses, armor, and law books (Bologna, Archivio di stato, Sant'Agnese
7/5597 no. 372). A helpful English comparison can be made with
the accounts of Wenlok of Westminster: Harvey, *Walter de Wenlok*,
155-214. The difference between Westminster household accounts and
Valdiponte convent accounts is, and should be, apparent; Miss Harvey's emphasis upon Wenlok's being "at home" out of the abbey
(p. 10) points up the immersion of Trasmondo in his abbey—an
abbot unfreed from his house.

[18] The last is Valdiponte, no. 25, fo. 104.

soldi to the notary for writing an account, twenty-three *denari*
for a *quaternus* for writing the income and expenses of the
account, twenty-five *soldi* for a piece of land. Equally detailed
and equally ordinary are the sales of barley and ground grain,
pears (16*s* less 1*d* in 1265) and cherries (45*s* in 1285), a yoke
of oxen (14*li* 12*d* in 1265). The great world, or at least the
little world, intrudes: money (18*d*) to a messenger bringing
letters, (100*s*) to a certain knight who was of use to the monastery, (18*s* 4*d*) to Dom Oliverio when he went to the papal
curia, (3*s*) to a doctor for medicine, (3*li*) to another for his
services, (25*s*) when a fraternity of clerks came to the monastery, (10*s*) for fish when a Baglione came to dine and (2*s* 6*d*)
for fish when the *plebanus* came, (12*s*) for meat when the
podestà of Perugia was entertained—and meat for the work-
men, meat for strangers, (7*d*) for Nicolò and his horse to go to
Perugia, (12*d*) for someone from Cardinal Simone, (12*d*) for
fish for the witnesses in the case against the men of Rance,
(6*s*) for Dom Angelo to go off and be ordained priest, money
(8*li*) for the monastery's council of four *sapientes*, money to
change money into other currencies—those of Florence, Tours,
and (particularly for salt) Ravenna.[19]

The wine is sold, and the barley; the shoes are bought, and
the chamberlain goes off to Perugia. But there is more than
this in the accounts. Dom Angelo becomes a priest. Meat must
constantly be bought for strangers—there was at least a strong
pretense in the house of observing the rule. In 1283, the monks
gave the friars of Saint Augustine twenty *soldi* for charity's
sake. Paupers, moreover, turn up and receive small amounts
of money from the monks: 4*d* in late 1271, 1*d* and 6*d* in 1267,
4*d* (for two) in 1265, and in 1285-1286, when an abbot died,
8*s* 8*d*. It is the romantic work of the monastery, of course mis-

[19] Valdiponte, no. 25, fos. 1, 1v, 2, 2v, 3v, 4, 5, 5v, 6v, 11, 14, 29,
104, 111v, 118. The account of the exchange for the three currencies
(fo. 113, in 1286) records that four florins then cost eight lire, eight
denari; for salt bought in the currency of Ravenna, fos. 111, 112v.
For a short discussion of the money of Perugia, see Luigi Bonazzi,
Storia di Perugia (Città di Castello, 1959-1960), 1, 268-270. For the
burden of hospitality to patrons in contemporary English houses, see
Susan Wood, *English Monasteries and Their Patrons in the Thirteenth Century* (Oxford, 1955), 103-105.

erably small and diluted. A *joculatore* (equally romantic, but at the other side of the exhortations and inhibitions of a prelate like Bonifazio Fieschi) got three times as much as the two 1265 paupers in 1283.[20] Valdiponte's gifts to paupers are not impressive, as is the Tavistock arrangement of Abbot Robert Champeaux who assigned the total income of West Liddaton to buy paupers' shoes and clothes. Presumably, however, the Valdiponte gestures represent something of the same impulse.[21]

The monks of Valdiponte were much involved in lawsuits. Nothing could be less surprising. Suits were a monastic pastime. Northern Italian Cistercian nuns have seemed to a close observer of their thirteenth-century habits "to derive intense emotional satisfaction" from their lawsuits.[22] In Rome the convent of Sant'Agnese on the Via Nomentana fought so long (for two centuries) with Santa Maria in Monasterio for certain lands that by the late thirteenth century, half a century before the dispute finally ended, the lands were called "mons de la questione" or "vallis de lite"—their topography less sure than the fact that they caused trouble.[23] A monastery without lawsuits is almost inconceivable, and Valdiponte certainly does not break the pattern. Valdiponte paid for its suits. Between August and December 1265 expenses amounted to slightly less than sixty-nine lire; three full lire of the December account were spent "for judges against the abbot of San Paolo" (as well as the twelve denari for fish for the witnesses against Rance in what seems a more important case), at a time, approximately, when two *corbi* of barley brought three lire seven *soldi*, and a *salma* of wine about twenty-seven *soldi*. In the

[20] Valdiponte, no. 25, fos. 2v, 11, 32v, 99v, 100, 111v; Gerolamo Rossi, *Historiarum Ravennatum libri decem* (Venice, 1589), 830-831 (Fieschi, canons I and II).

[21] Finberg, 226.

[22] Catherine E. Boyd, *A Cistercian Nunnery in Mediaeval Italy, the Story of Rifreddo in Saluzzo, 1220-1300* (Cambridge, Mass., 1943), 104.

[23] Isa Lori Sanfilippo, "Le più antiche carte del monastero di S. Agnese sulla Via Nomentana," *Bollettino dell'Archivio paleografico italiano*, NS II-III (1956-1957):2, 65-97, 70; G. Tomassetti, "Della campagna romana: Via Tiburtina," *Archivio della società romana di storia patria* [henceforth *ASRSP*], xxx (1907), 332-388, 357; P. Fedele, "S. Maria in Monasterio," *ASRSP*, xxix (1906), 183-227.

summer of 1266 the abbey spent ten *soldi* "on sentences against the men of Rance," and in the spring three *soldi* for the counsel of a judge.[24] But the unusual fullness of the Valdiponte accounts makes a rather surprising revelation: sometimes, at least, the money invested in suits seems to have paid off. In the account of income for the winter of 1265, a small account of slightly over twenty-two lire (accounts are seldom less than 100 lire), three successful lawsuits brought the monastery just short of an average of thirteen *soldi* apiece.[25]

At a great monastery like Montevergine near Avellino the scale of everything was different. In place of Valdiponte's cluster of rights, fields, and churches gathered around the valley of the Tiber, Montevergine had rich interests spread out over much of the whole Regno; instead of Valdiponte's close, complete accounts of income and expenses over two decades, Montevergine preserves a collection of over fifteen hundred thirteenth-century documents related in various (sometimes quite distant) ways to its rights and property.[26] Both monasteries were unusually competent, although different, keepers of records; and through the records of Montevergine, a very real monastery, pass the shadow figures of neighboring bishops, usually buttressed by their chapters: Felice of Lesina, Gilberto of Capaccio, Giovanni of Sant'Agata dei Goti, Benedetto of Ascoli Satriano, Pietro of Bovino.[27]

Montevergine claims stretched from Mercogliano, its town, and Avellino, to Naples, Aversa, Capua, Sarno, Nocera, Benevento, Mirabella Eclano, Salerno, San Severino, Eboli, Melfi, Lucera, Ariano, Bari, Bitonto, Troia, and even Collesano near Palermo; the web of properties of its sort of institution gave something of real coherence to the peninsular part of the

[24] Valdiponte, no. 25, fos. 1, 2v, 3v, 5, 6v; twenty years later two corbi of barley brought 4*li* 16*s* (fo. 103v), but there was constant minor fluctuation in the price of both wine and barley.

[25] Valdiponte, no. 25, fo. 1.

[26] Giovanni Mongelli, *Abbazia di Montevergine, Regesto delle pergamene*, II, III (Rome, 1957).

[27] Mongelli: II, 67 no. 1333; II, 167 no. 1722; II, 205 no. 1882; III, 96 no. 2279 and III, 166 no. 2534; II, 187 no. 1803.

Regno.[28] In a town as distant as Troia, Montevergine's claims
were thick and various: palazzi, houses and little houses, a
stable, vineyards, gardens, some olive trees, pieces of land scattered through the place—in the *piazza maggiore*, next to the
garden of the chapter of Troia, near various churches.[29] Montevergine's sources of income were various too: conventional
city and country rents and services, mills, eels, the income
from rabbit-hunting, the oaks of "lu domu" near Eboli, the
eight-day fair or long-market around the Feast of Saint Margaret in July, and a very noticeable number of chestnut groves
—chestnuts, like medical doctors and petty nobility, seem to
have filled the southern countryside.[30]

Claims were different from possessions in thirteenth-century
Italy. Like all monasteries caught in the papal-Staufen disorders Montevergine was repeatedly deprived of its rights, or
what it called its rights. The disorders were, perhaps above all,
a convenient excuse and cover for local disseisin. Of Montevergine disputes the most sharply preserved (in action though
not in cause), in the reality of ugly taunts, is the monastery's
fight with Roberto Janaro, whose misbehavior Abbot Marino
described in 1261.[31] Roberto had come with his gang to the
spedale of the monastery and called Abbot Giovanni Fellicola
a traitor and a bearer of the banner of the pope. Later Roberto
had said that he wanted to strangle the abbot. Finally when
the abbot died, Roberto said he mourned because he had
wanted to kill the abbot with his own hands. After the election
of Abbot Marino himself, Roberto had railed against him
("os suum in nos"); and Roberto stirred up dissension among

[28] See particularly Mongelli, III, 51-55 no. 2131, but also II, 225 no.
1965 and II, 19 no. 1112 and III, 3.

[29] Mongelli, III, 15-16 no. 2006: this is a claim which at least in part
speaks of possessions from which the abbey had been expelled by
imperial mandate; it is dated 2 August 1250.

[30] Mongelli: II, 125-126 no. 1565 (Raone, conte di Conza, gave the
monastery one of their mills on the Calore—one of his three near
Apice, of which he was signore); III, 32 no. 2062 (the rabbit-hunting,
from the profits of which they had been deprived in 1256); II, 194
no. 1836 ("lu domu"); III, 27 no. 2049 (eels); III, 139 no. 2437 (the
long market of Saint Margaret).

[31] Mongelli, III, 44 no. 2106.

the monks just as he had attacked and caused trouble in their town of Mercogliano. Marino ordered Roberto and all his tribe to be driven from the land of Mercogliano as traitors. He further ordered that none of Roberto's family ever be admitted to the habit of religion at Montevergine or be allowed to live in Mercogliano.

Another sort of rebellion against Montevergine was defeated, at least temporarily, in 1224. Leonardo, abbot of Santa Maria dell'Incoronata in Puglia, had said that he and his abbey did not want to live in obedience to Montevergine. The quarrel was submitted to the bishop of Ascoli who, in his devotion, not only bound the Incoronata to obedience but also gave Montevergine three churches.[32] There was treachery, too, within the house of Montevergine itself. In 1221 the monk Roberto admitted that he had represented the abbey at the Roman curia under a forged document and that he manufactured the fake seal at Pietrastornina. Roberto could not represent the abbey against the abbot, it was said, because ". . . abbatis et conventus est una et communis et in pari voto et unitate consistunt"—a cliché which under unlikely but convenient circumstances monks of Montevergine could bring themselves to utter.[33]

Montevergine, like almost everyone else, fought the battle of provisions. Their fight looks unamiable when, in 1227 before the archbishop of Benevento in his dwelling at Montesarchio, the abbot and the abbey's advocate (Canturberio), propose jurisdictional technicalities and appeal that they not be forced to give his benefice to Palmiero, a blind citizen of Benevento—while the archbishop insists upon the haste due in a "causa de alimentis pro miserabili."[34] Montevergine looks less unamiable when the Palmiero fight is seen in longer context, as in 1238 the abbey again resists before the archbishop of Benevento, this time against the provision of Andrea, clerk of Rome. The abbey lists provisions and pensions forced upon it by Popes Innocent, Honorius, and Gregory: two blind Beneventans (including Palmiero); a papal scribe (Pietro Ylario);

[32] Mongelli, II, 118 no. 1533.
[33] Mongelli, II, 103 no. 1472.
[34] Mongelli, II, 134 no. 1601.

and a converted Jew (Leucio).[35] The abbey was being pressed to a contemporary purpose which was not its own.

Gifts to the monastery seem to have declined, it is true, as the century progressed. By the last year of the century alienations far outnumber any other sort of Montevergine transaction; but these alienations were, at least in part, a phase of the abbots' constant effort to reshape the abbey's income, so that it would grow and, also, be easier to come by.[36] Abbot Guglielmo III's great exchange with the judge Pellegrino d'Arpino in December 1299, through which the abbot alienated a large collection of distant rights and possessions in exchange for more local ones, can be seen either as retrenchment or as simple good sense. Collecting rents from a great distance, and establishing distant rights, could cost more than the rents were worth. Besides, the archaic, extended distribution of monastic tenements through which great monasteries once "may have managed to provide for their essential needs without recourse to any market" was clearly anachronistic in thirteenth-century Italy (except for its value in diversifying income).[37] In a move not completely dissimilar from the Pellegrino exchange, the abbey, in 1268, pressed by heavy debts (200 *once*), released two sisters of Mercogliano from personal services that they had inherited from both their parents, in exchange for an *oncia* of gold and two *tari* a year.[38]

Although—perhaps partly because—they had debts, the abbots were careful estate managers: in 1291 Abbot Guglielmo confirmed a grant to a man of Maddaloni and his heirs "exceptis clericis et feminabus"; in 1254 the monk proctor for managing the monastery's goods around Eboli granted some land with four olive plants on it, in Malito, to a man who was

[35] Mongelli, II, 200-201 no. 1864 (for Pietro Ylario's—Ilario, de Lari —provision: II, 199 no. 1856).

[36] Mongelli, III:195 no. 2623, 196 no. 2626, and 2627, 197 nos. 2629 and 2631, 197-198 no. 2632, 198 no. 2633, 200 nos. 2635 and 2636, 203 nos. 2645 and 2646, 208 no. 2657.

[37] Mongelli, III, 208-209 no. 2657; cf. Mongelli, II, 18 no. 1106; the quotation about early extended distribution applies in its context (Luzzatto-Jones, 28) to nonmonastic ecclesiastical landowners as well as monasteries.

[38] Mongelli, III, 73-74 no. 2191.

within five years to convert it into an olive grove and then return half of the land to the monastery and keep the other half for himself and his heirs with the obligation, for the following fourteen years, of returning half the olives, or a tithe if the land were planted, to the monastery.[39] Like other monasteries, moreover, Montevergine was a creditor as well as a debtor: in 1273 the executors of Tommaso d'Aquino, conte d'Acerra, made provision that the monastery should not lose anything of the 160 *once* that it had lent Tommaso.[40]

Although monastic devotion and devotion to monasteries cooled in the thirteenth century, people continued, at a slackening pace, to make major offerings to Montevergine. Members of the local nobility still wanted to be buried there.[41] In May 1299 the noble Corrado d'Aversa arranged for the dispersal of his goods in his last will and testament: the payment of his debt, the provision for his wife if she remained unmarried, the selling of his books (ecclesiastical, legal, medical), the selling of his horses—except one named Sissino that he left to his nephew Corrado. The Franciscans and Dominicans are prominent, as one would expect in the will of a seemingly pious and learned and certainly noble late thirteenth-century testator. *Once* of gold are to be passed about: two to the Franciscans of Salerno for singing Masses; one to the Dominicans of Salerno; one to the sisters of San Lorenzo in Salerno and one to the sisters of Santa Maria Maddalena, and two *tari* to each Salerno hermit. But the great ecclesiastical bequests are for two, or one of two, old-fashioned institutions: for the priests of the great cathedral church of Salerno where Corrado wanted to be buried; for Montevergine, four *once* a year with the obligation of building a chapel, if he, Corrado, should die in the country, at Cotuniano, and be buried, as he wished in

[39] Mongelli, III, 157 no. 2501; III, 25 no. 2042.

[40] Mongelli, III, 92 no. 2266; the abbey of Staffarda's wealth "had made it the unofficial banker" of its district in the early thirteenth century: Boyd, *A Cistercian Nunnery*, 39.

[41] E.g., Mongelli, III:23 no. 2036, 24 no. 2041, 28 no. 2051, 40 no. 2114, 68-69 no. 2175, 135 no. 2423; Mongelli, II, 120-121 no. 1544 (in 1225 Rainaldo Lavareta, conte di Gesualdo, and his contessa, having chosen their place to be buried in the monastery, give it vineyards and unused land).

that case, at Montevergine. (It is easy to see why the old clergy fought against letting the Franciscans and Dominicans bury any but their own.)

Three of Montevergine's thirteenth-century documents go a long way toward explaining the sort of place or thing it was. Together they expose its heart—a silver votive heart perhaps— or three hearts, one within the other. The most external of the three is a major privilege that the monastery got from Urban IV in 1264, in the tradition of similar bulls from Innocent III and Alexander IV.[42] The Urban IV bull—the expense of which may explain, in some part, the abbey's 1268 debt—re-cites the abbey's individual possessions in great detail and then turns to more general rights: the abbey's exemption from tithe; its rights in interdict; its general exemption; rights of burial; its complete freedom of election and the elect's right to be consecrated by any bishop; its right to administer penance and baptism. The second document, an earlier one, from 1241, describes the contents of the monastery's treasury: the six sil-ver chalices, and the silver apple that was placed at the foot of the cross; the silver imperial image; the two crystal vases with silver work and silver tops; the precious cloths and vestments of silk and cloth of gold, reds and purples, with griffins flying; the cross of silver and the wood of Christ's own cross; and the relics of Saint James, Saints Cosmas and Damian, Saint Simeon, and Saint Clement.[43]

The third document is rather different (see Fig. 16). In it, in 1210, Abbot Donato arranges for the use of a gift given to the abbey through the hands of Fra Martino by a married couple for the remission of their sins' punishment. The provisions include the use of income from the gift for bread and beans for the poor on Holy Thursday.[44] The arrangement, as the document shows, was approved by Honorius III on 2 Decem-ber 1216, so that the actual document must have come from a

[42] Mongelli, III, 51-55 no. 2131 (plate facing p. 52): it exists in twelve copies of various date; see, too, III, 3.

[43] Mongelli, II, 212 no. 1907—I have of course only mentioned some of the treasures in the treasury.

[44] Mongelli, II, 59 no. 1297 (plate facing p. 480); A. Mastrullo, *Monte Vergine Sagro* (Naples, 1663), 131-136.

time after that date. The peculiar interest of the document is
due to the drawings which decorate it. At the top center of the
document, interrupting the lengthened letters of the invoca-
tion and date line (and those immediately below it) is the
figure of Christ the Redeemer. Halfway down the document
on either side of the extended letters of the abbot's "subscription" line are, to the left, sitting with his "subscription" cross
above his hand, the abbot, and to the right, the pope. In a broad
middle band extending down the lower half of the document
between the two "subscription" lists are three rows of figures.
In the top row is the Virgin flanked by two angels. Beneath
them, and identified, are three abbey obedientiaries, the claustral prior, the dean, and the provost. In the bottom row Fra
Martino holds the two donors, one by each hand. The tableau
explains the abbey's existence and its riches. The lay man and
woman, drawn, each with one hand on his or her heart, and
one hand in Martino's, through their gift, and the ladder of
the monastery, meet the Redeemer. The rich concatenation of
privilege, land, and silver had a reason for existing, and the
painter understood it.

Understanding seems to have been particularly strong at
Cassino under Abbot Berard (1263-1282).[45] Berard brought
physical and fiscal order to the great monastery with its di-
versified and elaborate eight-office system of obedientiaries,
its labors divided by type and by territory, its various jobs in
the hands of knights and clerks as well as monks.[46] Berard's
order was controlled and preserved by the records that Cassino
kept: Berard's own great register and the lesser filiated regis-

[45] The bibliography for Cassino in the thirteenth century is, as one
should expect, unusually long: Caplet; Tosti; Luigia Diamare, "L'orga-
nizza interna del monastero Cassinese nel secolo XIII," *ASRSP*, LXVIII
(1945), 33-61; Agostino Saba, *Bernardo I Ayglerio* [Miscellanea Cassinese no. 8] (Cassino, 1931); Berard, *Speculum Monachorum*, ed.
Hilarius Walter (Freiburg, 1901) intro., pp. vii-xxiii; *Regesto di Tommaso decano o cartolario del convento Cassinese (1178-1280)* (Cassino,
1915); L. Fabiani, *La terra di San Benedetto* (Cassino, 1950)—with a
helpful map; Mauro Inguanez, *Registrum sancti Angeli de Fortunula*
(Cassino, 1936); and much other work, particularly Leccisotti's in
volumes of Miscellanea Cassinese.

[46] See particularly Diamare, 41-55.

ters.[47] But Berard transcended all this. He also wrote his *Speculum monachorum*, his scholastic—flowered with learning—mirror for monks, modeled apparently on the work of Guillaume Perault. Through his *Speculum* Berard connected Cassino's surface order with the meaning of the rule and the purpose of the religious life as he understood them and thought Benedict had. Berard brought to his mirror some of the sentiment and spirituality of the anti-Cluniac feeling of his name-saint, Bernard of Clairvaux. Berard remembered the sweet praises of his former abbey of Lérins. But his predominant tone (except in the actual scholastic structure of the work) is perhaps best caught by his Senecan quotation: "What is wisdom? Always to want the same thing and always to not want the same thing."[48] In his reform of Cassino, Urban IV was solidly successful through the selection of this abbot from France, or rather from Lyons and Savigny and Lérins. Manfred had certainly been less successful in his nomination of Teodino, but Teodino had had little time.[49] Berard's articulate restoring and shoring up of monastic resources came at a time when the monks of Cassino appreciated the need for his work. The register of Tommaso the Dean, in an *arenga* that Matthew Paris would have understood completely although he might have felt it with less urgency, talked of the necessity of recording things, because of the growing treachery of his contemporaries, their enmity toward antique simplicity, truth, and rightness.[50] The virtue that insured monastic income seemed to have been slipping dreadfully away.

The action of thirteenth-century monasteries was repetitive and predictable. They protected their property. Large and small—San Pietro in Perugia, San Salvatore Castiglione in the

[47] See particularly A. M. Caplet's "Prolegomena, in *Regesti Bernardi*, xxiii ff.

[48] Perault: Walter, xv-xvii; Bernard: Walter, particularly 7, 18-19, 45, 122, 209-210, but also 6, 8, 11, 25, 46, 59, 60, 76, 77, 82, 84, 85, 111, 113, 117, 119, 121, 133, 135, 143, 169, 197; Lérins: Walter, 137; Seneca: Caplet (xlv) points out the quotation from ch. 2, "de stabilitate": Walter, 14. Mr. Paul Mosher is in process of preparing a fresh evaluation of Berard of Cassino.

[49] Diamare, 36-38, and Saba.

[50] *Regesto di Tommaso*, I.

diocese of Trivento—they invested in papal privileges.[51] They, as in the case of Santa Sophia in Benevento, recorded their long lists of holdings; and their records are very considerably better than those of neighboring diocesan chanceries.[52] Although they meant to be protected as much as possible from the government that ruled the rest of the community, secular and ecclesiastical, the monasteries, even those in rustic strongholds, could not and did not mean to be isolated from the community, although when not isolated they preferred to be dominant.

Sometimes the monasteries' entanglement was personal and complicated. In 1291 there appears the figure of a clerk named Mariano di Giorgio of Alife, who is described as "abbas" and rector of the church of Santa Maria de Campo in Sant'Angelo "de Rupetanina," Alife diocese, a church subject to the Benedictine monastery of Santa Sophia in Benevento; Mariano is also described as a clerk of the great church of Alife. Mariano di Giorgio, thus, like a spider hanging by two strands of web, connected the great abbey and the little cathedral.[53] Many other clerks similarly connected many other institutions.

Very frequently the entanglement of the monastery in more general society was direct and economic—and, in its multiplicity, at first sight, a little surprising. Much is revealed when the Staufen floods are over and the monasteries of the south can be seen scrambling to get what they consider, or call, their old rights, as popes and Angevins initiate the long detail of the inquest. Monreale, for example, was active even in the peninsular south: it can be seen, in the 1260's, trying to get its share of poor Bitetto's wealth or fighting for its two fishtraps or ponds (*trabes*) within the Mar Piccolo at Taranto.[54] Donors

[51] *Le carte dell'archivio di S. Pietro di Perugia*, i, ed. Tommaso Leccisotti and Costanzo Tabarelli (Milan, 1956), 134-152 nos. 29-32, particularly the last; Naples, Archivio di stato, Archivio Caracciolo di Santo Bono, Castiglione, abbazia di San Salvatore, no. 3.

[52] Archivio segreto vaticano, Archivio Aldobrandini, documenti storici, abbadie, 4 no. 53 (in 1278).

[53] Archivio segreto vaticano, Archivio Aldobrandini, documenti storici, abbadie, 4 no. 69.

[54] Carlo Alberto Garufi, *Catalogo illustrato del tabulario di Santa Maria Nuova in Monreale* (Palermo, 1902), 174-177, app., nos. 13, 15.

had given what they had had, and monasteries had wanted what they could get. San Giorgio, a convent for girls in Salerno, had, just before the century began, acquired rights over the market where greens (*folia*) were sold every day in Salerno's *piazza maggiore*.[55] Monasteries also dealt in churches (or in properties disguised by that name) as when, in 1279, in a twenty-nine-year lease of normal form, Abbot Nicola and the convent of Santa Sophia, Benevento, rented the churches of San Bartolomeo and Santa Lucia to a man named Adam for a yearly rent of half an *oncia* of gold to be paid on the Feast of the Twelve Brothers.[56]

Monasteries profited from the mercantile life of the city and from the feudal and seignorial life of the country where it was feudal or seignorial. The northern Cistercian nunnery of Rifreddo "was proprietor and seignior" of two small communities in the Valle del Po; and the abbey of Sant'Eutizio in Val Castoriana near Norcia is said to have flourished as feudalism flourished and declined as feudalism declined.[57]

In all this there is much similarity to the position of English monasteries—even Montevergine's fight for its eels from the Lago di Lesina recalls, though inversely, the "astronomical numbers of eels delivered by the fenland manors" of the abbey of Ely.[58] The similarity should not seem surprising. Monastic institutions, unlike bishops, in England as in Italy, were perforce stationary.[59] Monasteries, unlike bishops, in Italy as well as England, driven by their, at least once, purpose, were frequently established in rural fastnesses. But, in spite of much

[55] Leopoldo Cassese, *Pergamene del monastero benedettino di S. Giorgio* (Salerno, 1950), 96-99 no. 17; Carlo Carucci, *Codice diplomatico salernitano del secolo XIII*, 1 (Subiaco, 1931), 179-182 no. 89.

[56] Archivio segreto vaticano, Archivio Aldobrandini, documenti storici, abbadie, 4 no. 56.

[57] Catherine E. Boyd, *A Cistercian Nunnery in Medieval Italy* (Cambridge, Mass., 1943), 145; Pietro Pirri, *L'Abbazia di Sant'Eutizio in Val Castoriana presso Norcia e le chiese dipendenti*, Studia Anselmiana 45 (Rome, 1960), 65: I think that Pirri's "feudalism" would be conventionally described, outside of Italy, as a mixture of feudalism and seignorialism with a rather heavy emphasis on seignorialism.

[58] Mongelli, III, 27 no. 2049; Miller, 38.

[59] See Miller, 37, for the distinction between the monastery and the bishop at Ely.

similarity, real differences remain. English monasteries were much less likely to traffic in churches; there was more distinction between the sacred and the chattel. Up and down the Italian peninsula monastic houses made feast days (and not simply conventional or economically sensible ones like Michaelmas), particularly their dedication days, odious by fixing them as rent-paying days. The wax and the silver were gathered to the shrine on the cult's high day in a country in which, as opposed to England, feast days were not even used for normal dating purposes. Different countrysides, moreover, produced different incomes; the olives, the vines, the transient peasants, the twenty-nine-year and three-generation leases in Italy are different from their English counterparts. Although English monasteries like Faversham frequently claimed considerable properties in towns and Italian monasteries frequently hid in the country, the Italian monasteries were on the whole, like everything else in Italy, more urban in outlook and income than their English cousins. This looks very clear when the holdings of an Italian Cistercian country monastery like Fiastra are compared with those of English Cistercian houses like Rievaulx or Newminster.[60]

For the majority of reasonably healthy Italian monasteries and almost all English monasteries, nevertheless, the pattern is much the same: property, sometimes much property; little inspiration; hard fights; survival. Saint Albans, Sant'Eutizio, Valdiponte, Bury—most monasteries were much the same as far as anyone can really tell. But in a minority of Italian mon-

---

[60] See C.A.J. Armstrong, "Thirteenth Century Notes on the Rights of the Abbey of Faversham in London from a Manuscript of Grenoble," *English Historical Review*, LIV (1939), 677-685. For Fiastra, see below; for Newminster and Rievaulx: *Chartularium Abbathiae de Novo Monasterio*, ed. J. T. Fowler, Surtees Society 66 for 1876 (Durham, 1878); *Chartularium Abbathiae de Rievalle*, ed. J. C. Atkinson, Surtees Society 83 for 1887 (Durham, 1889), and Bryan Waites, "The Monastic Settlement"—see note 79 below. Although the distance is particularly sharply visible in this comparison of Cistercian houses, it is constantly clear; see for instance the distribution of the possessions of the priory of Saint Gregory in Canterbury: *Cartulary of the Priory of St. Gregory, Canterbury*, ed. Audrey M. Woodcock, Camden Series, 88 (London, 1956), 177-180. See, too, Eileen Power, *Medieval English Nunneries* (Cambridge, 1922), 98-99.

asteries something happens that sets them sharply apart from
English monasteries—so sharply that it makes a real difference between the two countries.

Looking at the decayed monasteries within their sight on
the Italian peninsula (and there was admittedly much decay—the whole monastic establishment can be made to look
like a medlar tree, with lots of rotten fruit hanging), sharp-
eyed, reforming thirteenth-century popes could allow, encourage, the wretched monks to be dumped right out of their houses.
The popes attached the depressed houses to houses they approved of; or they filled them with monks or nuns of orders
of which they approved. Small Benedictine houses cluttered
up the map of Italy in the thirteenth century, as little houses of
Austin canons did that of England just before the suppression. They almost asked, in fact sometimes they did ask, to be
put out of their misery.

As the boundaries of dioceses were insecure in Italy, so seem
the orders of religious houses. It was a country in which order
seems often not to have been worth mentioning in the description of small rustic houses, forgotten, almost unchosen, and
so presumably Benedictine. In England order was normally
carefully described and remembered—although there were
mistakes, as when in the 1230's the patron Margaret Lacy put
her house of nuns at Acornbury under the Hospitallers, unaware evidently of the difference between them and the Austin
canons.[61] Italian indefiniteness about order gives a peculiar
tone to a church in which the strongest, if not the liveliest,
element often seems monastic, in which the abbey like Farfa
is a great deal tougher and even more alive than the diocese
that attempted to surround it or its appurtenances. Italy was
also a country in which the local monastic patron, although he
existed, was dwarfed by that mammoth patron the pope.[62]

[61] Wood, 26-27.

[62] See Wood, especially, 3-11, 22; Boyd, *A Cistercian Nunnery*, 46-
47. For an example of a patron (in this case the bishop and chapter
of Melfi) fighting for its patronage (in this case of the monastery of
San Giovanni de Iliceto de Balnea), see Archivio segreto vaticano, Inst.
Misc., N.4291, 3-6 (from the 1280's); for the very interesting dispute,
early in the century, over the nature of the patronage of the house of
Santa Croce Lugnano in the diocese of Rieti, see Rieti, Archivio capi-

The early thirteenth-century popes were distressed by monastic decay throughout western Europe. They proposed remedies and attempted to establish reforms, like the organization of Benedictine chapters and both monastic and episcopal visitation, that were intended to occur in both England and Italy.[63] But in Italy the popes went farther than in England. In Italy they quashed and displaced. In displacing and reforming the old order in Italy the popes relied heavily on two "new" orders, the Cistercians and the Claresses. Both of these "new" orders seem rather surprising selections from an English point of view. The Cistercians of England do not by the thirteenth century seem either new or reformed; bankers by early century, bankrupt by late, it has been said; the Claresses hardly appear (in their slightly different English guise) in England in the thirteenth century.[64] But for Italy they are not at all inexplicable choices. The Cistercians did still provoke peculiar devotion in the Italian thirteenth century; never so splendid as in England, they had not collapsed so quickly. Too, Innocent III and Honorius III seem to have seen the Cistercians through a flattering romantic haze. Perhaps Honorius merely followed Innocent, and a man as hard and sharp and "realistic" as Innocent needed some areas of romantic illusion.[65] At any rate the Cistercians whom these popes saw were not exactly the Cistercians of contemporary records, but rather the Cistercians of Saint Bernard (with whom these popes did not have to deal) and of an almost real system of chapter and visitation.

tolare, IV.P.6, 1-11; for the normal action of the patron of an Italian church, see Rieti, Archivio capitolare, VII.F.5.

[63] U. Berlière, "Innocent III et la réorganisation des monastères bénédictins," *Revue Bénédictine*, XXXII (1920), 22-42, 146-159, and "Honorius III et les monastères bénédictins," *Revue belge de philologie et d'histoire*, II (1923), 237-265, 461-484; C. R. Cheney, *Episcopal Visitations of Monasteries in the Thirteenth Century* (Manchester, 1931).

[64] Sister James Eugene Madden, "Business Monks, Banker Monks, Bankrupt Monks: The English Cistercians in the Thirteenth Century," *Catholic Historical Review*, XLIX (1963-1964), 341-364; Knowles, *Religious Orders*, I, 5-6; David Knowles and R. Neville Hadcock, *Medieval Religious Houses in England and Wales* (London, 1953), 104-118; A.F.C. Bourdillon, *The Order of Minoresses in England*, British Society of Franciscan Studies, 12 (Manchester, 1926), 10-12.

[65] Berlière, "Honorius III," 245-248.

The Claresses were in a different position, and later. They combined the excitement of being attached to the romantic Franciscan ideal with a relatively quick and easy attitude toward accepting the sort of property of which Francis had, most people thought rather unreasonably, disapproved.

Not all thirteenth-century papal reform of monasteries resulted in a change of order, nor did all monastic decay. Berard's being sent to Cassino was a reform, as had been the temporary presence there of the Cistercian Raniero in 1217.[66] Gregory IX instituted reforms at San Pietro in Perugia, through his chaplain Giovanni da San Germano with the aid of Raymond of Peñafort, by calling San Pietro back to the proper observation of its own rule.[67] The wretched situation of the abbey of Santa Maria of Positano, whose three monk electors were bullied by a tough Capuano archbishop of Amalfi into electing an incapable drunkard as their abbot (or whose abbot was attacked by lying faction) could seem only to need a decent abbot and encouragement.[68]

In 1272, after the death of its abbot, there was only one monk, Crescio, in the Benedictine abbey of San Lorenzo at Ardenghesca in the diocese of Grosseto. Crescio, in rottenborough loneliness, proceeded to the election of an abbot. He chose Palmerio, monk of Sant'Antimo and prior of San Tommaso in the diocese of Pistoia. Gregory X, before approving the election, committed the investigation of its procedure to the cardinal deacon of Santa Maria in Cosmedin. The cardinal approved, and the pope confirmed; and in his confirmation the pope did not suggest that a monastery with one monk— or one monk and an abbot—should not exist.[69] San Lorenzo still existed in 1290 when, after two years of vacancy, two cardinals delegated by Nicholas IV had chosen as its new abbot Ventura, monk and proctor of San Saba in Rome.[70]

[66] Diamare, 38.

[67] Leccisotti and Tabarelli, 1, 152-155 no. 35.

[68] Berlière, "Honorius III," 256; *Regesta Honorii Papae III*, ed. Pietro Pressutti (Rome, 1888), 275 no. 1651.

[69] Siena, Archivio di stato, conventi soppressi, S. Maria degli Angeli (1272, Agosto 10).

[70] Siena, Archivio di stato, conventi soppressi, S. Maria degli Angeli (1290, Marzo 30).

Against these cases can be placed many others in which the
order was changed, by papal authority or by the house itself.
In September 1261 Adriano, abbot of San Nicola de Jaciano,
finding, in a recurring phrase, that his abbey was so collapsed
in spiritualities and temporalities that there was no hope of
its restoration, gave the abbey to the Cistercians through their
house of Sant'Angelo of Frigillo, although Adriano was permitted to retain a grange for himself for his lifetime.[71] In
June 1237 Gregory IX ended the dying struggle of the Benedictine house of Santa Maria di Tremiti (on the island of San
Nicola); he ordered the bishop of Termoli to install in the
monastery Cistercian monks from Casanova.[72] Tremiti's spiritual and temporal decay, much investigated, had been thor-
oughly established. The abbey had been the source of at least
intermittent papal concern since 1217.[73] In the years from 1234
to 1237 Gregory IX (and Raniero Capocci, cardinal deacon of
Santa Maria in Cosmedin) employed, or attempted to employ,
a number of clerics in dealing with the monastery: the bishops
of Troia and Lucera, the bishop of Dragonara, the subprior
of Trani, and the archpriest of Siponto.[74] A report from the
bishop of Dragonara and the archpriest of Penne adds a touch
of evil glamor to Tremiti's sad picture of poverty and decay:
it was not safe, they said, for them to go to the monastery itself on account of the danger of pirates and fear of the Slavs of
whom the abbot and monks were known confederates.[75] The
1260 description, from Luke, of neighboring San Leonardo
in Siponto, "not a house of God, but a den of thieves," seems
to have fitted Tremiti exactly.[76] The Cistercians of Casanova

[71] Alessandro Pratesi, *Carte latine . . . dall'Archivio Aldobrandini*
(Vatican City, 1958), 431-434 no. 186.

[72] *Codice diplomatico del monastero benedettino di S. Maria di
Tremiti (1005-1237)*, ed. Armando Petrucci, Istituto storico italiano
per il medio evo: Fonti per la storia d'Italia (Rome, 1960), III, 359-
361 no. 142.

[73] Petrucci, *Codice diplomatico*, III, 341 no. 128.

[74] Petrucci, *Codice diplomatico*, I, lxv-lxviii, and III, 341-361 nos.
129-142.

[75] Petrucci, *Codice diplomatico*, III, 355, in no. 138.

[76] *Regesto di S. Leonardo di Siponto*, ed. F. Camobreco, Regesta
chartarum Italiae, 10 (Rome, 1913), ix, 130 no. 195.

were asked to reform Tremiti, as they were also asked to reform other houses in the general area, Santa Maria di Calena,
San Giovanni in Lamis, and San Bartolomeo di Carbonara;
and Cistercian nuns from Romania were intruded in San
Benedetto of Conversano in 1266.[77]

An instrument of Cistercian reform in the eastern part of
Italy, in the duchy of Spoleto and the Marches, was the now
suppressed monastery of Santa Maria di Chiaravalle di Fiastra
or di Chienti, which is and was normally called Fiastra (see
Fig. 15).[78] The west façade of its imposing but reconstructed
twelfth-century church lies directly upon the modern highway
from Macerata to Urbisaglia in the eastern Marches. The monastery stands in a flat, fertile, relatively low area, about two kilometers long and one wide, within a crook in the river Fiastra. Beyond the Fiastra and a range of hills lies the Chienti, of which
the Fiastra is a tributary. To the south of the church lies the cloister, and to the north a cluster of farm buildings. Across the road
to the west, outbuildings form a shallow court and one of
them includes in its façade traces of arches with simple Romanesque decoration. The church itself is preceded by an enclosed portico. The church follows the simple Cistercian plan
of three aisles, with rectangular transept chapels, two on each
side of the presbytery.

The medieval monastery known by the names of its two
rivers was, of course, dedicated to the Virgin. Its "Chiaravalle"

[77] Walther Holtzmann, "Eine Appellation des Klosters Tremiti an
Alexander III," *Bullettino dell'Istituto storico italiano e Archivio mura-
toriano,* LXVI (1954), 21-39, 22; Petrucci, *Codice diplomatico,* I, lxvii;
and see Pratesi, *Carte latine,* xvi; Mongelli, "Le Abbadesse Mitrate di
S. Benedetto di Conversano," 371-373.
[78] For Fiastra see: Wolfgang Hagemann, "Studien und Dokumente
zur Geschichte der Marken im Zeitalter der Staufer, II: Chiaravalle di
Fiastra," *Quellen und Forschungen,* XLI (1961), 48-136 (there is a very
helpful bibliography in note 1); L. Janauschek, *Originum Cisterciensium*
(Vienna, 1877), 66 no. 162; J. M. Canivez, *Statuta Capitulorum Gen-
eralium Ordinis Cisterciensis,* III (Louvain, 1935); Ernesto Ovidi,
Le Carte della abbazia di Chiaravalle di Fiastra I (1006-1200), Fonti
per la storia delle Marche, 2 (Ancona, 1908); Filippo Caraceni, *L'abbazia di S. Maria di Fiastra o di Chienti* (Urbania, 1951); R. Brentano,
"Peter of Assisi as Witness," *Quellen und Forschungen,* XLI (1961),
323-325 (particularly n. 1).

indicates its ancestry. It was a daughter of Chiaravalle near Milan which, in turn, was a daughter of Clairvaux. It was established in the 1130's and 1140's by, primarily, a marquess of Ancona. Its holdings were partly the gift of the ancient Benedictine house of Santa Maria di Rambona near Pollenza, in the valley of the Potenza—the northern neighbor of the Chienti in that series of rivers and valleys, like the Esino to the north and the Tenna to the south, that cut through the Marches to the Adriatic.

Fiastra was, in the thirteenth century, the center of a network of fairly diverse properties. These properties (sometimes carefully measured) were clustered in neighborhoods around Fiastra and its granges and also around the houses that the monastery owned in a number of towns.[79] Of the granges—Santa Maria in Selva, Sarrociano, Montorso, Lanciano, Collalto, Val di Cortese, Montolmo (Corridonia), and the home grange of Brancorsina—Santa Maria in Selva, north of the Potenza and about five kilometers northwest of Macerata, seems through the actions of its granger to have been a particularly active center of thirteenth-century business in land and rents.[80] In 1290, pressed by specific need, distressed by the reduced rate of growth of income through gifts, or possibly merely intent upon rationalizing income, the abbey sold the rights to farm one grange, Sarrociano, to Gentile Buonconto, a citizen of Fermo, and his associates, for five years for a yearly rent of

[79] There is a very interesting study of monastic spheres of influence and "neighborhoods," especially those of Whitby, Guisborough, and Rievaulx, in Bryan Waites, "The Monastic Settlement of North-East Yorkshire," Yorkshire Archaeological Journal, XL:3 (1961), pt. 159, 478-495, particularly 489-493 and the description of Rievaulx for comparison with Fiastra—there is a map of Rievaulx interests on 488; see, too, T.A.M. Bishop, "Monastic Granges in Yorkshire," English Historical Review, LI (1936), 193-214; for a measurement see Fiastra, no. 2249 (it could be for some land of one of Fiastra's daughter houses).

[80] Perhaps Val di Cortese should be added to the list: Rome, Archivio di stato, Fiastra no. 1280; and Brancorsina, Fiastra no. 2234; the others are scattered through the pergamene, see, for example, nos. 367, 379, 417, 426, 669, 836, 911, 942, 958, 960, 964, 966, 1026, 1048, 1130, 1164, 1165, 1168, 1170, 1396, 1479, 1563, 1668, 1712, 1717, 1733, 1752, 1769, 1777, 1838.

280 lire of Ravenna-Ancona.[81] The town houses, in places like Civitanova, Macerata, and Montolmo (Corridonia) were, it seems, selected for the monastery's own use from the fairly large number of town properties that came to the monastery by gift or trade and that were for the most part merely used as sources of income.[82] Fiastra income came from very varied sources (as one sees when a 100-*soldi*, of Lucca, cow is exchanged for a mill wheel, within a few years of a time in the early thirteenth century when the monastery can and does buy four *staia* of woods for forty *soldi* of Lucca); and although this may not have helped much in the destruction of war, it may have helped in times of specific agricultural depression.[83] Much Fiastra income was in no way peculiarly Cistercian.[84] The grange and *conversi* system was maintained, although not in any purity. There may have been a slightly unusual amount of animal husbandry on Fiastra estates. But the Cistercian permission to maintain old feudal sources of income, originally forbidden, on lands inherited from old orders, seems to have facilitated a general erosion of the property rules; at least at Fiastra they seem not to have been inhibiting.[85]

Most visible Fiastra income came from long leases. Fiastra was, like many other monasteries in western Europe, a sort of central office for transactions in land that was located in several connected neighborhoods. As a sort of holding company it gave something of social and tenurial coherence to its area; and this was probably its greatest service to the community, and, in a way, its reason for being. It is as the chief administrator and formal source of authority in a sophisticated complex of tenements that the abbot (or sometimes his representative, like the prior when Abbot Ambrogio had gone to the Cistercian chapter general in September 1275), whom one

[81] Fiastra no. 1916; cf. Jones, "Camaldoli," *Journal of Ecclesiastical History* (1954), 173.

[82] See Fiastra nos. 1070, 1452, 1455.

[83] Fiastra nos. 411, 489.

[84] See Fiastra nos. 711, 1371; also 976.

[85] See Boyd, *A Cistercian Nunnery*, 98, who also uses E. Hoffmann, "Die Entwicklung der Wirtschaftsprinzipien im Cisterzienserorden während des 12 und 13 Jahrhunderts," *Historisches Jahrbuch*, xxxi (1910), 699-727.

watches, act, all those hundreds of times in the thirteenth century, surrounded by witnesses including many monks—in the cemetery at Chiaravalle, in the infirmary, under the apple tree in front of the abbot's chamber in Maytime, before the gate, under a portico, before the house of Chiaravalle "which is called 'obedientia muri,'" at the Chiaravalle shoemakers, in the piazza before the portico of the church where *conversi* and monks were prepared to give alms to the poor (one recalls Newminster), or, increasingly toward end-century, in the parlor "as is the custom."[86] Fiastra did not, however, deal, in this guise, in land alone. It was also a sort of bank and safety deposit box where people left money and valuables; and, of course, it was a borrower and a lender.[87]

In the early 1260's there seem to have been at least between forty and fifty monks at Chiaravalle, and in the 1270's at least about forty (when there were perhaps as few as twenty-five at a great Benedictine house like Farfa).[88] In the 1280's and 1290's the number of monks may have fallen below thirty (and the number may have been this low sometimes in the first half of the century); perhaps the decrease was partly due to the dispersal of monks to daughter houses. The figures are not very reliable. They come from lists of consenting monks

[86] See, for example, Fiastra nos. 410, 685 (*obedientia muri*), 721 (the shoemaker's), 877 (almsgiving *piazza*), 1188, 1260 (the apple tree in Maytime); there seems to be a correspondence between the customary meetings "in parlatorio" and the orderly work of the notary Buonconsiglio in the period between 1274 and 1294; for Newminster, see Fowler, *Chartularium Abbathiae de Novo Monasterio*, 88-89; for Ambrogio at the chapter general, Fiastra nos. 1520, 1521.

[87] See, for example, Fiastra nos. 1338, 893, 900, 906 (Florentine lenders in Tolentino in 1240), 2294 (in 1301 the noblewoman Forestiera, widow of the Magnifico Rainaldo, nominates a priest proctor to get back silver, books, arms, deposited at Chiaravalle); no. 1496 (stored documents), no. 1565. Compare with the situation in Normandy: R. Génestal, *Rôle des monastères comme établissements de crédit* (Paris, 1901).

[88] See, for example, Fiastra nos. 1284, 1471, 1579 (Farfa) (although 300 monks and *conversi* at Camaldoli: Jones, "Camaldoli," 169; and in an undistinguished house of nuns, San Giacomo di Monselice, in 1257, at least fifty-two: Archivio segreto vaticano, A.C.N.V., San Giacomo di Monselice, 6061).

and witness lists which fluctuate sharply presumably because of the monks' moving about on monastery business. For the most part the monks came from (or were identified as coming from) Chiaravalle's part of the Marches, from the general area into which most of its lands fitted, from Recanati, Macerata, San Genesio, Tolentino, Ripe, Urbisaglia, Monte Santa Maria, Montolmo (Corridonia), Morrovalle, Montemilone (Pollenza), Camerino, Fermo, Offida, that sort of place; but occasionally they seem to have come from as far away as Umbria or (like the abbots Ambrogio and Martino of Milan) Lombardy, the country of the mother house.[89]

The abbots were supported by a number of obedientiaries —a prior, subprior, major cellarer, sacristan, treasurer, occasionally a precentor—besides the group of grangers and, as in 1291, the abbot's *scutifer*.[90] Twenty-one abbots (if one includes the conspiratorially elected Benvenuto of 1235) are known to have presided over the thirteenth-century abbey.[91] Some abbots reigned long, like Oddone from at least 1208 to at least 1216, Giovanni from at least 1220 to 1230, Enrico from 1237 to 1246, Giacomo from 1256 to 1264, and Martino of Milan from 1290 to 1296; some reigned for only a year or two.[92] Their reigns were not all peaceful. A Fiastra conspiracy was reported at the Cistercian general chapter of 1211, a conspiratorial election at that of 1236, and a rebellion against the abbot at that of 1241.[93] There were also reports that the rule was badly kept in the abbey: in 1216 a report that wool was sold and fine cloth

[89] Fiastra nos. 1657, 1749, 1929, 777, 797, 872, 907, 1145, but cf. 807 (for Umbrians, see no. 797).

[90] Fiastra no. 1936 (*scutifer*); no. 809 (*cantor*).

[91] See Fiastra nos. 366, 370, 379, 382, 409, 574, 712, 800, 806, 842, 1028, 1074, 1145, 1303, 1390, 1460 (and 1513), 1609, 1687, 1748, 1817, 1916, 2040—for their initial *acta*; my list does not quite agree with Caraceni, 43-48—he has evidently found it possible to assume misdating in some difficult *acta*, but his omission of both Benvenuto and Berardo in 1235-1236 seems to me to avoid the Canivez evidence of the conspiratorial election (Canivez, II, 161) and the suggestion of faction in the witness lists (Fiastra no. 800 and its neighbors).

[92] Fiastra nos. 409-520, 574-708, 842-1020, 1145-1297, 1916-2034, 379-382.

[93] Canivez, I, 388; II, 161, 243-244.

bought; in 1278 that women came into the abbey.[94] Abbots
from other houses were sent to investigate; and in 1222 the
abbot of San Martino dei Monti was punished for not having
visited the monastery.[95] But abbots of Fiastra were used as
visitors and correctors, too; and there is no real suggestion that
the abbey was particularly disorderly or in particular disfavor
with the general chapter.[96]

During the century the monastery was engaged in a number of disputes before various sorts of judges. The governmental structure of the Marches provided a great variety of
judges in whose courts contestants could disagree. The proctors of the monks of Fiastra appeared before simple local secular judges: judges delegated by the *podestà*s of Macerata,
Montecchio (Treia), and Morrovalle, although the delegate
of the *podestà* of Morrovalle does not seem so simple when he
is Azo, doctor of the law, acting, in 1215, under his portico
in the Porta Steri of Bologna.[97] There were available the courts
of powerful local nobles like the d'Este and of local bishops
like Ancona and Fermo, and, stretching up above in tempting
complexity, of the often rival establishments of pope (local
delegate, vicar, rector, legate) and Staufen (until the fall of
Manfred).[98] The variety of Fiastra property interests took it
into disputes with lots of different kinds of lay and ecclesiastical opponents: with its old donor the abbey of Rambona;
with Orbisaglia; with the monks of Santi Filippo e Giacomo
in Macerata; repeatedly with men of Montemilone (Pollenza)
—disputes that involved wild Montemilone raids on Fiastra
granges and that centered in the 1250's around the men of

[94] Canivez, I, 454; III, 180 (the women may have caused the deposition of Ambrogio of Milan).

[95] Canivez, II, 16.

[96] Canivez, II, 38, 73; III, 160.

[97] For Azo, Fiastra, no. 515, and Hagemann, 76-78 no. 4; Fiastra nos.
375, 701.

[98] Hagemann's collection of documents is particularly valuable for
illustrating various jurisdictions; see, too, Fiastra nos. 520, 556, 736,
768, 1511, 1932, 1933; the Fiastra collection is particularly rich in fragments of cases before delegates, and for the use as delegates of relatively local bishops and archdeacons, and for the complementary (?)
jurisdictions of delegates and more powerful or permanent papal judges
like legates or vicars and rectors.

Montemilone's building a wooden bridge in Brancorsina in territory the abbey claimed, with the bridge's building interrupted in midstream by the dispute.[99]

The Fiastra picture is a normal and expected one. The only glaringly unusual thing about Fiastra is its collection of records. About 1900 Fiastra *pergamene*, a fantastic number in Italy, survive for the thirteenth century. Some of them, of course, but relatively very few, are not directly or obviously connected with the monastery. There are considerably more surviving documents than there are at rich Montevergine, although Montevergine is unusual too. (Much more normal for a monastery that has preserved any documents at all is San Pietro Perugia with its nineteen documents; even less normal —strikingly abnormal—is San Giorgio in Braida with over 4,000.) Fiastra's unusual preservation is, as usual, not really explicable. An occasional notary repeatedly employed by Fiastra, like Buonconsiglio Petrioli Alberti (eventually "notarius dicti monasterii Claravallis," active occasionally as early as 1267 and 1268 and active until 1294) may have been unusually efficient.[100] Buonconsiglio certainly kept a protocol that his successor could use.[101] There is even the beginning of, or a fragment of, a codex cartulary from the period between 1285 and 1306.[102]

Fiastra, then, seems normal but abnormally visible. In Fiastra's case the abnormal visibility has a particular advantage for the historian. Since Fiastra was one of those Cistercian houses which was employed in the reformation of decayed Benedictine houses, one can see in the case of one mother

[99] Fiastra nos. 610, 619, 786, 1465, 1652, 617, 1111, 1123, 1126, 1131, 1145; the list of objects stolen by the men of Montemilone from the granges of Santa Maria in Selva and Brancorsina makes a March grange sound very "cowboy, wild west": 2212, 2227, 2234.

[100] Fiastra nos. 1369, 1379 to 1996; he died or retired between April and August 1294 (see no. 1999); in 1268 he calls himself "Bonconscilius Petrioli Alberti Cincii de Petriolo": no. 1379; in August 1278 he is "once of Petriolo now of Urbisaglia": no. 1581; in October of that year he is "once of Petriolo now of Canalecchio," and he receives the 20 *li* Ravenna-Ancona dowery of his wife, Bernardessa, daughter of Actuccio Petrucci of Montecchio: no. 1584.

[101] See Fiastra no. 1993.   [102] Fiastra no. 1814.

house (or foster-mother house), better than usual, what really happened.

In the first place it must be repeated that in thirteenth-century Italy Cistercian houses and the Cistercian order were still attractive to some men and women who felt strongly pressed by religious enthusiasm. Throughout the century laymen, suddenly intensely interested in the welfare of their own souls (or sometimes of their own bodies, admittedly) or the souls of their ancestors (or the bodies and souls of their successors), submitted themselves, as oblates or as vassals, and their goods to Fiastra. Sometimes the picture is an impressive one, as when in 1263 Giacomo di Giovanni di Vigilio da Petriolo stood before the abbot, put his hands in the abbot's hands, and gave his body to God and the monastery; perhaps more impressive is Francesco di Corrado Caponegro, who in 1265 gave the monastery his goods but wished himself to live under Benedict's rule "in mundo militare"—but as usual, motives are not certain.[103] In 1255 what seems at least to have been the sort of religious enthusiasm that sought a more rigorous and ascetic rule moved a local Franciscan to seek admittance, and gain it, to the Cistercian order (and interestingly enough in 1258 the Cistercians of the affiliated community of San Antonio bought the Franciscans' old, relatively secluded house and church outside of Ascoli for 1000 lire of Volterra when the Franciscans moved to their present site in town— taking by concord the name San Francesco with them).[104] Fiastra also found its way, with the local friars and local parish churches and other local monasteries, into thirteenth-century wills from its part of the Marches.[105]

[103] See, for example, Fiastra nos. 417, 635, 655, 657, 704, 934, 1386, 1562, 1563, 1581, 1896. (Giacomo is no. 1294; Francesco is no. 1315.)

[104] Fiastra nos. 1107, 1195, 1197, and see Francesco Antonio Marcucci, *Saggio delle cose Ascolane* (Teramo, 1766), 238 (for Franciscans replacing Benedictines in 1215); in, or before, 1276 a dispute with the bishop of Fermo arose over the acceptance by the Cistercians of an oblate nun, Verderosa, who had been placed by the bishop in San Venanzio, Fermo, as a punishment, but who left that house in supposed Cistercian fervor: Fiastra no. 1535.

[105] See, for example, Fiastra no. 1282 (with a little gift, two *soldi*, to every church in Montolmo [Corridonia]).

Generally attractive, Fiastra was attractive to "romantic" popes and curias or disillusioned Benedictines, whichever—it is hard to tell—really initiated the movements of affiliation. If part of the motivation for affiliation had to do with financial as well as spiritual security, this makes it more rather than less like normal donations to monasteries, which often seem to have been partly suggested by the desire for increased security of tenure or for receiving an ample lifetime annuity.

In March 1256 John of Toledo, cardinal priest of San Lorenzo in Lucina, wrote, from Santa Croce in Gerusalemme in Rome, to the abbot and convent of Fiastra to tell them of the condition of the exempt Benedictine abbey of San Pietro in Ferentillo within the diocese of Spoleto.[106] Ferentillo is an ancient and very beautiful monastery built on one of the green hills that line the valley of the Nera (see Fig. 13). It conserves an eighth-century altar, twelfth-century frescos, campanile, building. But in 1256, the cardinal wrote, the prior and monks had made petition to the pope, in which they had said that the monastery was so gravely collapsed in spiritualities and temporalities that without papal aid there was no hope for its reform. They had asked the pope that the monastery be incorporated within the Cistercian order (and, in fact, as early as 1234 Matteo, abbot of Ferentillo, and his nine monks seem to have given themselves, ineffectually, to the Cistercian order and to Fiastra). The pope had commissioned the business to John, the "Cistercian cardinal." John gave Ferentillo to Fiastra, that Fiastra monks might teach Ferentillo Cistercian ways, until the next forthcoming Cistercian chapter general when the process could be gone into more formally. In December 1256, in a letter to Fiastra, Alexander IV confirmed John of Toledo's action.[107]

Trouble was not long in starting. Berardo, the former abbot of Ferentillo, did not mean to lose his living. He came to the pope to complain, got an auditor in Ottaviano degli Ubaldini, cardinal deacon of Santa Maria in Via Lata, and started a process. Ottaviano and John of Toledo were made arbiters in

[106] Fiastra no. 1136; Hagemann, 112-114 no. 58.
[107] Fiastra no. 1139; Hagemann, 115-116 no. 62; Fiastra no. 787.

the matter and they awarded Berardo 500 lire, of Ravenna, for his expenses and necessities, to be paid him by Fiastra. Since Fiastra did not, supposedly, pay within term, the abbot and convent were, in fact, excommunicated and Berardo was again given Ferentillo. By 20 February 1258, however, the abbot and convent had satisfied, with 500 lire, the papal chaplain Uberto de Coconato, who was acting as Abbot Berardo's proctor; Alexander IV wrote that they were to be freed of their excommunication and that Ferentillo was to be returned to them.[108]

It had cost Fiastra a lot, even more than appears on the surface. The abbey raised 200 lire and then had to borrow 300 more in December 1257.[109] When in 1265 the Florentine merchant Cante de Scala, for himself and his associates, sold the debt to Fango di Gaetano de Infangatis for himself and his associate Schiatta, citizen of Florence, the "residue" of the debt, of 300 lire, with its interest, was 420 lire.[110] In 1257 the counselors of Ferentillo—the lay body that, like lay *sapientes*, appears around Italian monasteries—committed to Guglielmo monk of Chiaravalle and a man named Palmiero the revocation of all Berardo's acts against Chiaravalle; and in 1257 it was the new abbot Guglielmo who was empowered to borrow the 300 lire (although in the following year Giovanni of Monte Santa Maria, the major cellarer of Fiastra, was empowered to borrow 250 lire from the Scala or from Nicola of Viterbo).[111] Some of the indebtedness was perhaps compensated for in 1258 when Fiastra seems actually to have begun to grant away Ferentillo properties.[112]

The physical relics of Santa Croce del Chienti are less impressive than those of Ferentillo; but, unlike Ferentillo, thir-

[108] Fiastra no. 1139; Hagemann, 117-119 no. 65; Fiastra no. 1167.
[109] Fiastra no. 1175.
[110] Fiastra no. 1305; the problem of contemporary high interest rates in Tuscany is discussed in two essays by Armando Sapori, "L'Interesse del denaro a Firenze nel Trecento," and "L'Usura nel Dugento a Pistoia," in *Studi di storia economica medievale* (Florence, 1940), 95-125.
[111] Fiastra nos. 1163, 1175 (and 1174), 1185; for *sapientes* see Valdiponte, fo. 110.
[112] Fiastra no. 1188: the debt discussed is even larger.

teenth-century Santa Croce (which was a few kilometers inland from the Adriatic near Civitanova and which is now a small farmhouse with chickens) has left a description of itself (see Fig. 17). The description is a romantic one in which the little abbey praises itself—in which in its century of decay and capture, it talks of its stored apples, the length of its grange walls, and the prettiness of its abbot's chamber.[113] The abbey listed its vestments (white, red, purple), its thirty-six altar cloths, and some of its claimed one hundred books. It had two rules of Saint Benedict, an epistle book, a gospel book, two missals according to the order, two breviaries of the order, two books of collects, two psalters of the order and two Roman ones, one *Dialogue*, one Basil, and one Isidore, two hymnals of the order, two diurnal antiphonals (one, of the order, "magnum multum crosse littere et crose note et pulcrerrimum multa"), two nocturnal antiphonals, one small Bible and one large one, and a homiliary for the whole year in two volumes. There are no splendid surprises in the library, like the mysterious Homer at Tremiti—or Tremiti's Terence, its Sallusts, its Lucan, its Ovid, its Boethius, its Cicero, its Catos, its *City of God*, its *Cur Deus Homo*, its Burchard of Worms; nor does Santa Croce's library have any of the up-to-date air of the thirteenth-century Franciscan library of Santa Croce in Florence, with its popular theology and logic.[114] Santa Croce del Chienti's is a very ordinary little Benedictine-turned-Cistercian library.[115] Still it is remarkable as one stands now amid the barnyard animals, or as one reads of Santa Croce's thirteenth-century litigations, to think that Gregory's *Dialogues*—which make the whole of Italy glow with sanctity—were once read there, or even that there were once there a Basil and an Isidore.

[113] Fiastra no. 2179.

[114] Petrucci, *Codice diplomatico*, III, 367-372 and "L'archivio e la biblioteca del monastero benedettino di Santa Maria di Tremiti," *Bullettino dell' "Archivio paleografico italiano,"* NS, II-III (1956-1957), part 2, 291-307; Charles T. Davis, "The Early Collection of Books of S. Croce in Florence," *Proceedings of the American Philosophical Society*, CVIII:5 (1963), particularly 407-410. For a short, comprehensive discussion of medieval Italian monastic libraries, see Penco, 513-525.

[115] If I am right in assuming its Cistercianness.

With its books the abbey listed its treasure: three chalices, one of silver, two of pewter ("piretro"); a silver cross with the wood of the true cross inside it; a silver box, and two ivory ones for relics. Then came the abbey offices and shops: the sacristy; the treasury joined to the church; the dormitory "long, large, and ample" with places for twenty-six monks and at its head seven seats with water arranged to flow under them continuously; a big kitchen with cellars, one for bread, beans, and oil, and, in another, things for the sick, and apples and salt; a place for grain; a shoemaker's house with its tools—on two floors, shop beneath; the abbot's chamber, pretty, high, and big, and with its latrine; the weaver's and tailor's; the wine cellar; the stable and the building next to it that could hold twenty horses; a woodshed; rooms for guests to eat and sleep in—for paupers, for familiars, for religious; the coops for chickens and ducks to provide for the abbot's chambers, for distinguished guests; the nearby walled grange with twenty pairs of oxen and hundreds of cattle, goats, and sheep. The abbey also told of its fine income in rents, apples, pears, nuts, oil, rents, its rents in emphyteosim from eight to ten thousand *modoli* of land, its possessions in Fermo, Macerata, and Civitanova—with five monks in San Martino in Fermo and two (though there ought to be four) monks at Santo Stefano in Civitanova. There were also the monks at home: the prior, the subprior, the cellarer, perhaps eight others, and at least two at the grange, as well as twenty or twenty-one *conversi*.

At about the same time that the abbey composed this descriptive inventory, it made another list. It had an inventory written in which it recorded its documents. This calendar is less warmly evocative than is the other list. It is, however, impressive; and it gives further evidence of Santa Croce's careful and detailed self-evaluation in the later thirteenth century.[116]

This abbey, Santa Croce, like Ferentillo, came into Fiastra's reforming hands in the thirteenth century. As at Ferentillo, the Santa Croce process started early and indecisively. In 1227 Lorenzo da Montolmo, monk and provost of Santa Croce, resigned himself and the seal of his monastery to the abbot and

[116] Fiastra no. 2196.

convent of Chiaravalle di Fiastra and to the order.[117] He chose, he said, as had Dom Corrado, once abbot of Santa Croce, the Cistercian way. In 1239, on 26 March, Filippo, bishop of Fermo, acting under a papal mandate which ordered Santa Croce to be given over to the Cistercian order, invested the proctor of Fiastra with Santa Croce by means of a ring; he acted in the church of San Pietro in Montolmo (Corridonia).[118]

In 1240, in January, an abbot Lorenzo of Santa Croce gave his horse as a pledge for seventy lire Volterra which he had borrowed from Gentile di Marco di Stefano of Fermo so that he might pay a royal exaction to that amount. The abbot or his monks had to pay back the principal by Lent with an interest of twelve denari per lira per month; they evidently managed, because the bond was slashed and returned. In the years from 1259 to 1263 under the abbots Angelo and Giacomo, Santa Croce had eight to ten monks, and it called itself Benedictine.[119] In 1264 there may have been as few as seven monks in the abbey, including the abbot, or there may have been six monks belonging to the abbot's party; but the abbey was not dead—one of the monks was an oblate.[120] An internal dispute seems clearly to have been in progress by June of 1265, when the abbot and monks appointed proctors to appear before Simone, cardinal priest of San Martino, papal rector of the Marches; the proctors were to contest the case of Angelo da Sant'Elpidio and Francesco da Civitanova, once monks of Santa Croce (Francesco as recently as 1262).[121]

In July of 1265 the abbot, still Giacomo, got himself freed from the excommunication he had incurred for being, or being suspected of being, too much on Manfred's side, for hav-

[117] Fiastra no. 659.
[118] Fiastra no. 882; Hagemann, 95 no. 26.
[119] Fiastra no. 900 for the horse pledge; for 1259 to 1263 see Fiastra nos. 1211, 1229, 1230, 1231, 1281, 1289 (Hagemann, 132-134 no. 92)—the monks Rainaldo and Rodaldo appear from the beginning in this series.
[120] Fiastra no. 1298: the notary Angelo has dated this very peculiarly "primo Kalend' Jun'."
[121] Fiastra nos. 1310, 1281.

ing helped him too much.[122] Abbot Giacomo protested his innocence. In fact the situation had been very difficult. As the dating of monastic letters shows, it was impossible to ignore the fact that Manfred did rule, and it would have been almost impossibly impolitic of any monastery to deny it. Manfred was also, as one gathers particularly from Thomas of Pavia, almost irresistibly attractive.[123] His attraction, however, held no lasting good for central Italian monasteries.

At least from April 1266 and into August of that year a process occurred through which Santa Croce was incorporated into the Cistercian order. On August 7 John of Toledo, now cardinal bishop of Porto, made Santa Croce a daughter of Fiastra, but the arrangements that preceded this filiation made it a very peculiar relationship.[124] On April 11 Abbot Servodeo of Fiastra and his monks had made Prior Festa their proctor for arranging a property settlement with Giacomo of Santa Croce and his monks.[125] A pact was arranged and sworn to by April 23, at which time Santa Croce still called itself Benedictine.[126] Giacomo was to remain a Benedictine abbot in the Cistercian house for his lifetime. He was to become a Cistercian only if he, of his own free will, ever decided to. His monks were to have livings carved out of Santa Croce holdings for their lifetimes. Giacomo was to rule without interference from Fiastra or from the Cistercians who would live in his house. He would, of course, not force the Cistercians to acts forbidden by the institutes of the order. Santa Croce property was to be respected as distinct from Fiastra property and to be in Giacomo's control. By June 14 Santa Croce was calling itself Cistercian, and by June 28 it could receive, as a Cistercian house, the subjection of the monastery of San Martino in Variano near Fermo.[127] By that time new members, like Santuzzo, presumably a Cistercian, appear, not too unobtrusively, in the house. The Santa Croce arrangement was one that could hardly have been seriously expected to work; but at Viterbo,

[122] Fiastra no. 1311; Hagemann, 135-136 no. 96.
[123] "Thomas Tusci Gesta imperatorum et pontificum," ed. Ernest Ehrenfeuchter, *M.G.H.,SS.*, xxii (Hanover, 1872), 483-528, 517.
[124] Fiastra no. 1333.   [125] Fiastra no. 1320.
[126] Fiastra nos. 1321, 2186.   [127] Fiastra nos. 1330, 1326.

on 26 November 1266, Clement IV confirmed the approval of his arbiter, Cardinal John, in a document with a rather arresting witness list: papal scribes; Lamberto, clerk of the cardinal bishop; but particularly Berardo, abbot of the so-called Cistercian monastery of San Giuliano sopra Spoleto.[128]

By 28 October 1275 trouble had arrived. On that day Guardo, clerk of San Giovanni de Casale, proctor of the abbot, Giacomo, and the convent of Santa Croce (calling themselves Benedictines again), refused judgment of Bernard, archdeacon of Narbonne, papal vicar for spiritual cases in the March, in a dispute with the Cistercian monastery of Fiastra.[129] Santa Croce had tried to use, and with some success it would seem, the court of Aldobrandino, bishop of Orvieto, papal vicar in cases of appeals over spiritualities in the Marches, Campagna, the Duchy of Spoleto, the Patrimony, and Tuscany, against the archdeacon's court. They claimed a suspect judge and got Cardinal Giovanni Gaetani Orsini as auditor—and also legal advice on how to handle the case, particularly if witnesses appeared to testify against them. They should say that hostile witnesses were few, light, of bad reputation, enemies, conspirators, unworthy of trust.[130] The Fiastra-Santa Croce dispute turned, on its surface, into a dispute between the courts, and it continued at least through early 1276.[131] Although a new abbot, Guglielmo, appears at Santa Croce in 1277, with monks like Rainaldo and Rodaldo who had been in the abbey as early as 1259, and with Santuzzo as his prior, the disputes were not over.[132] In 1278 the Cistercian chapter general took cognizance of a dispute between the houses of Fiastra and Santa Croce.[133] In 1280 Abbot Buonguadagno of Santa Croce, with Santuzzo as his prior, was again calling the house Cistercian; and monks of the old dispensation, like Rodaldo, lived on.[134]

[128] Fiastra no. 1340.
[129] Fiastra no. 1522.
[130] Fiastra no. 2212, undated.
[131] Fiastra nos. 1523, 1532.
[132] Fiastra no. 1557.
[133] Canivez, III, 181.
[134] Fiastra no. 1627, 703; I assume that one Rodaldo was not quickly inserted after the deletion of another.

The monastery of San Giuliano over Spoleto is a romantic
ruin (see Fig. 14). Its church stands high and almost isolated,
amid flocks of sheep, on a rosemary-covered hill. It, like Ferentillo and Santa Croce, was attracted and attached to the Cistercians in the thirteenth century. Less than a month after the
bishop of Fermo, acting under a mandate of Gregory IX, had
attached Santa Croce to Fiastra, Gregory wrote, on 7 April
1239, to the bishop of Spoleto to incorporate San Giuliano
within the Cistercian order.[135] Gregory's involvement in these
affairs was probably encouraged by his own sense of knowing
something special of what the religious life could and ought
to be; his treatment of the Franciscans suggests that he thought
he knew very well what was best for religious men.[136] But
Gregory's letter says that the monks of San Giuliano had
wanted to and asked to be admitted into the Cistercian order.
In 1239 San Giuliano had an abbot, a prior, and at least six
monks.[137]

By 1244 and perhaps considerably earlier Fiastra's connection with San Giuliano had led it into litigation with the
bishop of Spoleto; but the great war between Fiastra and San
Giuliano came in the 1260's.[138] The Fiastra dispute with San
Giuliano, like that with Santa Croce and even more that with
Ferentillo, seems to have centered around the personality
of a strong or at least troublesome abbot of the daughter house
(although San Giuliano was initially a very tentative daughter—it seems to have freed itself after the initial connection).
The Fiastra-San Giuliano dispute also fell into the hands of
John of Toledo.

Berardo, abbot of San Giuliano, seems to have been an unusually difficult monk, although he may have thought of himself as unusually tried and harried. Berardo appears in 1262
warning his claustral prior and three other monks and the
oblates of his monastery that they ought to obey the rule of
Saint Benedict in fasting and dress and chastity and silence.[139]

[135] Fiastra no. 910; Hagemann, 95-96 no. 27.
[136] See Rosalind Brooke, *Early Franciscan Government*, 56-76.
[137] Fiastra no. 893.
[138] Fiastra no. 999.
[139] Fiastra no. 1273.

In the same year and again in the next he and his convent are seen making Altegrado di Angelo da Loreto their proctor general at the Roman curia and particularly before the auditor Uberto, cardinal deacon of Sant'Eustachio.[140] In August 1262 Giacomo, the abbot of Fiastra, and his monks were negotiating a loan for money to pay their expenses in their case against the monks of San Giuliano and "him who calls himself abbot."[141] In the 1263 San Giuliano document making Altegrado proctor, Berardo, calling himself Berardo Henrici, named Fiastra as his house's enemy.[142] In April 1265 Cardinal Uberto issued letters of citation (under his red wax seal with the stag of his titular church on it) in a San Giuliano case over the hospital of San Catallo de Gavelgis in the diocese of Spoleto; but various courts were in action.[143]

In a composite, four-part document, some of which comes from April 1266, Abbot Berardo twirls about in interesting poses.[144] In the first part Berardo consents, on 28 April 1266, to John of Toledo as arbiter. In the second part, with essentially the same witness list and in the same house in Spoleto, Berardo makes the reservation that he consents only if the arbitration proves satisfactory after a year's trial and does not prove injurious to his interests; to this second part is attached a statement that that instrument is false in which Berardo and his monks promise submission to Fiastra and to the Cistercian institutes and renounce the time of probation and privilege of novices. In the third part of the composite document the abbot protests against certain statements, implying his subjection to Fiastra, before George of Tonengo, canon of Dublin, auditor of causes for Cardinal Uberto. The fourth part of the document, acted in Viterbo in the Piazza San Silvestro, is a clear denunciation by Berardo: the Cistercian order does not please him; Fiastra does not please him; he does not want San Giu-

[140] Fiastra nos. 1275, 1291 (Hagemann, 131, no. 89) (the initial one in the cloister of Sant'Isaia in Spoleto); Altegrado made Lanzelotto his proctor: no. 1275.

[141] Fiastra no. 1278.

[142] Fiastra no. 1291 (in a house of Sant'Isaac); and see Brentano, "Peter of Assisi as Witness," and Fiastra no. 2225.

[143] Fiastra no. 1307.

[144] Fiastra no. 1318.

liano and its monks to be subject to Fiastra and to Servodeo
its abbot. Berardo, in this segment of the document, revokes
any promise of obedience for himself or his monks, and he
returns San Giuliano to its pristine state of unsubject
Benedictinism.

In spite of Berardo's undated reservations, he with Servodeo,
as abbots of their two monasteries, accepted John of Toledo as
arbiter, in the presence of Giacomo of Santa Croce, in Viterbo
in May 1266.[145] Both Berardo and Servodeo, according to a
document that looks perfectly legitimate, accepted the normal
sort of arbitration agreement, including a penalty for non-
compliance of 10,000 lire Ravenna-Ancona. Nevertheless, in
early 1267 Berardo "once abbot" was being cited in a criminal
case by Giorgio da Recanati, papal scriptor, on the authority
of the once-bishop Brugnato, the penitentiary of Cardinal
Simone, in a case that had moved from Cardinal Uberto's
court.[146]

The final act—extreme rather than chronologically last—in
this little bellicose drama between Fiastra and San Giuliano
seems to have happened over and over again, to appear in frame
after frame, because it survives in the repeated statements of
six witnesses, whose notarized depositions were copied by
Lanzelotto da Loreto, acting as a notary for George of Tonengo's court.[147] There is nothing but their oaths to make one
believe that the witnesses are impartial; two were brothers,
one a nephew, and one an in-law of Berardo. The incident
they describe happened on an April 27 in the same house in
Spoleto in which on April 28 in 1266 Berardo consented to
John of Toledo's position as arbiter; it occurred reasonably
soon after Servodeo's succeeding Giacomo as abbot of Fiastra
in early 1265.[148] It could not have happened after Martino
succeeded Servodeo in 1269.[149] In the incident in the house at

[145] Fiastra no. 1325.
[146] Fiastra no. 1349 and no. 1345 for the Fiastra connection.
[147] Fiastra nos. 2211 and 2213: one document in, as Lanzelotto wrote,
three pieces, but two are stitched together; the heading is lost, rotted
away.
[148] Fiastra no. 1303—well before April.
[149] Fiastra no. 1390—well after April.

Spoleto, Servodeo and Berardo argue. Servodeo says to Berardo, "You should come to an agreement. You are doing a bad thing with this litigation of yours, ruining our monastery economically, and destroying your own." At this point a monk of San Giuliano named Tommaso jumps up. (He is shown to be a monk of San Giuliano: one of the witnesses says that Tommaso has been a monk for twelve years; he has seen him dressed as a monk, behaving like a monk, obeying the abbot, doing the monastery's business.) Tommaso says to Servodeo, "You have done worse. You have deceived us. Not satisfied with taking our goods, you steal our rights." Servodeo then jumps up, full of wrath, and with his right hand he hits Tommaso in the mouth, or in the nose and mouth. Blood runs from Tommaso's nose and mouth. The words vary a little from witness to witness, but the picture is the same. Then the witnesses are asked if Berardo was involved in sending an armed band against Abbot Giacomo of Fiastra, and they say no. Servodeo's act, in the Spoleto scene, is the act of a Cistercian who could stand no more, and it is understandable. It is very far, however, from the scene by the fire in Walter Daniel's story of Ailred of Rievaulx's charity.

In a document of 1278 the mother and three daughters—Fiastra, Santa Croce, San Giuliano, and Ferentillo—appear together in an act that talks of their collective privileges.[150] There is nothing on the act's surface to suggest anything less than smiling familial harmony; but thinking of it in a longer context one can only remember (with a twist of time) those little family collections of Roman imperial portrait busts in the Capitoline, smiling or genteel, before the kill. Still its thirteenth-century experiences did not leave Fiastra impotently embittered, incapable of further reform. Late in November 1299, Paola, abbess of Santa Margherita in Monte Granaro, said that she and her (perhaps twenty-two) nuns wanted to embrace the Cistercian rule and to submit themselves to Abbot Giovanni of Fiastra.[151] Paola knelt before Giovanni and accepted, and declared, his right to visit, reform, institute, and replace. Early in December, on Saint Nicholas's day, the abbot

[150] Fiastra no. 1571.
[151] Fiastra no. 2129.

visited the nunnery.[152] He insisted that the office be better and more devotedly celebrated in the church, that the nocturnal hours be properly celebrated, that laymen and clerics alike be kept outside the monastery doors and not even come into the parlor without two auditors to conversations, that silence be better kept. He enjoined punishments—enthusiasm undimmed.

Moved to reform monasteries, thirteenth-century popes were of course moved to reform the rotten monasteries of Rome, their see's city. The city was pocked with little clerical and monastic establishments. There were too many for any city to support; but they remained and retained some remnant of their ancient endowment, purposes, and populations. These establishments pursued uneven courses through the thirteenth century, even those, some of them, with famous names, like the Pantheon, Santa Maria Rotunda. In spite of its image of Gregory and its new (in June 1270) bells and belfry (of which a stone panel, with the names of its archpriest and clergy, fixed on the façade of the Pantheon, under its portico, still boasts), Santa Maria Rotunda was, in 1283, a seat of crime and a cause of scandal.[153] Martin IV, writing from Orvieto in April of that year, sent the bishop of Tivoli and the guardian of the friars minor within the city of Rome to reform the Rotunda.[154]

In Rome as elsewhere the popes introduced orders that seemed well ruled and respectable into dubious houses. In 1198 Innocent III confirmed the concession of Santa Prassede to the monks of Vallombrosa.[155] In 1231 Gregory IX gave Sant'-Alessio all'Aventino to the Premonstratensians.[156] In 1285 Honorius IV gave San Silvestro in Capite (which had, a few years before its transfer, at least an abbot and four monks) to the nuns of Palestrina, the community of Saint Margaret

[152] Fiastra no. 2130.

[153] For the Gregory see Rome, Archivio di stato, San Cosimato, no. 311, and above, Chapter III; for the bells see the portico of the Pantheon and Vincenzo Forcella, *Iscrizioni delle chiese e d'altri edifici di Roma* (Rome, 1869), I, 289 no. 1098.

[154] *Martin IV*, 134 no. 312.

[155] P. Fedele, "Tabularium Sancti Praxedis," *ASRSP*: xxvii (1904), 27-78, 33; xxviii (1905), 41-114, 79-81, no. 44.

[156] A. Monaci, "Regesto dell'Abbazia di Sant'Alessio all'Aventino," *ASRSP*: (1904), 351-398; xxviii (1905), 41-112, 151-200; xxvii, 355.

Colonna, who took for themselves or were given the rule of the Franciscan Minoresses.[157] Perhaps the most spectacular of thirteenth-century Roman changes was a double switch in, probably, 1250. The Augustinian Hermits, protected by Ricardo Annibaldi, were given the Franciscans' church of Santa Maria del Popolo. The Franciscans, at the height of their popularity, were given the Benedictine's great senatorial church of Santa Maria in Capitolio, the Aracoeli. The Benedictines were given nothing.[158] In Rome, as all over the peninsula, the new orders of friars, increasingly housed, moved into old churches and old houses—so the Dominicans of Florence, in 1221, took Santa Maria Novella, as the Dominicans of Rome took Santa Sabina in 1222 and Santa Maria sopra Minerva (given them by the city) in 1275.[159]

Among the Roman houses that changed orders was Santi Cosma e Damiano (San Cosimato) in Trastevere (see Fig. 18).[160] San Cosimato lay in a part of Trastevere less closely built than it now is. The monastery was surrounded by vineyards, closed gardens, houses, and other churches and monasteries whose properties stretched down to the river, with its mills, and to the Trastevere gates, with their suburban gardens. For all Rome's urbanity, this part of it, like some others, had a curious village air in the thirteenth century; although Trastevere was always a village with an unusual number of important families and ecclesiastical corporations.

The holdings of San Cosimato, many of them leased out,

[157] V. Federici, "Regesto del monastero di San Silvestro in Capite," *ASRSP*: xxii (1899), 213-300, 498-538; xxiii (1900), 67-128, 411-447; J. S. Gaynor and I. Toesca, *S. Silvestro in Capite* (Rome, 1963), 26.

[158] Francis Roth, "Cardinal Richard Annibaldi," *Augustiniana*, ii (1952), 118.

[159] Stefano Orlandi, *"Necrologio" di S. Maria Novella*, i (Florence, 1955), xviii.

[160] For Santi Cosma e Damiano, see P. Fedele, "Carte del monastero dei Ss. Cosma e Damiano in Mica Aurea," *ASRSP*: xxi (1898), 459-534; xxii (1899), 25-107, 383-447—the documents go to the twelfth century; and Riccardo Capasso, "Un contributo allo studio delle suppliche pontificie nel secolo XIII," *Bullettino dell' "Archivio paleografico italiano,"* ns, ii-iii (1956-1957), part i, 169-174: the document examined (Rome, Archivio di stato, San Cosimato, no. 262) is now in Cassenza 5, not, as here described, in Cassenza 4.

were interwoven among the village gardens, along the streets of Trastevere, near its churches and the river. San Cosimato had collected lands outside the Porta Portese and the Porta San Pancrazio. It acquired holdings nearer the sea in the diocese of Porto, particularly those connected with the church of San Cornelio; it got them from the church of Santa Maria in Farneto in the diocese of Arezzo in a rather elaborate transfer of possessions, supervised by Gregory IX, in 1238, through which Farneto got the monastery of San Crispolto of Bettona in the diocese of Assisi.[161] These Porto holdings of San Cosimato's were threatened in the 1240's by the chapter of Saint Peter in the Vatican, from whom San Cosimato had to be protected. San Cosimato had interests in Nepi and particularly in Sutri, where it held a whole complex of properties and incomes through its subject church and hospital of San Giacomo of Sutri.[162] Throughout the century there is evidence of San Cosimato's rearranging and consolidating its holdings. It is even possible that Abbot Nicola's excessive zeal for consolidation ruined the Benedictines of San Cosimato. In the latter part of the century San Cosimato seems to have become increasingly interested in investments in and around Tivoli, a town that resembled Sutri in many ways but that differed from it in one very major way. Tivoli was a papal residence, a summer capitol. It promised, as Sutri could not, immense profits during periods of papal residence.

San Cosimato, like other churches, had a hoard of relics. A list of them survives, in copy, from 1246, when by order of Stefano cardinal priest of Santa Maria in Trastevere, urban vicar of Pope Innocent IV, a bishop consecrated, at San Cosimato, the altar dedicated to Saints Cosmas and Damian and to Saint Cornelius.[163] The relics range from the very sacred to the usual local, Roman ones: from wood of the cross, a part of the crucifixion sponge, of the stone from which Christ ascended, and of the clothes of the Virgin, to relics of Prassede,

[161] See San Cosimato, nos. 212, 214, 217, 218, 254, 266, 267, 273, 275, 278, 280, 289, 290; and Fedele, "Carte . . . Ss. Cosma e Damiano"; for Farneto, San Cosimato nos. 262, 265; and Capasso.

[162] See San Cosimato, nos. 217, 257, 329.

[163] San Cosimato, no. 258.

Prisca, Pudenziana. There were relics of Peter and Paul, Luke, and of Andrew's cross, of Lawrence, Blaise, Sebastian, Sixtus pope and martyr, Nereus and Achilles, Pancras, Valentine, Vincent, Peter and Hyacinth, Felix and Agapitus, Nicholas, Damasus, the Quattro Coronati, Martial, Pantaleon, Lucy, Margaret, Dorothy, the 11,000 virgins, and a number of others. At the heart of the hoard were the church's own particularly appropriate relics: Saints Cosmas and Damian and Cornelius, and by 1246 a relic of the stigma in Saint Francis's hand.

The Franciscan relic and the Assisi holdings are signs of a new order in the old house. By 18 August 1234 San Cosimato had been taken from the Benedictines and given to the Claresses (or Damianites). On that day Gregory IX granted a Franciscan, Giacomo, the power to select an *yconomus* to manage the business affairs of the monastery, as in April of the following year (but perhaps also earlier) Giacomo did.[164] In 1232 the Benedictines of San Cosimato, still busy with the affairs of the house, had had an abbot, Massario, an *yconomus*, a monk and five *conversi* to represent their little community.[165] In the early years of the century the number of San Cosimato monks seems to have hovered around seven.[166] After the change of order, at least in the early years, there were more nuns. In 1244 there seem to have been about thirty of them, although in 1261 only about fifteen.[167] As late as 1220 men and women had been granting their possessions to the Benedictine house for the love of God and the good of their souls (although of course these words may have disguised additional practical motives), but gifts seem to have been sparse between 1220 and 1234.[168] After the house had been transferred to the Franciscans the gifts began again and, intermittently, continued.[169] In 1277 Bartolomea di Gentile di Gentile di Pietro di Leone explained her gift as being "out of reverence for almighty God, the blessed martyrs Cosmas and Damian, the blessed

[164] San Cosimato, no. 238.
[165] San Cosimato, no. 230.
[166] San Cosimato, nos. 196 (1207), 200 (1213).
[167] San Cosimato, nos. 252, 284.
[168] San Cosimato, nos. 214, 215, 217.
[169] San Cosimato, nos. 257, 301.

Clare, and for the remission of all her sins"; Clare had joined the older saintly recipients.[170]

The Claresses quickly involved themselves in the problems of San Cosimato's property management—in exchange, dispute, and settlement. They worried their documents with the conventional Roman insuring phrases: should mills be destroyed, should precious metals be found.[171] They combined the privileges of their order with the special privileges of the house; and they sharply opposed, and with papal privilege, the interference of the bishop of Sutri in their jurisdiction over San Giacomo and its properties.[172] The nuns exchanged vineyards for rents—to be paid in one case, at least, on the feast of "Sanctus Cosimatus."[173] In 1239 the nuns rented the church and hospital of San Giacomo Sutri to Cencio, the archpriest of Capranica, and to Pietro Zillo, a canon of Sutri, for eight years.[174] Cencio and Pietro were to pay their yearly rent of thirty-four lire of Siena, if they could get to Rome safely, half on the feast of All Saints, and half, in high unrealized irony, on the Sunday on which is sung "I am the good pastor (or shepherd)." The community of Claresses had crawled, like a hermit crab, within the Benedictines' old, protecting, but in the end debilitating, shell of property.

The supervision of shifting monasteries as well as of their shifting possessions was attempted by local Italian prelates as well as by the papal curia. The diocese of Amalfi under Filippo Augustariccio provides a good example of local supervision. There the archbishop watched over the acquisition and dispersal of monastic holdings in Amalfi, Atrani, and the hinterland. He approved the insertion of monastic tenements between the storeys of the hill buildings and the exchange of mills and conduits along the fast little rivers.[175] In September 1269 Archbishop Filippo presided over a major change.[176] The

[170] San Cosimato, no. 306.
[171] See San Cosimato, nos. 250, 264.
[172] See San Cosimato, nos. 242, 243, 278, 280, 292.
[173] San Cosimato, no. 310.
[174] San Cosimato, no. 250.
[175] Riccardo Filangieri, *Codice diplomatico amalfitano*, II (Trani, 1951), 139 no. 389, 167-169 no. 424: for types of monastic property.
[176] Filangieri, *Codice diplomatico amalfitano*, II, 135-139 no. 388.

document (or rather the triplicate set of identical documents) in which the archbishop described his action and its purpose was begun with a solemn harangue on the pastoral office: *si pastores ovium*—how much more serious and exacting ought to be the care of souls, the job of the shepherd of God's sheep, than even the exacting, day and night, watch of the shepherd of sheep. The document is one of those that embodies the connection between the careful statement of the nature of pastoral duty and a specific pastoral act.

Filippo's act involved the moving of four monasteries in Atrani. There were, he said, three Benedictine nunneries in Atrani (directly under his diocesan supervision) so badly located or endowed, so unsuitably placed, that the nuns lived irregularly, not according to the rule, and immorally. These were the nunneries of Santa Maria de Fontanella, San Tommaso, and Sant'Angelo di Atrani. There was also a Benedictine monastery in Atrani (also directly subject to the bishop), San Quirico, where, because of the scarcity and decay of Benedictine vocations, the abbot alone, or the abbot and one monk, lived. The archbishop wrote that he had discussed the situation with Amalfi laymen and clerics and that he had gotten consent for his action from the chapter of Amalfi, as he certainly had from a long list of the patrons of Sant'Angelo (who gave up every right but their rents).[177] The archbishop said that the four convents also consented to his decision. His decision was to unite the three nunneries and move them to San Quirico, which in effect became Santa Maria de Fontanella, and to move the almost defunct old monastery of San Quirico to the old Fontanella, with what seemed an appropriate division of properties; and the monks in their new monastery were bound to visit the doorstep of Saint Andrew at Amalfi on his two feast days, in November and May, to help insure, presumably, that their discipline would hold.

The new arrangement seems to have worked well, at least for a time and in part. From 1272 through 1280 Letizia, abbess of the combined nunnery of Santa Maria at San Quirico, was active, repeatedly with the archbishop's supervision, in rear-

---

[177] Filangieri, *Codice diplomatico amalfitano*, II, 132-135 no. 387.

ranging, seemingly profitably, her house's holdings.[178] In 1284 after Letizia was no longer abbess, the house was involved in dispute with a Salerno knight over a debt and a deposited instrument, before Andrea d'Alagno, canon of Amalfi and delegate of the archbishop, who found the nunnery's case as presented by their two Scalese proctors less compelling than the knight's.[179] Still, as recently as 1279 the widowed mother and siblings of a girl named Mariella Cappasancta (of, it seems, a prominent Atrani family) inspired, in their document's words, by God in their hearts, were willing to promise half an *oncia* of gold to the nunnery annually as long as Mariella, a nun there, should live.[180] Even if the Cappasanctas were not really moved by pious appreciation of the combined nunnery's holy purposes, they must have felt that it could, with help, survive for a girl's lifetime, in reasonable respectability.

The history of monasticism must, in a way, always be a dismal history. It is the sad story of the luxurious wildernesses of expiring Italian Certosas, of the monks of the "Canonica" of Amalfi futilely trying to keep their house (now the Albergo Cappuccini) a Cistercian place, and, in another direction, of a fourteenth-century English Benedictine's making himself a hermit at Farne—the death of dreams. At the end of the thirteenth century, as the friars joined the monks in decay, the story is particularly dispiriting—the propertied friars, the Claresses grasping for their rents, Sant'Agnese fighting for the Baysio inheritance. The *necrologio* of Santa Maria Novella in Florence boasts of the friar Francesco di Durante de' Chiermontesi (who died in 1304) that he had by heart the whole corpus of the Decretals and the better part of the Decretum.[181] Profitable, perhaps, and up to date, no doubt—but disappointing to find that thus even Dominican hearts were filled. Insofar as it was dominated by the fall of the friars the scene was more dismal in Italy than in England because the friars had

---

[178] Filangieri, *Codice diplomatico amalfitano*, II: 149-151 nos. 402-404; 152-158 nos. 406-412; 159 no. 414; 162-163 nos. 417-418; 166-167 no. 423; 170-176 nos. 426-432; 178-179 no. 435; 192-193 no. 451.

[179] Filangieri, *Codice diplomatico amalfitano*, II, 184-186 no. 442.

[180] Filangieri, *Codice diplomatico amalfitano*, II, 173 no. 429.

[181] Orlandi, I, 25.

been more brilliant in Italy and more generally important—
although to this pattern there had been exceptions: the friars
of the Sack, essentially Provençal, seem to have been stronger
in England, and the Franciscans of Oxford were not dull by
any standards.[182]

Italian thirteenth-century monasteries look very different in
different focus. With their real property and their hoard of
charters, they look tough and alive against the diocesan
church: as the massive monastery of Montevergine does
against the shadows of surrounding bishops. With their dull
spirituality and their crumbling religion, they look shabby and
broken against the enthusiastic friars: as Benedictine Aracoeli
does against Franciscan Aracoeli, or as any thirteenth-century
monastery does against Saint Francis.

The monastic histories of thirteenth-century Italy and thirteenth-century England are different histories. The English
monastery embedded in the land was, as at Saint Albans, stable
in an ecclesiastical society that moved. The Italian monastery,
as at Santa Croce Chienti, was mobile in a religious society
that refused to move, that cracked instead into reaction and
enthusiasm. The Italian church was more persistently monastic than the English church; the monastery retained more of
its relative importance in Italian ecclesiastical society, although
individual Italian monasteries shifted their boundaries and
their orders, and friars flew about the countryside.

In close Italy the popes employed a policy of monastic re-
juvenation which they did not need to, or did not dare to, try
in distant England. They moved old orders out of and new
orders into religious houses (but not boldly enough to protect the new orders from the financial claims of the old). They
chose orders like the Cistercians and the Claresses. In choosing them, and particularly the Cistercians, they chose the more
restrained and conventional branch of the religious revival,
respectability rather than violent enthusiasm. They did not,
for the most part, choose the branch represented by the more
frenetic orders of friars like the extreme Augustinians. This
papal policy in Italy was sustainedly Romanesque, redolent of

[182] For the Friars of the Sack, see Richard W. Emery, "The Friars
of the Sack," *Speculum*, xviii (1943), 323-334, particularly 326.

the odor of Saint Bernard, in its relatively frequent use of monasteries rather than bishops (of estate managers rather than bureaucratic administrators) for the reformation of monasteries.

By the end of the thirteenth century the monastic economic picture was not so discouraging as it was to become. Monastic landlords shared in late thirteenth-century prosperity.[183] But it is hard to believe that there was not at least a confused awareness of the dangers due to the exhaustion, through development, of monastic wasteland. The statement of the provost of the great church of Mantua in 1233 that within the one hundred preceding years all of the church's lands had been "cleared, ploughed, redeemed from wood and marsh, and converted to the production of food" is a rather chilling one.[184] There is no reason to feel that this sort of exhaustion, particularly half-understood, did not frighten to conservatism thirteenth-century ecclesiastics. Its sense probably encouraged thirteenth-century popes to the reformation of those monasteries visible to them in Italy, although the eventual danger may have been much graver in northern, more purely agricultural, countries.

The popes, who were necessarily sensitive to local demands, were, although probably not consciously so, conservative in their Italian innovations; their innovations preserved the order of society. Old religious orders in decayed monasteries which were no longer at all enthusiastic no longer aroused the sort of external enthusiasm that would bring them gifts. They were no longer a strong source of new income for themselves or the church; to attract new income, more attractive orders had to be introduced. More dangerously, the lack of monastic enthusiasm threatened the very existence of monastic establishments. Beneath the surface agitation about individual abbatial incomes, monasteries (those great estate managers, holding companies, "agricultural banks") were an integral part of the organization of society and particularly of tenure and tene-

[183] See, for example, E. M. Halcrow, "The Decline of Demesne Farming on the Estates of Durham Cathedral Priory," *Economic History Review*, VII (1954-1955), 345-356, particularly 356 for late century prosperity; see, too, and compare Jones, "Camaldoli," 168-169, 172-173.

[184] Quoted and translated in Luzzatto-Jones, 99.

ments.[185] That they might go on serving society as estate managers and accountants they needed their reason (or excuse) for existence, their heart (or façade), enthusiasm (within and without). Thus in a land that desperately needed sustained order and organization the reforming popes aided society (its conservation) by substituting Cistercians and Claresses for Benedictines.

[185] Sister James Eugene Madden has used the term "agricultural banks" recently ("Business Monks," 347-348), a term borrowed, as she says, from Léopold Delisle (*Études sur la condition de la classe agricole et l'état de l'agriculture en Normandie au moyen âge* [Évreux, 1851], xxxix). The argument of this chapter does not mean to imply that there were no monastic suppressions or changes of order of any sort in England until the period just before the Reformation: see particularly J. C. Dickinson, "Early Suppressions of English Houses of Austin Canons," in *Medieval Studies Presented to Rose Graham*, ed. Veronica Ruffer and A. J. Taylor (Oxford, 1950), 54-77, 57.

V · THE WRITTEN CHURCH

CCLESIASTICAL documents—the distillation, the crystallization, of their dioceses, or monasteries, or churches—lie in hundreds and thousands of Italian armadios, in sacristies and bishops' palaces, in secluded rural monasteries, in the *conventi soppressi* fonds of state archives.[1] Archives are complicated and peculiarly verbal physical remains. They are promising archaeological digs, dumps of documents articulate at various levels and in various directions. The document in the archives is a live connection with the past; it pierces the past's crust. It talks directly of the society that produced and preserved it. Italian documents say very different things from English ones. The two sets of documents speak clearly of the differences between the two churches in the thirteenth century.

The most obvious difference between the two churches' documents has to do with bishops' registers. Registers existed in England; they did not in Italy. The first surviving English registers come from Lincoln (1217) and York (1225). Thirteenth-century registers survive from Canterbury, Bath and Wells, Coventry and Lichfield, Exeter, Hereford, Norwich, Salisbury, Winchester, Worcester, and Carlisle.[2] In some of

---

[1] For a brief introduction to Italian archives see Hilary Jenkinson and H. E. Bell, *Italian Archives during the War and at its Close* (London, 1947); I believe that the best guide to the archives of the peninsula lies in the volumes of Paul Kehr's and later Walther Holtzmann's *Italia Pontificia*.

[2] There are a number of valuable discussions of English episcopal registers: E. F. Jacob, *The Medieval Registers of Canterbury and York*, St. Anthony's Hall Publications, No. 4 (London, 1953); Irene J. Churchill, "The Archbishops' Registers" in *Mediaeval Records of the Archbishops of Canterbury* (London, 1962), 11-20; C. R. Cheney, *English Bishops' Chanceries* (Manchester, 1950), 100-110, 147-149; Alexander Hamilton Thompson, "The Registers of the Archbishops of York," *Yorkshire Archaeological Journal*, XXXII (1935), 245-263; C. W. Foster, "The Lincoln Episcopal Registers," *Associated Architectural Societies Reports and Papers for 1933*, XLI (1935), 155-168; Claude Jenkins, "Some Thirteenth Century Registers," *Church Quarterly Review*, XCIX (1924-1925), 69-115; R. C. Fowler, *Episcopal Registers of England and Wales*, Helps for Students of History, No. 1 (London,

these dioceses the registers start only at end-century; in some, early registers have probably been lost. There is no doubt, though, that the English register of institutions to benefices swelling to general administrative *acta* is a product of the thirteenth century. Archbishop Gray, bored in his northern isolation, remembered the administrative efficiency of his days in King John's chancery.[3] This personal memory almost surely swept York into that movement of enrolled government, with its neatly effective official memory, that characterized John's England, Philip Augustus's France, and Innocent III's Rome. But although the York instance may have had a personal cause, the register was a sort of record that exactly fitted the diocesan government that was evolving in thirteenth-century England. The importance of Lincoln, perhaps the best-governed diocese in Christendom, in the evolution of the episcopal register emphasizes the naturalness of the development. In Lincoln, diocesan records were carefully and systematically kept from 1209 at the latest, and probably from 1200.[4] The naturalness of the development is also emphasized by the adjustment of the York register through the century until it reached its neat bureaucratic compartmentalization (particularly by archdeaconries) during the episcopates of Archbishops Romeyn (1286-1296) and Corbridge (1300-1304). The movement from roll to codex, from casual to fixed form, from few to many registers' being written, is a movement that was propelled by the very real and active administration of the English church.

Italy, close to the observing papacy with its own magnificent

---

1918). But the best introduction to the register is probably through a well-edited one with a good introduction, like *The Register of Thomas Corbridge, Lord Archbishop of York, 1300-1304*, ed. Alexander Hamilton Thompson, Surtees Society, 138, 141 (Durham, 1925-28), or like Rosalind M. T. Hill's edition of *The Rolls and Register of Bishop Oliver Sutton, 1280-99* (Hereford, 1948-65) for the Lincoln Record Society.

[3] For Gray's boredom see C.A.F. Meekings, "Six Letters Concerning the Eyres of 1226-1228," *English Historical Review*, LXV (1950), 501.

[4] Rosalind Hill, "Bishop Sutton and his Archives: a study in the keeping of records in the thirteenth century," *Journal of Ecclesiastical History*, II (1951), 43-53, 52.

thirteenth-century registers, saw no such movement.[5] The only diocese (except perhaps for the monastic quasi-diocese of Cassino) from which something close to papal or English episcopal registers is known to survive is Città di Castello.[6] In the surrounding stillness the achievement of Città di Castello is deafening. Città di Castello preserves nine books of episcopal documents which also include some stray gatherings of not strictly pertinent material.[7] There are in all something over 1,500 folios, collected in gatherings, or *quaterni*, of four pieces of parchment doubled into eight folios, with occasional variations from the regular pattern. The material in the bishops' books stretches from the late twelfth century, at least in copy, and the early thirteenth century through the early fourteenth century, to 1340, and then thinly through the fifteenth century. The material in the books is particularly concerned with the late thirteenth century, the episcopates of Pietro V d'Anagni (1252-1265), Nicolò (1265-1279), and Giacomo d'Enrico Cavalcanti (1280-1301). The gatherings within the

[5] For a recent summary of the material available on thirteenth-century papal registers, see Edith Pásztor, "Contributo alla storia dei registri pontifici del secolo XIII," *Bullettino dell' "Archivio paleografico italiano*," ser. 3, 1 (1962), 37-83; the best introduction to the registers is through themselves in the excellent edition of the Bibliothèque des écoles françaises d'Athènes et de Rome and through the introduction by Robert Fawtier to *Les Registres de Boniface VIII*; Harry Bresslau, *Handbuch der Urkundenlehre für Deutschland und Italien* (reissued Berlin, 1958) is the best general introduction to papal diplomatic, and Peter Herde, *Beiträge zum päpstlichen Kanzlei- und Urkundenwesen im 13. Jahrhundert* (Kallmünz, 1961), the best specific guide to the thirteenth-century papal chancery; R. L. Poole, *Lectures on the History of the Papal Chancery down to the Time of Innocent III* (Cambridge, 1915), is still helpful; see, too, Robert Brentano, " 'Consolatio defuncte caritatis': a Celestine V letter at Cava," *English Historical Review*, LXXVI (1961), 296-303 and references therein.

[6] For Cassino, see above, Chapter II (notes 18, 19, 20), Chapter IV (notes 45-50), and Tommaso Leccisotti, "La Tradizione archvistica di Montecassino," *Miscellanea Archivistica Angelo Mercati*, Studi e Testi, 165 (Vatican City, 1952), 227-261.

[7] Robert Brentano, "The Bishops' Books of Città di Castello," *Traditio*, XVI (1960), 241-254, in which the structure of the books is examined more fully; and see above, Chapter II (notes 46, 98, 126, partic. 161-170), Chapter III (note 32).

modern books do not maintain their medieval sequence, but in some cases the intended medieval sequence is clear. This is particularly noticeable in some forty numbered *quaterni* of the episcopal notary Pietro da Canoscio, which could perhaps be reassembled into an almost complete register for Bishop Pietro V d'Anagni and the beginning of one for Bishop Nicolò.[8] In the 1270's the notaries Guido di Giovanni and Rainaldo Armanni were similarly successively active in organizing their *quaterni* for Bishop Nicolò. These thirteenth-century *quaterni* were organized rationally, not merely chronologically, as early as the notary Urso's 1230 visitation *quaternus* during the episcopate of Matteo.[9]

Although the episcopal chancery at Città di Castello is in an extreme and rather isolated position in Italy, in one way it recalls every other observable Italian chancery. It was notarial. The keeper of the bishops' records was a notary public, usually by imperial authority. The *quaterni* themselves, although sometimes specifically organized around episcopal business like visitation or around a specific period of activity like the vacancy after the death of Bishop Nicolò in 1279, were essentially notarial cartularies restricted to episcopal business, much like the notarial cartularies that preserve so much of the non-ecclesiastical activity of late medieval Italian towns.[10]

The Italian church was a notarial church. A painting, in Siena, by Pietro Lorenzetti makes the point with wonderful, pictorial clarity (See Fig. 19). In the 1320's Lorenzetti painted a predella panel of Honorius IV's approving the rule of the Carmelites.[11] In it Lorenzetti had Honorius hand a sealed notarial instrument—in protocol and eschatocol clearly notarial —to the friars; and three of Honorius's predecessors, supported by angels, hold similar notarial instruments over his head.

[8] Brentano, "The Bishops' Books," 244-245.

[9] Brentano, "The Bishops' Books," 246.

[10] Preservation and activity are described together in David Herlihy, *Pisa in the Early Renaissance* (New Haven, 1958), particularly "The Notarial Cartulary," 1-20, with its initial quotation from Federigo Visconti; compare, for another region, John H. Mundy, *Liberty and Political Power in Toulouse, 1050-1230* (New York, 1954), 115-121: "The Notariate of Toulouse."

[11] Siena, Pinacoteca no. 84.

Lorenzetti's Italian perception has made notarial the papal bull. His new naturalism has made clearly apparent his revealing inexactness, an inexactness probably derived from the assumption that a serious document would of course be notarized (but possibly from the observation of a safely notarized copy that could have existed in the archives of the Carmine in Siena). In Italy to prefix the word "notarial" to the word "instrument" is as much a redundancy as in England it is a curiosity.[12]

The bishops of Italy fit into Italian urban society, and in the greater cities of Italy, living within the concepts of Roman law, hundreds of notaries were active at a time.[13] The bishops used the towns' notaries. Sometimes specific notaries became for a time the bishops' or churches' notaries or scribes as they did at Taranto and Frigento at the end of the twelfth century, at Milan, Salerno, Ravello, Bari, Trani, Foligno in the thirteenth century, Camerino at the beginning of the fourteenth century. They became notaries of an abbey like Fiastra or at least for one case of a person like the dean of Nola. By the end of the thirteenth century the citizen of Rieti and papal notary, Giovanni Petri, was the episcopal "notarius" or "scriba"; and his intermittent tenure at least from 1265 until his death after 3 May 1314, considerably outlasted that of his episcopal superiors.[14]

[12] For a general discussion of notarial acta see Alain de Boüard, *Manuel de diplomatique française et pontificale* (Paris, 1925-1948), II: *L'Acte privé*; for the work of an English notary see that of Edmund de Verduno or of Canterbury in Brentano, *York Metropolitan Jurisdiction* (index), or William Somerdeby, in the same place, 77 and n.

[13] Herlihy, *Pisa*, 10-11.

[14] Dieter Girgensohn and Norbert Kamp, "Urkunden und Inquisitionen der Stauferzeit aus Tarent," *Quellen und Forschungen aus italienischen Archiven und Bibliotheken*, XLI (1961), 137-234, 169: Sellitto di Salva da Taranto, notary of the church of Taranto (1194); Alessandro Pratesi, "Note di diplomatica vescovile beneventana, parte II: vescovi suffraganei," *Bullettino dell' "Archivio paleografico italiano,"* NS, I (1955), 19-91, 80: Giovanni de Sancto Nicholao, notary of Agapito bishop of Frigento (between 25 December 1192 and 24 March 1194); Giacomo C. Bascapè, *Antichi diplomi degli arcivescovi di Milano e note di diplomatica episcopale*, Fontes Ambrosiani, 18 (Florence, 1937), 90 (Montino Corono da Gallarate, notary and scribe of Archbishop

In one case at least a notary's attachment to an Italian prelate, his movement about the countryside with him, is sufficiently apparent to recall the great case of John of Schalby at Lincoln. Schalby followed Oliver Sutton, bishop of Lincoln, about his diocese for eighteen years. Schalby was Sutton's registrar and he was accompanied by at least two scribes and a notary. Schalby carried his work with him, "the rolls and

---

Ottone—1268), 93 (Antegrado Croceo, ? Crotto, notary public of the city of Milan and scribe of Archbishop Ottone—1282), 97 (Antegrado Crotto, notary public of the city of Milan and scribe of Archbishop Ottone, also Bernardino Fossano, notary public of the city of Milan and chancellor of the fabric of the Great Church—1292), 98 (Beltramino da Robiano, notary public of the city of Milan and scribe of Archbishop Francesco—1301), 102 (Redolfo, notary of the curia of the archbishopric of Milan—1302); Cava, Archivio della Badia di Santissima Trinità, arca LVIII, no. 114 (Tomasio, described as our notary by Archbishop Filippo of Salerno, and described by himself as notary of the curia of the archbishop—1287); Luigi Enrico Pennacchini, *Pergamene Salernitane (1008-1784)* (Salerno, 1941), 176 (Bartolomeo Baraioli, canon of Ravello, notary public of the church of Ravello and of the acts of the curia of the bishop Tolomeo of Ravello—1290); there is another original copy of this document—see Antonio Balducci, *L'Archivio della Curia Arcivescovile di Salerno*, 1 (Salerno, 1945), 49 no. 160 (in this document Bartolomeo decorates and elongates the letters of his name; Bartolomeo's position as a canon notary should be noted); *C.d.b.*, II, 52-54 no. 24 (Pietro di Giovanni da Mansolla, notary public of Bari and of the lord archbishop—1274); *C.d.b.*, VI, no. 21, 35-36 (Nicola, priest and notary of the church of Trani and of Bartolomeo, archbishop of Trani—1207); Michele Faloci-Pulignani, "I Confini del Comune di Foligno," *Bollettino della regia deputazione di storia patria per l'Umbria*, XXXIII (1935), 217-247, 244-254 (Bartolo di Giacomo, the notary of Bishop Berardo of Foligno—1289); for Fiastra see above, Chapter IV, notes 100-102 (Buonconsiglio Petrioli Alberti); Cava, arca LIX no. 114 (Bonuto, notary of the city of Nola and of the dean of Nola in this case—1292); Rome, Archivio di stato, Fiastra, no 2259 (Francesco Massei, notary by imperial authority and now notary of the bishop, Rambocto, of Camerino—1301); Rieti, Archivio capitolare, armadio II, fasc. B, no. 2, and fasc. E, no. 6; armadio III, fasc. C, no. 4, and Rome, Archivio di stato, Sant'Agostino di Terni, no. 5; for a comparison with French practice and a more extended one with English practice see Cheney, *English Bishops' Chanceries*, 25-27, 28-43; for Canterbury, see also Irene Churchill, *Canterbury Administration* (London, 1933), I, 9-25, and for York, Brentano, *York Metropolitan Jurisdiction*, 81-82.

quires which comprised Sutton's register" and also apparently "the rolls of the bishop's four immediate predecessors," all this on a packhorse or packhorses as the bishop's party rode through the huge diocese. And Schalby wrote until his hand grew so tired that his writing showed it. The Italian who recalls Schalby is Pietro da Ceprano, Federigo Visconti's "chamberlain and scribe or notary," who went with him on his great Sardinian visitation of 1263. Pietro, like John, was involved physically in following his prelate and in carefully recording his acts and, in Pietro's case, his statements. At journey's end Pietro went over Federigo's accounts with him.[15]

The difference between what John of Schalby and Pietro da Ceprano compiled is, however, a significant difference. Pietro's records were incorporated in a lively and articulate book of sermons, an eccentric and personal codex, very different from Schalby's official, orderly, administrative compilation. The distance from Italy to England is made clearer (and too the distance from the 1260's to the 1280's) if the Pisan records are also seen against the late thirteenth-century registers at York which, from the time of Romeyn, from 1285, used archdeaconries, administrative territories, as categories for recording the general business of the diocese.[16] Pietro da Ceprano, like the registrars at York, used geography—but he to trace the personal and heroic quest of the sermon-giving Federigo Vis-

[15] Hill, *The Rolls and Register of Bishop Oliver Sutton*, III, xxvi-xxxii; Hill, "Bishop Sutton and his Archives," 53 (tired-looking hand-writing); J. H. Srawley, *The Book of John de Schalby* (Lincoln, 1949), 3; above, Chapter III; Florence, Biblioteca Medicea Laurenziana, Plut. 33, sin. 1, fos. 141, 144v.

[16] *The Registers of John le Romeyn, Lord Archbishop of York, 1286-1296, and of Henry Newark, Lord Archbishop of York, 1296-1299*, ed. William Brown, Surtees Society, Nos. 123, 128 (Durham, 1913-1916); and see Jacob, *Mediaeval Registers*, 16; the register of Romeyn's predecessor, William Wickwane, which is for the most part preserved in duplicate, contains sections, particularly the *Visitacio provincialis in dyocesi Dunelmensi*, which bring its structure a little closer to that of continental quasi-registers like the Pisan visitation: *The Register of William Wickwane, Lord Archbishop of York (1279-1285)*, ed. William Brown, Surtees Society, No. 114 (Durham, 1907); Thompson, "The Registers of the Archbishops of York," 248-249.

conti and they to mark the territorial administrative boundaries within their diocese.

The Italian notary active in ecclesiastical affairs is omnipresent and almost always an integral part of a general community, itself relatively literate and given to expressing itself in the constant production of notarial instruments. The Italian notary is, however, though common, not at all necessarily a personally unobtrusive figure. He is sometimes very obtrusive and calls attention to himself in obvious ways. In some parts of Italy he developed a peculiar hand and in some parts a peculiar style. The notaries of the coastal centers around Naples and Salerno maintained into the fourteenth century a peculiar curial script, based on Beneventan. The script seems through its illegibility to have distinguished the notary from his literate contemporaries in a too literate area. It also probably gave his documents that air of pompous legality that seems, like a whiff of "whereas," to add self-conscious validity to important instruments. Frederick II opposed the curial script, but Robert the Wise tolerated it. It was used less frequently than before in the thirteenth century (perhaps as notaries relaxed into being licensed public officials rather than peculiarly skilled curial scribes), and it seems to have disappeared in the fourteenth century. The curial script has long been known to have survived after 1315. The last of the published and now destroyed Amalfi documents in Naples to be written in the script was written by the notary Benenato de Amoruczo in 1332.[17] Benenato is also the last notary for whom an example

[17] Riccardo Filangieri di Candida, "I 'Curiales' di Amalfi," *Bollettino del Bibliofilo*, no. 11 (1920), 277-287; "La 'Charta' Amalfitana," *Gli Archivi italiani*, VI (1919), 35-47, 133-162; *Codice diplomatico amalfitano*, I (Naples, 1917), xxv-xxviii; Leopoldo Cassese, *I Notari nel Salerno ed i loro protocolli dal 1362 alla fine del '700*, Estratto da *Notizie degli archivi di stato* (Rome, 1948); Robert Brentano, "The Archiepiscopal Archives at Amalfi," *Manuscripta*, IV (1960), 98-105, 101; an illustration of the curial hand of the area (Ravello, 1199) is to be found in Jole Mazzoleni, *Esempi di scritture cancelleresche, curiali e minuscole* (Naples, n.d.), pl. VII; for persistence after 1315, E. A. Lowe, *The Beneventan Script* (Oxford, 1914), 44; for considerably later dates, Mauro Inguanez, "La Scrittura Beneventana in codici e documenti dei secoli XIV e XV," in *Scritti di paleografia e diplomatica in onore di Vincenzo Federici* (Florence, 1944), 309-314. The 1332 docu-

of the old curial script is preserved in an instrument within the archives of the Archbishop of Amalfi.[18] It is dated 1347. But as early as 1310 Benenato himself was using the conventional Carolingian-based script.[19] In his family, ability to read the curial script seems to have survived its use. In 1376 Sergio de Amoruczo read and transcribed "de littera curialista," a grant, from 1279, by the archbishop of Amalfi, Filippo Augustariccio, of four large shops to be built for Masses to be said for his and his family's souls in the cathedral church at Amalfi.[20]

Across the peninsula on the Adriatic coast, in Bisceglia, Canne, Conversano, Molfetta, Monopoli, Siponto, and Terlizzi, notaries decorated and made personal their instruments by inserting the rhymes and rhythms of florid poetic phrases into the incarnation phrase of their dating clauses.[21] Up and down the peninsula and in the islands notaries identified themselves with their hands, their sometimes arresting names —Achilles or Lanzelotto or (appropriately in turn of the century Bologna) Aristotle, and sometimes even their peculiar spelling, like that of the notary for Torgotorio de Muru, archbishop of Oristano (1224-1253), who wrote of him as "Donnu Trudori de Muru archipiscobu de Arborea."[22] Notaries sometimes described the property they held and its proposed disposition, as when a notary left *domum unam meam magnam* to the clergy of the Duomo at Bari.[23] Buonconsiglio, Fias-

---

ment is in Filangieri (*Codice diplomatico amalfitano*, II [Trani, 1951], 287-288 no. 582).

[18] Amalfi, Archivio arcivescovile, A.P., sec. xiv, No. 65.

[19] Amalfi, Archivio arcivescovile, A.P., sec. xiv, No. 13.

[20] Amalfi, Archivio arcivescovile, A.P., sec. xiv, No. 140.

[21] Giovanni Antonucci, "Rime e ritmi nella diplomatica pugliese," *Japigia*, III (1932), 215-226; Francesco Babudri, "La poesia nella diplomatica medievale pugliese," *Archivio storico pugliese*, VI (1953), 50-84; Robert Brentano, "Sealed Documents of the Mediaeval Archbishops at Amalfi," *Mediaeval Studies*, XXIII (1961), 21-46, 40 n. 38.

[22] Achilles: Gennaro Maria Monti, *Codice diplomatico brindisino*, I (Trani, 1940), 134-136 no. 77; Lanzelotto: Rome, Archivio di stato, Fiastra, nos. 2211, 2213; Aristotle: Bologna, Archivio di stato, Sant' Agnese, 8/5598, G432, G433. Raimondo Bonu, *Serie cronologica degli arcivescovi d'Oristano* (Gallizzi-Sassari, 1959), 33.

[23] *C.d.b.*, II, 110 no. 45 (1295).

tra's notary, recorded his genealogy, the itinerary of his life, and the dowry of his wife.[24] All notaries identified themselves with their notarial signs.[25] The signs range from simple geometric patterns to quite elaborate and elegant drawings—the fish and flowers, the fleur-de-lis, iris, or sheaf and ribbon of various Città di Castello notaries, the splendid little horse's head of a notary from Monte Granaro, a hanging fish from Rieti.[26] In Città di Castello the notaries came to favor small, vertical signs, often geometrically stylized natural forms, usually on steps, often with a cross on their tops; in Amalfi notaries often chose horizontal signs and frequently they constructed them of their monograms.

Notarial characteristics are a glass through which almost all Italian ecclesiastical acts are seen. What is said is, almost everywhere, said in the notary's style. There are exceptions. Girardo, a much-maligned bishop of Fermo, issued sealed letters with no particular notarial characteristics.[27] Three of his preserved *acta* begin with his name, with extended letters in the originals; the originals preserve a conventional style (*dei gratia*), address, salutation, abbreviated explanatory *arenga*. They are, in the broader European sense, normal, straight through to their closing dates, and normal too in their physical structure—small (21.5 cms by 13.5 cms; 25.5 cms by 15.5 cms) rectangles, with folds and holes, and in one case red silk strings for the now missing seal.[28] A 1287 letter of Fra Tom-

[24] Rome, Archivio di stato, Fiastra, nos. 1379, 1581, 1584; see above, Chapter IV, note 100. I have not run across an Italian notary who, like Edmund of Canterbury at Durham, sometimes refers to the location of his notarial license in the papal registers: Brentano, *York Metropolitan Jurisdiction*, 162 n. and pl. 3.

[25] For examples of notarial signs in England: J. S. Purvis, *Notarial Signs from the York archiepiscopal records* (London and York, 1957); in Italy: *Exempla scripturarum*, II: *Epistolae et instrumenta saeculi XIII*, ed. B. Katterbach and C. Silva-Tarouca (Vatican City, 1930).

[26] Rome, Archivio di stato, Fiastra, no. 1959 (Monte Granaro); Rome, Archivio di stato, Sant'Agostino di Terni, no. 5 (Rieti); Brentano, "The Bishops' Books," 250-251.

[27] Rome, Archivio di stato, Fiastra, nos. 1207, 1412, 1451.

[28] The silk is on no. 1412; the other original is no. 1207.

maso, bishop of Terni, in which he grants a chapel to the Augustinian friars is similarly conventional and non-notarial.[29] It is rather larger (37 cms by 21 cms) than the Fermo letters, begins with the enlarged F of its Frater, and retains some red and yellow silk but not its seal. A 1293 letter (33.5 cms by 20 cms) of Todino, bishop of Senigallia, begins with the general address "Universis Christi fidelibus ad quos littere iste pervenerint" with an extended initial U; the address is followed by "Todinus divina miseratione Senegal*lensis* episcopus" and by a letter on plumbed parchment devoid of notarial characteristics and with its last line extended, like that in a papal letter, so that it stretches across the parchment.[30] Not only does a very beautiful, rather unusual 1267 letter of Ottone Visconti, still carrying the "great seal of Saint Ambrose," not show any notarial traits, it would have been a worthy and generally unsurprising production of any of the great chanceries of Europe.[31] And a many-sealed, ragman 1296 letter granting an indulgence for the benefit of the Augustianian friars of Terni, flamboyantly proclaims its non-notarial style and thus, in a way, its ecclesiastical independence.[32] The document bore or was meant to bear the seals of at least fifteen bishops whose names appear in its text and on its flap among the twenty holes pierced there to carry seal strings. The document was probably prepared in Rome, where it was dated; it was probably prepared before any of the signatory bishops was secured and surely before the total number of signatories was fixed because the space between "permissione divina" and "episcopi, salutem" would admit several more names, as would the spaces

[29] Rome, Archivio di stato, Sant'Agostino di Terni, no. 4.

[30] Rome, Archivio di stato, Fiastra, no. 1983.

[31] Bascapè, *Antichi diplomi*, 85-86 no. 16; pl. vi is an excellent reproduction of the letter with its seal.

[32] Rome, Archivio di stato, Sant'Agostino di Terni, no. 6. But there could be notarial ragmen, too, like the instruments of the notary Ciabatto, which publish the Lucchese elections of 1256 and 1269 and which each canon of Lucca sealed with his own seal (ed. Martino Giusti, "Le Elezioni dei vescovi di Lucca," *Rivista di storia della chiesa in Italia*, vi [1952], 218-219, 220-222). The 1269 instrument, with its seal slits, survives in original: Lucca, Archivio arcivescovile, +0.44.

between the holes pierced for the seals' strings. The scribe, like some scribes in provincial courts—Milan's for example, shows the clear influence of papal proximity and of the constant market for papal documents in the Roman area; he succumbed to no notarial attractions and produced a splendid letter patent.[33]

The provincial Italian church was exposed to the practice of the papal curia through the presence in the provinces of papal officials and their *acta* (and of course through provincial reception of papal letters). Cardinals were perhaps particularly affected by papal style, persuaded to difference from local practice by the high dignity of their office as well as their cosmopolitan backgrounds.[34] The diplomatic practice of cardinals, although not local, could be bizarre: the cardinal deacons of Santa Maria in Porticu and San Nicola in Carcere wrote a letter, now dated 1284, from Spoleto, to the officials and commune of Perugia, in normal letter form, but written on paper and sealed close with their wax pointed-oval seals.[35] Still the papal curia and its affiliates and subordinates offered examples of conventional cosmopolitan form to the Italian countryside. On the whole the countryside, insofar as it was represented by provincial episcopal chanceries, rejected the example. The high neighboring papacy proved less generally compelling than the surrounding notarial community. Of the influences acting upon these chanceries the political was, in this sense, less potent than the social.

Patterns of influence from chancery to chancery are apparent in Italy. The episcopal chancery at Bologna responded to the influences of Ravenna, its metropolitan mother see. The copying of form is particularly noticeable in a diploma privilege, a document of great formality, of 1133 in which the met-

[33] See particularly pls. III through VI in Bascapè.
[34] For papal diplomatic and cardinals' letters see, for example, Perugia, Archivio di stato, Cass. II, no. 45 (and see the illustration in *Gli Archivi dell'Umbria*, Ministero dell'Interno, Pubblicazioni degli Archivi di Stato, xxx [Rome, 1957], facing p. 96), Brentano, "'Consolatio defuncte caritatis,'" 298n.; and Palermo, Archivio di stato, Cefalù, no. 500.
[35] Perugia, Archivio di stato, Cass. II, no. 61.

ropolitan example and the suffragan copy both survive.[36] But it is demonstrated in a series of formal privileges issued by bishops of Bologna between 1133 and 1230.[37] The elegant and solemn diploma of 1230, issued by Bishop Enrico for Santa Caterina di Quarto, is, in spite of its solemnity, less bound by the regular form of the privilege than its predecessors; it helps to herald the new regular form of the Bolognese chancery, a patent letter form used by the cosmopolitan Bishop Ottaviano I degli Ubaldini.[38] In this form, like its predecessor, the episcopal chancery of Bologna was, for an Italian episcopal chancery, unusually regular and unusually closely connected with the common form of non-Italian chanceries. The connection is not surprising in the instance because of Ottaviano's sophistication and more generally because of Bologna's papal, and particularly because of its academic, connections. The chancery not surprisingly followed the local university's formularies; it is close to Giovanni da Bologna.[39] But even in Bologna itself, in its thirteenth-century regularity, the pressure of notarial practice is observable. The "mixed form" (half-episcopal, half-notarial), familiar in Italian archives, is present.[40] Perhaps it was too common, too ordinary, really to be seen.

In the province of Benevento, less a really coherent entity than the province of Ravenna, the influence of the mother see and the development of common form in suffragan chanceries seems to have been very slight. At the end of the twelfth century the see of Frigento, although seemingly inspired by the papacy rather than by Benevento, developed something of chancery organization and episcopal diplomatic.[41] In this it seems, among its co-suffragans, to have been essentially unique. The diocese of Larino could in 1240 achieve a certain solem-

---

[36] Giorgio Cencetti, "Note di diplomatica vescovile bolognese dei secoli XI-XIII," in *Scritti di paleografia e diplomatica in onore di Vincenzo Federici* (Florence, 1944), 159-223, 164-166, 197.

[37] Cencetti, 166-173, 197-201, pls. 3 and 4.

[38] Cencetti, pl. 5.

[39] Cencetti, 201-204, and nn. 20-22.

[40] Cencetti, 198-199.

[41] Alessandro Pratesi, "Note di diplomatica vescovile beneventana," *Bullettino dell' "Archivio paleografico italiano,"* NS, I (1955), 19-91, 41-43, 76-80.

nity in its work, but the documents remained semi-public, semi-notarial. The diocese of Avellino stresses the Benevento suffragan type. Its documents are repeatedly merely notarial instruments, not infrequently indistinguishable from those of the surrounding community.[42] The diocese seems to have had no coherent isolated chancery.

At the end of the thirteenth century two documents issued by Beneventan suffragans were actually prepared in the archiepiscopal curia. To letters modeled after one issued by the Benedictine Beneventan Archbishop Giovanni da Castrocielo in 1293, the bishops of Frigento and Telese, in 1299 and 1300, had their own seals affixed (and a copy of the Telese document notes that the seal was of red wax on silk string). In 1297 the bishop of Sant'Agata dei Goti issued a similar copy, but from Sant'Agata rather than Benevento. Each member of this little node of documents following the relatively orderly pattern of the archdiocesan chancery is a letter of indulgence for the confraternity of Santo Spirito in Benevento.[43] It emphasizes the importance of the grantee, not the grantor, the governed rather than the governor. It also emphasizes the ordinary Italian episcopal chancery's lack of independence from the total community.

In general the ordinariness of Italian notarial practice prevailed in ecclesiastical writing offices. Some bishops, like those of Fermo and Bologna, did issue documents free of notarial signs. There was some connection between ecclesiastical chanceries, like those of Ravenna and Bologna, relatively undeflected by the surrounding mass of notarial practice. But for the most part notarial practice carried all before it. Ecclesiastical chanceries defined themselves too poorly—they had too vague and interrupted a view of their specific function within the community—to break away from the practice of the unusually literate and incessantly writing notarial community which surrounded them.

[42] Pratesi, "Note," 43-45, 35-38.
[43] Pratesi, "Note," 41, 49, 48; for Benevento, see F. Bartoloni, "Note di diplomatica vescovile beneventana, parte 1: vescovi e arcivescovi di Benevento," in *Rendiconti dell'Accademia nazionale dei Lincei*, Classe di scienze morali, storiche, e filologiche, ser. 8, v (1950), 425-449.

In superficial contrast with this pattern of ordinariness one finds those occasional documents, particularly from the south, bedecked, encrusted, ornamented with a huge and tawdry showiness that would certainly have startled any English chancellor.[44] The great *acta* of Pietro III Paparone, archbishop of Brindisi, are Byzantine barges that carry a heavy load of formulae, trapping, harangues, witness lists, and seals.[45] They are reminiscent of the sporadic showiness of Pietro's pastoral activity. They sharply recall the actual barges upon which Pietro and his floating court descended upon island monasteries. But, in spite of the superficial contrast, some of this flamboyance is closely connected with simple notarial practice. The notary's subscription, decorating and validating, is frequently one of the encrustations on the great *acta*. The witness list, spacious and impressive (and proclaiming the importance of the cathedral clergy), is formally closer to the witness list of contemporary southern notarial instruments than it is to that of the papal privilege. The list of the great southern episcopal document is archaic as the privilege's is but archaic in the way that the southern instrument's is. Finally, the great southern *acta*, like the prevalent notarial practice of the Italian church, show the refusal or the inability of the Italian provincial churches to develop distinctive chanceries using the common forms of thirteenth-century public documents—particularly letters patent—ordinary to the papal curia and to the episcopal chanceries of northern Europe. Italian chancery practice in these two opposite but related directions shows as clear a withdrawal from what would seem the dominant mode of western European practice as does Italian hesitance in the use of Gothic.

The connection of the great *acta* with ordinary notarial practice can be seen if one turns to a specific set of archives,

[44] It has been noted that in the course of the twelfth century English episcopal letters under papal influence seem, unlike English royal letters, to have become increasingly elaborate (F. M. Stenton, "*Acta Episcoporum*," *Cambridge Historical Journal*, III [1929], 1-14, 11-12); papal practice in the thirteenth century would not have encouraged further elaboration, nor would it have been appropriate to the very real press of business in thirteenth-century English episcopal chanceries.

[45] See above, Chapter II.

a collection of documents, which remains, in part and with additions, essentially in its original site. Two striking qualities distinguish this sort of local Italian archive from its English counterpart. There are a great many of these archives scattered through the countryside; they are generally very small. The scattering is due in part to a history without Reformation, early national unity, or a strong group of nineteenth- and twentieth-century archival historians. The smallness is due in part to natural depredations like earthquakes and fires and to the documents' having remained in casual local hands. But both scatteredness and smallness also result from the administrative geography and the principles of record-keeping already in existence in the thirteenth century. Smallness, too, although a general quality of Italian local archives, is not a universal one. Some exceptions are obvious: Cava, Cassino, and overwhelmingly, if one can admit collections that have been moved, Fiastra and San Giorgio in Braida. These are noticeably monastic, not diocesan, exceptions; but there are also, though fewer of them, diocesan exceptions like Lucca. Monastic archives survive locally, of course, in a country like Italy, which did not have a general, successful monastic suppression, in a way that they do not in England (although the suppression in England preserved monastic records in the king's hands and in those monasteries like Durham which changed without interruption into new foundations, and the nineteenth-century suppressions in Italy disturbed both monastic and diocesan archives). But, too, here as in very many other ways thirteenth-century Italian survivals preach that the monasteries had a sort of reality that the dioceses did not.

The three armadios of documents in the archiepiscopal archives at Amalfi are a curious nest of remnants of the see's past.[46] The archives are not complete: some members have strayed in Amalfi; some were taken to Naples and later

[46] See Robert Brentano, "The Archiepiscopal Archives at Amalfi," *Manuscripta*, IV (1960), 98-105, and "Sealed Documents of the Mediaeval Archbishops at Amalfi," *Mediaeval Studies*, XXIII (1961), from the latter of which much of the material in the following few pages is repeated.

burned.[47] The archives are not pure: local conventual collections and some of the Ravello archives have been added to
them. In some obvious ways the Amalfi archives, like the
Amalfi church, are atypical even for the Italian south. In spite
of all this, and perhaps also because of it, the Amalfi archiepiscopal archives (deposited in a room in the *arcivescovado*,
by the chancellor's office, above the cloisters of Paradise) form
a nice little unplanned sample of the Italian church's history.
They are seen provocatively against the collections at Lincoln
and York—particularly if the thirteenth-century Amalfi documents are seen, at least first, as part of the total medieval
deposit.

The Amalfi archives are essentially a collection of notarial
instruments. Of these instruments, 554 survive from as early
as the eleventh and as late as the seventeenth century.[48] There
is also a small group of 105 papal and 9 royal letters. There
are thirty-five documents sealed by the chapter, vicars, chancel-
lors, and various bishops.[49] There is a miscellany of codices
and transcriptions. There are thirty-one letters issued over the
seal of the archbishop of Amalfi; they come from as early as
1274 and as late as 1847.[50] Of this general collection only a
small percentage comes from the thirteenth century. There are
three bulls (all Alexander IV), sixty-two notarial instruments,
and three letters over the archiepiscopal seal. There is no sign
of a thirteenth-century Amalfi archiepiscopal register or cartu-

[47] The Amalfi archives in the Archivio di stato were destroyed by
the Germans in 1943; they have fortunately been edited through the
beginning of the fourteenth century: Riccardo Filangieri di Candida,
Codice diplomatico amalfitano (Naples, 1917-Trani, 1951); for the
destruction see therein ii, vi.

[48] They are classified at Amalfi as "A.P., sec. xi, 1" through "A.P.,
sec. xvii, 14" in which the category "A.P." represents "Atti privati,
semipubblici, notarili." A microfilm copy of a crude hand-list of the
archbishops' *pergamene,* or parchment documents, is deposited in the
Library of Congress. I have corrected slightly the original list which
is deposited in the archives.

[49] Amalfi, Archivio della curia arcivescovile, pergamene sigillate
(P.S.): classified under "royal," "papal: bulls and briefs," and "miscellaneous."

[50] Amalfi, Archivio della curia arcivescovile, P.S., Arciv. Amalf.

lary and no suggestion that there was any sort of thirteenth-century enrollment in the archiepiscopal chancery (although there does survive at Amalfi a cartulary recording the Tramonti holdings of the convent of San Lorenzo, in Beneventan script which might be thirteenth-century).[51]

The segment of the Amalfi archives that catches the eye is the collection of medieval sealed archiepiscopal documents. Twenty parchment documents that were issued over the archbishops' seal between 1274 and 1490 survive. The overwhelming impression that these documents give is the common Italian one that the clerks of the archiepiscopal chancery were unable or unwilling to involve themselves in that long evolution of regular form which, from the eleventh to the fourteenth centuries, shaped the products of the royal and episcopal chanceries of western-central Europe into a conventional sameness. The reluctance of the Amalfi clerks to conform to the northern or papal pattern is apparent in large and in small, in the bold and obvious physical appearance of the total documents and in the wording of their internal formulae.

The Amalfi documents are huge; and, with only three exceptions (1362, 1411, 1461),[52] they are longer than they are broad. A 1281 regulation of the celebration of the Feast of Saint Andrew is 66 1/2 cms by 59 cms.[53] A 1485 license for the hermit Gabriele Cinnamo is 71 cms by 55 cms.[54] A 1371 license for constructing a chapel is 63 1/2 cms by 31 1/2 cms.[55] To this bigness there are a few exceptions, and the most extreme is a 1411 document in almost normal letter patent form that creates a "cardinal" canon of Amalfi: it is 17 cms by 23 1/2 cms.[56]

Much of the space of these documents is taken up by autograph witness crosses and subscriptions (or crosses and subscriptions elaborately pretending to be autograph); and the smallness of the 1411 document is connected with its having

[51] Amalfi, Archivio della curia arcivescovile, codices e misc., no. 6.
[52] Amalfi, P.S., Arciv. Amalf., sec. xiv, no. 6; sec. xv, nos. 1, 4.
[53] Amalfi, P.S., Arciv. Amalf., sec. xiii, no. 2.
[54] Amalfi, P.S., Arciv. Amalf., sec. xv, no. 6.
[55] Amalfi, P.S., Arciv. Amalf., sec. xiv, no. 8.
[56] Amalfi, P.S., Arciv. Amalf., sec. xv, no. 1.

no subscriptions except the archbishop's. This practice of appending crosses and subscriptions is common, as has been noted, in both conservative diploma-privilege forms and in southern notarial instruments. The use of these witness lists in Amalfi archiepiscopal letters illustrates their connection with both of these forms. But some Amalfi documents were extreme; the 1281 document regulating the celebration of the Feast of Saint Andrew is bedizened with the subscription of fifty-eight witnesses.[57]

The most noticeable quality about the internal formulae of the Amalfi letters is their lack of consistency and regularity. The three sealed *acta* of the thirteenth century, all issued by the same archbishop, use three different styles for the archbishop: "divina paciencia humilis Amalfitanus archiepiscopus" in 1274; "miseracione divina humilis Amalfitanus archiepiscopus" in 1281; "reverendus pater dominus Philippus Amalfitanus archiepiscopus" in 1292 (the last in a document actually issued under the name of the witnessing judge, the notary, and the witnesses).[58] This fluctuation continues during the medieval period, in both sealed and unsealed documents, except for a fairly regular use of the style "permissione divina" between 1359 and 1439. The same sort of irregularity is present in the dating clauses. The place date is sometimes in the locative (actum Amalfie) and sometimes, through 1371, in the accusative ("aput," or after 1359 "apud," "Amalfiam"). Of the three thirteenth-century dates, one is in the locative, two are in the accusative. The time dates are very various, with different ingredients moving in and out—but never including a feast-day date. The dates are either in the initial protocol or in the eschatocol, moving from one to the other throughout

[57] Amalfi, P.S., Arciv. Amalf., sec. xiii, no. 2. The number of witnesses is generally something between four and ten in these documents. A splendid example of a multi-witnessed Amalfi document from 1253 is reproduced in Pietro Pirri, *Il Duomo di Amalfi e il chiostro del Paradiso* (Rome, 1941), fig. 19, facing p. 60; in it the formal arrangement is more than usually suggestive of the privilege form.

[58] Amalfi, P.S., Arciv. Amalf., sec. xiii, nos. 1-3 (see Ughelli, vii, cols. 228-229, 224-226, 226-228; and Matteo Camera *Memorie storico-diplomatiche dell'antica città e ducato di Amalfi* (Salerno, 1876-1881), I, 158-160).

the whole period. But, again, in the period of the late fourteenth and early fifteenth century they are relatively consistently within the eschatocol.[59]

Until 1477, when a Florentine archbishop used a northern
notary, the Amalfi documents were written by Amalfi
notaries.[60] They, the scribes or quasi-chancellors of the archbishops, were chosen from the community of Amalfi notaries.
The production of sealed archiepiscopal *acta* was (at least
from the early fourteenth through the late fifteenth century)
only a quantitatively minor part of their professional activity,
even of their professional activity for the church of Amalfi.
They were often from prominent Amalfi notarial families;
they acted sometimes under imperial and sometimes under
papal authority. They were probably a select body within the
whole group of Amalfi notaries, but it is impossible to be sure
how many men were actually active at any one time. At least
in the period from 1370 to 1439 (the general period of Amalfi
regularity) their office developed a name: notary of the *acta*
of the archbishop's curia. The first two of the three surviving
thirteenth-century *acta* were redacted by Pietro Montincolli,
"clericus et publicus ecclesie Amalfitan' notarius" and "dia-
conus et publicus ecclesie Amalfitan' notarius." The third of
the thirteenth-century *acta* was redacted by Giacomo Sabbatino, "publicus civitatis Amalfie notarius."[61]

Three unsealed instruments by Giacomo survive in the
Amalfi archives.[62] The survival of both sealed and unsealed
documents becomes regular for his successors; and the sealed
and unsealed are startlingly similar. The existence of the inter-
mediate document signed but not sealed by the archbishop

[59] Brentano, "Sealed Documents," 33-37, 40-44.

[60] Amalfi, P.S., Arciv. Amalf., sec. xv, no. 5.

[61] Brentano, "Sealed Documents," 25-28. A sealed document from
1269 edited by Filangieri (and from the archiepiscopate of Filippo
Augustariccio, like those surviving at Amalfi) was written by Albiczo
Ramulo, "clericus et puplicus notarius domini archiepiscopi et ecclesie
Amalfitane"; the lengthy witness list includes a number of other
"clerks" of Amalfi, the church of Amalfi, and the great church of
Amalfi: Filangieri, *Codice diplomatico amalfitano*, II, 135-139, partic-
ularly 138-139.

[62] Amalfi, A.P., sec. xiii, nos. 56a, 57; sec. xiv, no. 2.

makes clear the lack of real separation in content and form between sealed *acta* and notarial instruments. The huge archaic-
looking *acta* which seem unfreed from their past are in fact
unfreed from their contemporary surroundings. The lack of
distance is visually clear if, for instance, a 1333 document
sealed by the famous Franciscan Archbishop Landolfo Caracciolo and redacted by the notary Benenato de Amoruczo is
seen against a 1361 document subscribed but not sealed by
Archbishop Marino del Giudice and redacted by the same
notary. They look very much alike.[63]

The archiepiscopal *acta* carry two particularly flamboyant
stigmata: their seals and their *arengas*. No wax archiepiscopal
seals survive at Amalfi from before 1488, but the archbishop
probably used a wax seal for some documents as early as the
thirteenth century. The 1274 document with which Archbishop Filippo Augustariccio made proctors for the Council
of Lyons has lost its seal ("sigillo nostro pendenti"), but a single slit, 1 cm long, in the document's fold must have held a
parchment tag that carried a wax seal.[64] The seal that does
survive and that is described repeatedly ("tipario nostro
plumbeo" and variations) is made of lead. The lead seal survives on documents dated 1292, 1333, 1370, 1426, 1461, and
1485;[65] a number of other documents from 1281 to 1490 say
that they bear it. The surviving seals are, as is conventional in
lead, approximately circular, with diameters of about 3 1/2
cms, and with obverse impressions with diameters of about
2 1/2 cms. The reverse impressions of the seals are all different
from each other and are all variations of the names and styles
of the issuing archbishops, showing in general a slight increase
in elaboration with the passage of time.[66] The obverse impression, centering around a half-length, full-face figure of Saint
Andrew, remains the same from 1292 to 1485.

[63] They are reproduced in Brentano, "Sealed Documents," facing pp.
26 and 27.
[64] Amalfi, P.S., Arciv. Amalf., sec. xiii, no. 1.
[65] Amalfi, P.S., Arciv. Amalf., sec. xiii, no. 3; sec. xiv, nos. 1, 7; sec.
xv, nos. 2, 4, 6.
[66] There is a list of the reverse inscriptions in Brentano, "Sealed
Documents," 32.

The Andrew of the Amalfi seal belongs to a mid-Byzantine iconographical type common in twelfth-century Sicily.[67] The Andrew of the seal is bearded and haloed; he holds a book in his right hand and a Greek cross on a staff in his left hand. The figure is flanked by the capped initials "S" and "A"; and the whole is within an encircling rim. The whole place of Amalfi is the setting for a medley of Andrew iconographical types; but it includes one other striking sample of the seal type (though without a halo and reversed). It is the Andrew in a niche on the side of the sculptured sarcophagus of Pietro Capuano (c. 1360) now in the cloisters of Paradise.[68] Compared with the seal, the Capuano Andrew has a remarkable, classical fluidity and naturalism. By comparison with the sarcophagus Andrew, the almost contemporary 1370 seal looks archaic. The 1485 seal is iconographically as well as stylistically archaic, still adding its leaden gravity to its archaic sort of document.

Saint Andrew was, by the beginning of the series of sealed *acta*, the dominant cult figure at Amalfi.[69] A body purported to be his had been brought by a cardinal, an Amalfi Capuano, from sacked Constantinople. It became the brilliant centerpiece of Amalfi's hoard of relics. The spiritual strength from the local cult moved to the archiepiscopal *acta* through the image on the seal.[70]

The doctrine of the universal church was caught by the *acta* in their *arengas*. The *arenga* is that part of the document's protocol which explains the individual action in more general terms and in the terms of Christian literary and spiritual tradition.[71] It combines quotations and paraphrases of biblical

[67] For a discussion of the type with bibliography: Otto Demus, *The Mosaics of Norman Sicily* (London, 1950), 318-321.

[68] The Capuano Andrew is reproduced in Brentano, "Sealed Documents," facing p. 32. One of the Nicholas ends of the Capuano sarcophagus is reproduced in Pirri, *Il Duomo di Amalfi*, fig. 36, facing p. 85; Pirri contains a good sampling of the Amalfi Andrews.

[69] See Pirri, *Il Duomo di Amalfi*, 135-148.

[70] See Cyril Mango, *The Brazen House* (Copenhagen, 1959), 137 and fig. 22, for a seal whose reverse points out its involvement in a sort of spiritual vision: "The Lord Himself is the most secure seal...."

[71] For the *arenga*, see: Heinrich Fichtenau, *Arenga (Mitteilungen des österreichischen Instituts für Geschichtsforschung, Supp.* xviii:

text with pious sentiment and learned commonplace. It is an exercise in rhetoric. Harangues repeatedly borrowed from one chancery by another or repeated in successive generations in the same chancery expose administrative memory and administrative connections, a web of coherent and understood purpose. But it is understanding that precedes, chronologically, the understanding of purpose illustrated by the quick efficiency of the administrative writ.

In 1292 at Amalfi, Filippo Augustariccio issued his regulations concerning the stipends of the cathedral clergy. The elaborate document, which retains its lead seal, contains an elaborate, eighty-nine word *arenga*: *Pii patris imitantes vestigia.* . . . It echoes around two passages from Matthew (20:12 and 11:28) and a commonplace about men of the altar living of the altar distorted from Paul (I Corinthians 9:13).[72] Harangues related to the Pauline *divinus cultus* part of this Amalfi example can be found used in Salerno in 1256 and 1260, in Giovinazzo in 1266, and in Naples in 1317.[73] The 1256 Salerno document uses the phrase "cum secundum apostolum qui altari servit vivere debet de altari," which clari-

---

1957); Cheney, *English Bishops' Chanceries*, 72-75; Kathleen Major, *Acta Stephani Langton*, Canterbury and York Society (Oxford, 1950), xxviii-xxxiii; Bartoloni, "Note," 435-436; Karl August Fink, "Arengen Spätmittelalterlicher Papsturkunden" in *Mélanges Eugène Tisserant*, IV, Studi e Testi, 234 (Vatican City, 1964), 205-227; and see the extended lists of *arengas* in: Avrom Saltman, *Theobald, Archbishop of Canterbury* (London, 1956), 197-208; Maria Kopczynski, *Die Arengen der Papsturkunden nach ihrer Bedeutung und Verwendung bis zu Gregor VII* (Berlin, 1936), 104-119; Antonie Jost, *Der Kaisergedanke in den Arengen der Urkunden Friedrichs I* (Münster, 1930), 42-101; Gerhard Ladner, "Formularbehelfe in der Kanzlei Kaiser Friedrichs II und die 'Briefe des Petrus de Vinea,' " *Mitteilungen des österreichischen Instituts für Geschichtsforschung*, XII (1932), 115-142.

[72] Amalfi, P.S., Arciv. Amalf., sec. xiii, no. 3 (Ughelli, VII, cols. 226-228; Camera, I, 158-160).

[73] Giuseppe Paesano, *Memorie per servire alla storia della chiesa salernitana*, II (Salerno, 1846-1857), 401 n. 1, and 391-401; *C.d.b.*, II, app. (Giovinazzo, Canosa, e Putignano), 206-207 no. 23; Luigi Parascandolo, *Memorie storiche-critiche-diplomatiche della chiesa di Napoli* (Naples, 1847-1854), III, app. I, 196-197 no. 34; for the commonplace, see, too, R.A.R. Hartridge, *A History of Vicarages in the Middle Ages* (Cambridge, 1930), 36.

fies the connection between Amalfi's "cum qui altari servit vivere debeat de altari" and a letter of Innocent III's which was selected for inclusion in Gregory IX's Decretals.[74] It is characteristic of late thirteenth-century Amalfi that its most noticeable connection with the diplomatic of the great Church of the outside world should be found in the rather grotesque and antiquated device of the *arenga*. The later use of the *arenga* at Amalfi is equally characteristic: the *arenga* is long preserved but irregularly used in Amalfi's irregular and archaically ornate documents.[75]

Ornate, showy, revealing of the chancery that composed them as these documents are, they should not, one might suppose, be preserved as they are in the archives of the issuing chancery. They should, simple reason would argue, have remained in the hands of their recipients or beneficiaries. Why did they not? Some of the Amalfi *acta* answer the question explicitly. A document through which Archbishop Marino del Giudice in 1371 gave license for constructing a chapel dedicated to Saint Catherine in the church of Santa Maria, Tramonti, says that several copies of itself have been prepared as a precaution.[76] Two 1333 licenses granted by Archbishop Landolfo Caracciolo permitting the construction of chapels in or near the cloisters of Paradise tell of the making of two "publica instrumenta . . . uno penes nos retento aliud in archivio ipsius ecclesie."[77] The 1292 Filippo Augustariccio document regulating clerical stipends talks of the preparation of two "publica consimilia instrumenta bullata," of which one should

[74] c. 16, x, iii, 5; Potthast, no. 71.

[75] Brentano, "Sealed Documents," 37-40; the 1269 document edited by Filangieri (*Codice diplomatico amalfitano*, II, 135-139) in which Archbishop Filippo arranged for the disposition of a number of decayed monasteries (see above, Chapter IV) uses a *si pastores ovium* arenga, pertinent to thirteenth-century reform, of widespread European use in various variants, one of which was used as late as 1477 in Amalfi in Archbishop Giovanni Niccolini's disposal of the property of the church of Santa Trofimena to the convent of Santa Maria Dominicarum (Amalfi, P.S., Arciv. Amalf., sec. xv, no. 5).

[76] Amalfi, P.S., Arciv. Amalf., sec. xiv, no. 8.

[77] Amalfi, P.S., Arciv. Amalf., sec. xiv, nos. 1, 2.

be preserved in the "vestiario" of "nostre ecclesie Amalfitane" and the other at the Cistercian monastery of the Canonica in Amalfi. The dorse of the preserved 1292 document says "hoc privilegium est in vestario Amalf'."[78]

These documents were the rich, cumbersome recording of a registerless chancery. They are the decorated, as the notarial instruments are the plain, signs of the Amalfitan rejection of the sort of ecclesiastical administration embodied in the registers of Lincoln and York. Filippo Augustariccio himself, the archbishop responsible for the three thirteenth-century sealed *acta*, was a reformer, at least (and the reservation is of obvious importance) in his concern for orderly monastic houses. But Filippo's work with his diocese was not reflected, except narratively, in the documents his chancery produced. The lead-sealed documents plumb an already elaborate form, the subscribed instrument, to give it, clumsily, an imposing validity, in duplicate.[79] They seem violently different from the mass of preserved instruments dealing repeatedly with the transfer of property; but the difference is bridged by the subscribed instruments. The full force of Amalfi peculiarity is seen only in the long run of three centuries' documents; but the thirteenth-century documents predict every phase of later eccentricity except longevity.

Amalfi is a neat but extreme sample of the diplomatic of the Italian church. The peculiarities, from a non-Italian point of view, of Amalfi diplomatic are obvious, tangible, and visible; and they can be seen at one time, in the little collection still preserved in the Duomo complex. Elsewhere in Italy, inexpert and unpracticed chancery scribes, that is, inexpert and

[78] Amalfi, P.S., Arciv. Amalf., sec. xiii, no. 3; the 1269 Filippo document edited by Filangieri says that it was prepared in three copies (*tria similia scripta*), one for the nuns, one for the monks, and the third for the church of Amalfi: *Codice diplomatico amalfitano*, ii, 137-138.

[79] This effect is brought out particularly forcefully in the validating clause of the 1269 Filippo document edited by Filangieri (itself actually in triplicate) with its list of validations: notary, lead seal, archbishop's subscription, other subscriptions (*Codice diplomatico amalfitano*, ii, 137-138).

unpracticed in specifically ecclesiastical business and documents, produced a sort of document archaic and cumbersome, as at Salerno, or unsure and quasi-notarial, as in the province of Benevento.[80] Inexplicably, in 1220, a Beneventan notary might, and did, merely notarize, with judges' subscriptions, the judicial confirmation by papal delegates of a sentence which the earlier judges (from Scala) had sealed.[81] In 1274 Guglielmo of Camaldoli might, and did, add his convent's or his own seal to a notarized instrument making a proctor for the convent; and so, in 1277, might, and did, the chapter of Verona, following what seems to have been their practice, add a seal to a notarized instrument making proctors for them.[82]

The problem of sealing or notarizing was obviously a bothersome one in the thirteenth-century church.[83] It is not really surprising that Filippo Augustariccio sealed (and probably with a conventional wax seal) his instrument making proctors for Lyons, a council of the whole Church assembled far outside the local neighborhood.[84] In England prelates involved in negotiations with the external church "proved" the seals of pertinent documents by describing them in notarial instruments.[85] The proctors of English debtors sometimes appended their seals to the notarized Italian bonds of their creditors, and English ecclesiastics sometimes sealed notarial instruments

[80] Good examples of archaic, cumbersome Salerno documents are: Salerno, Archivio della curia arcivescovile, arca III, nos. 142 and 153 (calendared in Antonio Balducci, L'Archivio della Curia Arcivescovile di Salerno, I, 45, 47); for the province of Benevento see Pratesi, "Note."

[81] Ravello, ex-cattedrale, bolle, no. 9; Robert Brentano, "A Ravello Document," Traditio, xv (1959), 401-404.

[82] Florence, Archivio di stato, conventi soppressi, Camaldoli, 18 Febb. 1274; Verona, Archivio capitolare, c. 48, no. 2 (and see c. 43, no. 3).

[83] This is emphasized by a collection examined in Giacomo C. Bascapè, "Bolle e sigilli di notai," Bullettino dell' "Archivio paleografico italiano," NS, II-III (1956-1957), pt. I, 59-68, and plates; see, too, the legate's 1237 enactments for England: Powicke and Cheney, 257-258.

[84] Amalfi, P.S., Arciv. Amalf., sec. xiii, no. 1.

[85] Durham, Dean and Chapter Archives, Loc. XIV.2.m for example; see Brentano, York Metropolitan Jurisdiction, 254-255.

appointing proctors to act on the continent.[86] But the general problem seems particularly acute in the Italian church; and this, of course, is perfectly consistent with the general development of its chanceries and their position in the total community.

Lead seals were not peculiar to Amalfi, although they were probably peculiarly persistent in that long-decaying city. Archbishop Cesario of Salerno used a lead seal on documents that survive from 1252, 1260, and 1261.[87] Archbishop Giacomo of Capua used a lead seal on documents from 1230, 1239, 1241, and 1242.[88] Bishop Richerio of Melfi used a lead seal on documents from May and June 1224.[89] Bishop Leonardo of Giovinazzo, active in confirming the deeds of his predecessors, used a lead seal in June 1254; and Archbishop Gervasio of Taranto used one in 1193.[90] In the eighteenth century Giannone believed that the many-prerogatived archbishops of Benevento still used their lead seals in imitation of the popes of Rome.[91] The Beneventan lead seal is mentioned as early as 988. It survives in an example from 1158, and its obverse carries the images of the Virgin and of Benevento's Saint Bartholomew.[92] Lead seals were certainly not uncommon south of lead-sealed Rome; it was once even thought that lead seals were regularly used by the ecclesiastics of the Regno from the ninth

[86] Durham, Dean and Chapter Archives, Miscellaneous Charters, 7028 and 5820 f; Brentano, York Metropolitan Jurisdiction, 220-223, 224-225. For Westminster's notaries, see Harvey, Walter de Wenlok, names listed in index under "notaries," and then indexed individually.

[87] Salerno, Archivio della curia arcivescovile, arca III, nos. 142, 151, 153; Balducci, I, 45, 47.

[88] Jole Mazzoleni, Le Pergamene di Capua (Naples, 1957-1958), I, 117-118, 130-133, 145-148, 148-150 (nos. 56, 64, 71, 73).

[89] Angelo Mercati, "Le Pergamene di Melfi all' "Archivio segreto vaticano," Miscellanea Giovanni Mercati, v, Studi e Testi, 125 (Vatican City, 1946), 262-323, 288-298 (pergamene di Melfi, II, nos. 8, 9).

[90] C.d.b., II, 198-202, nos. 19, 20; Girgensohn and Kamp, "Urkunden und Inquisitionen der Stauferzeit aus Tarent," 167-170.

[91] Pietro Giannone, Ragioni per le quali si dimostra che l'Arcivescovado Beneventano, non ostante, che il Dominio temporale della Città di Benevento fosse passato a'Romani Pontefici, sia compreso nella grazia conceduta da S.M.C.C. a'nazionali e sottoposto al Regio Exequatur, come tutti gli altri Arcivescovadi del Regno (n.d.), 9.

[92] Bartoloni, "Note," 432-433.

to the fifteenth centuries.[93] Provincial seals were undoubtedly affected by the usage of Rome.[94] The practicality of lead in "warm countries, in which an impression in wax would not retain its distinctness" has been noted (and exaggerated).[95] But the lead seals of the south are essentially a remnant of ancient Byzantine domination.[96]

Lead seals were common, but even in the south the theme was not lead but variety. Italy was more various in its seals than is the Apocalypse. In the late twelfth century Agapito of Frigento was using an oval wax seal with a standing mitered figure carrying his pastoral staff.[97] There was a wax seal at Benevento probably more antique than the lead one; and at Monreale both the archbishop and the prior used wax seals in the thirteenth century. At Cassino in the 1270's the dean's black wax made contrast with the abbot's lead. At Rieti the friar bishop, Rainaldo, used a white wax seal, and the political bishop, Pietro Gerra, used a green one.[98] At Bari a 1221 wax seal of Archbishop Andrea survives.[99] The most impressive, probably, of all Italian thirteenth-century seals, the great seal of Saint Ambrose of the archbishops of Milan, is wax and

[93] Michele Russi, *Paleografia e diplomatica de' documenti delle province Napolitane* (Naples, 1883), 162-163; Russi's statement, if I understand it correctly, seems much too sweeping, but not all of the samples upon which it was presumably based are now available.

[94] The papal bull is clearly described in Poole, *The Papal Chancery*, 119-122.

[95] Reginald L. Poole, "Seals and Documents," in *Studies in Chronology and History* (Oxford, 1934), 95.

[96] See: Gustave Schlumberger, *Sigillographie de l'Empire Byzantin* (Paris, 1884), 231-234; Arthur Engel, *Recherches sur la numismatique et la sigillographie des Normands de Sicile et d'Italie* (Paris, 1882), particularly pls. III-V; and also: Anton Eitel, *Uber Blei- und Goldbullen im Mittelalter* (Freiburg, 1912), 70-72; Bresslau, *Handbuch*, II, 588-613; Ludovico Muratori, *Antiquitates Italicae*, III (Milan, 1740): "de sigillis medii aevi," cols. 135-140.

[97] Pratesi, "Note," 42.

[98] Bartoloni, "Note," 431; Carlo Alberto Garufi, *Catalogo illustrato del tabulario di Santa Maria Nuova in Monreale* (Palermo, 1902), 52-53, nos. 115-116 (1269, 1273): the archbishop used a ring counterseal. For Cassino, see Chapter II above; for Rieti, Archivio capitolare, armadio II, fasc. B, no. 1, and fasc. E, no. 3.

[99] *C.d.b.*, I, 165-166 no. 88.

round.[100] Wax seals are common, and seal slits that once held tags that can only have carried wax are much more common.[101] They echo the cardinals' wax (like the red stag seal of Sant'-Eustachio or the white horse of San Giorgio) against the papal lead.[102] They echo too the wax of noble, communal, and regal, against some few imperial seals.[103] But, always, they are afloat in a great sea of simple notarial instruments.

The Amalfi *arenga*s and witness lists are even less unusual than the use of the leaden seal. *Arenga*s that are often moving, often apt, and often repetitive, decorate the documents of Brindisi and Benevento, and of Fermo and Milan: the *debita pastorum officia* provoke; the *viscera caritatis* open; and the apostle speaks.[104] (They do even in England.)[105] About the south of Italy witnesses subscribed their names to make large *acta* look more solemn and valid—at Cosenza, at Santa Severina, where, as elsewhere in the Greek south, Greek subscriptions mix with the Latin.[106] In the north witnesses subscribed to episcopal privileges. On the foot of a 1230 document of Bishop Enrico of Bologna the canons of the church of Bologna

---

[100] Bascapè, *Antichi diplomi*, pl. vi.

[101] Examples of this sort of slit: Cava, arca LVIII, no. 114 (Archbishop Filippo of Salerno in 1287); Rome, Archivio di stato, Fiastra, no. 2130 (Abbot Giovanni in 1299).

[102] Uberto of Sant'Eustachio's seal is described (in 1265) in a Fiastra document: Rome, Archivio di stato, Fiastra, no. 1307; for San Giorgio: Rieti, Archivio capitolare, armadio IV, fasc. D, no. 3; this does not mean to imply that each cardinal always used wax of the same color.

[103] For noble example see an Aldobrandini document with a seal of Pietro Ruffo of Calabria in white wax, round, with a horsed warrior on the obverse and arms on the reverse: Archivio segreto vaticano, Archivio Aldobrandini, documenti storici, abbadie, 4, 54; for a communal example, see Sandro Degani, "Note sul prospetto del Duomo di Cremona," *Palladio*, NS, V (1955), 109-123, 119 figs. 12, 13.

[104] Monti, *C.d.br.*, I, 84 no. 53 (1293); Bascapè, *Antichi diplomi*, 97 no. 23 (1301); Ughelli, VIII, cols. 136-137; Rome, Archivio di stato, Fiastra, no. 1207 (Fermo).

[105] See, for example, the relatively elaborate *arenga* with which in March 1281 Archbishop William Wickwane of York announced to his suffragan Robert of Holy Island, bishop of Durham, that Wickwane intended to visit Holy Island's diocese: *Wickwane*, 154.

[106] Pratesi, "Note," 308-309 no. 131; Archivio segreto vaticano, Archivio Aldobrandini, documenti storici, abbadie, 4, 55.

sit, in their subscriptions, as does the Mary of the bishop's *arenga* sit at the feet of Christ, and thus they too serve as does the *arenga*'s Martha.[107]

Just as the Amalfi validation of documents which are not simply notarial is at the showy extreme of a general Italian way of doing things, so is the Amalfi way of keeping records (or the Amalfi denial of record-keeping) an unusually pronounced and emphatic statement of the general Italian way. At Amalfi archbishops did not enroll, they made elaborate, ornate, repeatedly validated, plumbed duplicate copies, to save. As in much else, the Italian method is not completely different from the English one; it is the shading and emphasis in the patterns of the two churches which make them in fact different patterns. Duplication was certainly not unknown in England. It was used, for example, by the priory of Saint Gregory in Canterbury in the first half of the thirteenth century.[108] If the form of duplication known as the chirograph is considered, it can be seen as a generally common form of preservation in western Europe in the thirteenth century. A really important statement, one that helped define the constitutional structure of an ecclesiastical province, survives in chirograph form from the province of York and from the year 1286.[109] A

---

[107] Mazzoleni, *Esempi di scritture*, pl. xxiv. (The subscription of signatories could prove a problem for English scribes and prelates. On 11 June 1293, Archbishop-elect Winchelsey of Canterbury wrote Canterbury, as he said he had repeatedly before, for fresh copies of his electoral "Decretum" with the signatures of individual monks [and a formula statement and mark by any monk who might prove illiterate], not signatures all in one clerical hand like those in the copy of the "Decretum" originally given to the Canterbury clerk, William of Sardinia: Rose Graham, "Archbishop Winchelsey: from his Election to his Enthronement," *Church Quarterly Review*, cxlviii [1949], 169-170.)

[108] Audrey M. Woodcock, *Cartulary of the Priory of St. Gregory, Canterbury*, Camden Third Series, 88 (London, 1956), 113 no. 152 (. . . *cartam nostram . . . dupplicauimus*) and (chirographs) 169-170 nos. 1, 6-7.

[109] Brentano, *York Metropolitan Jurisdiction*, 252-253 and pl. 1; this, significantly, is not an exact duplication of the other parts of the chirograph: each party kept a segment with its opponent's but not its own seal, with appropriate and related variation in the actual wording of the document; for this in Italy (Monreale): Garufi, 59 no. 131.

1206 agreement between Abbot Samson of Bury and the men of Southwold was written as a chirograph.[110] But both these sorts of chirograph are different from Italian duplication in its most extreme form: they are not kept as the record of unenrolled episcopal *acta*. They are instead the guarantees kept by the two sides of a compromise, a patent compact, not one obscured by the process of administrative government. Even the Saint Gregory documents represent transactions in land and rent or agreements for which duplications (chirograph or not) are natural and helpful recording documents. This is distinctly less true about a document granting a license for constructing a chapel or regulating incomes among cathedral clergy. In a practiced episcopal chancery of the late thirteenth-century English sort, these documents would demand to be enrolled in an official register.

The Amalfi kind of duplication went on elsewhere in Italy: at Melfi, at Larino, at Orvieto.[111] But there was, of course, some enrollment. Monasteries kept cartularies. Cassino under Berard was a great enroller.[112] Camaldoli recorded its documents carefully.[113] In the rich collection of documents from Fiastra there is the beginning of a codex cartulary from the period between 1285 and 1306, and the Fiastra notary Buonconsiglio kept a protocol that his successor could use.[114] There is even a little beginning to enrollment from the Benedictines of San Cosimato at the end of the twelfth century.[115] But, with the exception of Città di Castello and of course Rome (and Roman officials) and in a way Cassino, one does not really

[110] R.H.C. Davis, *The Kalendar of Abbot Samson of Bury St. Edmunds and Related Documents*, Camden Third Series, 84 (London, 1954), 151 no. 130.

[111] Angelo Mercati, 288-298, nos. 6-7 (see 297 for retention in "armario ecclesie Melfiensis"); Pratesi, "Note," 82-84 no. 15; Luigi Fumi, *Statuti e regesti dell'opera di Santa Maria di Orvieto* (Rome, 1891), 86-89, no. 5; and for Vercelli, see Domenico Arnoldi, *Le Carte dello archivio arcivescovile di Vercelli* (Pinerolo, 1917), 324.

[112] See above, Chapter II.

[113] See the great collection in conventi soppressi, Archivio di stato, Florence.

[114] Rome, Archivio di stato, Fiastra, nos. 1814, 1993.

[115] Rome, Archivio di stato, San Cosimato, no. 178.

find the enrollment of episcopal administrative *acta*; and the discovery of a few more exceptions would not change the picture.[116] Italian ecclesiastical enrollment, where it exists, is dominated by two very qualifying characteristics: it is generally notarial in that the notary employed to do the church's business records it as he does his other business, although sometimes in a roll or codex restricted to the church's business; Italian enrollment generally records only transactions in property (or, as at Valdiponte, money) and thus is not in any way either particularly ecclesiastical or (in a nonfiscal sense) administrative.[117] The memory of Italian official ecclesiastical administration did not seem an important memory—that was not where Italian life was.

The pattern of enrollment is echoed in the pattern of preservation. There are magnificent dumps of documents—Fiastra, Montevergine, Camaldoli, Cassino—that were obviously purposefully preserved. The church of Veroli still keeps 257 thirteenth-century documents. Amalfi kept its lead documents in archives; and Melfi had its *armadio*. Bishop Guglielmino Ubertini of Arezzo carefully regulated the keeping of archives in the *canonica* at Arezzo. Careful bishops and heads of houses, like Leonardo, bishop of Giovinazzo, and Isabella, abbess of Conversano, had old documents copied to save them from decay—the sort of activity that in another geographical context should have suggested enrollment.[118] But the record-

[116] See, for papal officials, D. P. Waley, "A Register of Boniface VIII's Chamberlain, Theoderic of Orvieto," *The Journal of Ecclesiastical History*, VIII (1957), 141-152, or Conrad Eubel, "Der Registerband des Cardinal grosspönitentiars Bentevenga," *Archiv für katholisches Kirchenrecht*, LXIV [N.F. LVII] (1890), 3-69.

[117] For a nice description of the distinction between different kinds of enrollments—cartularies as opposed to registers and letter-books—see W. A. Pantin, "English Monastic Letter Books," in *Historical Essays in Honour of James Tait*, ed. J. G. Edwards, V. H. Galbraith, and E. F. Jacob (Manchester, 1933), 201-222; for a descriptive analysis of the medieval manner of keeping one important set of English ecclesiastical archives, see Jane E. Sayers, "The Medieval Care and Custody of the Archbishop of Canterbury's Archives," *Bulletin of the Institute of Historical Research*, XXXIX (1966), 95-107.

[118] Camillo Scaccia Scarafoni, "L'Archivio capitolare della Cattedrale di Veroli," *ASRSP*, LXXVII, 3rd ser., VIII (1954), 91-96, 93. Corrado

ing of the Italian community's important actions did not de-
pend upon the preservation of records in ecclesiastical, and
particularly, episcopal archives. The community's notaries
were its memory.

The peculiar pattern of the survival of documents in Italy
is due in large part to a succession of natural disasters—earthquakes, floods—to wars and suppressions; but it is also due to
the original deposit. The pathetic remnant of the Verona
capitular archives, with its four thirteenth-century documents,
is much more representative of the bulk of Italian ecclesiastical
collections than is the rich hoard of Fiastra with its thousands
of documents; and this is true in part because of the relatively
casual attitude the thirteenth-century Italian church took toward preserving the records of its official acts and because of
the broad dispersion of its thin and limited authority. What
was preserved has a particular shape: it is connected more
with monasteries than with the thirteenth-century adminis-
trative-episcopal church; it is overwhelmingly concerned with
property; it is notarial; a relatively disproportionate amount
of it (in the absence of other material) is concerned with the
work of papal delegates and officials; when it is more than all
this implies, as in the case of Federigo Visconti's records, it is
sometimes very personally connected with the figure it
surrounds.

The Italian documents that survive are a constant denial of
the existence of a truly important governmental church with
a major role to play in the Italian community (even as the
expression and repository of the community's spirituality).
The diplomatic of the single document of Manasses, bishop
of Volturara, fits the business of the document exactly.[119] The
twenty-nine-year lease is preserved in a rather elegant but
otherwise ordinary notarial instrument with a judge's sub-
script. The document is no more episcopal than the act.

The distillation or crystallization of Italian dioceses in

Lazzeri, *Guglielmino Ubertini* (Florence, 1920), 151; see Leonardo
above; Giovanni Mongelli, "Le Abbadesse Mitrate," 377-381.

[119] Archivio segreto vaticano, documenti storici, abbadie, 4, 3; see
above, Chapter III; of course it is possible, and probable even, that other
(unknown to me) Manasses documents may exist.

Italian archives confirms one's impression that the Italian diocese was not, at least relatively, an extended, administered,
geographical thing. The episcopal chancery was not shaped by
isolation in an illiterate community. It was not freed from the
surrounding, corroding, supporting society. The episcopal
chancery was not free, partly because of the nature of the en-
veloping society. That society was given much of its tone by
an urban, notarial, literate, business community. In general,
the chanceries employed ordinary local notaries for occasional
ecclesiastical business. Giacomo Sabbatino at Amalfi and John
of Schalby at Lincoln were different sorts of clerks; and they
looked out at, and saw, and wrote about very different
churches.

A church writes about itself in many ways. The thirteenth-
century English and Italian churches wrote their autobiog-
raphies unceasingly and at very various levels of sophistication, self-awareness, and intellectuality. Aquinas and Pecham
were writing, among many other things, of Italy and England. But, in their scholastic writings, they were both so much
more obviously writing of Paris and of its international world
that it would take the most learned sensitivity in the observer as
well as the sharpest preconception of what is, in the scholastic,
English or Italian, to isolate their national strains.

The difference between those composites of talking scholars,
the universities, is more susceptible to a crude and general
examination. There are noticeable differences between Italian
and English universities, and they echo and amplify other differences between the ecclesiastical and literate communities
within the two societies. Oxford was a second Paris.[120] It was
a center for the study of arts and theology serving locally the

[120] For Oxford see particularly Hastings Rashdall, *The Universities
of Europe in the Middle Ages*, new edition, ed. F. M. Powicke and A.
B. Emden (Oxford, 1936), III, 1-273, especially 140, and H. E. Salter,
Medieval Oxford, Oxford Historical Society, 100 (Oxford, 1936), 90-
112: I think that Salter's view of Oxford and civil law is mistaken (see
p. 95).

international Gothic clerical community of which Paris and the papal court were the centers (although Oxford was relatively more concerned with the law than was Paris, because, no doubt, of its isolated English position).

Bologna was not another Paris either in constitution or curriculum.[121] Although overwhelmingly preeminent, Bologna was not nearly so alone in Italy as Oxford was in England. The Italian universities, although swept into the organized structure of thirteenth-century *studia* and not devoid of the arts, were, very strongly, professional schools interested in the law and medicine; and these professions were, particularly in Italy, not very distinctly ecclesiastical.[122] They were certainly not ecclesiastical in the sense that the theology of Oxford was. The universities of Italy were also clearly more municipal than were those of the north; of this Piacenza is an outstanding example.[123] It is perfectly consistent with the general nature of the Italian community and the relatively slack and unformed structure of the church within that community that the Italian universities should seem less specifically engaged than were the English in a separate ecclesiastical society.

The difference between universities is, however, a difficult and technical one. It does not lend itself to elucidating an historical comparison of which it is not the center. This is true, a little more, a little less, at least in the thirteenth century, for most intellectual and all academic disciplines. Professional thought (like the professional practice of law) was a very elaborate game. Only unconvincing generalizations can be drawn from its surface. But some thought—articulate, written and preserved at length, elaborately descriptive—was fortu-

[121] For Bologna see particularly Rashdall, I, 87-268.

[122] For a list of the distinguishing characteristics of Italian universities, as they seemed to Rashdall, see Rashdall, II, 58-62; for a deeper and more recent examination of the complexity of one university center see Helene Wieruszowski, "Arezzo as a Center of Learning and Letters in the Thirteenth Century," *Traditio,* IX (1953), 321-391; see, too, F. M. Powicke, "Bologna, Paris, Oxford: Three *Studia Generalia,*" in *Ways of Medieval Life and Thought* (London, n.d.), 149-179, particularly 168.

[123] Rashdall, II, 35-38.

nately not professional, at least in the academic sense. Of this sort of written thought, the most obvious to an historian is history.

Through the mid-twelfth century, history was probably as respectable an intellectual discipline as any other; but the hardening of the university curriculum, which of course excluded history, and that curriculum's and its method's domination of all formal academic thought removed history to the intellectually frivolous periphery of serious studies. In its frivolity history became (or in some descents remained) garrulous, straightforward, and helpfully obvious and informal.

In comparing thirteenth-century England and Italy two historians demand to be considered. They have loud, obtrusive, unsubtle voices; they have a great deal to say in great detail. They, like very many of their colleagues, write from within the church (however it be defined); and their writing constantly describes the church (again however it be defined) both consciously and accidentally. They are of course Matthew Paris and Salimbene de Adam—the first an English Benedictine monk, the second an Italian Franciscan friar. They were not exact contemporaries. Matthew Paris was born at an unknown place in about 1200 and died in 1259, probably in June and almost surely at Saint Albans. Salimbene was born on 9 October 1221 in Parma and he died sometime after 8 September 1287 at an unknown place.[124] (The difference between what is known and not known in these dates is, it will be seen, clearly connected with other differences between the two historians.)

In selecting Matthew Paris and Salimbene as the representative historians of their two countries, one is, in spite of their loud obviousness, being in some senses arbitrary. There were lots of other historians in both countries. Some of the others, like the Cassino notary Richard of San Germano in Italy and the Saint Albans monk Roger Wendover in England, are quite distinguished. Of the less distinguished particularly,

---

[124] For Matthew Paris's life, including dates, see Richard Vaughan, *Matthew Paris* (Cambridge, 1958), 1-20; for Salimbene's life, see the preface by B. Schmeidler to O. Holder-Egger's edition of Salimbene in *M.G.H.*, vii-xx.

Matthew Paris and Salimbene are not typical, not so much because their attitudes are noticeably different as because the lesser historians' attitudes are often not very noticeable at all. Matthew Paris was an influential historian, but Salimbene was not.[125] The two are chosen because they have so much to say. The arbitrariness of the selection, like the articulateness of the historians, is meant to make a sharp contrast with the relatively random selection of the relatively inarticulate documents in archival hoards. If in fact in their differences the two categories of writers seem in some ways to be saying the same things it might make what both say sound more convincing.

In many ways Matthew Paris and Salimbene are very much alike. They both represent very clearly a category of historians that can be called for convenience "thirteenth-century." It is a category that makes particular sense when it is made to contrast with a chronologically immediately preceding category that can be called, again for convenience, "twelfth-century." When compared with their predecessors, "thirteenth-century" historians can be seen to have common qualities both negative and positive. In the first place, their interests and abilities are more confined to contemporary history than are their predecessors', whose general histories the later historians in many cases continued. Partly in connection with this (and of course with the expansion of written government) the "thirteenth-century" historians have a "wider technique" in their command of "more extensive sources."[126] (Both Matthew Paris and Salimbene, although attracted to quite different sources, are remarkably imaginative, at least on the surface level, in their uses of sources.) "Thirteenth-century" historians are more interested in man as an intricately political and social animal than are "twelfth-century" historians; and they are less interested in man alone with God, in the patterns of the psyche, than are "twelfth-century" historians. (In this they exactly

---

[125] Vaughan, 152-155 (Matthew's influence was greatest through his *Flores Historiarum*, not his *Chronica Majora*).

[126] The phrases are from V. H. Galbraith, *Historical Research in Medieval England* (London, 1951), 30, a lecture-essay which boldly attacks the changes in medieval historiography as does no other work (to my knowledge) and which is thus of unique value.

parallel and record the change in the nature of ecclesiastical enthusiasm and reform between the two centuries.) Closely connected with this difference is another. "Thirteenth-century" historians are interested in the surface of event and the description of things—individual events and things. They turn away from the "twelfth-century" probing of interiors, ideas, minds, "reality." The "twelfth-century" historian threw away the husks of things to get at the important meaning inside. The "thirteenth-century" historian, like the thirteenth-century natural scientist or theologian, knew that the husks were important, but he did not, as they did, know or explain why. The "thirteenth-century" historian was no longer Augustinian really (and the "twelfth-century" historian had been the finest product of the school); his surfaces are often held together by simple prejudices, persuasions, and emotional attitudes, not by the grand controlling ideas of his predecessors. He is very far from Otto of Freising.

Example is clearer than generalization. A great water image can be taken from an historian on either side of the twelfth-, thirteenth-century break: one from William of Malmesbury's *Historia Novella*, written in the years around 1140 and one from Jean, Sire de Joinville's *Histoire de Saint Louis*, finished in the early years of the fourteenth century but written from thirteenth-century memories. In writing background to his examination of the troubles of Stephen's reign, William of Malmesbury goes back to the last years of Henry I's reign and approaches Henry's death from the other side. Henry died in Normandy in December 1135, but the scene around which William arranges the discussion of Henry's death occurred in August 1133. It is the last crossing of Henry from England to Normandy. "God's providence jested strangely then with human affairs" (echoing Ovid); it was the anniversary of Henry's happy crowning.[127] The universe, at least the literary universe, is caught in the action: "The elements accompanied with their sorrow the last crossing of so great a prince."[128] Virgil remembering Caesar's death in the Georgics offers appro-

[127] K. R. Potter, *The Historia Novella by William of Malmesbury* (Edinburgh, 1955), 11-12.
[128] Potter, 12.

priate words for the eclipse on the day of sailing, and William himself steps forward to say he saw (apocalyptically) the stars around the sun.[129] And in the earthquake a few days later William saw the wall of his house rise twice and fall. This movement of the universe and strangeness of numbers, with Virgil and William watching together, set Henry's tragic death and the fall of ordered government in a universal setting. The essentially undescribed crossing is followed by a counting of the days and months to the night on which Henry died.

On Saint Mark's Day 1254, Louis IX set sail for France, back from crusade. It was the king's birthday, and Joinville jested that in leaving for France he was born again. On the way home, probably after the company had sailed by Pantelleria, the scene that makes high contrast with William's takes place. The queen had gone to bed in her cabin. One of her women threw the kerchief from the queen's head too close to a candle. It and the queen's clothes caught fire. The queen jumped up naked and threw the kerchief into the sea, and she put out the fire in her clothes. Some men in the barge following the ship cried "Fire" but not loudly. Joinville raised his head and saw the burning kerchief on the sea. It burned clearly and the sea was still.[130] The scene is described in detail. Joinville finds it visually interesting, but not in any major way significant. It is immediately followed by a little scene of interchanged conversations, of the king's unrest, of precautions against similar dangers in the future. The episode is followed by another related to it because it too was an incident at sea.[131]

[129] The Virgil is Georgics, Bk. 1, line 467. It is rearranged in William, who says "ut poete solent dicere." The source is a remarkably appropriate one: Virgil talks of the sun as omen and echo of human activity in the incident of Caesar's assassination. Miss Linda Mackersie, in a seminar paper delivered at the University of California, has pointed out that William's classical allusions repeatedly show a familiarity with and understanding of the surrounding classical text, and the reference in William is more effective if the reader recalls the source.

[130] Natalis de Wailly, *Jean, Sire de Joinville, Histoire de Saint Louis, Credo, et Lettre à Louis X* (Paris, 1874), 354-355 (Frank T. Marzials, *Memoirs of the Crusades* [New York, 1958], 298).

[131] Wailly, 356-357 (Marzials, 299).

A squire, trying in the morning to keep the sun from shining through a hole in the ship on his lord's face, fell into the sea. He prayed to the Virgin, who miraculously held him up in the water. Joinville, having found this out from him, later had the scene painted in his chapel at Joinville and put in stained glass at Blécourt.

Joinville is literal and descriptive and interested in the individual incident. Malmesbury is literary and allusive and interested in the connections between the individual incident and the universe. Malmesbury's insertion of self heightens the reality of the nonphysical; Joinville himself treasures the physical—the sight, the painting.

The difference between "twelfth-" and "thirteenth-century" is seen again if Joinville's tale of the squire's not drowning is cast against the repeated twelfth-century scene of the sinking of the White Ship and the death of Henry I's only legitimate son. The twelfth century muses slowly on the vanity of earthly values and the transitory quality of earthly glory; Joinville produces his quick miracle.

Perhaps the clearest notion of the change is seen in contrasting biographies, and never more clearly than in the contrast between Walter Daniel's portrait of Ailred of Rievaulx and Jocelin of Brakelond's of Samson of Bury.[132] Walter Daniel, writing about 1170, described Ailred by describing the qualities of his mind and soul, his emotions and his books; Walter Daniel described Rievaulx, the Cistercian Yorkshire house of which Ailred was abbot, essentially in terms of the affections which inhabited that "haunt of peace."[133] Jocelin wrote his Chronicle into the early thirteenth century. His Samson is a man with bald head, thick lips, and a red beard turning white, a man who grew hoarse with even a slight

[132] F. M. Powicke, *The Life of Ailred of Rievaulx by Walter Daniel*, Nelson's Medieval Classics (Edinburgh, 1950); H. E. Butler, *The Chronicle of Jocelin of Brakelond*, Nelson's Medieval Classics (Edinburgh, 1949). I do not mean to disguise the differences in order—Cistercian, Benedictine.

[133] Powicke, *Life*, 37; Walter Daniel does count the monks, but, I think, to give force to his image of the monastery as broad sea; still his work is not devoid of physical detail where it can heighten the effect of spirituality.

cold.[134] Bury, the Benedictine abbey of which Samson was abbot, is a place of buildings and acres, income and rights. In the movement from Walter Daniel to Jocelin of Brakelond reality has become physical, and sentiment has turned into act.

Matthew Paris and Salimbene are safely on the thirteenth-century side of this divide. Neither of them breaks through to the kind of piercing greatness in history that their fellows Jocelin of Brakelond and Joinville do. Jocelin watches and stays within a small and personally known scene (with, at a flaming center, a saint's relics); and he describes it with a talent so stunning and visual that the talent disguises certain reticences of spirit and defects of intellect.[135] (Talent serves him rather as it does Stubbs and Parkman.) Jocelin is a monk in his monastery, Joinville a layman in the great world. Joinville's being a layman is connected with his greatness. Uneducated in the conventional sense, relatively unread, he may have been unaware that he wrote a sort of work that was no longer intellectually respectable. This allows his work (in spite of an occasional sense in it of aged feline conservatism) its glistening intensity. Matthew Paris and Salimbene lack Jocelin's and Joinville's brilliance, but they are big, long, widespread, and literate.

They are also quick, physical, prejudiced and gossipy, interested in scandal, appearance, and action. Their minds fall easily into verbal and conceptual cliché when they approach motive, significance, internal reality.[136] They are as far as the thirteenth century can take them from the slow brooding spirituality of William of Malmesbury—with its love of mind and of learning, its interest in the reason of generalization and the understanding of government, with its contempt for the world and its love for William's island, glowing with the glory of remembered saints in the places where their bodies had been and were.[137] Against William's depth, Matthew and Salim-

---

[134] Butler, 39.

[135] For the great relic: Butler, 106-117.

[136] Vaughan has made lists of the repeated vocabulary, imagery, and allusion of which Matthew Paris was particularly fond: 126-129.

[137] William of Malmesbury's biography has been summarized recent-

bene are facile, if attractive, prattle. Their thoughts are, like the rivers of Japan, short, swift, and shallow.

In all this Matthew and Salimbene are very much alike. But in many ways they are also very different. Their most stunning difference, and one that is very significant in them, can be seen physically—in their movement, in their collection of sources. Matthew Paris stayed still, behind his monastery walls, and listened to the tales of visitors. Salimbene moved about northern Italy and southern France gathering his information.

The two modes are not literally mutually exclusive. In 1248 Matthew Paris went to Norway because he had been asked for by the monks of Saint Benedict Holm on the island of Nidarholm to visit and reform them according to the rule of Saint Benedict. Besides his great trip across the sea, Matthew Paris sometimes left the monastery to be present at the great events of the kingdom of England as he was at Westminster in 1247 on Saint Edward's Day when he talked to the king.[138] But generally Matthew stayed at home, in his abbey at Saint Albans. His sources came to him: the king visited the monastery at least nine times between 1220 and 1259; Otto the legate, Richard earl of Cornwall, the queen, the archbishop of Canterbury, the bishops of Norwich and Bangor, royal councillors and papal emissaries came.[139] Matthew got his information from people like the king of Norway, the bishop of Beirut, a messenger of the king of Castille, a goldsmith, a Cahorsin moneylender, people who brought or sent stories of distant places to Matthew.[140]

Salimbene, the Parman, lived in many places in Italy, at Bologna, Ferrara, Modena, Ravenna, in Franciscan house after Franciscan house. But he traveled too, to Genoa, to Lyons, to Auxerre. He went to the place where Innocent IV was, and listened to him talk, and wrote down what he said. He found the bustle of a seaport fascinating and learned from listening

---

ly by Dom Hugh Farmer: "William of Malmesbury's Life and Works," *Journal of Ecclesiastical History*, XIII (1962), 39-54.

[138] The Norwegian trip and Matthew's other movements are examined carefully in Vaughan, 2-7.

[139] Vaughan, 11-13.

[140] Vaughan, 13-17.

to travelers who sailed in and out of it. He sat in foreign re-
fectories at dinner, tasted the foreign food, and remembered
the foreign tales.[141] In his Chronicle, he followed a character,
like Rainaldo of Rieti, about, learning his plot on the move.[142]
He tasted the wines, white and red, of Auxerre and compared
them with the wines of northern Italy; he looked at country
against country and compared them with his own eyes, walking about to get a better view.[143] "I have seen much and lived
in many provinces. . . ."[144] Salimbene went on quest, and
Matthew Paris kept the hoard.

The difference between the two historians, one gathering
things behind his walls, the other chasing the world, is of
course the difference between their two orders. One is very
Benedictine, the other very Franciscan. But they chose their
orders—or at least Salimbene chose his, fighting his father
to do it, offending his father for life. If Matthew Paris did not
choose the Benedictine life because he thought it appropriate
for himself (and one cannot know), it was chosen for him
by his parents or guardians—an even more complete contrast
with Salimbene's rebellion.

One can know about Salimbene's early life and his family as
one cannot know of Matthew Paris's, because Salimbene is
anxious to tell about it—parents, ancestors, siblings, cousins,
connections, home, personal detail—to write it all down and
save it, to have it noted. In this, too, Salimbene was Franciscan. In spite of their early illiteracy the Franciscans were a
very literary, or at least much-writing, troop. They liked anecdote, and presumably—but not certainly—they liked it better
if it was didactic and lent itself to effective sermonizing.[145]
They also liked the personal, the odor of sentiment and do-
mesticity more fragrant when crushed, rejected, and lamented.
Sharp anecdotal scandal and sweetness are sometimes curi-

[141] Salimbene, vii-xx, and for example, 206, 217-221, 313-318.
[142] Salimbene, 324-328.
[143] Salimbene, 217-221.
[144] Salimbene, 38.
[145] For a discussion of Franciscan chronicles see A. G. Little, "Chronicles of the Mendicant Friars," in *Franciscan Papers, Lists, and Documents* (Manchester, 1943), 25-41.

ously intertwined around the latticework of Franciscan chronicles. They are in Salimbene.[146]

One anecdote that Salimbene tells of his own childhood is particularly striking. It is of an experience that he cannot have remembered, of which he had to be told, because it happened in 1222, the year after his birth. Salimbene in fact says that it was something of which his mother used to tell him when she told stories of the great earthquake that shook northern Italy in 1222. Salimbene's parents' house was right next to the baptistry at Parma. When Salimbene's mother felt the force of the great quake she was terrified. She thought that the baptistry might fall on the house. She ran to the house of her father and mother and brothers for safety. She took Salimbene's two sisters, one under each arm, with her. But Salimbene himself, an infant in a crib, she left. And Salimbene says, "And for this I loved her less surely because she should have cared more for me a boy than for her daughters. But she herself said that they were easier for her to carry because they were a little bigger."[147]

This mother, named Inmelda, Salimbene called a humble lady and devoted to God, much given to fasting and alms, never angry, never striking anyone, but rather each winter taking into her household some poor indigent from the hills. She died a Claress and was buried at the Clares; and as Salimbene says this he bursts into a prayer for her soul. Of his mother's mother, the lady Maria, Salimbene says little more than that she was pretty and fleshy and that her family lived next to the church of Saint George.[148] Of his father's mother the lady Enmengarda he says more. She lived one hundred years, and fifteen of them in Salimbene's father's house while Salimbene was alive and there; and she taught him to seek good company and to be good and wise. These two women were not alone in Salimbene's father's life. The woman Rechelda was Salimbene's

[146] There seems to be a good deal of similarity between the taste or tone of Salimbene and that of Ubertino da Casale: Decima L. Douie, *The Nature and Effect of the Heresy of the Fraticelli* (Manchester, 1932), 143.

[147] Salimbene, 34.

[148] Salimbene, 55.

father's concubine and the mother of Salimbene's brother Gio-vanni—a handsome man and a good warrior, who voluntarily exiled himself from Parma, went off to fight for the emperor, then in penance went to Compostela, then stopped and mar-ried in Toulouse, and there died and was buried in the friars' house.[149]

Salimbene tells of these women, of his bastard brother, and of his two, presumably older, legitimate brothers, and his three sisters, and of the greater extended family (decorated with romantic, paladin names) and its connections—extended out through the streets of Parma as well as the rungs of consan-guinity. At the center of all is Salimbene's father, Guido de Adam, handsome, brave, well connected and a crusader.[150] He was the conscious antagonist against whom Salimbene moved when he was seventeen and became a friar. Salimbene cut him-self free from the nest by the baptistry where he had been left as an infant. His father never forgave him, but Salimbene won to Franciscan allegiances many members of his family, in-cluding of course his mother.

Salimbene was conscious of the fact that he had said much about his genealogy, even though he had been forced to leave out many important historical events, and he said so. For do-ing it he had numbered reasons, its usefulness, the example of the ancients, Saint James on the transitory quality of life, but also and first because he had been asked to by his niece Suor'Agnese, of the Parma house of Clares: and Paul wrote to Timothy of the care of one's own.[151] (Suor'Agnese, like Henry Adams's nieces, excuses this history; and for her sup-posedly the style was made simple.)[152]

The whole Chronicle is a personal affair. It blossoms at Salimbene's birth.[153] It is an extension of Salimbene's self. His movement gives it its pattern. The chronological sequence, the little boxes of yearly events, with which, moving out of Sicard of Cremona, it begins, are soon shattered and discarded. The opposite is true of Matthew Paris's *Chronica Majora*. To him the years are very important. They are in fact boxes,

[149] Salimbene, 54.
[150] Salimbene, 37.
[151] Salimbene, 56-57.
[152] Salimbene, 187.
[153] Salimbene, 34.

or drawers, which give coherence to almost accidentally adjacent events. The effect is emphasized by his yearly sum-
maries in which he sums up the general nature and most important events of each year, and by his fifty-year summary in
1250.[154] The difference between the chronological organization of Salimbene's *Chronica* and Matthew Paris's *Chronica
Majora* is reminiscent of the difference between the geographical organization of Federigo Visconti's visitation book and
John Romeyn's register—the former following the movement
of the man, the second divided into archdeaconries.

Instead of the stories of a personal youth, Matthew Paris
tells the history of his monastery. Instead of a difficult fight
with his father embedded in a pattern of consanguinity, Matthew Paris has a list of abbots, succeeding each other to the
same institutional position, with whom he has a running "constitutional" argument concerning the power of abbot over
monk, spiritual father over spiritual son.[155] Salimbene fought
for freedom to leave his father's house; Matthew Paris condemned abbots who tyrannically sent monks away from the
motherhouse of Saint Albans to distant cells.[156] But (to twist)
the most gently moving, familial scene in either is probably
that in Matthew Paris in which the child prince Edward
stands on the shore crying as the sea carries the king, his father, Henry III, from his sight.[157] Emotion between members

[154] Matthew Paris, *Chronica Majora*, v, 191-197; Reginald Lane Poole
seems to me to miss the point rather grotesquely with his "only the
annalistic framework remains. The book is a History": *Chronicles and
Annals* (Oxford, 1926), 73.

[155] For a recent discussion of Matthew Paris's "constitutionalism"
see Vaughan, 139-140, 187-188; it is interesting to compare Matthew's
attitude with Jocelin's—Jocelin identifies with the choir monks but
does not apply the identification to external politics.

[156] William Wats, *Matthaei Paris . . . Historia Major . . .* (London,
1684), 990-1074 ("Vitae viginti trium abbatum S. Albani"), e.g. 1045
(2)—i.e. the second page so numbered; or see more conveniently in
Gesta Abbatum Monasterii Sancti Albani, I, ed. Henry Thomas Riley,
Rolls Series (London, 1867), 217-253, Matthews' entire consideration
of the abbacy of John de Cella; see a reference to this attitude in
Vaughan, 187-188, where it is placed in its context with Matthew's
other views.

[157] Matthew Paris, *Chronica Majora*, v, 383; cited and translated in
Vaughan, 130.

of the same family is such a usual device for Salimbene to use
in connecting the individual people in his world with each
other that it cannot ever in his history find the fresh power
that it does in Matthew Paris's unusual instance.

Both Matthew Paris and Salimbene are interesting on foreigners and foreignness. Matthew Paris is a xenophobe.
Strangers are always threatening England and the English
church, prying into its treasure; they are clothed by Matthew
in his sexually suggestive imagery of hatred. Salimbene on the
other hand is the amateur sociologist interested in foreign
mores. Salimbene talks of meeting and spending time with
the friar John of Plano Carpini (Pian del Carpine), who was
then carrying, and explicating, his book on the customs of the
Tartars; and in the same passage he writes of the difference
between the black monks of France (and Burgundy, where
he was) and of Italy.[158]

In the first year (1235) of that part of the *Chronica Majora*
which is original to him, Matthew Paris writes of the friars.[159]
They are a threat. They insinuate themselves into the territory
of noble monasteries. They pretend that they will preach and
go; but they linger and steal away the hearts and gifts of the
laity. It is an absolutely characteristic passage, and a central
one, in various ways. It is suspicious of an intruder, untrusting.
It states a preference for the way things are and have been.
It is concerned with money and property. It speaks in terms of
institutions and territories. It does not recognize any just attraction in spiritual enthusiasm.

Under the year 1246 Matthew Paris tells of the bishop of
Carlisle, Walter Mauclerc, who resigned his see and became a
Dominican.[160] The act does not capture Matthew's imagination or interest. He explains it by saying that the bishop was
afraid that he did not hold the see legitimately. The contrast

[158] Salimbene, 206-207, 210-213.
[159] Matthew Paris, *Chronica Majora*, III, 332-333; Margaret (Mrs.
William) Coit has allowed me to read her essay on the response of the
English monastic chroniclers to the friars in the thirteenth century. It
would make Matthew's reaction seem typical, except in its articulateness, for the chroniclers of his time and later.
[160] Matthew Paris, *Chronica Majora*, IV, 564.

with Salimbene's long concern with Rainaldo's contemporary resignation of the see of Rieti is very sharp.[161]

Salimbene's interests are centered in the acts of enthusiasm of individual men, the often sudden dominance of one element in a checkered psyche. With this sudden dominance he connects texts—particularly biblical ones, Paul, Psalms. In the arguments around Rainaldo's rejection of the see of Rieti, in which Salimbene takes personal part, there is a search for a text which will be a key to spring Rainaldo's mind. In his own rejection of his father Salimbene finds the key in Matthew 10, "Who loves father and mother more than me. . . ."[162] That it contradicts his lighter argument from Paul about genealogy is not pertinent; they are separate. Both texts are like keys in a drawer full of keys, the sacred texts of the past, to be chosen for the individual case; it is a drawer that is opened in moments when Salimbene feels some desire for spiritual enthusiasm. The elevation of enthusiasm and the sacred memory are all the connection that the individual incidents demand.

Salimbene is involved in a sort of intellectuality of magic. Sometimes he seems aware of divine purpose in the universe; sometimes he seems only to be playing a game with texts he has heard more learned men speak. With his major characters, mixed bishops like Obizzo of Parma, sometimes he seems to be searching for classical reformation, real conversion; sometimes he seems only an alchemist watching the external manifestations of the disparate parts of the brain.[163] But he is almost always personal, and his Chronicle is a group of men and texts floating fairly freely in an observed universe—their connection, when it exists, a sort of magical-spiritual assumption about reality, Joachimite-Franciscan.[164]

Matthew Paris is stable and institutional. He is fixed in his monastery. His constant fear is that his monastery, which is

[161] Salimbene, 324-328, and above, Chapter III.

[162] Salimbene, 40.

[163] Salimbene, 62; above, Chapter III; for a flash of Salimbene and the God-directed universe, the scene in which the old friar at Città di Castello convinces him to change his name: Salimbene, 38-39 ("nemo bonus nisi solus Deus").

[164] The Chronicle is shot through with Joachim, but see Salimbene, 236ff.

very rich, will grow less rich, which is very powerful, will grow less powerful. In great wealth he fears institutional poverty. Nagging at the periphery of his consciousness is, perhaps, the awareness of the fact that Saint Albans wealth is, in the new set of values of his day, unexcused and purposeless. But on the surface of his mind is his awareness of his existing essentially as a part of Saint Albans. His group is the monks of his monastery. In the disputes between monastery and abbot, his position is clear; and so it is in disputes between monastery and pope or king. But also Matthew's placing himself within a group, his seeing himself as essentially part of an institution, is reflected by (or reflects) his external world organized into similar groups and institutions; and in their disputes his sympathies are foreordained. He is a "constitutionalist" not just because Saint Albans is a baron against the king, but also for the now familiar reason that the barons against the king are oligarchs like the monks against the abbot. When a bishop or archbishop visits and corrects the religious institutions of his diocese, Matthew's Chronicle does not record a mere clash of personalities, it describes the opposition of two conventional institutions; and they are seen also as physical institutions, geographically placed. Matthew's England is a pattern of contiguous dioceses covering the land, mapping it.[165] They enclose distinct geographical peculiars and exempt areas. His Saint Albans is very much a place of walls and fields, roofs and belfries, charters.

Matthew Paris reveals his position in dealing with Robert Grosseteste and Hugh Pateshall.[166] Grosseteste is a saintly bishop, a conservative concept that Matthew is perfectly willing to accept and honor, one that his universe even needs. Grosseteste is a university intellectual, a concept that Matthew Paris is incapable of understanding—his own learning is conservative and monastic, and his attitude toward universities is

[165] For example, a bishop of Bath tells Matthew of an earthquake in his diocese (*Chronica Majora*, v, 46); Grosseteste descends upon his; see, too, *Chronica Majora*, III, 517.

[166] Matthew Paris, *Chronica Majora*, for Grosseteste examples, III, 523, 528-529, 638-639; IV, 151, 232; V, 389-392, 429, 448, 692-693; for Hugh, IV, 1-2, 121-122.

vague and ambiguous.[167] Grosseteste is a man who resists the impositions of the foreign pope, and thus is a hero, and very particularly to Matthew, of the local national church. In his opposition to the pope the bishop preserves the integrity of the local church, preserves the walls of the old institutions. But Grosseteste is also the reformer and visitor of monastic houses within the diocese of Lincoln—the hammer of the monks, the persecutor of the monasteries. In visiting too harshly Grosseteste destroys the ancient constitution and threatens institutional integrity. He is here a destroyer of old walls. And it is always the protection of old walls (on land, in geography) that Matthew wants.

Hugh Pateshall is a smaller figure than Grosseteste, but he obtrudes himself upon Matthew's view of the world; and he is the source of obvious and characteristic confusion for Matthew. In Matthew's recreation of the year 1240 he presents the scene of Hugh's giving up the job of treasurer to accept that of bishop of Coventry and Lichfield. The drama of the scene is of exactly the type, and at exactly the level of intensity, to attract Matthew. Hugh says to the barons of the exchequer that he could never really give them up, of course, but that he gives up forever the exchequer itself. Tears, kisses, farewells follow. As the barons cry, Hugh tells them that although he is all unworthy the Lord has called him to another governance, that of souls. The scene ends well; but in the following year, 1241, Matthew must look at Hugh again, as Hugh dies, after having actually applied in his short episcopate the cliché that Matthew had thought in Hugh's speech he approved. Here, in 1241, Matthew must see in Hugh the persecutor of monks, the hammer of the religious, and particularly, Matthew says, of his own religious, who had made him their bishop. Hugh had lived his whole life well, but in the end he had relied on evilly unbalanced counsel. Matthew is dealing with a man whom he knows to be good, and whom he himself has shown to be lovable. But Matthew can hardly conceive of attacks upon the independence of a monastic establish-

---

[167] It is not always hostile, openly; he condescends to plead for Oxford (the second school of the church) to the king: *Chronica Majora*, v, 618.

ment as a function of goodness. He must explain them away as, in this case, the result of bad counsel—a verbal shield with which Matthew and his contemporaries frequently protected themselves from hard and painful thought. When Matthew sees a hand, even a saintly hand, raised against a monastery, his fears freeze his thought.

Matthew's fears allow his political persuasions to become the reason of his book. Torrential rains and disastrous political events, and earthquakes, can lie together in his Chronicle without suggesting ominous connection. In the *Chronica Majora*, in his description of the night of 26 July 1243, Matthew specifically denies his responsibility as an interpreter of omens. The description is a handsome piece; it calls to mind Joinville at sea, or the *Merchant*—on such a night. The night was very clear; the air was very pure. The Milky Way hung down as on the stillest night in winter. Suddenly the stars seemed to jump and dance and fall. They seemed to throw themselves around the sky and, in great numbers, to fly together, so that if they had been real stars (as no one, Matthew feels, with any sophistication could think them), there would have been none left in the sky. Matthew includes in his description a pleasing and rather surprising reference to Aristotle's *Meteors*. He concludes: "It is the job of astrologers to consider what sort of portent all this really is, but to every perceptive man it must seem amazing and portentous."[168]

In the *Gesta Abbatum* Matthew uses a line from Ovid: "ludit in humanis divina potentia rebus."[169] The way he uses it (so differently from the way it is incorporated in William of Malmesbury) suggests his approach to fortune and the universe—frivolous, uninterested, casual, sometimes literarily effective. Events lie together, chronologically adjacent to each other. In November 1237, in the *Chronica Majora*, the winds

[168] *Chronica Majora*, IV, 249; see, too, for example, *Chronica Majora*, V, 529.

[169] Ovid, *Epistulae ex Ponto*, IV, 3, line 49; Wats, 1042(2). Professors Louis MacKay and Charles Witke identified the line for me. It is also identified in Riley, 228. The line itself, or a paraphrase of it, is that used to different effect in William of Malmesbury on Henry I's last crossing, where it helps to tie the incident to the movement of the universe.

were heavy and the clouds were dark; the planets gathered together under the sign of Capricorn. The prelates of England gathered together in Saint Paul's in London to attend the council of the legate Otto. The setting is very effective; but the only reality is the political one of Otto's activity and English reaction to it. The heavens are trimming.[170]

Matthew is afraid that something will be taken away from him. Heavy with his house's possessions, he fears movement. Salimbene is, in a Franciscan way, possessionless; his security is in freedom and movement. The difference between the two men is a personal, psychological difference; it is a difference in religious order. It is also the difference between the economies of two societies: an agrarian one in which wealth is slowly come by and, generally, slowly lost, and in which economic security means conservation; and a much more commercial society, where great fortunes can be seen to be lost and won quickly, in which freedom from the past and its institutions can be seen to mean adventure as well as ruin.

Salimbene's church is a series of personal popes: Innocent IV, the family connection, reformer of the church, fighter against the Staufen; Gregory X, the man of great religion, the lover of the poor. It is the Alleluia and the flagellants, the bishops, the cardinals, memories of Francis, friars moving from city to city, and monks, quotations from Isaiah and Augustine—pennants flying. It is the concept of the whole church, East and West, meeting at Lyons, at least in Gregory's mind.[171] Matthew's church is the diocese of Lincoln and the diocese of Bath and Wells; it is a physical church with Westminster and, in the distance, the Sainte Chapelle, being built around their relics, and Beaulieu, a place for Isabella of Cornwall to be buried in.[172] It is the order of archbishops facing the order of bishops, the order of bishops facing the order of monasteries —a church of categories. It is the protective stability of the

[170] The legatine council is that, of course, with which Chapter I of this book begins.

[171] See particularly, Salimbene, 268 (position of pope), 468 (Gregory X), 70-71 (Alleluia), 465-466 (flagellants), 495 (Lyons).

[172] Matthew Paris, *Chronica Majora*, IV, 156-157, 92, 2.

old religious houses threatened in a new and dangerous age by insidious friars, disturbed prelates, and foreign agents. Matthew's English church is one in which bishops consult their archdeacons, or pretend to, in order to avoid the financial demands of curial legates, and in which the rectors of Berkshire form a community that can be gathered and consulted.[173] It is a church which is anti-papal but not heretical in Matthew's sense: that sort of strange enthusiasm, heresy, existed only far away in places like Milan, a city that seemed to Matthew full of heresy.[174] For Matthew political rebellion within the church could be salutary, even necessary, but enthusiastic spiritual rebellion was exotically repulsive. Matthew's history, with its simple texture of rowed series of stories (*exempla abundant*), is made protective by conservative monastic quotation, as Horace and particularly Ovid intrude, for example upon the year 1241, and make seem old and unfrightening the new and threatening events, threatening to Matthew's church, a thing to be desolated.[175] What each historian—Matthew Paris and Salimbene—saw was shaped, in the most obvious way, by the shape of his own mind, but it was also shaped by the external church of his own country—by the country church, by the city church.

In his attack upon Brother Elias, Salimbene produced a scene in many ways characteristic of his work—characteristic in one way in its use of oral evidence.[176] (Songs and poems heard are sources useful to Salimbene as charters seen are to Matthew Paris.) Quoting Ecclesiasticus, Salimbene said that Elias gave bad example to peasants and other laymen. He said that, because of Elias, peasants, and boys and girls, used to taunt friars as they walked along the roads of Tuscany,

[173] *Chronica Majora*, IV, 37.
[174] *Chronica Majora*, IV, 63.
[175] The internal structure of the *Chronica Majora* can be examined by looking at the contents of one year's annal and their connectives: for example, 1246 (*Chronica Majora*, IV, 503-589); for *exempla abundant* and the church waiting to be desolated, *Chronica Majora*, IV, 100, 173.
[176] Salimbene, 160.

as Salimbene himself had heard hundreds of times, by singing at them:

> Hor attorno fratt Helya
> Ke pres' ha la mala via.

It is a rustic scene of country lanes and farm people. But in Salimbene even country lanes are roads from one town to another. His is a map of urban centers—like Florence, an extreme case, whose joking citizens Salimbene makes to say of the Preacher Giovanni da Vicenza: "For God's sake let him not come here, for we have heard he raises men from the dead, and we are so many that our city cannot possibly hold any more" (and, says Salimbene, it sounds stronger in the Florentine dialect).[177] Salimbene's life and Chronicle happen in and between towns; by every implication his subject and his audience are urban. He goes down to the country, just as Matthew Paris goes up to town.

Most of Italy and most Italians were not really urban, statistically, in the thirteenth century, but Italy's prevailing literate idiom was urban.[178] Idiom is important and noticeable—as it is in Tennyson's "Princess," turning industrial, or in much late medieval writing mocking in rusticity the urbanity of the continental world. Town forms Salimbene's idiom, and country Matthew Paris's, not because one's country depended for its livelihood on commerce and industry and the other's for its livelihood on agriculture, but because the importance of urban commerce and industry in Italy was great enough to catch the eye and guide the tongue and shape the mind, and it was not in England.

Matthew Paris and Salimbene were men, intricately articulate men. Fortunately even the most superficial and simple individual man (even only partly revealed) is too complex and contradictory to fit into a stylized model of the English or Italian church built to contrast with a model of the other. Still, these two men fit their models, and see them, surprisingly

[177] Salimbene, 83.
[178] Luzzatto-Jones, 161: for the continuing majority of workers on the land, even in industrial areas, and the impossibility of drawing a sharp line between industrial and agricultural Italy.

clearly. Matthew Paris is a conservative monk attached to a cult center. On the surface, in this, he seems very far from the diocesan church and pastoral enthusiasm of Robert Grosseteste; and, unlike Salimbene, Matthew is in fact far from the center of new activity in his nation's church. But, actually, seen against Salimbene, Matthew makes Grosseteste's point against Manasses of Volturara or Rainaldo of Rieti very well. Matthew Paris is a dark Grosseteste, a Grosseteste in shadow. His fear finds an escape to the same sort of pattern as does Grosseteste's enthusiasm. Matthew, conventionally but significantly, chooses to praise an abbot by calling him a lover of order (or of the order).[179] What Matthew fears (even from his cult center) is the breakdown of ecclesiastical institutions, just as what Grosseteste hopes for is their enlivement (the enlivement of those he understands). Salimbene and Rainaldo of Arezzo, across Europe, live in an ecclesiastically patternless world, but one that admits great, undisciplined enthusiasm. Moved by their own personal persuasions, guided by prophet and preacher, they swing freely from point to point through a world that has no ecclesiastical walls of any real significance—and in which sanctity is the denial of the lust for property.

[179] Wats, 1046(1) or Riley, 217: from Matthew's biography of John of Cella, a mixed portrait, and an interesting one. In beginning, it plays with the image of Martha and Mary and calls John a Mary with something of the same hesitance that Jocelin of Brakelond (p. 1) shows in speaking of Abbot Hugh's contemplative virtues.

CONCLUSION

THE TWO contrasting churches that have been built in this book are not meant to be fixed and permanent structures. Like temporary festa altars, they are for a time and a place; and there is about them some of the deliberate hyperbole of impermanence. They are meant to expose the thirteenth-century church without pretending that they expose it more effectively than other comparisons and other approaches could, than would, for example, a comparison of Benedictine and Franciscan, of monk and friar. Religious order constantly cuts across these churches even as they stand. It does in the comparison of Salimbene with Matthew Paris, in the figures of John of Toledo and Prospero of Reggio. It was Stephen the Englishman who, as an intense Franciscan, encouraged Rainaldo to give up the bishopric of Rieti, while Salimbene, in the instance less intense (in the pose of the moderate narrator "I") urged, though Italian, the appreciation of the value of office— so involved can the pattern become. These national church buildings can be dismantled, obviously, and the materials which were used to build them reassembled in other combinations.

Artifice admitted, however, the contrast is a clear one. Image after image reiterates the distance between the styles of the two churches. The distance is as great as that between the styles of thirteenth-century rebuilding at the cathedrals of Salisbury and Cremona. It is seen in the contrast between Grosseteste's brave speech to Innocent IV at Lyons and Bishop Guido of Assisi's surprise at finding Francis in Innocent III's Rome—and in Adam Marsh's writing to tell Grosseteste that he should look at Joachim of Flora's work.[1] Facing Celestine V in the Abruzzi, Archbishop Winchelsey of Canterbury must have been "bewildered and fascinated." Like one character observing another in an Iris Murdoch novel, he must have "felt himself confronted with an entirely unfamiliar moral world,

[1] "Adae de Marisco Epistolae," ed. J. S. Brewer, in *Monumenta Franciscana*, I, Rolls Series (London, 1858), 75-489, 146-147.

a world which seemed to have its own seriousness, even its own rules, while remaining entirely exotic and alien."[2] So, if they could have brought themselves to look, would the English and Italian churches have seen each other, although they both read the same Bible and *Corpus Iuris* and believed in the same miracle of Transubstantiation.

The English church was a church of bishops. They were its saints. They ruled its contiguous dioceses, divided into geographical archdeaconries. They admitted no open and lost spaces as they fought closely defined exemptions. They believed that administrative continuity was both desirable and possible. These bishops ruled through carefully supervised officials; they wrote their records. During vacancies their dioceses were ruled by officials appointed by the bishops' administrative superiors. Their's was, when it worked successfully, an orderly governmental church (in a relatively orderly governmental state). The English church participated—much more fully than it seems to have when it is seen by itself—in the activism of thirteenth-century Paris and Rome (of the Lateran).

Italy's participation was different; reality in its church was differently defined. Even in most of its better-ordered sees there was only the intermittent governmental memory of Vercelli, the dependence upon the notarial community of Città di Castello. Was there anything to be administered in vacant Italian dioceses? If there was, it was primarily the property that the proprietary chapters held; and they, the chapters, in fact guarded the vacant sees. Chapters and monasteries were collections of property, around cult centers and their relics, ill-adapted to participate in Parisian-Fourth Lateran reform. To these capitular and monastic centers the Italian church was drawn, its pattern puckered further, in small, to ancient *pievi*, collegiate churches recalling the ideals of eleventh-century reformers. The bishoprics of the Italian church were essentially decorated towns, not parts of provinces. But into this elderly

[2] *An Unofficial Rose* (Viking Press: New York, 1962), ch. xii, p. 110. For a study which recasts material closely related to that of this book in a startlingly successful and different pattern see Lester Little's forthcoming book on the friars in a changing economic world.

and rather empty, yet cluttered, stillness rushed a violent enthusiasm, the movement of friars and flagellants. The Italian
church participated fully in the activism of thirteenth-century
Assisi and Santa Maria del Popolo. It was a church of mute
bishops and listening birds.

In thirteenth-century Italy the episcopal church was not, in
John of Salisbury's phrase, the soul in the body of the com-
monwealth. In thirteenth-century England it was. The two
churches penetrated, were integrated with, their societies in
quite different ways. In England the literate official church
held a specific place with a specific set of functions connected
with "pastoral care." It was, almost, a corporation within a
corporate society. It had its own integrity, but it penetrated
more general society, informed and enlightened it. The church
was teacher and writer, in neatness recalling Villard de Hon-
necourt's star caught within an eagle—balance, pattern, and
style. Interpenetration of church and society was unlike this
in Italy, where the church was not isolated in its literacy,
where bishops used their communities' notaries, where laymen
sometimes elected their *pievani*, and where cities came to control the *opera* of their duomos. The Italian episcopal chancery
was not a unique office shaped by its isolation in an illiterate
community, nor one which defined writing for the surrounding community. Similarly the Italian official church lacked
neat formal boundaries; and it was not expected completely
to define religion for—it did not completely satisfy the religious
needs of—the surrounding community. Italian society did not
demand of its church the specific Gothic form of the thirteenth-century northern European church.

In Italy the church was broken into parts: the relatively ineffectual episcopal establishment; violent popular and "Franciscan" enthusiasts; propertied colleges and monasteries. The
monastery seems in many ways to have remained more important, relatively, in Italy than in England; it retained its
material reality within the shadowy structure of diocese and
province. But in conservatively monastic Italian ecclesiastical
society, exact monastic order sometimes seems to have meant
little; and in decaying monasteries it seemed appropriate to

replace one order with another so that the general proprietary
establishment might survive.

In both England and Italy the church offered its subjects a
sort of government. "Justice," a modern historian has written,
"was almost the only service which a mediaeval government
owed its subjects."[3] A justice, which often supplemented and
sometimes replaced local ecclesiastical justice, was offered by
the universal papal government through the media of the local churches' establishments. Boards of judges (very local in
Italy), drawn from the rungs of the hierarchy, from *pievano*
through archbishop, sat as delegates to hear cases. Their justice
seems at first glance to have been inhibited by technical and
frivolous objections, by the constant opposition of litigants to
partisan judges, by constant contumacy. Seen more closely,
the church's ineffectual justice looks different. It seems to have
allowed parties to find for themselves relatively workable and
realistic compromise and to maintain during their search, although at considerable expense, relative order. This was the
real function of most contemporary government—to officiate
while disputing subjects found the line at which their interests
met; one thinks of Edward I and *quia emptores,* of the English in Gascony making it possible for rich merchant and poor
warrior to live together, taxing one and paying the other. The
direction and speed of the maneuvers which masked the
search for ecclesiastical compromise (including in Italy compromise over real property) differed slightly and reasonably in
Italy and England. The reality which the compromise recognized differed a good deal. Delegate justice, the church in the
ward, local and locally applied, was in some ways very far
from the statement of the general council and the university
lecture.

The localness of delegate justice should not, however, be
unduly stressed. Papal justice was a skein that caught, in its
own way, the entire West. The general structure, as opposed
to some of the detail, of its techniques and its arguments was

[3] Joseph Reese Strayer, *The Administration of Normandy under
Saint Louis,* Mediaeval Academy of America (Cambridge, Mass., 1932),
12.

universal. It constantly touched the crucial commonplaces and assumptions of the whole Church. It loudly proclaimed the principles of compromise and consensus. It demanded the proctor representing the corporate community. Its judges consulted with the learned in the law, and echoed the monastery consulting with its counsellors, the bishop with his chapter, the pope with his cardinals.

The churches of England and Italy actually met in the papal curia. But its repulsiveness maintained their distance. In 1254 Eudes de Châteauroux, the crusading cardinal bishop of Tusculum, made lament to Joinville over his leaving crusade and crusaders, the fresh band of holy warriors, to return to the staleness of the Roman curia, the *desloial gent* who were there. Roman treachery was loyalty to money. It was a liege whose tyranny was exaggerated but whose court did not encourage the remodeling of church after church through the exchange of ideas and serious observation.

If the churches of Italy and England, tied in Rome, were different, why were they different? If causality is not taken to be too simple, chronologically progressive, or definite, there are answers. The feudal, agrarian North and the more mercantile South were different societies: they worked differently; they built differently; they prayed differently. The South's prayers were urban prayers and piazza prayers, paupers' prayers and prayers paid for by relatively fluid incomes. They were also in part antique prayers (Byzantine against northern Gregorian—from a differently remembered history). A residual inertia lay beneath the frantic Italian surface movement, the inertia of the difficult, accumulated Italian past— "All of the incongruous things of past incompatible ages"— the Roman neighborhoods, the honorific archbishoprics, the collegiate *pievi*, the network of monastic tenure. A miscellany of vested interests was set to resist or misunderstand the message of Lateran episcopal reform. Its church could no more use the governmental ideas of Langton's Paris than it could use Gothic. It could better rest in the past and wait for future changes more its own.

It seems very likely that the connection between the structure of religious action and the way money was made in the two societies was not just vague and general—the difference in a sort of assumed audience demand. It does not seem too far-fetched to find a connection, not very far from the conscious areas of mind, between the way active northern prelates thought about ecclesiastical reform and the way they assumed one conserved and increased episcopal (and family) income. The slow-growing accumulation of wealth, the thought-out planning of intensive farming, on the well-run manor of the North and the patient conservative reformation of the northern prelate do seem to stand together against the adventure, the relatively sudden riches, loss of riches, disgust with riches, of southern merchant and friar. The connection is suggested by the biography of Saint Francis and, more persuasively but less bluntly, by the biography of Grosseteste, who himself (like some manorial Robert Owen) made the connection by composing in "The Rules of Saint Robert" a treatise on estate management.[4] None of this is meant to obscure England's involvement in the wool trade or the pertinacious rusticity of much of Italy. It is meant to point out relatively similar modes of proceeding and to suggest that perhaps the economic mode helped shape the ecclesiastical one.

Italian reluctance to accept and take effective part in the organized administrative government of extended geographical areas is notorious. That reluctance in the specific area of thirteenth-century ecclesiastical government is a central theme of this book. It is a reluctance so strongly continuous and so unlimited by specific racial or territorial boundaries in Italy, so built into the culture, that it compels the observer to suspect that Italians had been inhibited by the facility of subsistence in the peninsula, that they had not been persuaded as had the inhabitants of some harsher climates, like England, to appreciate the value of a carefully regulated and administered community. In the thirteenth century, a primitive governmental lethargy remained as an odd companion to sophisticated and advanced mercantile life. Its explanation is difficult; but it was not due initially to the presence of foreign rulers. It coincided with a long persistent Italian localism, which is also notorious

[4] See W. A. Pantin, "Grosseteste's Relations," in D. A. Callus, ed., *Robert Grosseteste* (Oxford, 1955), 204-205.

and which is also clearly visible in the organization of the thirteenth-century church.

The tangle of cause and coincidence is a difficult one, but it remains perfectly clear that the different interpretations of the office of archdeacon in Italy and England, for example, were closely connected with more general differences between the two societies. Each of the two churches themselves had a group personality in which the arrangement of traits and parts, although not logically necessary, was logically consistent. They are essays in correspondence, examples in harmony.

In each church were all the qualities of the other. No significant element of either church, with the exception of "heresy" (as opposed to anti-papalism) and except at the very specific level (the actual register), is its alone. But the arrangement of their parts (their related parts), the emphasis, produces the clear difference in their styles. They are churches dominated by different elements or different humors. One undervalues memory (recent memory), and the other enthusiasm. They have, again, quite different personalities—as different as the Dashwood sisters, or as Redcar and Rome. In this they break, with the breadth of their distance, any narrow definition of thirteenth-century church. They also offer, in their two styles of being, a definition of difference as clear as, and more historical and much richer than, that of choleric and phlegmatic, or fire and water.

BISHOPS AND SAINTS

I wrote the third chapter ("Bishops and Saints") of *Two Churches* on the Via di Villa Ruffo in Rome during the summer of 1964. I wrote it at Eric Bercovici's big desk in a bay window looking out over the north flank of Santa Maria del Popolo and (like a barbarian on the Pincio) looking into the city. The room in which I wrote, a bedroom, was extraordinarily pleasant. Its other windows looked into the park of the Villa Borghese at the level of the trees' branches and beyond them of the internal roads of the park, so that the aspect was sometimes rural and sometimes very urban, with the urbanity of great nineteenth- and twentieth-century city parks. I hope that by the time this essay is finished it will be clear that this fact, the fact of the room on the Via di Villa Ruffo, is as important as any to the way in which the chapter was made.

What I wanted to do, I thought, as I began to write *Two Churches*, and particularly as I wrote its first chapter, was to break something. I wanted to protest against everything "vague and arranged and fine" on the dead surface of contemporary historical writing, to shout like Thomas Carlyle or Gertrude Stein that life and truth, present or past, are rough, difficult, and to be felt. I tried to signal this point by quoting Carlyle, although Stein was probably more important in forming my attitudes. This sort of signal may not be much noticed. In my first book (*York Metropolitan Jurisdiction*), I echoed a line from *Sense and Sensibility* to make a point and perhaps even more to give simple pleasure by recalling the complicated but disciplined tone of Jane Austen's book. Most people did not, I think, see, so this time I used quotation marks.

Most particularly I wanted to object to the sugary good taste that seems to me to dominate historical writing, at least in America. Good taste, although one may recall it with simple longing sometimes, is and must be the deadliest enemy of anything creative. And it seems clear to me that if history is not creative, is not art, it is not worth the sustained effort of any serious man. Good taste protects the reader from experience and the writer from experiment. It gives them both an excuse for rejecting what they do not understand.

Beyond that, I felt that *Two Churches*, like all written history, had a right to be as difficult, intricate, hard to get at, even unintelligible, as I wanted to make it. I thought my job was to create something that would have its own existence, not to provide a simple, pretty, light guide to a classical countryside unconfusing in the convention of its imagery and arrangement. I think, and thought, that history should be allowed to be, should be made to be, as demanding (and always as complex) as a play or a novel. I cannot understand the chasm. Why should people who listen in patience through a play like *Waiting for Godot* in the hope that they will have some little understanding of it, some experience from it, turn to history and demand the slick prettiness and intelligibility of Trevelyan or, at the other extreme, the statistical, sociological firmness of clear answers in matters in which they must know there are no real answers? I cannot understand why, or at least I cannot accept the fact that, only history should be permitted to be, forced to be, unreal. (Perhaps both reader and writer are placated by history's "factual" texture; because it is "factual," it need not be real.) If history is worth writing at all, it must be written "real," with the violent and complex reality of serious fiction.

My talk of audience is something of a red herring. I am of a generation some of whom grew up believing those of its predecessor's poets who talked of creation rather than communication. I do not believe much in communication. At most, I think it should be a by-product. Again, it seems to me that my job is to make something, perhaps to make it for myself, not to keep thinking, "Will this get across to an audience?" *Make* does not, of course, mean "to make from nothing or without rules." The particular niceness of medieval history is that it has unusually rigorous rules and that it demands rather peculiar skills; at best, the remaining, discoverable, hard-sought past (as it is seen, not, of course, as it existed) controls one's hand as much as the shape of a sonnet does. In the matter of audience, teaching seems different from writing. Teaching is like ballet—not that the connection with the audience is like the connection with the audience in ballet but that the connection with the audience is like the movement of ballet (perhaps it could be so even in writing).

In the first chapter of *Two Churches* ("The Connection") I tried very hard to create something in which the convolution of prose and matter would make them inseparable so that the total shape of the whole chapter would express the active repulsiveness of the thirteenth-century papal curia and the feverish, greedy insecurity there. Although I had only fragments of people to work with (and more than fragments would probably have disturbed the text), I wanted the fragments to suggest real people in real places. Within the chapter I tried to show this in at least four ways. I tried to sharpen the presence of the fragment figures in the curia by presenting them with a blunt physiological-chemical mixed metaphor. I played with the figure of one curial proctor, Pietro of Assisi, at some length, so that I could show one fragment being slowly extended by additional evidence and then stopping with lack of evidence so that the remaining growth had to be imagined. I tried to expose the relatively full humanity of the English cardinal, Hugh of Evesham, by talking at length of his will. Wills are excellent documents, reservedly formal, but rehearsing much of the donors' experience and affection. Hugh's will makes little maps of university towns and of the locations of his livings. I also tried quickly to suggest a combined image of crowd-piazza-stage by using a real papal piazza, Orvieto (and I intended to include a plate of it), a suggestion of repeated figure line by mentioning Guardi crowds, and a nightmare image of a general council from Matthew Paris—all tied to a masque at a stage court. I wanted the small hard pieces of proctors that dominate the center of the chapter to be eased into large comprehensible polygonal crowd-stage image. And I wanted Matthew Paris, pieces at the end, particularly with Hugh and the extravagant who opens the book, to keep turning up, but not as a chorus, more perhaps as an inverted Polonius, with foolishness in a shrewd mouth.

The chapter is not so bold as I intended it to be. The brutal business of presentation of evidence and transition works hard against any imagined pattern. Besides, historians are timid by profession. We are all hiding among external, previously formed patterns. My most blatant timidity changed the first sentence of the chapter. The chapter begins with Matthew Paris's talk of heavy winds around a council in 1237. I meant the first sentence to be dizzying, to swing around, careeningly announcing the tone of the chapter. It had, originally, seventy-nine words in it. It should have stayed as it was. But, finding it more than my flesh could bear, I dropped a conjunction and cut the sentence in two. Too much time passed in writing the book for me to sustain the courage that the original chapter required. My taste changed. Even the chapter's title, "The Connection," which had seemed to me pleasingly to suspend the chapter between Marx and the then "scene," palled and grew dated. Still, even in its tamer form, the chapter seems to me a pretty violent expression of revolt, in a way that the third chapter, "Bishops and Saints," is not at all, or hardly at all.

Since this is true, it may seem odd that I have chosen to write about the third rather than the first chapter of the book (although the chapters are not really separable). There is a simple reason for my selection. I enjoyed writing the third chapter a great deal more than the first. Writing it really gave me a great deal of pleasure, surprisingly, probably suspiciously, unalloyed with the usual pain of historical writing. I have felt this sort of pleasure only in writing an essay on Stubbs, the description of the character of William Wickwane in *York Metropolitan Jurisdiction*, some small parts of the *Early Middle Ages*, part of chapter five ("The Written Church") of *Two Churches*, and a couple of papers that I wrote for the American Historical Association. (I am better at writing things to speak.) It seems to me worth noting this obvious thing, that an historian, this historian at least, chooses to write about things because he likes them. I think the historian is all too often viewed as a sort of machine (a vacuum cleaner? a baler?), all too little as a man and a writer. I think that this view robs both the writing and reading of history of its proper resonance.

I felt pleasure in writing "Bishops and Saints" in part because of the Via di Villa Ruffo, but I wrote chapter four ("Fortresses of Prayer") at the same desk during the same summer, and I have written very painful chapters in very beautiful rooms. The summer in which I wrote "Bishops and Saints" was, in general, a particularly happy one for me. It followed a personally difficult period during which I had written the earlier chapters of the book. I remember with particular clarity the earlier joy I had felt when I wrote the Stubbs essay in a wonderful, primitive penthouse on the Via del Mattonato in 1960. I sat at a table by a large window and looked out into the yellowing leaves of the Gianicolo and the Fontana Paola, as the older children, then both under two, played in the sun on the terraces. Although personally painful things were happening in America, it was in lots of ways a golden autumn. The period between it and the summer of 1964 was for me much less golden. I can remember writing chapter two ("Provinces, Dioceses, and Paths of Appeal") through a whole Swarthmore winter, and surely part of its somber tone is due to my somber mood. (It seems to me that this is important, that the Roman senate looks bright or dull to the historian and his reader depending upon the one's mood when he writes as well as the other's while he reads.) But the summer of 1964, for some reason, largely I suppose intellectually inexplicable and connected with the passage of time, seemed fresh and bright and full of joy. In it, with the preliminary research already done, I sat down, as I have said, with pleasure to write "Bishops and Saints."

There is another reason for my choosing to write about "Bishops and Saints." In a book which calls itself an essay, "Bishops and Saints" is more truly an essay than any other chapter. It is less a hoard of faceted stones, of small pieces of examined evidence, painfully collected, to give in mass a general idea. It moves in relatively broad sweeps; it has relatively extended passages of continuous prose. It states most boldly the thesis (the wrong word, perhaps the "idea") of the book. It is the center of the book.

The book as a whole is meant to be a general comparison of the total styles of the English and Italian churches in the thirteenth century. Its first chapter talks about the connection between the two churches, particularly in the Roman curia. It spends a long time with curial proctors. The second chapter talks about the administrative and judicial structures of the two churches and their attempts at diocesan reform. It spends a long time with cases in courts of law. The third chapter compares the sorts of men who became bishops and who were considered saints in the two churches. The fourth chapter describes monasteries, particularly decayed ones, and deals at greatest length with the monastery of Fiastra and her daughter houses. Finally, the fifth chapter concerns itself with the ways in which records were kept in the two churches and the ways in which their histories were written—two aspects of the way in which each church wrote about itself.

It is hard to remember exactly when and how I first decided to write the book in its present form. It took a long time to work out and write, a long time for me or it to find its final shape. Some of its elements had been in my mind a long time. In the first place, I had never liked what seemed to me conventional history. "Conventional" is a dangerous and perhaps silly adjective, particularly in the mouths of rebels. We often rebel because we need the movement, not because there is something real and appreciated to rebel against. My "conventional" may not be anyone else's "conventional," and it may in fact not exist, or it may be a thing of straw. The pejorative "conventional" may seem particularly dubious from me since my first medievalist hero, the first writer of medieval history who tempted me to follow his field through the beauty of his work, was T. F. Tout in his *The Place of the Reign of Edward II in English*

History. Tout is not normally considered inflammatory. He was for me. I had not known that his sort of written art could exist until, as a sophomore at Swarthmore, I read him.

Like most students, my first real connection with history had been through historians acting as teachers rather than writers— Jean Wilson, Mary Albertson, George Cuttino. They, like Tout, encouraged in me a taste for tough beauty created out of rigor. Certainly none of them ever suggested any killing kind of conventional, proper thought in history. They asked questions which were dry and sharp and provocative. One of them, George Cuttino, persuaded me that it was a normal and desirable thing to spend my junior summer on a raft with Johnson and Jenkinson (*Medieval English Court Hand*) and my senior winter reading microfilms of fourteenth-century pipe rolls. I learned from George Cuttino, or at least I learned when he taught me, to dislike finding things out from secondary sources and even to dislike using printed editions. There is something terribly boring, it still seems to me, about a printed edition of almost anything, and something very interesting about any unedited document, at least from the years between 1000 and 1400. This attitude is obvious in my work. I cannot help choosing, whenever possible, the unprinted rather than the printed source.

When I was at Swarthmore, I was equally committed to medieval history and Victorian poetry. In a way I am always trying to make the two things meet. It really is a sort of basic tension, and I think it explains, or is at least consistent with, the way I work.

At Oxford I was overwhelmed by Sir Maurice Powicke. Both he and his successor, V. H. Galbraith, seem to me explosive. Their existence encourages the throwing away of old patterns. They effect this, at least with me, in very different ways. I think, though, that a sensitive observer could look at *Two Churches* and tell pretty easily that I am an Oxford product of the Powicke-Galbraith period and that I was taught by Kathleen Major and W. A. Pantin.

Powicke's influence on me was direct and personal. I listened to him very intently, in scenes that are fixed in my mind, walking through wet bracken at Boot and thinking about Furness, listening to him read *Persuasion*. I could not, having known him, accept a lesser view of history than his. His Langton and his Winchelsey and his Henrician-Edwardian community are clearly my models, and his Maitland. I do not always like what he wrote. He is sometimes too softly Christian for me, and even, in his essays, particularly the rather popular ones, just too soft. (He himself was anything but soft.) Even his generally accepted masterpiece, *King Henry III and the Lord Edward*, sometimes seems a little loose and slack to me. But I think that the idea of *Stephen Langton* dominates, as it should, the most interesting—to me—medieval work of this century. *The Thirteenth Century*, with its tight, uncompromising execution of a fantastically elaborate but fully imagined pattern just at the edge of human comprehension, never cheapened by labeling phrases but expressed complexly in the reflecting arrangement of exact and exactly described particulars—this seems to me the real book of history, even surpassing *Domesday Book and Beyond*. Certainly *Two Churches* is written to *The Thirteenth Century*. It is, implicitly, always talking about Powicke's Langton, Powicke's Grosseteste, Powicke's Edward, and Powicke's Winchelsey. They are the model human structures for the men who live in my book, they and the great extended Grosseteste of Father Daniel Callus's collection of essays, particularly his own and Pantin's.[1] But the debt to Callus is very explicit in the *Two Churches*. The debt to Powicke is different. The *Two Churches* swims around in Powicke's mind. The world it believes in is the world he created. Its people and ideas try to touch each other in his way—or in his way cracked and spangled by an Italianate American who lives and teaches in Berkeley.

Powicke, however, was not deeply interested in documents. He was not really an archival historian. There is nowhere in

---

[1] D. A. Callus, ed., *Robert Grosseteste* (Oxford, 1955).

his work the sort of fierce beauty that a single piece of parchment, perfectly exposed and understood, creates. This is Galbraith's sort of beauty. He combines it, in a way particularly seductive to me, and more so as I grow older, with the sweep of rash generalization, the nominalist's generalization, which pretends to be neither true nor false, but brilliantly enlightening.

I am directly involved with Galbraith's own thought and work, but at Oxford my closest contact with an historian who made beauty out of the perfect handling of a specific piece of parchment was with Kathleen Major. Her quiet classes in diplomatic within the miserable Maitland library in Schools were as satisfyingly and involvingly theatrical for me as any performance I have ever seen. I have never been able not to want to work in diplomatic since. The purest excitement I find in history is still, and from that time, looking at a new, strange document in a set of archives. The dismal, cold room at Farfa disappears when I see a document. This has obviously given me much pleasure. That it forms my work, the slightest glance at my footnotes should make apparent, particularly in a chapter like "Provinces, Dioceses, and Paths of Appeal" and, overwhelmingly, in "The Written Church." But it is also destructive to my work, because I am inherently incapable of being a decent diplomatist. I only like the initial step. I like to find, to puzzle, to read, to understand, to transcribe—and at all of these things I am competent enough. But I cannot take legible notes; I detest searching journals for references to related documents; I am incapable of proofreading perfectly. The edition of a single document like my own " '*Consolatio defuncte caritatis*': a Celestine V letter at Cava" is valueless or at least unbeautiful if it is not perfect and perfectly introduced and annotated, and mine is not perfect.[2] I am, in diplomatic, hopelessly attracted to work for which I am unsuited. The edition of a papal letter should be like a haiku. But a haiku is written and created; the edition of

[2] *English Historical Review*, LXXVI (1961), 296–303.

a papal letter involves the patient use of tedious machinery. That the form of "Bishops and Saints" demanded my eschewing most diplomatic was probably one of its advantages.

The way I worked in *Two Churches* could not, I think, be understandable at all if it were separated from my background. But I should not like to imply, since it is the very opposite of what I believe, that significant background is essentially academic, or even that my pertinent academic training was limited to college and university, or history. The particular ways in which, at school, Brother Daniel taught Virgil, and Brother Jareth, Milton, were more important to me than much university history. As both teacher and historian I have been violently influenced by the way W. H. Auden taught a little course in Shakespeare's sonnets and the way Ethel Brewster taught Terence at college. Beyond that, my whole approach to history is very much formed by my own teaching and by my students at Berkeley. My work, I think, screams Berkeley—not the Berkeley of computers or even of learned colleagues (although it may indeed scream them too, particularly George Guttridge), but the Berkeley of the freshman section of Western Civilization and the junior section of historiography, of the undergraduate course, the Berkeley of activist, morally directed, intelligent, eccentrically educated young people. I could never understand Gregory IX so well, or hate him so much, I think, if I had not taught at Berkeley. Texts from my teaching (a letter to Boniface, Walter Daniel) appear specifically in chapter three; they have become inseparable from me. Historians whom I teach, Bede, William of Malmesbury, Parkman, Carlyle, direct me.

But Berkeley like Oxford is academic, if in a different way. The real background that forms an historian can hardly be described to an historian's audience, to other historians. It would embarrass them. It is the background of sibling position (as one of my most brilliant students endlessly points out), of family, of class, of village. It is at the simplest level apparent to me that my strong sympathy with both Powicke and Honorius

IV has much to do with my being a late child of old and un-
believably attractive parents. My sympathy for the Frangipane in
the thirteenth but not in the twelfth century has everything to
do with my growing up surrounded by gentle people living on
smaller and smaller incomes and remembering the past. Most
of all, my mind is equally expanded and imprisoned by the
beauty of the small Indiana river town in which I spent summers and some winters as I grew up. What I always want to
write is the way the white path above the hill meadow runs
parallel to the blue river beneath it, the way a rotten, brown
apple hangs on a bare, black branch in the November evening,
Pyramus and Thisbe in the moonlight by the mulberry tree
above the river, the mist in the southern cypresses. It seems to
me that when I wrote of Federigo Visconti in Sardinia in
"Bishops and Saints," I was coming as close as I dared to these
real images in my mind. It seems to me worth embarrassing
readers with these minor revelations, because in different ways
they must be true of all historians. They are almost too obvious
to mention; but things that are too obvious to mention are
often forgotten. The historian is a man, a human being, and
in his way an artist, and he is trying hard to express the images
in his mind, his real and full mind, within the constricting,
disciplining event of the past. In very different ways he sometimes succeeds—look at Maitland, look at Parkman, and above
all look at Ranke.

My Oxford dissertation, which I finished in 1952 and published in a slightly revised version in 1959, was a study of the
metropolitan jurisdiction of the archbishops of York, that is,
their jurisdiction over the suffragan dioceses within their province in the later thirteenth century. In fact, the dissertation became also, because of what I found in the archives, a study of
papal judges delegate. Most of my research was done at Durham,
in the Dean and Chapter archives, and at the British Museum,
but I also came to Rome to do a little work. I had already come
to Florence for a vacation and stayed, like most of my friends,
at the Lanini near the Ognissanti and the Arno. Italy was just

recovering from the war. It was quiet and poor, and parts of Florence were still broken. It did not occur to me in Florence that I might work on Florentine history, but it did become clear to me that I liked the winter sun, the air, the countryside, the buildings, the paintings, and, as much as anything else, the food.

When I finished my dissertation, I found that I had moved in a peculiar direction. Although I had intended to do at York, for a short time, part of what Irene Churchill had done at Canterbury, my results were very different from hers.[3] She had managed to control herself and present an outline; I had broken out into an untidy assortment of people and cases. And I was unhappy about working on York, on England, on the north of Europe in isolation. It had also become apparent to me, as it must to most Americans as they work, that it is almost impossible for an American to be, or be allowed to be, a local European historian. We are not from Cornwall or Wensleydale. Even before I had finished the dissertation, W. A. Pantin had suggested that I write to Evelyn Jamison to ask her, since I wanted southern comparisons, about the south of Italy. Miss Jamison suggested that I begin looking at Bari, and I myself was increasingly attracted to Salerno.

In the years between 1952 and 1956, when I arrived in Italy for a Fulbright year, I became more certain that I wanted to do a comparative study of English and Italian ecclesiastical institutions. My plan was not very well formed, but I thought that I wanted to work in the south, at some place like Catanzaro or Reggio Calabria (Gissing country). But, as always with archival historians, my plans were re-formed by archives. In those days the Fulbright Commission sent scholars to Perugia for an initial month to be taught Italian. I could not stand the idea of being near archives and not working in them. The archives of Umbria were not then catalogued as they are now, but I had looked at Paul Kehr's Umbria volume of *Italia pontificia*. Kehr did not profess an interest in documents after 1198 (when In-

---

[3] Irene Churchill, *Canterbury Administration* (London, 1933).

nocent III and my real interests begin), but he and his successor Walther Holtzmann in their regional volumes compiled by far the best guide to Italian local archives (although Mazzatinti is good on the things he covers).[4] Their work stands like a *faro* over the wastes of Italian medieval history. Kehr suggested that there might be interesting things at Città di Castello.

I went over from Perugia and found the bishops' books of Città di Castello, and I have been involved with them, and the extraordinarily active bishops they record, ever since, but never so profoundly as I then assumed I would be. The bishop's registry at Città di Castello was my first real introduction to Italian local archives, and I was lucky in it. I was treated kindly, allowed to read, and put next to the stove. I was allowed to find out what riches could exist in a local collection without having to face the rude, stupid hostility that guards the doors to so many Italian collections. I also went to the Archivio di Stato in Perugia and there found the records of Santa Maria di Valdiponte, and particularly its detailed chamberlain's accounts from the period between 1265 and 1288. I had, then, and meant not to lose, the monks of Valdiponte, as I had the bishops of Città di Castello, but I did not know exactly what I was going to do with them. I also went to Bologna and found the rich fond of the Dominican convent of Sant'Agnese so attractive in its litigiousness. I was also becoming interested in curial proctors (a few of whom had been important in my first book). I bought in November in Florence a small red leather notebook, and in it I copied the name of the proctor from the dorse of every papal letter that had one. I went about the Italian countryside, to Gubbio, to Verona (beginning, as Pantin noted, a sort of *iter Italicum*), demanding to see papal letters. I thought I would write something on proctors.

I was still bound for the south, although initial inquiries about archives had been discouraging. At the beginning of December I went with my wife to Salerno so that I could work

---

[4] For example, Mazzatinti on Rieti: Giuseppe Mazzatinti, *Gli archivi della storia d'Italia*, IV (Rocca San Casciano, 1906), pp. 208–68.

there. It was hard to find a place to live. Amalfi, in winter, seemed a good place to find a flat or house, and a place from which I could commute to Salerno. Because I believed in looking for archives everywhere, I sent a note to the chancellor of Amalfi to ask if I could see his archives. After some time, the chancellor, Don Gabriele Vissicchio, wrote to say that I might work in the archives if I would sort them. Until May, on ferial days when there was no funeral, my wife and I worked together sorting and making a handlist. When there was feast or funeral, Don Gabriele played the organ, and so the chancellor's office and the archives remained closed. Don Gabriele, although his eyes were poor and it was difficult for him even to get home to Atrani, also worked at a local orphanage. He was a very busy and a very good man. His archives were high above the cloisters of Paradise. Their documents stretched from the eleventh to the twentieth century. Our work (which was annoying to some Neapolitan archivists because it was done by foreigners) was done in a sort of vacuum without scholarly tools, but it was absorbing and informative. It was Pitt Rivers, the opposite of Collingwood. I immersed myself in the documents and learned from them, let them form my questions. The cupboards in which the documents were stuffed were like a dig. From Amalfi I went to Monsignor Balducci's archives in Salerno and the Archivio di Stato, to Ravello, to Naples, to Palermo and Bari, and finally through Sardinia north again to Perugia, Assisi, Bologna, and Città di Castello. The year was an Amalfi-centered general *iter*.

Amalfi was like going to school again. The things I learned were various, but I was most interested in the documents issued by the archbishops of Amalfi, as late as 1490, over a lead seal. I was particularly pleased by a practical archival joke, a document with the wrong seal attached to it by shopkeepers' string, as if it were designed to point out the collection's diplomatic queerness. Through the winter, as I looked at these sealed documents, I became increasingly intent upon trying to define for myself the peculiarities of a society that could produce them, a society in which they would seem natural. This was pure Collingwood. The seals were my Albert Memorial. The curious artificiality with which Collingwood, in his *Autobiography*, presents his Albert Memorial experience (perhaps because it is an example, unlike the Bath Gorgon, so far from his professional interests) should not disguise its central validity, its real helpfulness in the understanding and explaining of the development of historical research. My friend and colleague Gunther Barth looking at and wondering about Victorian buildings in Oregon seems to me like me looking at and wondering about lead seals in Amalfi; we both seem to have been following the Collingwood pattern.

By the time I came back to Italy, to Rome, for a year in 1960–1961, the plan of a general book comparing the two churches had formed in my mind, although the patterns of its chapters had not. A group of ideas now moved in my mind around the Amalfi seals, the Bologna cases, the Valdiponte monks, and the Città di Castello books and bishops. I had already decided to compare bishops and saints and historians, and I already thought that the historians would be, as they are (in chapter five), Matthew Paris and Salimbene. I knew that I wanted to combine in the book the most minute local archival work with, at least by implication, the broadest generalization about two societies.

In Rome that fall I found the documents of the Cistercian monastery of Fiastra in the Marches. There are still, in the Archivio di Stato in Rome, about nineteen hundred thirteenth-century documents in the Fiastra collection. I went through them all. (No one who has not worked in the Archivio di Stato in Rome can know what that means. The Archivio collects archival absurdities in its beautiful building—della Porta, Borromini—whose porticos are stained by the oil slicks of the cars that use its *cortile* as a parking lot.) I became so interested in Fiastra that I almost deserted my general plans to work on it alone. Just as I finished reading, I discovered that Wolfgang

Hagemann had been through the fond a short time before I started. The heart of his findings was published in *Quellen und Forschungen* for 1961.[5] I was kept from deserting my general book by work at the German Institute, just as, earlier, Peter Herde's work had helped keep me from hiding completely in proctors (and it should be known that work at the German Institute, unlike much medieval work in Italy, has been consistently excellent). It became clear to me that I really could not escape the general book, and I began more seriously to plan the shape of its chapters.

I imagine that no historian can really remember the chronology of this sort of planning. (It seems to me a fault in us that we do not use more our own uncertainty about time and the difficulty of fixing it, stopping it in imagination, as an historical tool.) I myself have a particularly bad memory, except for scenes, patterns, conversations—a difficult and unpleasant fault in an historian. I have notes that show stages of composition and ideas, but they are, of course, not dated. As I remember it, the general shape and function of my chapters at this point formed themselves in my mind rather quickly. Increasingly I thought of the chapters as five movements in some sort of musical composition. My knowledge of music is too thin for the analogy to have been very detailed, but it was helpful to me; it was the best way I could think of for dealing with the structures I wanted. The first chapter, ugly and discordant (and, as the book's preface says, about what the book is not about—the connection between the two churches) was meant to establish my tone and terms. Its themes are not the themes of the book, but they were meant to prepare the listener's ear and to separate him from his preconceptions. The second chapter was meant to be a long slow movement, uningratiating and difficult, in which all the themes of the book were to be stated,

---

[5] Wolfgang Hagemann, "Studien und Dokumente zur Geschichte der Marken im Zeitalter der Staufer, II: Chiaravalle di Fiastra," *Quellen und Forschungen aus italienischen Archiven und Bibliotheken*, XLI (1961), 48–136.

but in fragments not easily to be grasped. It is the chapter of administration, visitation, lawsuits. The third chapter was meant to be a fast movement, in which the themes were to be restated in a relatively attractive, even pretty, and obvious way, so that the reader-listener would be reassured about what he thought he had read or heard in the previous chapter, and also convinced of it because he had moved from difficult illustration to bright statement. This is the first chapter about relatively whole people, bishops and saints, and, as I have said, of relatively extended ideas and patches of prose. The fourth chapter, on monasteries, was again meant to be slow, to recall earlier themes in difficult and relatively unmelodic and inarticulate surroundings, to prepare the reader for more difficulty. The fifth chapter was designed in two parts. The first of its parts was meant to be the most difficult of the book, hard and very discordant talk of diplomatic with even measurements in centimeters in the text— a set of footnotes and a bibliography broken into the text, a sort of kidnapping into prose of the mechanics of historical work. Then in mid-chapter there was to be a switch to the fastest, brightest, hopefully most easily perceptible part of the whole book, in which all the themes would be restated in the comparison of Matthew Paris with Salimbene, and the movement would be back and forth, back and forth, like, almost, the sawing of violins. I liked this whole concept and, once having perceived it, I kept it in my mind.

But my perceptions are much more usually visual. Like Italo Svevo's Emilio Brentani (and probably for some of the same bad reasons), I have the "habit of always thinking in images" (and partly the images of whatever novel I happen to be reading). I always thought of chapter four as being square, like a box, a cloister, or just a square. Chapter three I thought of as a physical movement, a trip, a journey. My hardening of this image and deciding how to use it is one thing that I can date roughly, because I can remember the physical circumstances that surrounded it. I was walking home from the Vatican to the Via del Mattonato at noon on a sunny day in the winter of

1960–1961 and thinking of Federigo Visconti. (Walks are, I think, very helpful to historians; it seems to me in fact that the walk is the most readily convincing part of Collingwood and the Albert Memorial.) Just as I got to the Porta Settimiana, I realized that I wanted Federigo's 1263 Easter visitation of Sardinia, his long trip, to be the central knot of my chapter, the thing that would tie it together. I wanted it not just because I was fascinated with Federigo, the things he said and did and wore, but also because I remembered traveling something of the same path, before I had paid any attention to Federigo, at about the same time in the spring of 1957. I wanted the green Sardinian spring (and it was still the old Sardinia) and the Pisan churches that I had seen, and particularly Santa Giusta, at the center of the book and chapter. Since then Federigo has been inextricably connected in my mind with the Porta Settimiana, and he probably really walks and rides, at least in part, there or on the roads of the Borghese or on a street in Indiana.

There is a long (for me, three and one-half years) and often very painful time between the arrival of that sort of general idea and the actual composition of a piece of history. Even with the material found and the more detailed pattern of the work established, the writer has to decide exactly what part of his discoveries he wants to use, and how. I have a full sheet of blue stationery divided into five parts on which I tried to separate my material, to decide what should be emphasized in each chapter. It is an odd-looking thing. The third chapter has pairs or groups of names in it like "Celestine V Winchelsey" and "Filippo Benizi. Grosseteste. Manasses of Volturara Oliver Sutton" (with Oliver Sutton circled in red). "Louis of Toulouse" is underlined; "Obizzo" written in red crayon; "Peter Lo." in pencil and in a penciled square. There is a note reading "~~physica~~ absorption in material / rejection of / Rainaldo of Rieti in S." In a series of ellipses are: "Francis—Celestine," "Langton—Winchelsey," "E. of A." There is more, some illegible. Around this scheme were piles of papers, notes, often illegible in parts. I have never been able to keep my notes on file cards (although, ironically, for years I taught Berkeley juniors how to do it; and I always intend to do it myself with the next book)—like the graduate student–professorial brief case, it is something I have not yet been able to bring myself to. As a result, everything is harder and messier. Working conditions have not changed much for me since at Oxford on John's Street I used to get up each morning and spread out my great sheets of foolscap all over the floor and gather them all up again in the evening.

Now, some months after *Two Churches* has been published, I can make myself look at "Bishops and Saints" coldly to see if I can tell why I chose the people and examples I did. They were for the most part not inevitable—lots of bishops and saints would seem to have done much the same job.

First of all, two people dominate the chapter, Francis and Grosseteste. For me at least, they were inevitable. But they are treated very differently in the chapter. Grosseteste, already wonderfully exposed by the Callus collaborators, did not need to be completely exposed again; but he is dealt with relatively straightforwardly and is, I think, normally introduced into the chapter. Francis is spiritually and bibliographically very different from Grosseteste. I could not deal with him straightforwardly for various reasons. His words and acts are surrounded by a great mass of uncertainty. They were hidden by his successors, and they are argued over by our contemporaries. They are not easy and clear. Moreover, I myself am too much in awe of Francis, and something more than that, to reduce him to an illustrative character in a chapter. I tried in a way to make Francis shine above the chapter ("like the sun out of Ganges"). In any case he and Grosseteste, as the two ideals, were to dominate the chapter. I also found Winchelsey and Celestine V inescapable. I was intrigued by their meeting in the Abruzzi. Powicke and Rose Graham had made me see how extremely interesting Winchelsey was; Celestine V (on whose feast Malcolm X, Ho Chi Minh, and I were born), I disliked with a particular intensity.

The chapter begins with a paragraph about Philip Benizi as

a pre-contrast with Grosseteste. I am not sure exactly why I chose him. I like the story of his crying for his book, and I like looking at him on San Marcello on the Corso. I think, though, that I chose him because he makes my point about Italian saints and their anti-activist position familiarly and respectably (and so he makes an easy beginning) and also because I thought my first sentence about him ("Saint Philip Benizi, flaming with love, wanted not to be a bishop"), which arrived at my mind whole, dove nicely into the matter. From Benizi I moved to Grosseteste and through him to Hugh of Lincoln, the last twelfth-century bishop of Grosseteste's see. I wanted to use Hugh because I wanted to stay in Lincoln, to use it in a way for itself and also to build up to a successor of Grosseteste's, Oliver Sutton. But also, accidentally, I happened to be paying attention to Hugh because I had been reviewing an edition and translation of one of his lives, so his great change from "contemplative" to "active" was in my mind. It struck me that it would be very helpful to the book.

I wanted very much to use Oliver Sutton, who comes next. For a long time before my actual writing, I had played with the idea of his "bursting mind" filled with the minutiae of an English bishop's job; I wanted it in a long bursting-pudding paragraph. I wanted physical things in the paragraph, like Ralph Paynel's swans and Robert of Wootton's copy of Gregory's *Moralia* on Job (partly because I had grown to love that book when I worked on the *Early Middle Ages*). But the reason I had particularly chosen Sutton (besides his being from helpful, great Lincoln, to which good registrars and Kathleen Major had attracted me), rather than some other conscientious late thirteenth-century bishop, seems to me quite clear. It is because Sutton was edited by Rosalind Hill. It is not just that it is an edition in which one has complete confidence, but also that Miss Hill has, in introductions and essays, made Sutton (and his companion Schalby) interesting and attractive in a way that his contemporary bishops are not. I suspect that if she had edited one of the others, I would have been attracted to, and would have written about, him. There was, however, a catch in my having become so sure that I wanted to use Sutton. In Rome in the summertime it was impossible for me to find a full text of Hill, and my notes were impressionistic and a mess. My point was clear; but it would be no point without names, pages, dates—and these were inaccessible. This is the sort of headache that constantly troubles a scholar working on two countries in two countries—the documents and the books are often not available at the same time. Nothing (except the perversity of Italian archivists and my own terrible handwriting) has made my work harder than the books missing from Italian libraries.

I moved from Oliver Sutton, so beautifully recorded, to Bishop Manasses of Volturara, from whom, insofar as I know, only one document, the grant of a house by Trajan's gate in Benevento, survives. The contrast is obviously a nice one; but there are lots of poorly recorded Italian bishops. I chose Manasses because I noticed the document when I was going through the Aldobrandini archives in the Vatican and liked it (in some part because of Trajan's gate, which is very beautiful, and because of the document's church bell). Manasses is followed by a quick juxtaposition of two clusters of tenants under trees, a cherry and an ash, near Genoa and Saint Albans, which I chose because I wanted a quick introduction of the property-holding Church with something memorably physical (I also got a misspelling), because I like things that happen under trees, because I like Miss Levett on Saint Albans, and in spite of the fact that I would if I could steer forever clear of Genoa—in spite of its editions.[6]

The point that I am trying to make is that the historian chooses his actual examples for complex and partly personal and, at least in my case, visual reasons. Louis of Toulouse, for example, obviously caught my attention because of Margaret Toynbee's book about him, and also—this was true for everyone

[6] Ada Elizabeth Levett, *Studies in Manorial History* (Oxford, 1938).

else as well—because of Simone Martini's painting in Naples, but I also found irresistible a life (full of splendid rejection) that tied together the Castel dell'Ovo and the Ara Coeli.[7] I obviously am attracted to Margaret dedications because I have a young daughter named Margaret who looks for her name-saint. On the other hand, if I were writing "Bishops and Saints" now, I would write much more of Peter Martyr, because I now have thought more about him and have come to understand better his historical significance. Some of the people whom I chose when I did write, Rainaldo of Rieti, Rainaldo of Nocera Umbra, Pietro the Lombard, are figures meant to be more central in later work of mine. It should be clear that my chapter three, and I should think every historical essay, is caught in a web and connected with its author's earlier and later work.

At least for me, it is often very difficult to decide (although sometimes immediately obvious) how an idea or a figure should be presented in the text. I found a problem in deciding, for instance, in taking the figure of Rainaldo of Rieti from Salimbene, how much Salimbene to retain. I decided that I wanted Salimbene at least as much as Rainaldo and that I wanted to use the narrative of Rainaldo to illustrate Salimbene's techniques and persuasions, so I kept to a close paraphrase of his text. When I was writing about Federigo Visconti, I was aware of something curious nagging at the back of my mind, an echo of some English visitation. I suddenly realized that this great Italian visitation, in some ways, in some lights, reminded me of the most notorious of thirteenth-century English visitations, of Boniface of Savoy at Saint Bartholomews. I decided to present my discovery as it occurred. The odd connection seemed to me useful, but useful to the reader only if he could discover it, going in the right direction, as I had. So I took a chance and stuck my own mind, observed, rather forcefully into the chapter. Again, in reading of Federigo, I was—perhaps partly for very superficial

---

[7] Margaret R. Toynbee, *St. Louis of Toulouse* (Manchester, 1929).

reasons (his name, for example)—reminded of Federigo Borromeo in Manzoni's *I promessi sposi*. I then read Dora Lucciardi's similar reaction.[8] I decided, for conviction, to try to preserve the sequence of discovery in my book.

To bishops and saints I needed to attach other things. I needed the tone, the realization of the existence of heretics, Greeks, and Saracens. I did not, in this book, at this time, want to explore any of them in depth. I had to talk about them just enough to get their sound or scent in the chapter's later pages. I also wanted relics, miracles, and dedications. The last are particularly hard. They are slippery and indistinct, and the work that has been done on them is not reassuring. But I felt that I needed so much to have their sort of evidence apparent, for the reader to be aware of it, that I decided to use a sampling of dedications and at the same time to make perfectly clear through my notes how provisional my use of them was. This obvious device has advantages. Footnotes (although all historians must hate the drudgery of writing them correctly) bring tension to the page of history. The real life of the page depends on that tension between footnote and text; and at best, I think, it is apparent, taut, and complicated.

In "Bishops and Saints" I was particularly anxious to press the connection between the sources of episcopal income and, also, episcopal backgrounds and the nature of episcopal reform. It seemed, and seems, to me very important to examine this provocative connection. I thought it was an opportune place to try to introduce a neat socioeconomic model and "quantification." At the very least, it would have seemed natural to count different types of bishops in economic-class categories. I was forced in the end to realize that even this gesture would be destructive and misleading. My categories were shaky, my information in crucial areas very light and, even more, uneven. About some aristocratic bishops, for example, I knew as much

[8] Dora Lucciardi, "Federico Visconti arcivescovo di Pisa," *Bollettino storico pisano*, II, 1 (1933), 16.

as one could hope to know from the thirteenth century. About some I had only an adjective, the suggestion of a name, a hint in Ughelli.[9] I knew specific incomes, but not total incomes; but I knew more than that alone would imply if I could express it in words rather than numbers. To put these people and incomes together in blocks would suggest completely unwarranted certitude. Numbers are very clear, hard-edged. They would be an absurdity for a country, Italy, in which I could not even count the bishops. (Even if one feels sure about which dioceses to include, one's actual count may be several hundred off due to defective lists based on defective evidence.) So after much thought, with hands clean, in the service of exactitude, I gave up counting. Instead of avoiding selectivity and disguising the unevenness of my evidence, I decided to press them upon the attention of my reader. It was, in a way, fortunate for me. I find computerized history deeply boring. The things that it can discover can almost never be the things that I want very much to know. It eliminates the most exciting part (the uneven, jagged connection, the perceived individual) of historical investigation. Still, although I think that I was right to back away, there is always something disturbingly feeble about retreat.

About categories themselves I tried to be exact in example. I also, however, in perhaps a rather cowardly way, depended upon other people, for example on Gibbs and Lang, whose categories of elected bishops I used as an adjustable model. In a book that extends itself as mine does, one almost must rely on other people and move where they have moved. Because of Lazzeri I could talk of Arezzo; because of Russo, of Cosenza (although it would be wrong to imply that I depended equally upon these two books or that they were of the same quality).[10] In the other direction, just because so many people, particularly

---

[9] Ferdinando Ughelli, *Italia sacra* (Venice, 1717–1722).

[10] Marion Gibbs and Jane Lang, *Bishops and Reform, 1215–1272* (Oxford, 1934); Corrado Lazzeri, *Guglielmino Ubertini, vescovo di Arezzo (1248–1289) e i suoi tempi* (Florence, 1920); Francesco Russo, *Storia dell'arcidiocesi di Cosenza* (Naples, 1957).

so many able Americans, work in and on Florence, I tried to avoid it. I wanted my book to complement rather than to use their work.

Like other historians, I imagine, I am concerned with the problem of morality in history. Why write about saints? Do they have specifically saintly values? Should the moral values of the subject and the historian move back and forth and touch each other? I follow Acton and, at a greater distance, the Spiritual Franciscans. I disagree with what I take to be Rosalind Brooke's and M. D. Lambert's forgiving understanding of the later conventional Franciscans.[11] I think their perversion, their ugliness, is part of their appearance. The historian's disapproval of them (if he has it) is a tool for reviving them, and making them live again. I do not suggest that it should replace understanding, but rather be a part of a more complex understanding. I do not disguise, I think, my feelings, but in "Bishops and Saints" they had to be expressed in a rather complicated way: I really believe that the English church was morally positive in a way that the Italian church was not, but that Grosseteste for all his greatness was morally pale and even inept beside Francis. Moral persuasions shape historical essays and books. The sharply observable difference in shape between my book and William Bouwsma's book *Venice and the Defense of Republican Liberty* (a book also different from almost all other contemporary books of history because of its incredibly sustained brilliance) is owing in some little part at least to our, for the moment, different attitudes about judging historical figures.

All the historian's grandiose plans for the writing of history, at least all my plans, are threatened by error, by simple mistakes. They grow like lichens on a text. The quickly or carelessly written note is easily misread; one of many typing and typesetting fingers can be put on the wrong key and the mistake not noticed. Years of careful work come to look silly. Beyond

[11] Rosalind B. Brooke, *Early Franciscan Government* (Cambridge, England, 1959); M. D. Lambert, *Franciscan Poverty* (London, 1961).

that simplest and most plaguing sort of error is the kind that comes from ignorance. In a book as broad as *Two Churches* (at least one written by me) there were bound to be errors of ignorance. Beyond them, there are errors of direction, errors that come when one looks at something the wrong way, in the wrong connection: an oath that comes from, and that I had read in, the *Corpus iuris canonici* looked to me, as I was writing *York Metropolitan Jurisdiction* and thinking of local things, local and feudal; and I said so. The structure of *Two Churches* begs for this sort of error (but, fortunately, also for the awareness of it).

All these errors eat away at the effectiveness of a piece of history and make it seem pretentious and foolish and hollow. But the only way, at least for me, to avoid them, if it is at all possible, is to write a little, narrow, closed piece of history. And I do not want to do that. Of course, not all histories that look subdued on the surface are dead. Edward Miller's *The Abbey and Bishopric of Ely*, for example, may seem a quiet, closed book to the superficial observer, but for some fortunate reason its conventional order seems, at least to me, to burst with life. The book does not parade its vivacity, but within the pattern of its good order, conventional prose, carefully examined evidence, persuasive logic, it simply lives.

Like many, perhaps all, historians, I assumed when I was young that I would grow old writing in verse. I am still much attracted to, perhaps incapable of avoiding, the poet's ordering of material. He need not, even in a narrative poem (think, for instance, of Arnold's *Tristram and Iseult*) worry with dull, soggy transitional passages, with tedious explanations. He can present his series of images and ideas whole, clear, bright, and let the transition occur, as it should, without the dullness of written words, in the reader's mind. Without words, transition becomes beautiful. If I ever have enough nerve, I shall write history completely without transition. "Bishops and Saints" is an easy start. Its pattern does not require, in many places, more than the juxtaposition of contrasting figures.

I also envy the poet sound, particularly as in Clough—crazy, daring, ugly sound. I have tried using it, but not, I think, very interestingly, except sometimes in the timing of phrases, in *Two Churches*. Three hundred and fifty pages of sounding history has to be pretty subtle to be bearable; it is not, unfortunately, like a song from *The Princess*.

I am also constantly bothered by being unable to reproduce visual things. The Princeton Press did an imaginative job in *Two Churches* with plates seven to twelve. These plates scramble thirteenth-century representations of bishops and some of the ecclesiastical buildings inhabited in the text: bishops and buildings move together. I like the arrangement very much, although I did not work it out. Still for years I have lived in, intermittently, and written about Italy. The things that really interest me most in Italy, that stop me, hold me in one place, are things like the way folds of drapery cut the grilled rectangle of a church transom, the way the arches of a Tiber bridge cut into quay and river or frame a monastery. While I am absorbed by these patterns, I write of the way in which senators ruled— not uninteresting, but there seems an odd and somehow destructive distance between what I look at and what I do. This essay itself should more pleasingly be the description of enclosed and open spaces, the way my room moves toward the Mattei and Campitelli. Sometimes these things come together. As I wrote "Bishops and Saints," I stared day after day at Santa Maria del Popolo; and (as I discovered Roth's work at the same time) the Popolo's new order, the wild Augustinian hermits, pressed their way first into the chapter, then to importance in it.[12]

If I wrote as I should like to write, this long essay would have been very Japanese, a little George Herbert, the length of a paragraph but not a paragraph, a series of sounds, pictures (or rather molds and mobiles—spatial relations) and phrases. The vapid, soggy words would be evaporated. Images (the piazza

[12] Francis Roth, "Cardinal Richard Annibaldi, First Protector of the Augustinian Order, 1243-1276," *Augustiniana*, II (1952), 26-60, 108-49, 230-47; III (1953), 21-34, 283-313; IV (1954), 5-24.

at Bologna, the castle at Wallingford, Pecham's three gold pins), hard, bare ideas, quotations, and noisemakers would be dispersed and three-dimensional in a complicated and sounding pattern (reflecting in some way the room on the Via di Villa Ruffo) on the page—and the footnotes would be exact and obvious, or completely absorbed.

INDEX